CONTENTS

Key to Map Pages	2-3	**Postcode Map**	122-123
Map Pages	4-120	**Index to Streets**	124-176
Index to Places	121		

REFERENCE

Motorway	A1(M)	Map Continuation	⬇50
'A' Road	A19	Buses Only	▭▭▭
'B' Road	B1380	Car Parks (Selected)	P
Dual Carriageway		Church or Chapel	†
One Way Street	traffic flow →	Cycleway	🚲
One Way traffic flow on 'A' roads is indicated by a heavy line on the driver's left.		Fire Station	■
Restricted Access		Hospital	H
House Numbers 'A' & 'B' Roads only	2 45	Information Centre	i
Railway	Station Level Crossing	Police Station	▲
County/Unitary Authority Boundary	+ · + · +	Post Office	★
District Boundary	— · — · —	Toilet Disabled Toilet	▽ ♿
North Yorkshire Moors National Park Boundary	▒▒▒▒		

SCALE:
4 inches to 1 mile

0   ¼   ½ mile
0   250   500   750 metres

1:15,840

Geographers' A-Z Map Co. Ltd.

Head Office:
Fairfield Road, Borough Green, Sevenoaks, Kent, TN15 8PP
Telephone 01732 781000

Showrooms:
44 Gray's Inn Road, London, WC1X 8HX
Telephone 020 7440 9500

Copyright © Edition 4 1996
      Edition 4A (Part Revision) 2000

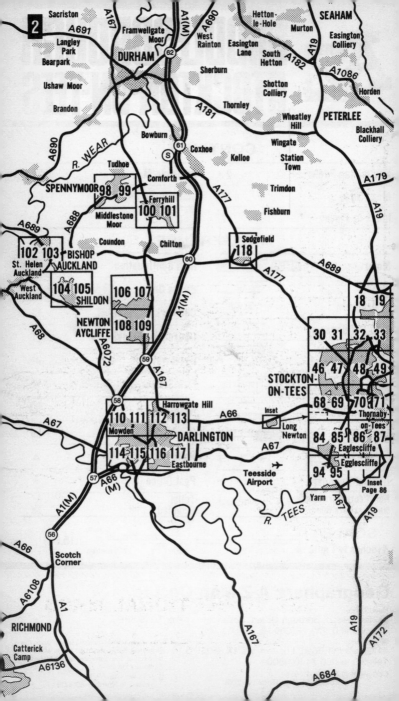

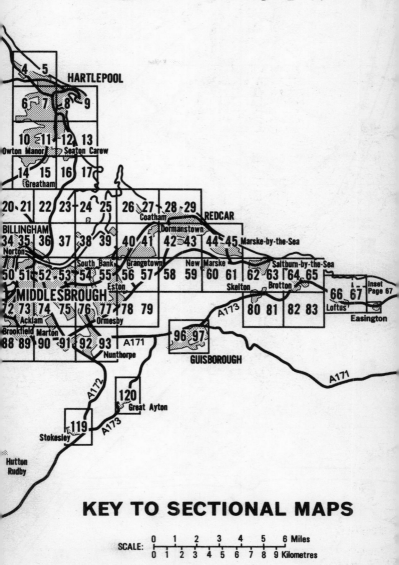

3

N O R T H   S E A

HARTLEPOOL

4 5
6 7 8 9
10 11 12 13
Owton Manor Seaton Carew
14 15 16 17
Greatham
20 21 22 23 24 25 26 27 28 29 REDCAR
Coatham
BILLINGHAM
34 35 36 37 38 39 40 41 42 43 44 45 Marske-by-the-Sea
Norton Dormanstown
South Bank Grangetown New Marske Saltburn-by-the-Sea
50 51 52 53 54 55 56 57 58 59 60 61 62 63 64 65
Eston Skelton Brotton
66 67 Inset Page 67
72 73 74 75 76 77 78 79 80 81 82 83 Loftus
Acklam Ormesby A173 Easington
Brookfield Marton
88 89 90 91 92 93 96 97
Nunthorpe A171 GUISBOROUGH
A171
A172
120
Great Ayton
119 A173
Stokesley
Hutton
Rudby

KEY TO SECTIONAL MAPS

SCALE: 0 1 2 3 4 5 6 Miles
        0 1 2 3 4 5 6 7 8 9 Kilometres

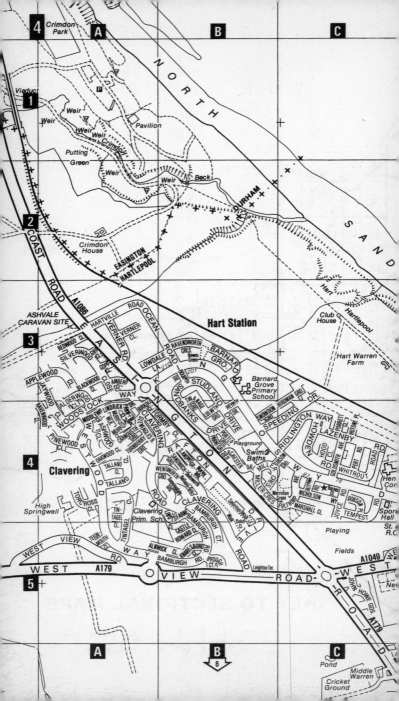

D **E** **F** **5**

1

NORTH

SEA

2

3

HART
WARREN   Golf

Lake

Course
Pond   Lake

Pipe
Pipe   Pipe

Pipe
Outfall

Outfall

Pipe

Pipe

Pier

4

Smith
. Sch.   DOWSON

ROGERI
PL

KESANT
RD

Cemetery
Junction
North

Works

Pipe

North
Sands

R.C. Prim.
Sch.
GILBERT PL

RUNCIMAN

BRUNTOFT
LAMBERD RD.   AVE.

er's
Sch.

ROAD

WEST

VIEW   ROAD   AVENUE

Brus
Corner

SMITH

Palliser
Works

OLD

CEMETERY

ROAD

VIEW   ROAD

Cemetery

WEST

SKELTON

BRUCE

ST.

ANNANDALE

DAVISON

MIERS

BRADSW
EMERSON
CT.

ELLET
ST.

Clinic

Library

CRESCENT

Bagley
Walk

WEST

AVENUE

Tennis Cts.

VIEW

Old
Cemy.
ROAD

5

Old Cemy

West View

CRES

ARKLEY

Cmty.
Cntr.

CARRICK

Playground

Sports
Grnd.

ROAD

Hartlepool
R.L.F.C.

Tun

Mayfield Park
(Hartlepool R.U.F.C.)

CRES

WINTERBOTTOM

CRESCENT

GRIT ST

MILLPO

A1049

ROAD

GRIT ST

JONES

D

NDRY

POUND

RUNCIMAN

RD

WELLS

SURGY

RD

CRESC

West View
Inf. & Jun.
Schs.

WARREN

DRIVE

WINTERBOT

SWAP

RAWS

E

7

SKERNE

Works

HARTLEPOOL

ROAD

ROAD

OAKESWAY

F

House
Factory

Factories

MANSPOOL

Leisure
Gdns

MILLPO

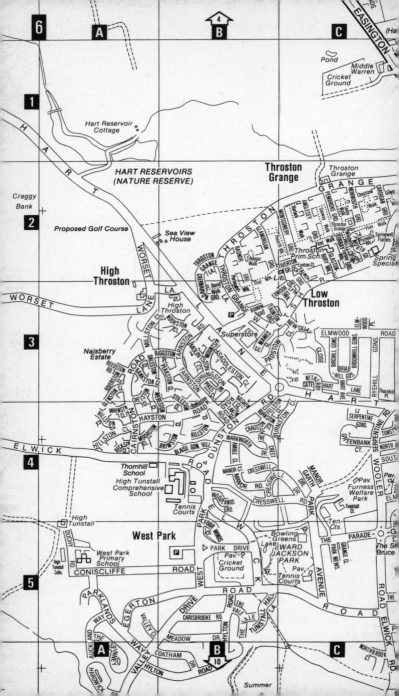

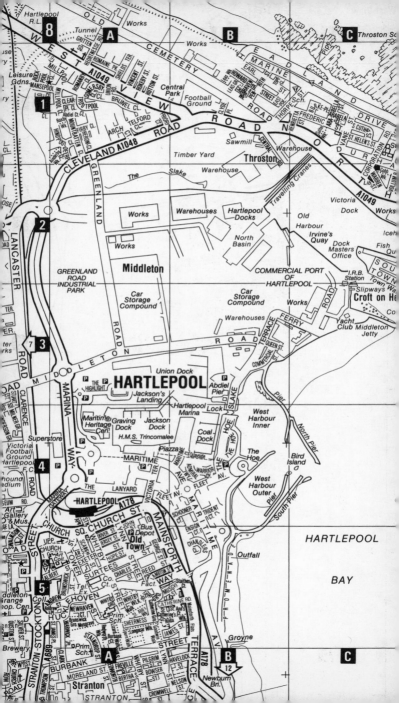

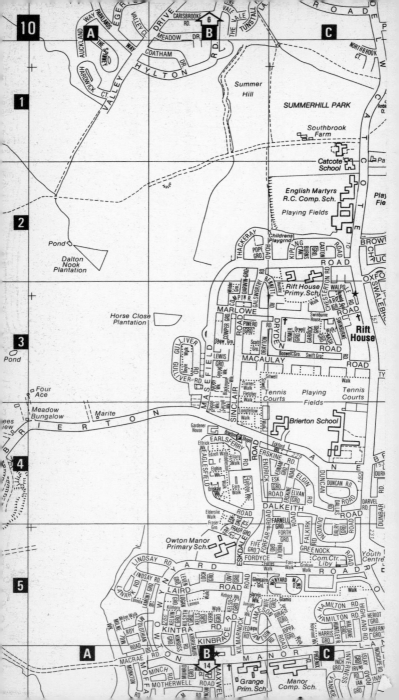

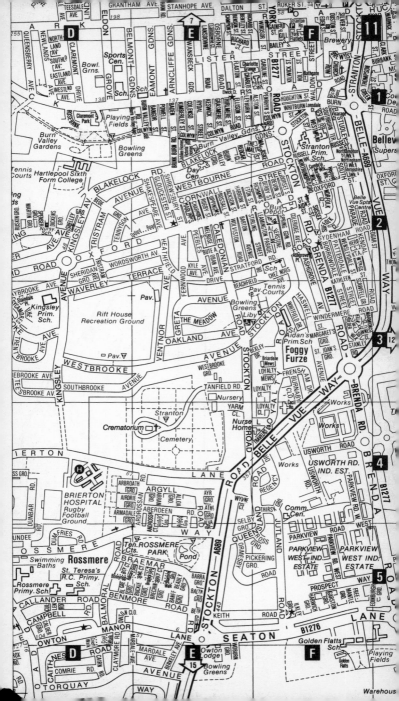

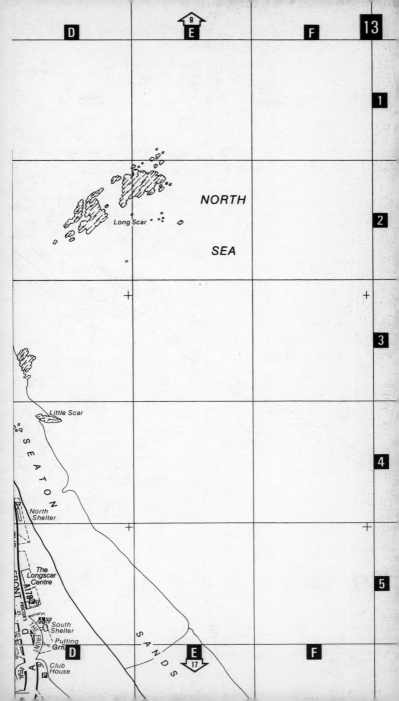

9

1

NORTH

2

Long Scar

SEA

3

Little Scar

4

S
E
A
T
O
N

North
Shelter

The
Longscar
Centre

5

South
Shelter

Putting
Grn.

S
A
N
D
S

Club
House

17

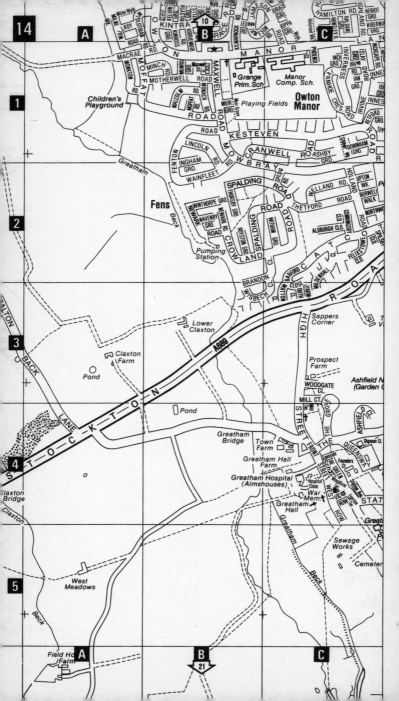

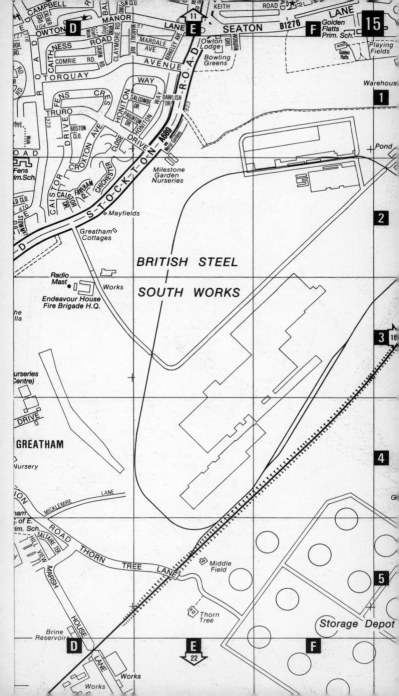

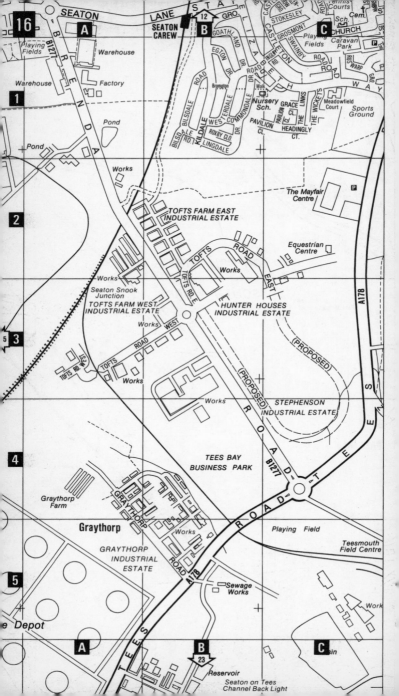

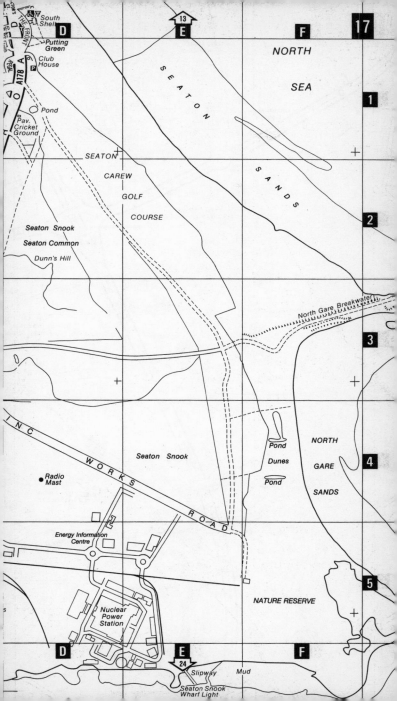

THE FRONT

South Shelt

D

Putting
Green

Club
House

A178 A

P

Pond

Pav.
Cricket
Ground

SEATON

CAREW

GOLF

COURSE

Seaton Snook

Seaton Common

Dunn's Hill

13

E

SEATON

SANDS

NORTH

SEA

17

F

1

2

North Gare Breakwater

3

INC

WORKS

ROAD

Seaton Snook

• Radio
Mast

Energy Information
Centre

Nuclear
Power
Station

D

Pond

Dunes

Pond

NORTH

GARE

SANDS

4

5

NATURE RESERVE

E

24

Slipway   Mud

F

Seaton Snook
Wharf Light

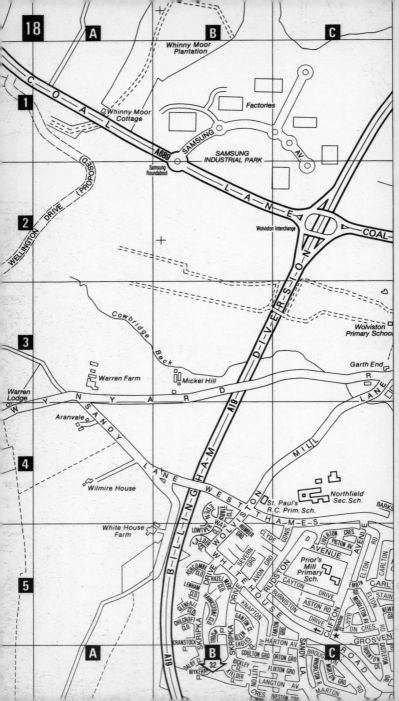

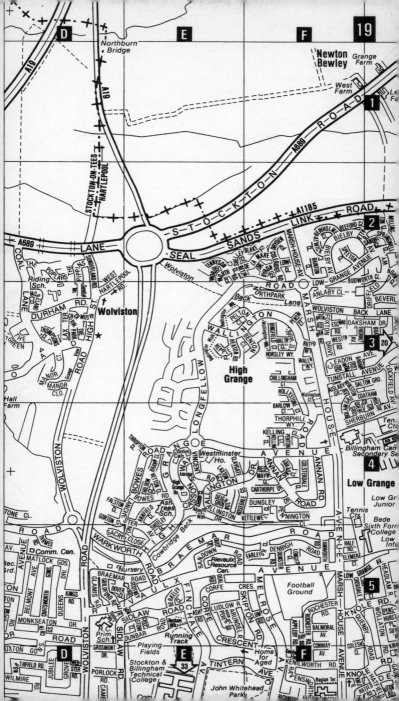

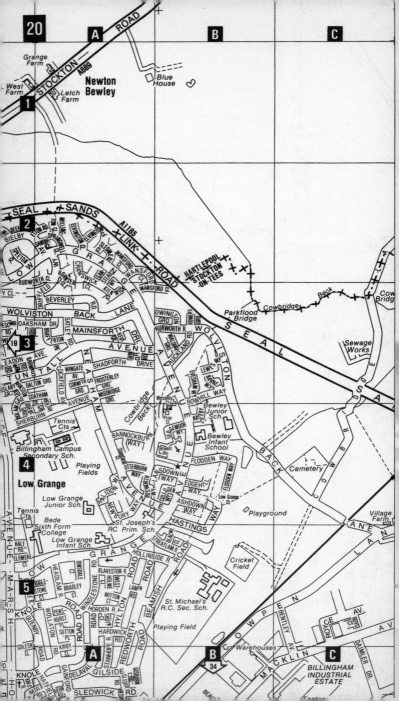

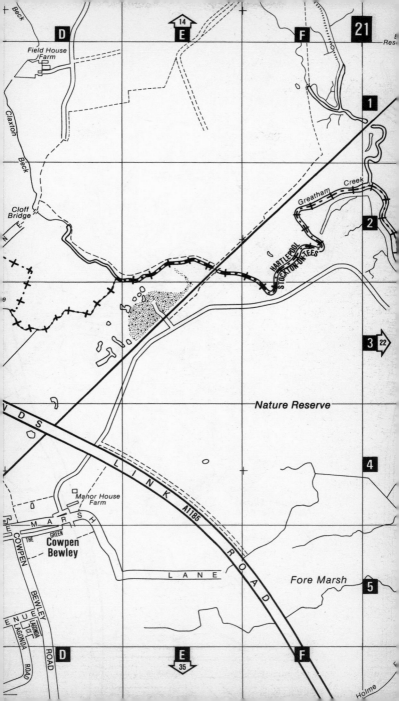

D   ▲ 14 **E**   **F**   **21**

Field House Farm

Claxton Beck

Cloff Bridge

1

Greatham Creek

2

HARTLEPOOL
STOCKTON-ON-TEES

3 ▶ 22

Nature Reserve

LINK ROAD A1185

Manor House Farm

MARSH

THE GREEN

Cowpen Bewley

COWPEN

BEWLEY

ROAD

L A N E

Fore Marsh

4

5

LAGONDA CT

LAGONDA ROAD

D   ▼ 35 **E**   **F**

Holme

A

B

C

1

2

3

4

5

21

15 Thorn Tree

Storage D

Brine Reservoirs

MARSH HOUSE LANE

Works

Works

Marsh House Farm

Marsh House

Creek

HARTLEPOOL

STOCKTON-ON-TEES

Cote Hill

Greatham Creek

Gr Cr

North End

Todler's Fleet

Mucky Fleet

Rough Marsh

Swallow Fleet

Cowpen Marsh Nature Reserve

Holme Crook

Holme Fleet

SEATON CAREW ROAD

A178

rsh

Holme Fleet

A

B

C

36

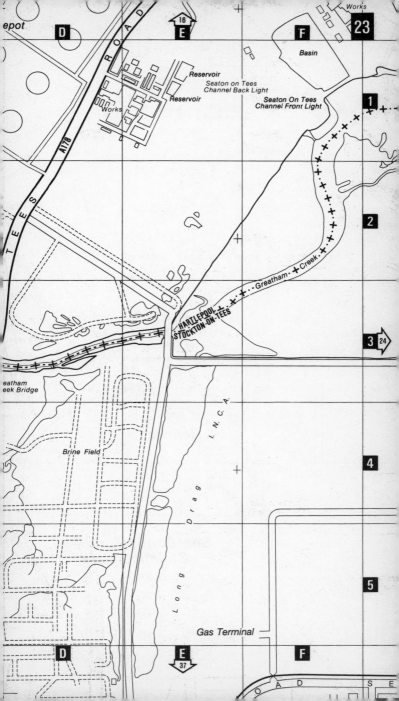

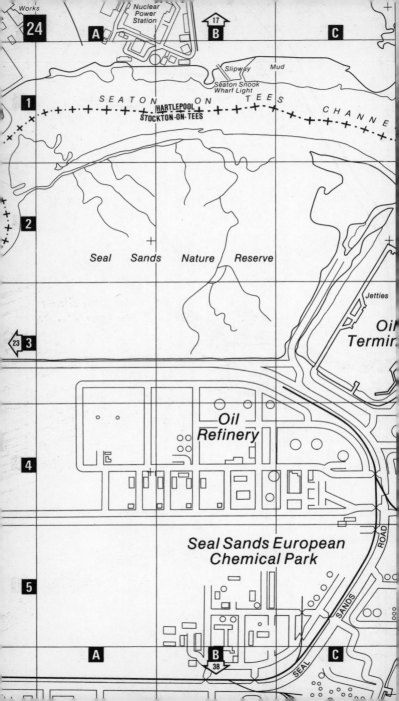

Works

24

Nuclear Power Station

A

B

17

C

Slipway

Mud

Seaton Snook
Wharf Light

S E A T O N   HARTLEPOOL   O N   T E E S   C H A N N E
STOCKTON-ON-TEES

1

2

Seal   Sands   Nature   Reserve

Jetties

23 3

Oil
Termir

Oil
Refinery

4

Seal Sands European
Chemical Park

5

A

B

38

ROAD

SANDS

SEAL

C

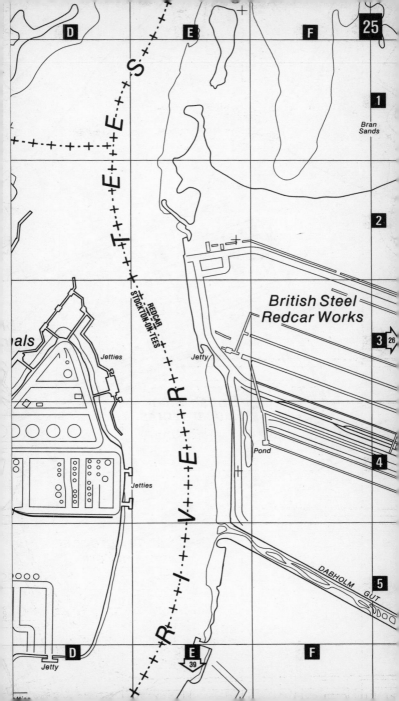

D   **E**   **F**   **25**

1

Bran
Sands

2

British Steel
Redcar Works

3 ▷26

REDCAR
STOCKTON-ON-TEES

Jetties

Jetty

Jetty

Pond

4

als

Jetties

5

DABHOLM GUT

D   **E**   **F**

Jetty

▽39

RIVER TEES

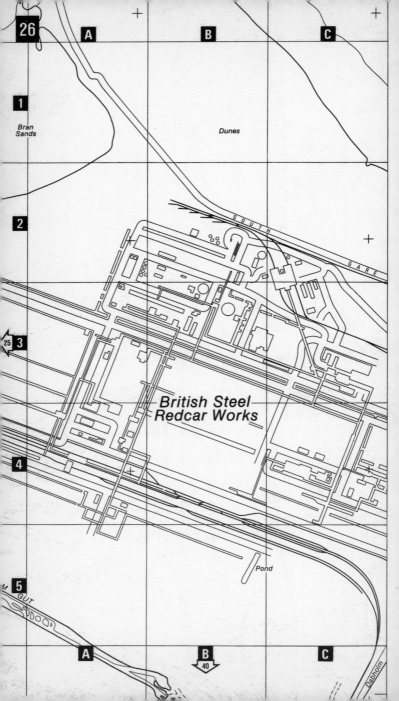

A   B   C

1

Bran
Sands

Dunes

2

SOUTH

GARE

25 ◄ **3**

British Steel
Redcar Works

4

Pond

5

GUT

A   B
40

C

Dabholm

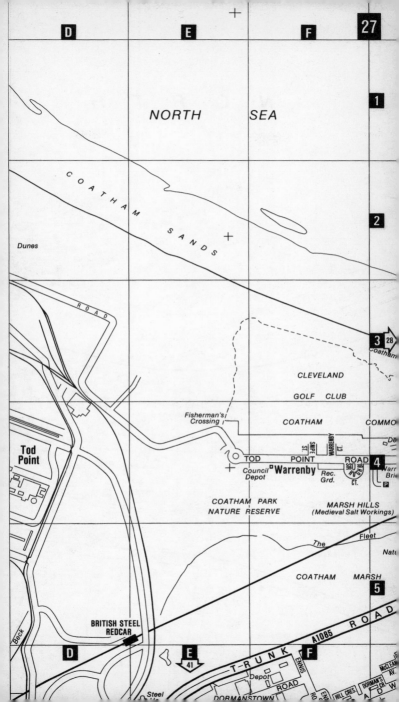

A **B** **C**

1

N O R T H

2

Westcar Head

Inner Height

West Flashes

The Hampstead

27 **3**

Coatham Sand Banks

Roller Skating Rink Boat Ho.
Swimming Baths
Amusements
MAJUBA ROAD
Club Cen. Ho.
Cleveland Golf Club
NEWCOMEN ROAD
Coatham
QUEEN STREET
WEST
NEWCOMEN TCE.
ARTHUR ST.
HENRY ST.
KING ST.
ANSON ST.
PIERSON
ELLIOTT ST.
CLIFFORD ST.
R O

COATHAM COMMON

Depot
Coastguard Station
MARINA AV.
York Terrace
HIGH ROAD
York Ter.
BRIG.
COATHAM
Prim. Sch.
KIRKLEATHAM
Coatham Lodge
Victory Ter.
St. Vincent St.
TRAFALGAR T.
Cricket Grd. Pav.
NELSON ST.
Youth Cen.
Cherry Trees
Health Centre
Council Offs.
STR
REDCAR C

4
SIR W.A.
TOD POINT RD. YORK
Warrenby Bridge
Caravan Park
Works
Laing Caravan Site
HARVAL RD.
KIRKLEATHAM
THORNABY GRO.
PRIORY GRO.
HORNLEIGH GRO.
STEAD MEM. HOSP.
BLENHEIM
Cleveland Tertiary College
Ten. Cts.
SAND
H
The Kennels
'SH HILLS (Salt Workings)
Fleet
Coatham Bridge
LANE
Bowling Grn.
LOCKE PARK
Tennis Cts.
Boating Lake
Pav.
LOCKE RD.
Playing Flds.

The
Lake
Nature Reserve
CORPORATION
A1085
MERSEY ROAD

5
MARSH
TRUNK A1085 ROAD
Recreation Ground
Playground
GORDON
LOVAT AV.
DUNCAN AV.
AINOL GRO.
KIRKLEATHAM
A1042
ROAD
EAST
SEVERN RD.
SEVERN
GRETA ROAD
DERWENT ROAD
FORTH ROAD
Sacred Heart R.C. Sec. Sch.
Playing Flds.
St. Dominic's Primary Schs.
ROAD
ROAD
MERSEY ROAD
Cleveland College (Redcar F.E. Centre)
Playing Fields
Westfield
RYDAL RD.
THIRLMERE

A
CRANLETON AV.
McCLEAN AV.
DORMAN'S CR.
BROADWAY
STAITHES
KETTLENESS AV.
GRINKLE
RUNSWICK RD.
ASHBY RD.
HINDERWELL RD.
B
42
THAMES LA.
TWEED
TRENT
TYNE ROAD
TEES ROAD
ROAD
ROAD
BUTTERMERE
C
HAWE RD.
ELLER RD.
WATCH
NEWLANDS
RD.
HOW
RD.
WINDERMERE

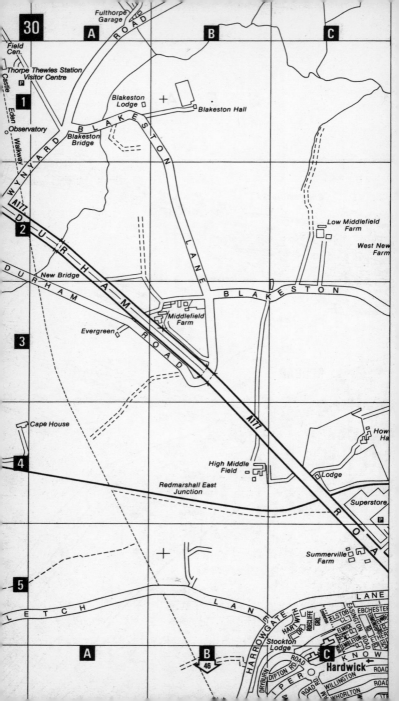

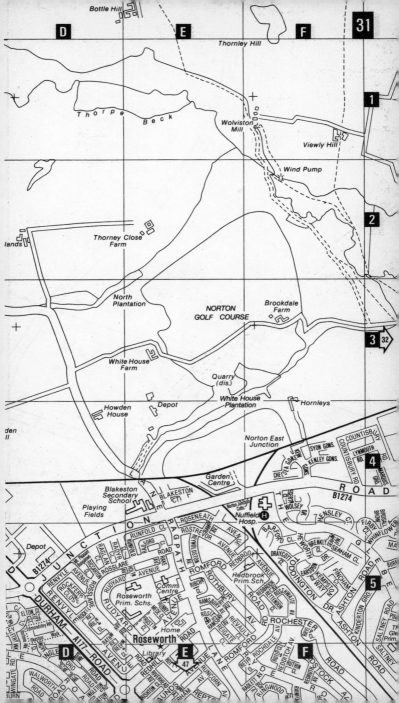

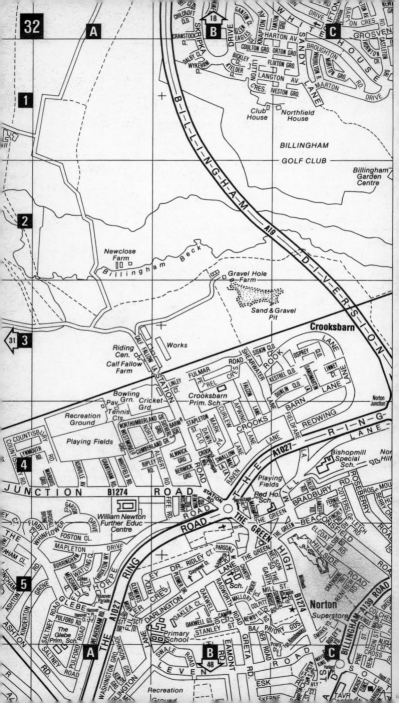

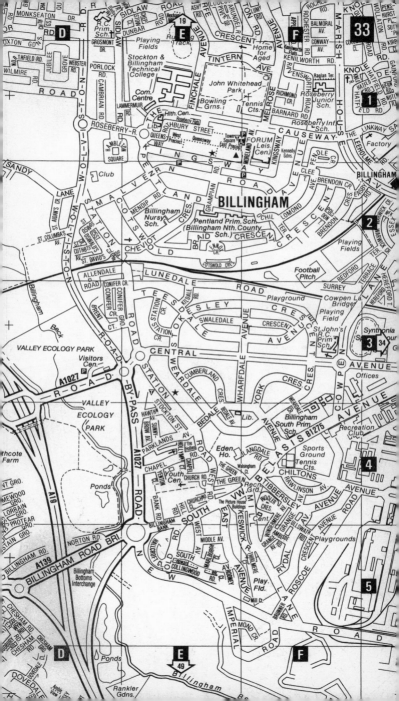

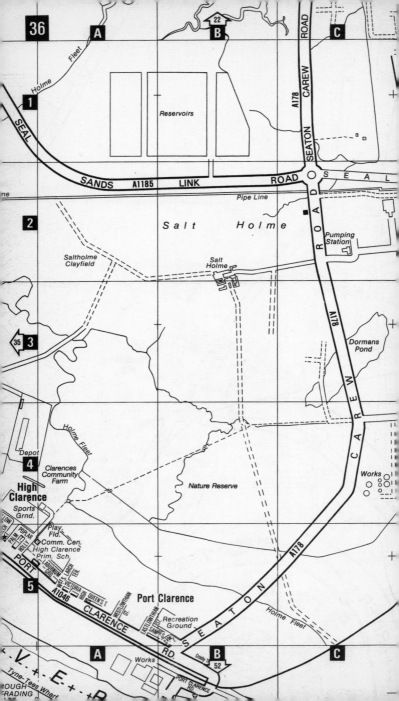

D **E** **F**

23
Gas Terminal

1

S A N D S   R O A D

Pipe   Line

2

Reclamation
Pond

Reservoir

3 38

+

Riverside Road

4

Hargreaves
Quarry
Pond

Jetty

5

River   Tees   Eston   Wharf

SMIT

D **E** **F**

53

Wharf

Dry Docks

38

A   B   C

24

SEAL SANDS

1

Jetty

Jett

Pipe Line

Oil Refinery

2

ROAD

Jetty

Reservoir

Res

RIVERSIDE

STOCKTON-ON-TEES
REDCAR

37 3

Jetty

Jetty

ROAD

RIVERSIDE

Works

4

Works

R·+I·+·V·+E·+·R·+

South Bank Wharf

Works

Jetty

Wharf

Eston Wharf

SMITH'S

5

Wharf

Dry Docks

DOCK

Works

ROAD

Conveyor

Works

Wharf

A   B   C

TEES OFFSHORE BASE

54

ROAD

Conveyor

Works

Training

Works

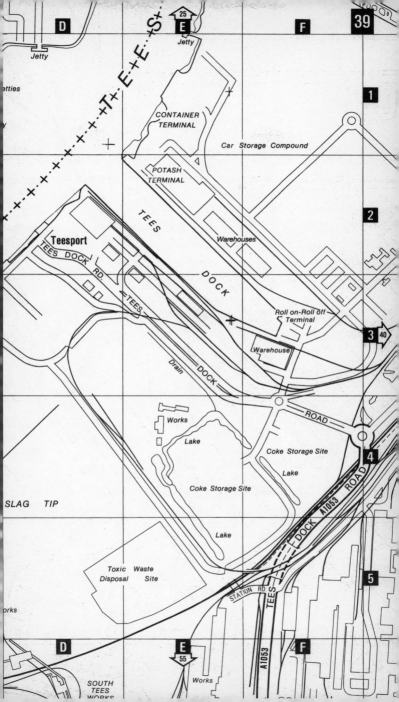

D   E   25   F   39

Jetty

Jetty

etties

CONTAINER
TERMINAL

Car Storage Compound

1

POTASH
TERMINAL

T E E S

Warehouses

2

Teesport

TEES DOCK RD.

D O C K

TEES

DOCK

Roll on-Roll off
Terminal

3   40

Warehouse

Drain

Works

ROAD

Lake

Coke Storage Site

Lake

Coke Storage Site

4

SLAG   TIP

Lake

DOCK A1053 ROAD

Toxic Waste
Disposal Site

STATION RD.

TEES

5

orks

D   E   55   F

A1053

SOUTH
TEES
WORKS

Works

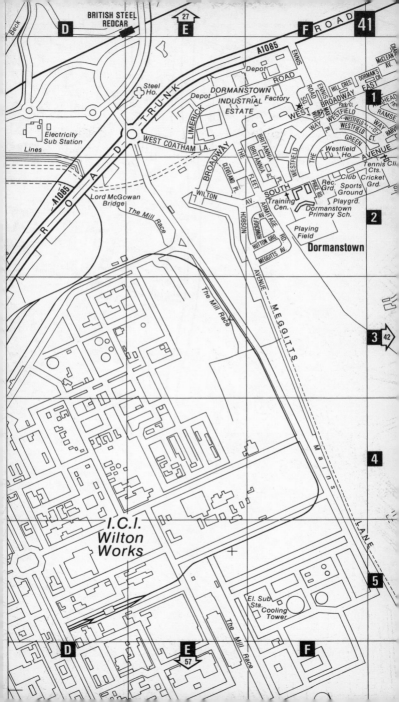

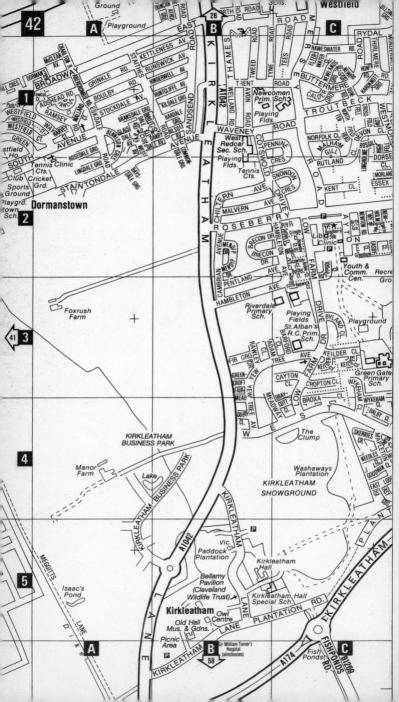

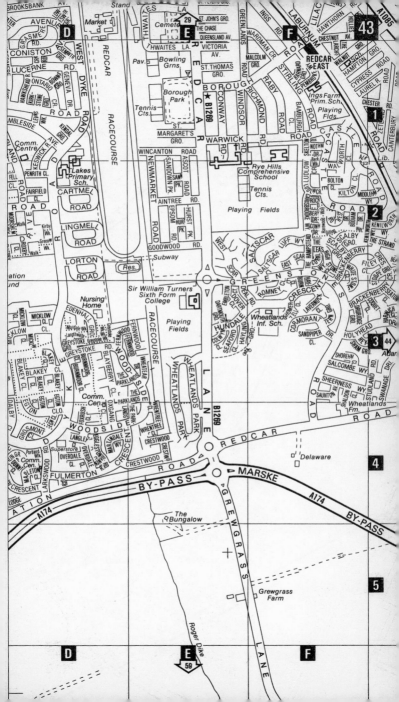

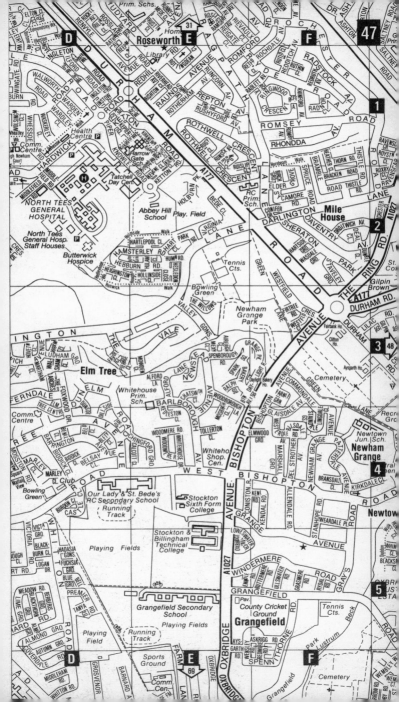

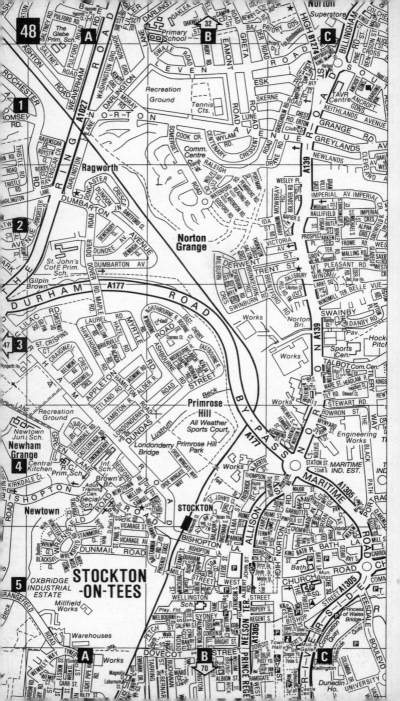

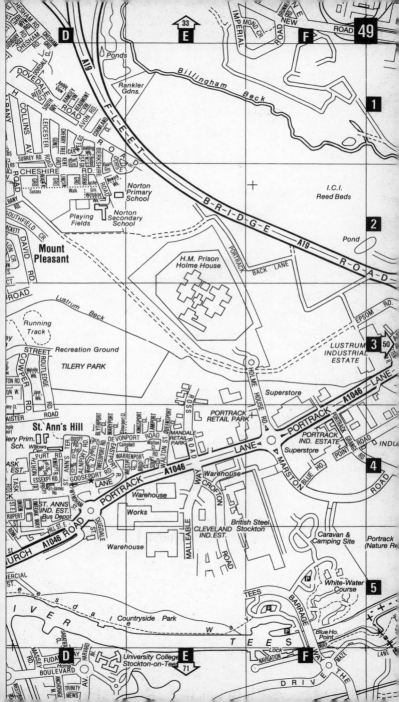

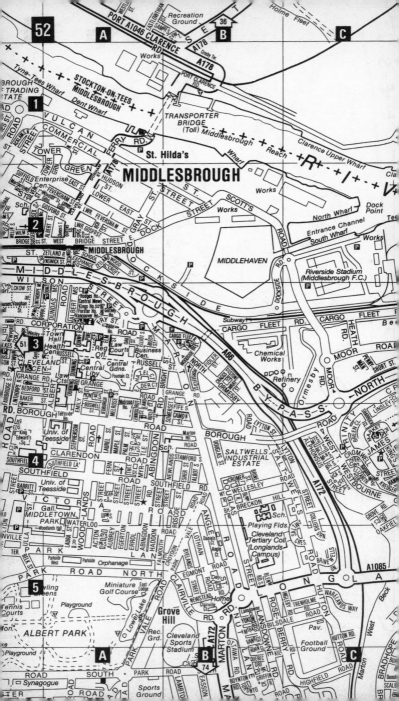

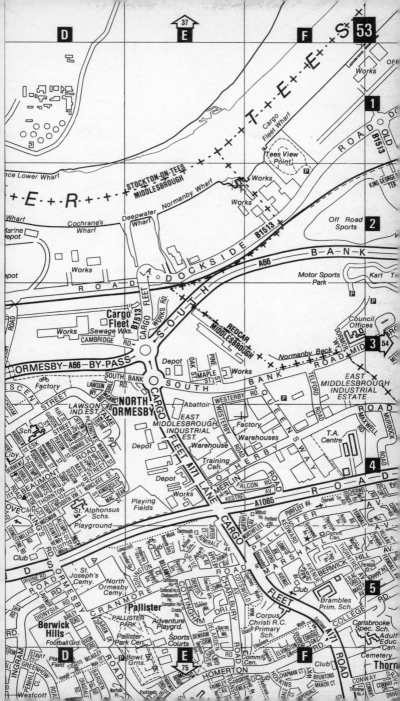

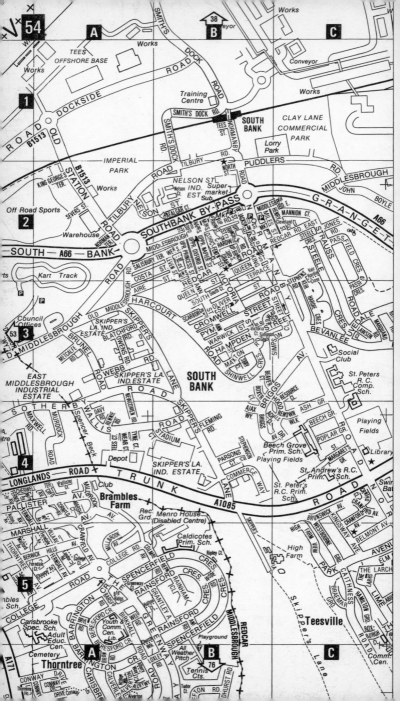

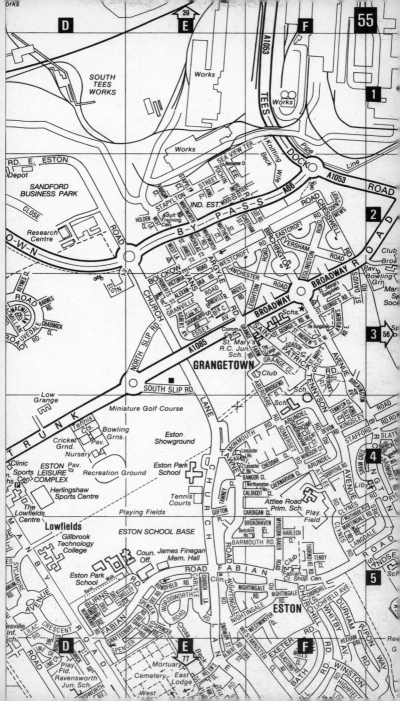

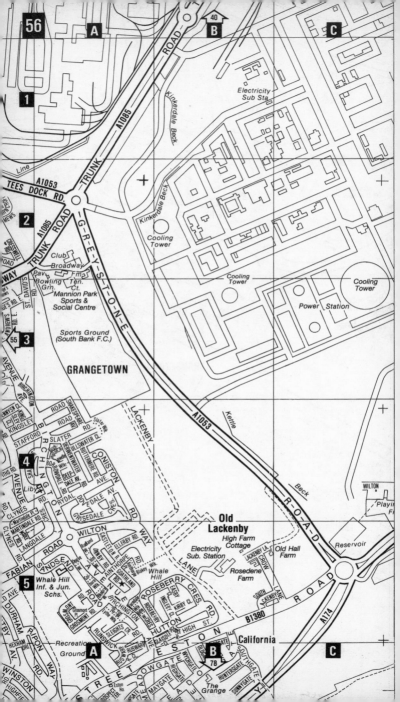

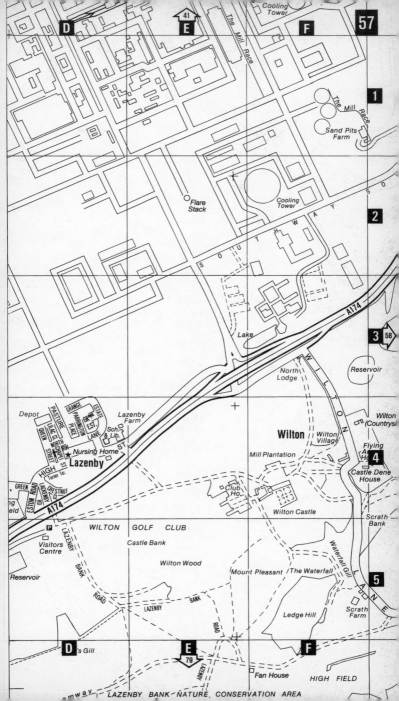

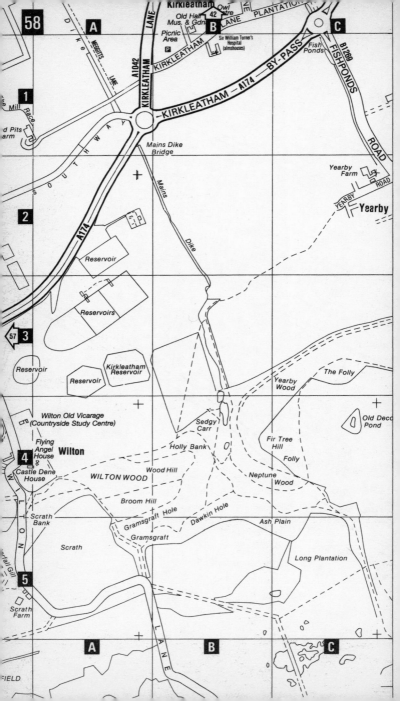

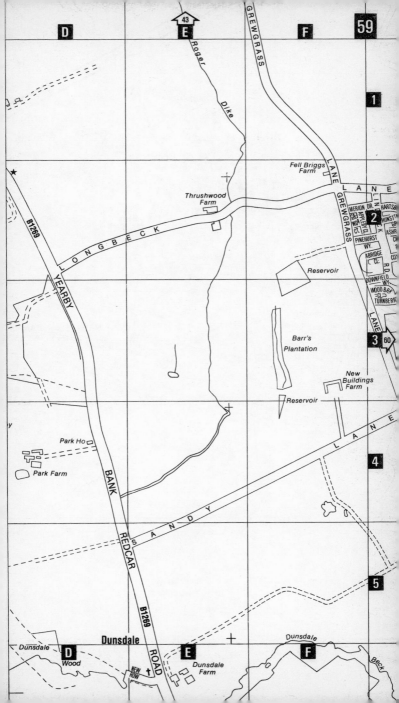

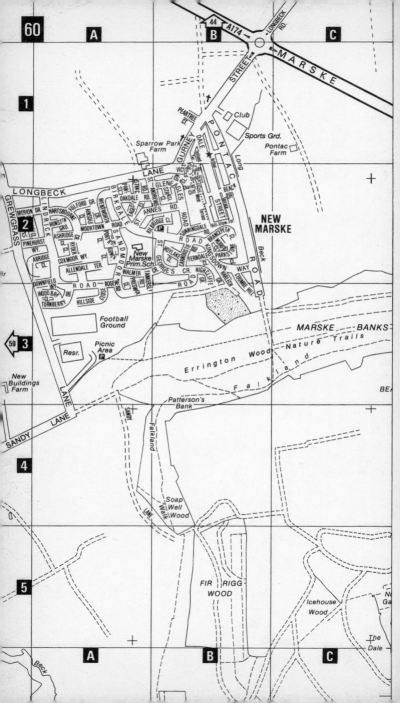

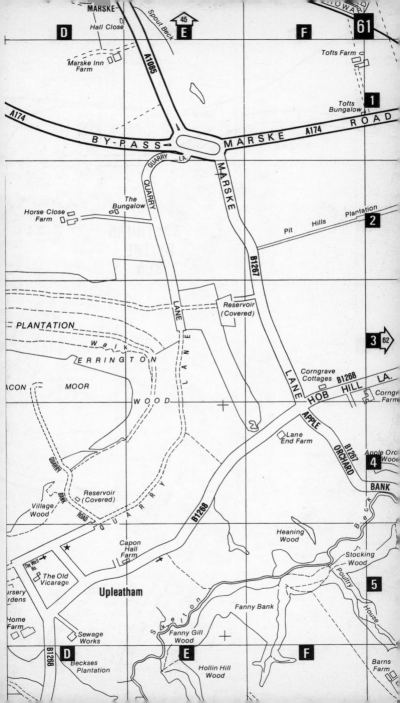

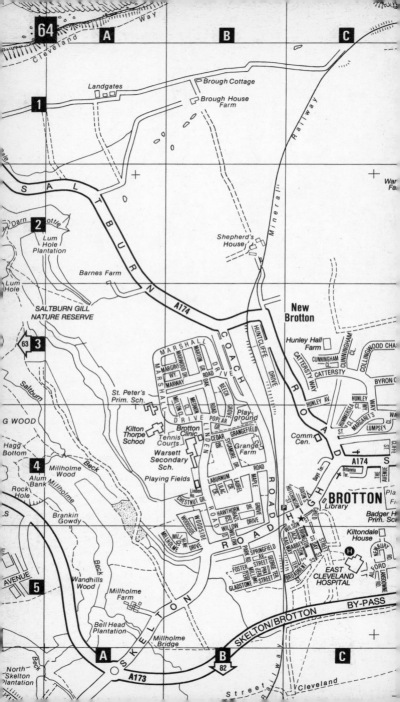

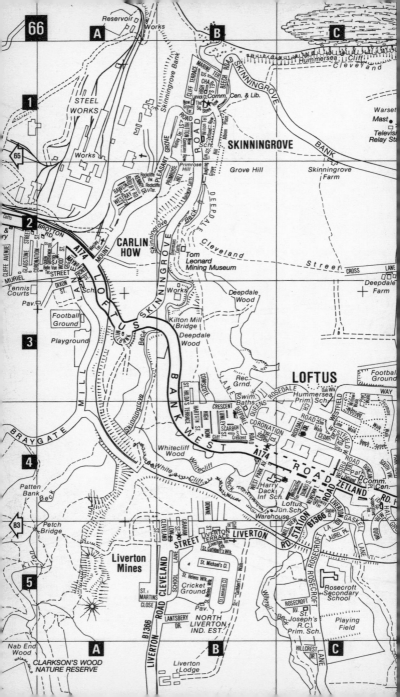

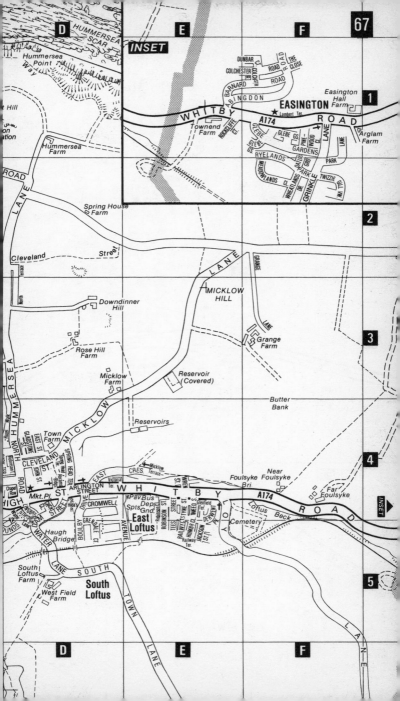

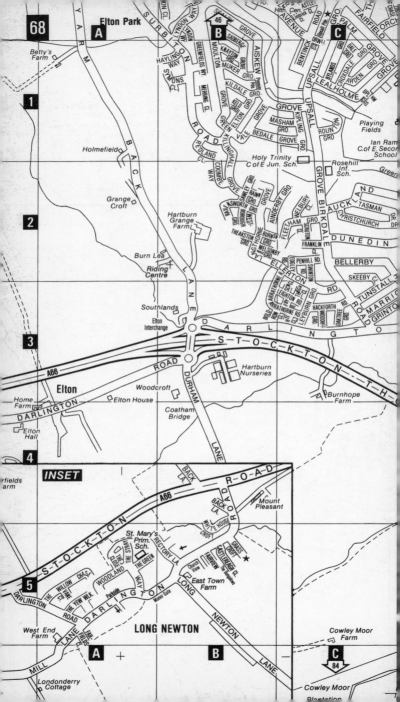

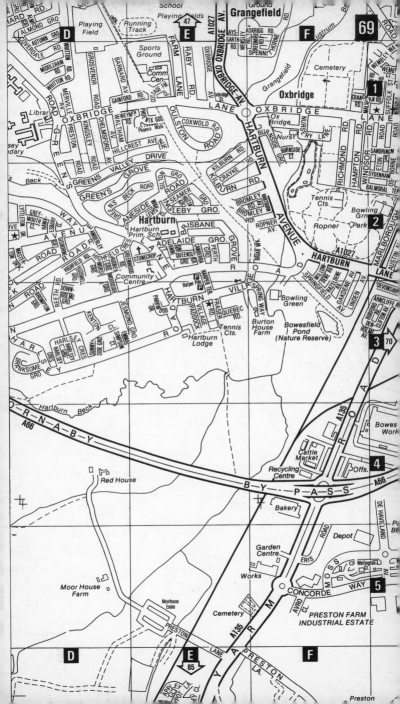

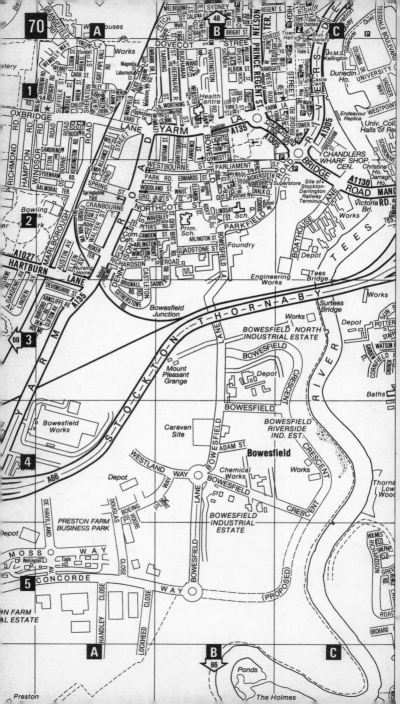

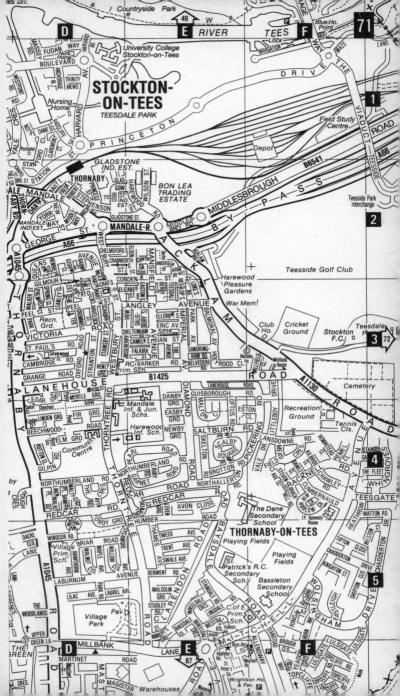

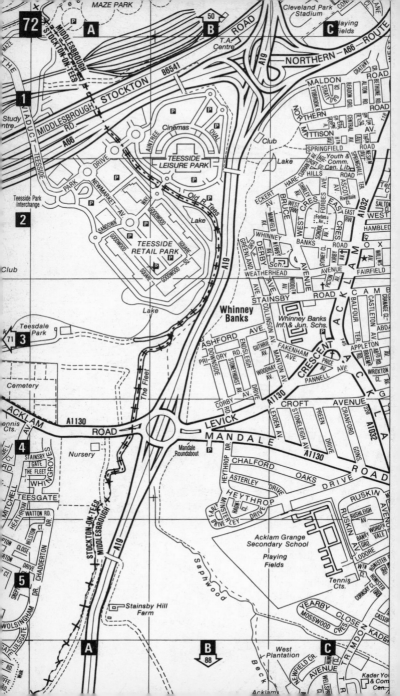

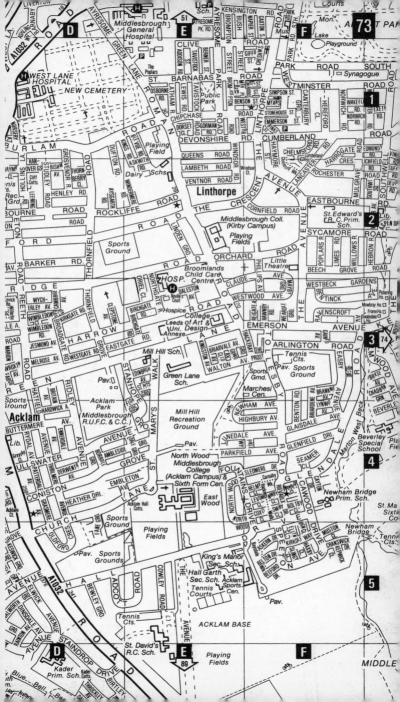

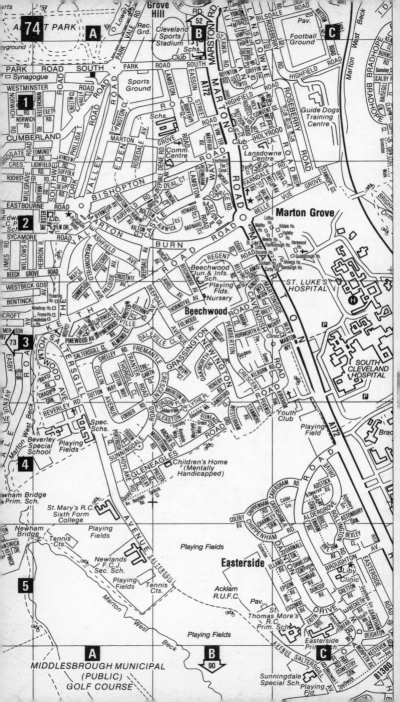

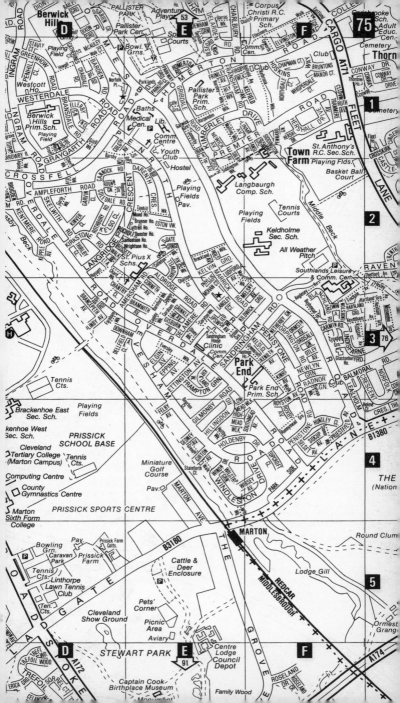

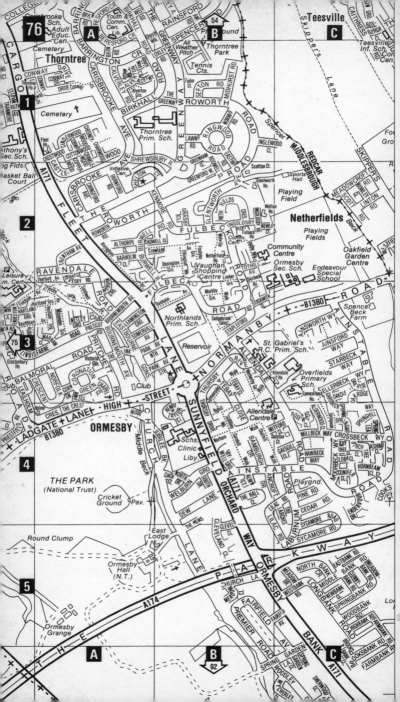

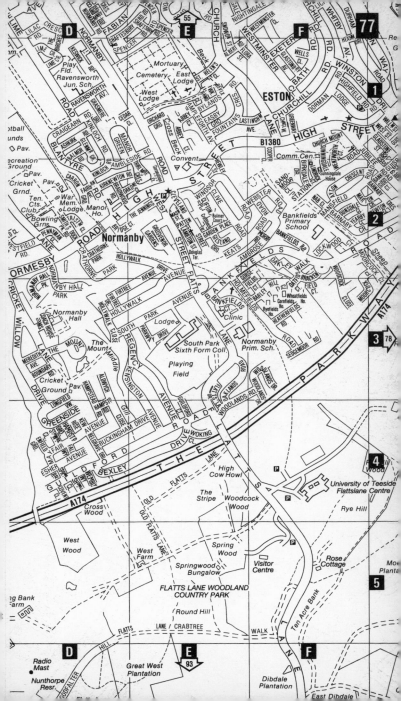

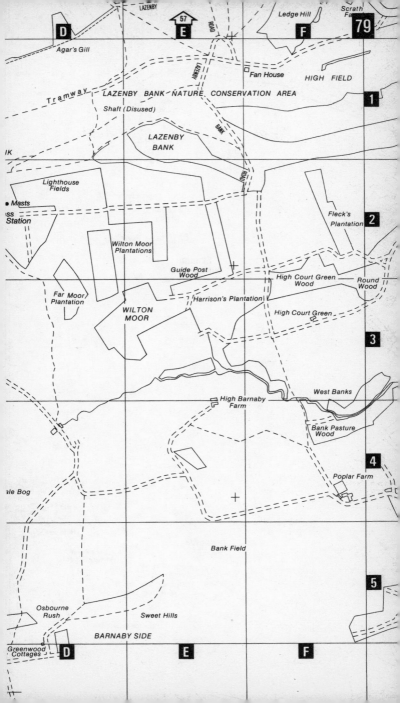

LAZENBY

Ledge Hill

Agar's Gill

Fan House

HIGH FIELD

Tramway   LAZENBY BANK NATURE CONSERVATION AREA

Shaft (Disused)

LAZENBY
BANK

Lighthouse
Fields

Masts

SS
Station

Fleck's
Plantation

Wilton Moor
Plantations

Guide Post
Wood

High Court Green
Wood

Round
Wood

Far Moor
Plantation

Harrison's Plantation

WILTON
MOOR

High Court Green

West Banks

High Barnaby
Farm

Bank Pasture
Wood

Poplar Farm

ale Bog

+

Bank Field

Osbourne
Rush

Sweet Hills

BARNABY SIDE

Greenwood
Cottages **D**   **E**   **F**

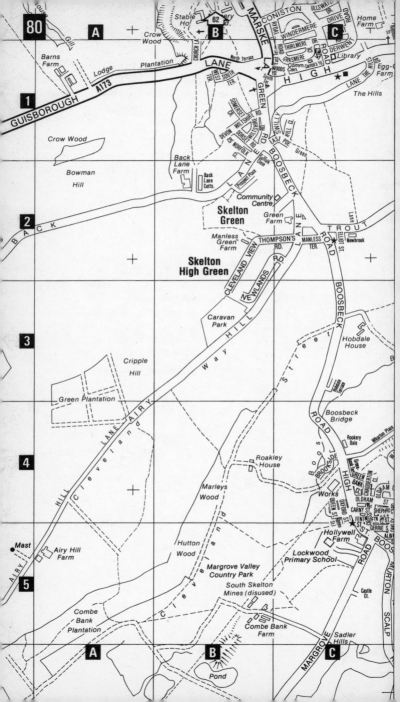

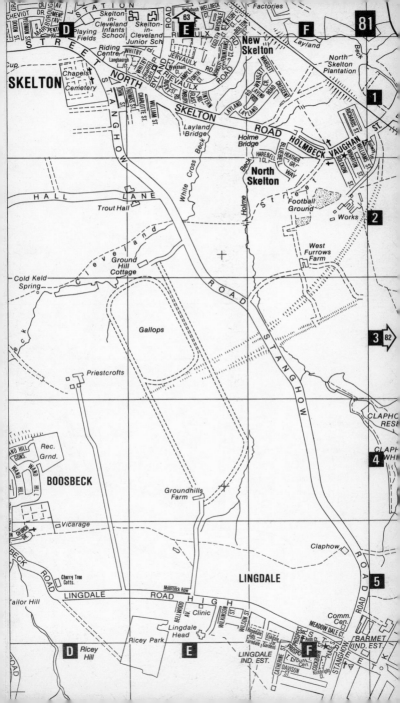

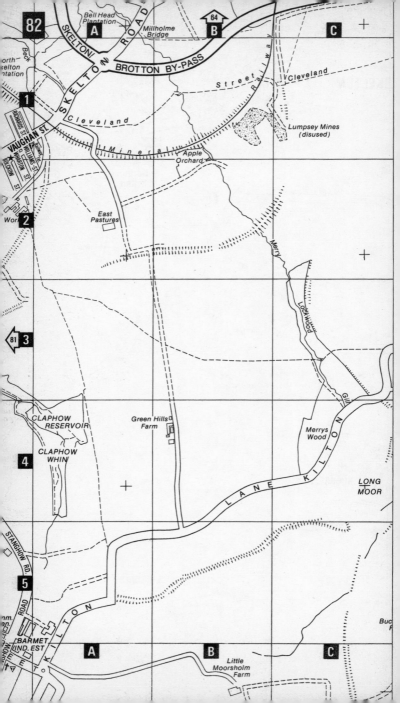

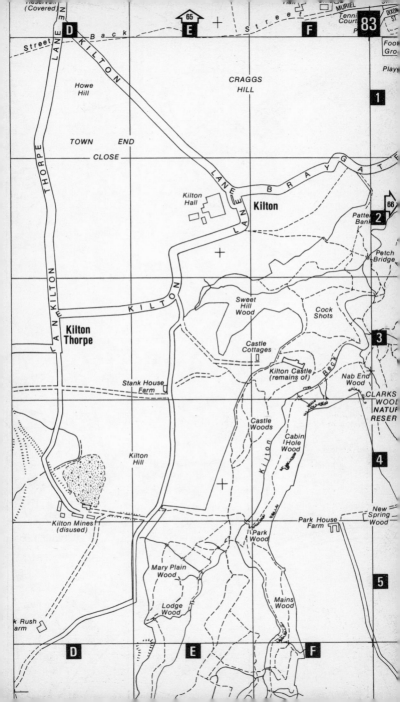

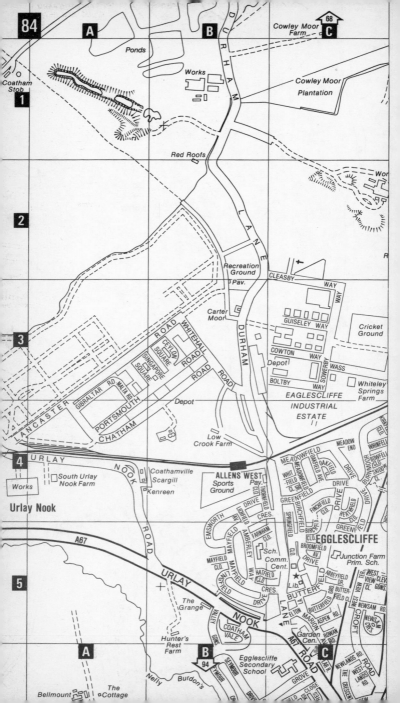

84

A B C

1

Coatham
Stob

Ponds

Works

Cowley Moor
Farm 68

Cowley Moor
Plantation

DURHAM LANE

Red Roofs

Wor

2

Recreation
Ground
Pav.

CLEASBY WAY

WAY

Carter
Moor

GUISELEY WAY

Cricket
Ground

3

ROAD

WHITEHALL ROAD

CEYLON
SQUARE

SINGAPORE
SQUARE

MALTA RD.

ROAD

DURHAM ROAD

COWTON WAY

SOWERBY WASS

Depot

BOLTBY WAY

Whiteley
Springs
Farm

LANCASTER

GIBRALTAR RD.

PORTSMOUTH

CHATHAM

Depot

Low
Crook Farm

EAGLESCLIFFE

INDUSTRIAL
ESTATE

4

URLAY

South Urlay
Nook Farm

NOOK

Coathamville
Scargill

Kenreen

Works

Urlay Nook

ROAD

ALLENS WEST
Sports
Ground

Pav.

MEADOWFIELD

MEADOW
END

OAKFIELD DRIVE

WHIT...
FIELD CL.

MEADOWFIELD NE.

DRIVE

DUNNMOOR DRIVE

BOWFIELD CL.

WHINFELL

EMSWORTH DRIVE

THORNFIELD

GREENFIELD

SPRINGFIELD

BIRCHFIELD CLO.

FINCHFIELD CLO.

HEATHFIELD

GREENFIELD DRIVE

EGGLESCLIFFE

5

A67

URLAY

NOOK

ROAD

The
Grange

Hunter's
Rest
Farm

MAYFIELD
CLO.

MAYFIELD CLO.

LINFIELD AV.

AMBERLEY

FARNHAM WAY

Sch.
Comm.
Cent.

HATFIELD CLO.

MAYFIELD
CRES.

CRES.

BROOMFIELD DRIVE

CLO.

BROOMFIELD
AV.

Junction Farm
Prim. Sch.

ABBEYFIELD
DR.

BUTTER-
FIELD CLO.

WEST
VIEW CL.

TER
MAIN RD.

NEWSAM RD.

VALLEY GDNS.

COATHAM
VALE

Lib.

BUTTERFIELD

ELTON DRIVE

MARION CLO.

BUTTERFIELD RD.

ASPEN RD.

Garden
Cen.

ROMAN RD.

A67 ROAD

CROFT

WEST-
LANDS RD.

NEWLANDS RD.

THE CRESCENT

NEWS...
CRES.

Bellmount

The
Cottage

Nelly

Burdon's

SEYMOUR

SEYMOUR

94

Egglescliffe
Secondary
School

GROVE

CLOSE

Egglescliffe

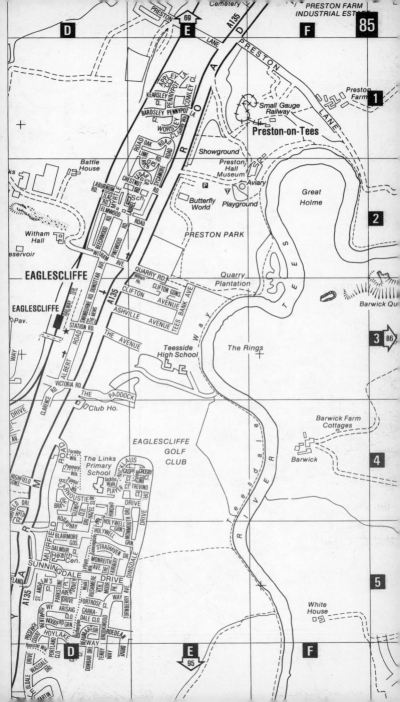

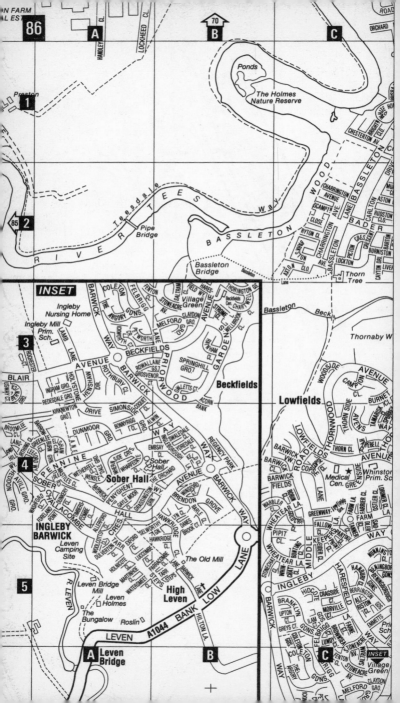

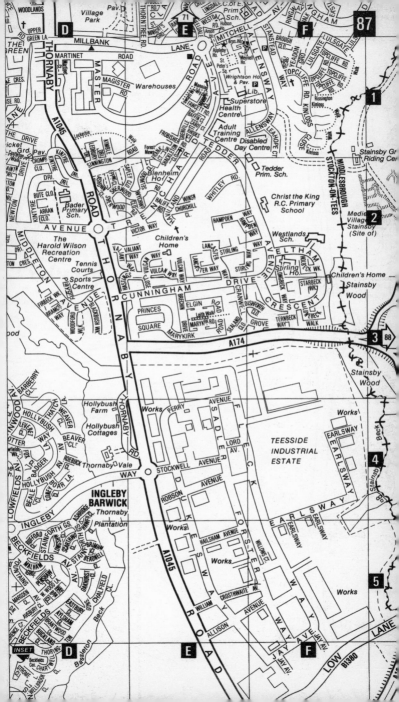

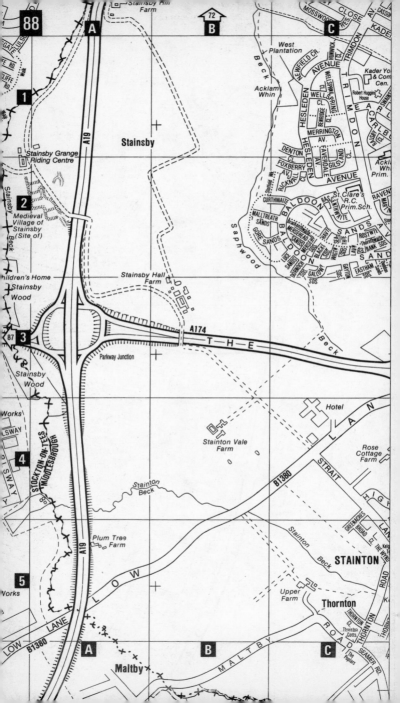

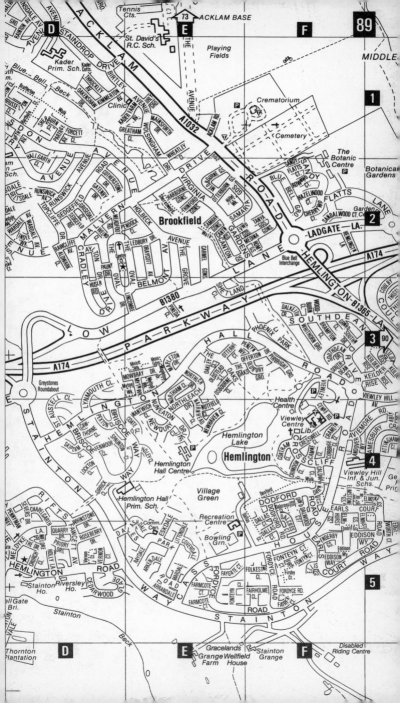

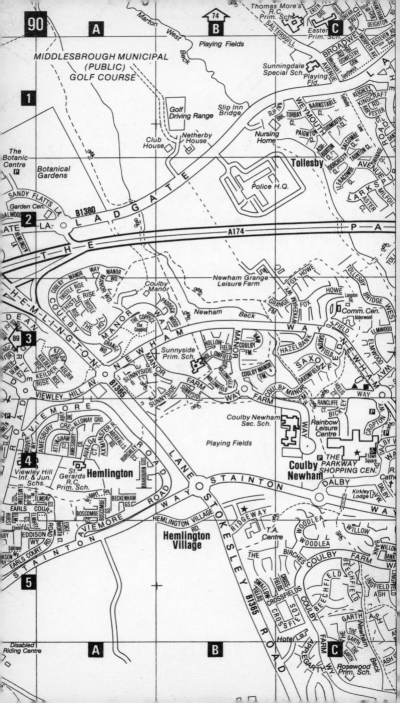

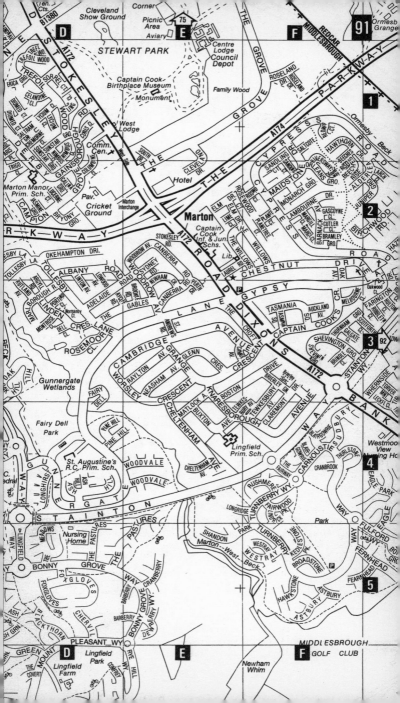

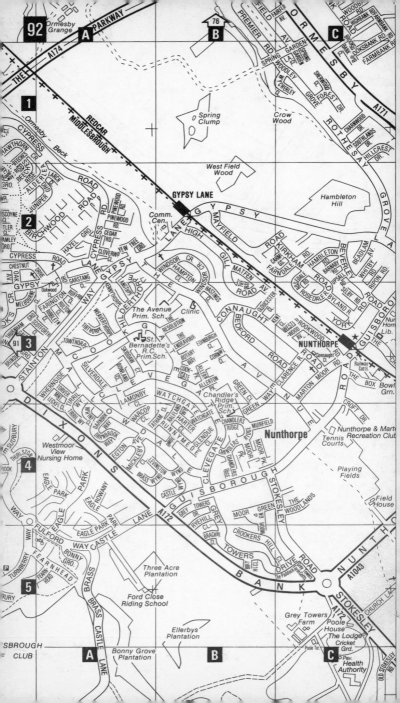

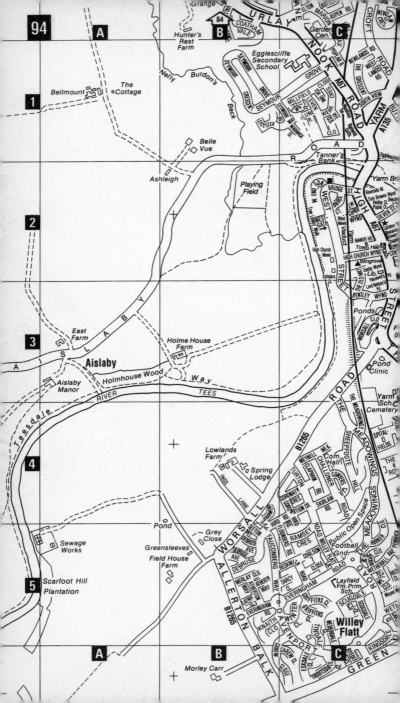

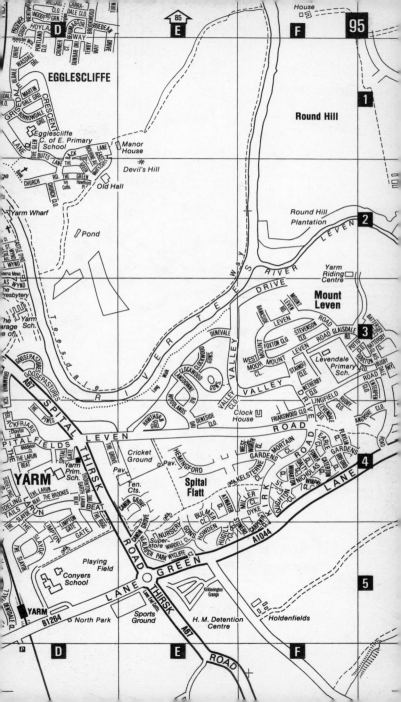

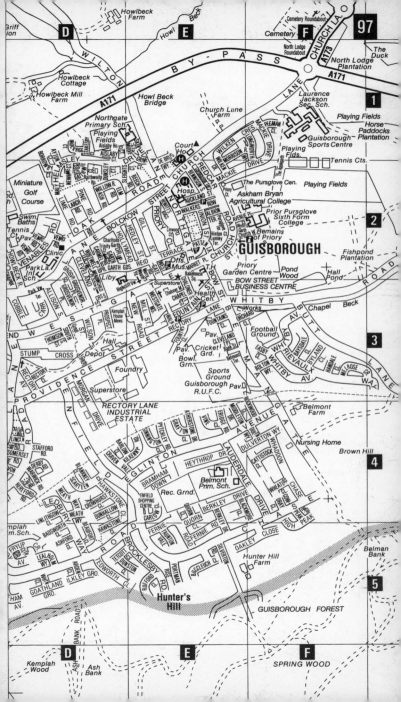

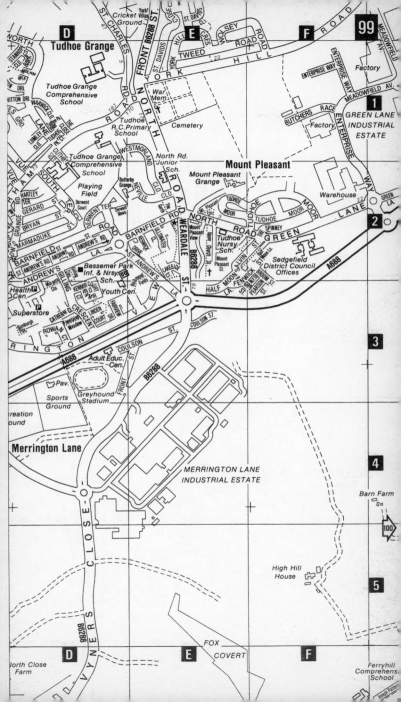

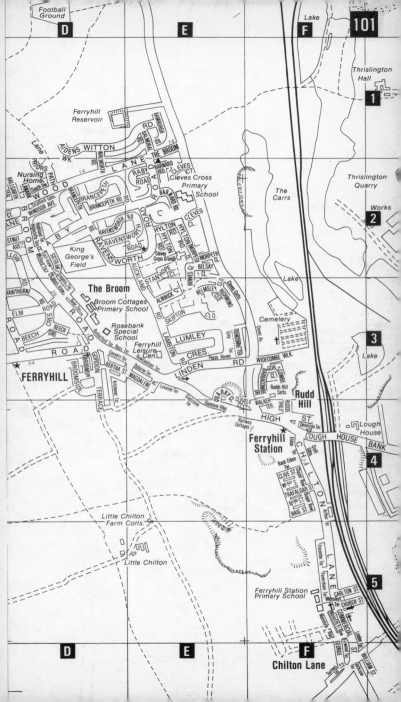

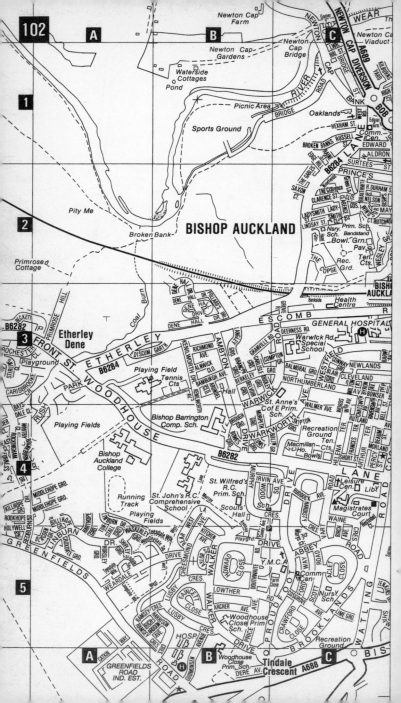

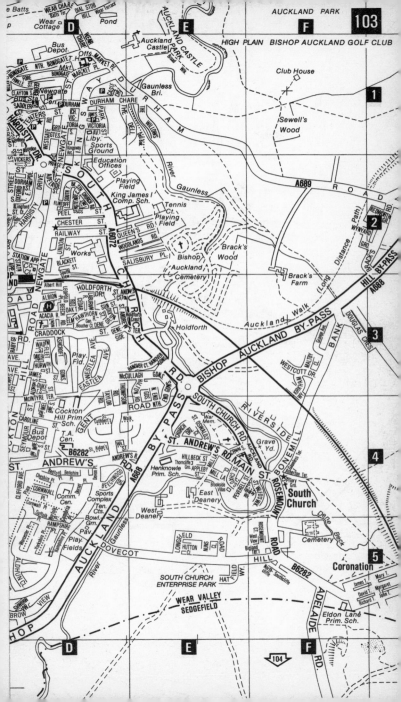

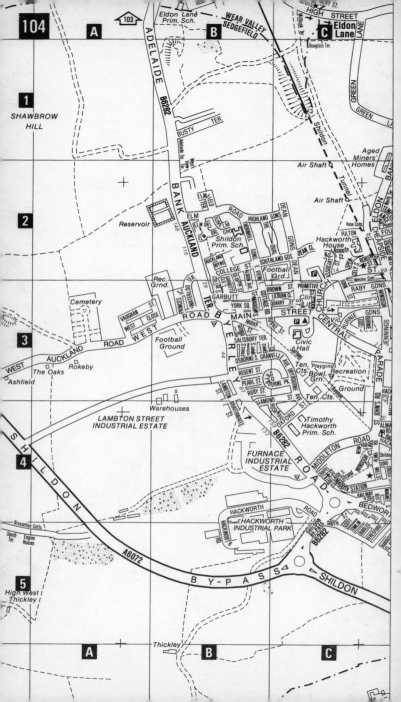

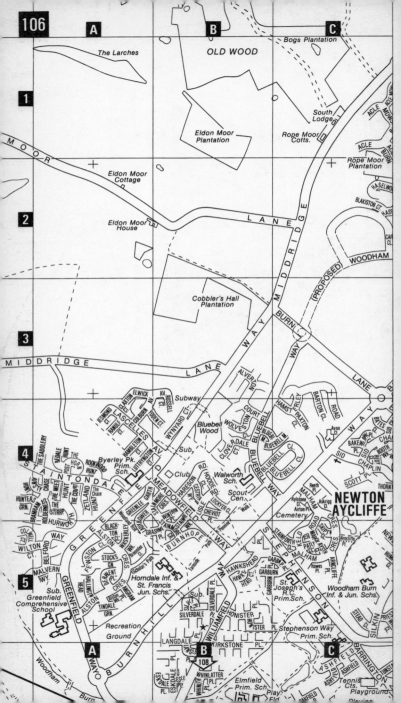

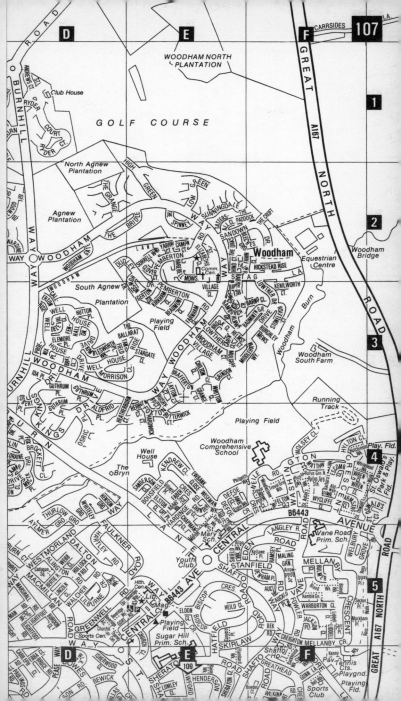

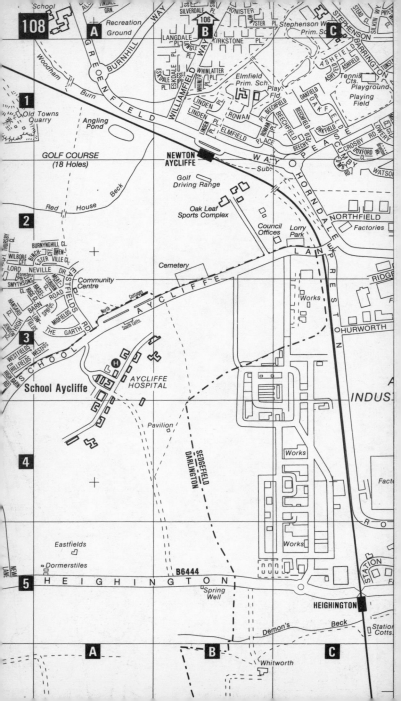

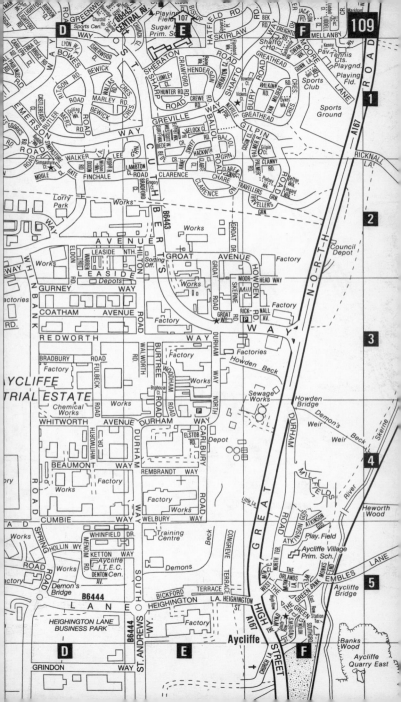

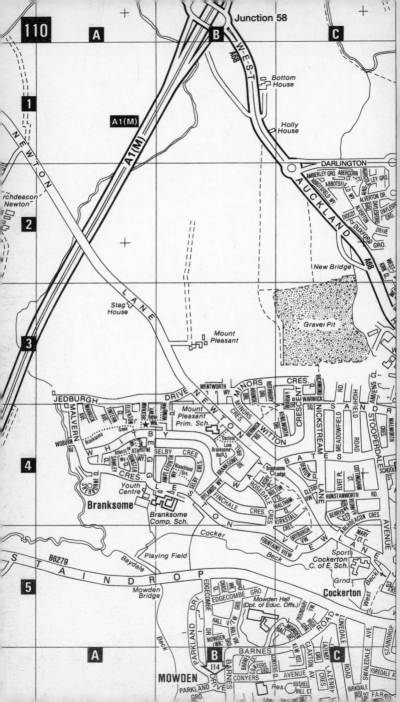

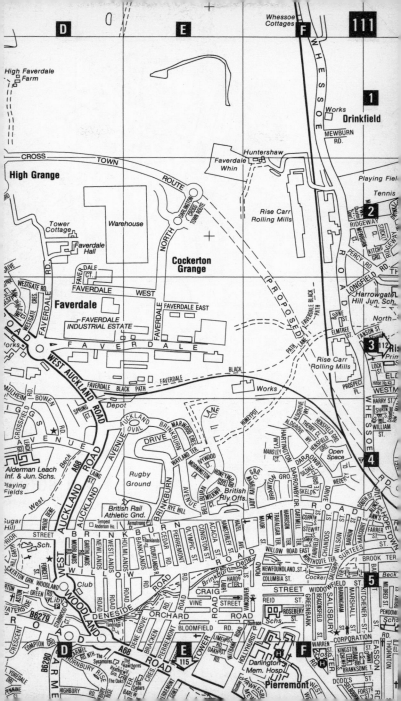

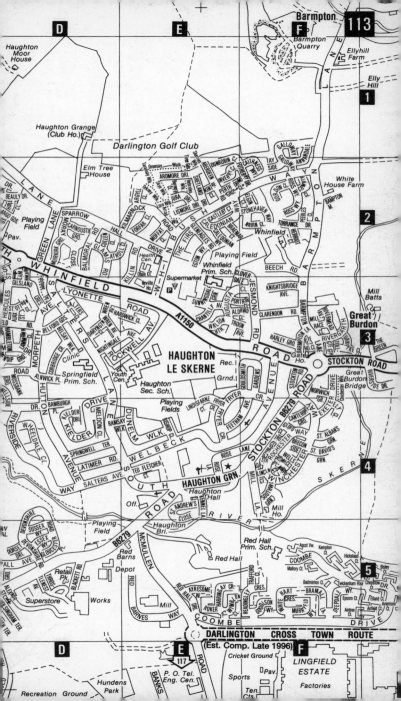

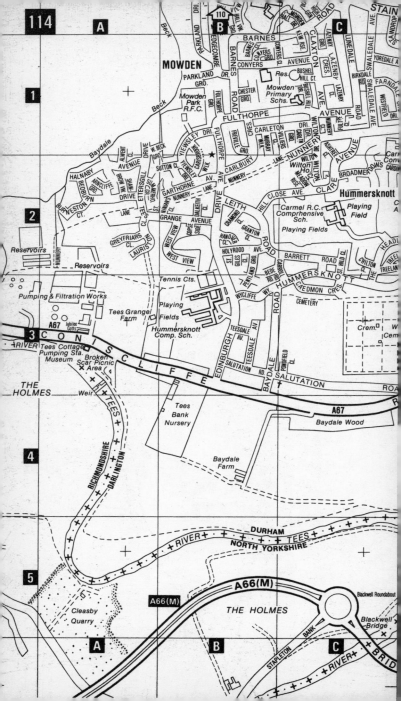

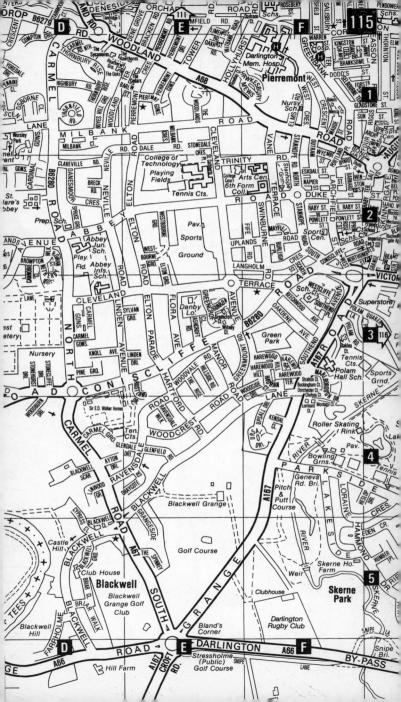

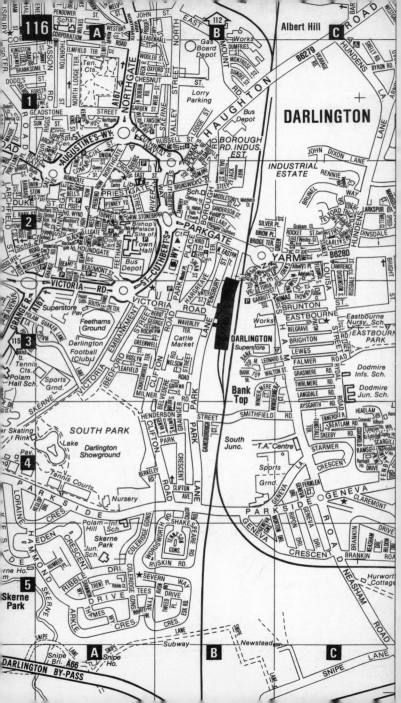

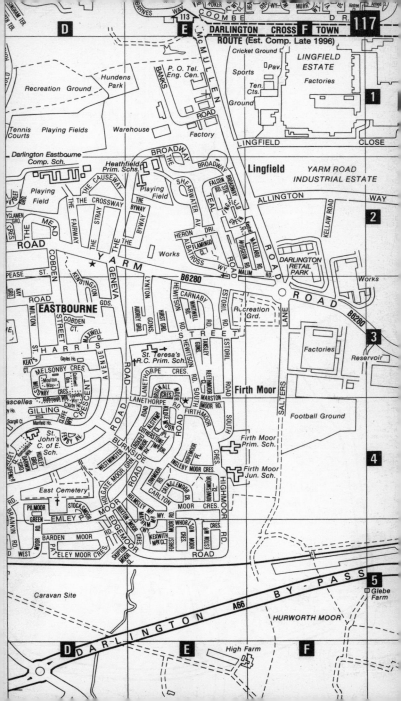

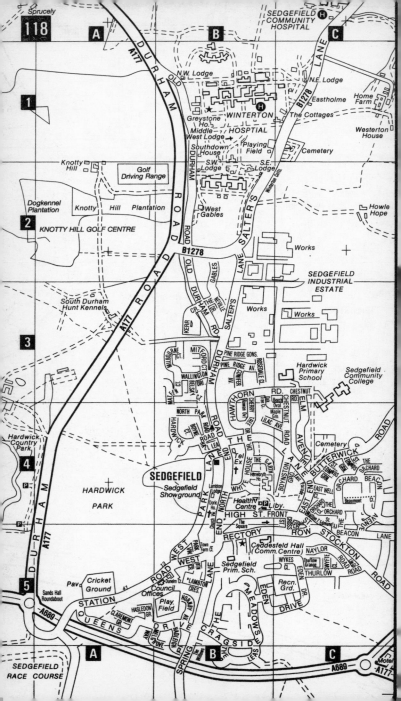

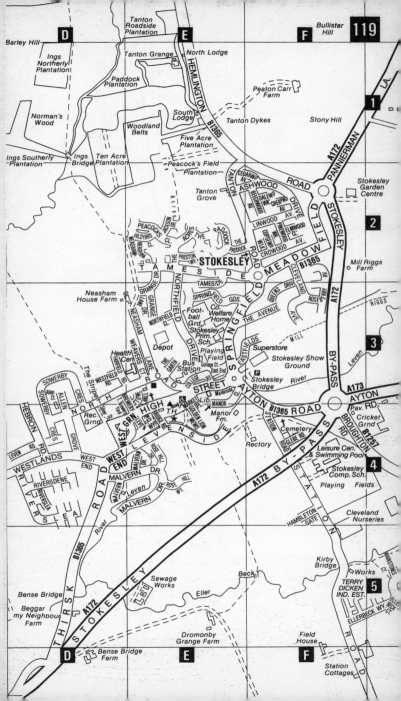

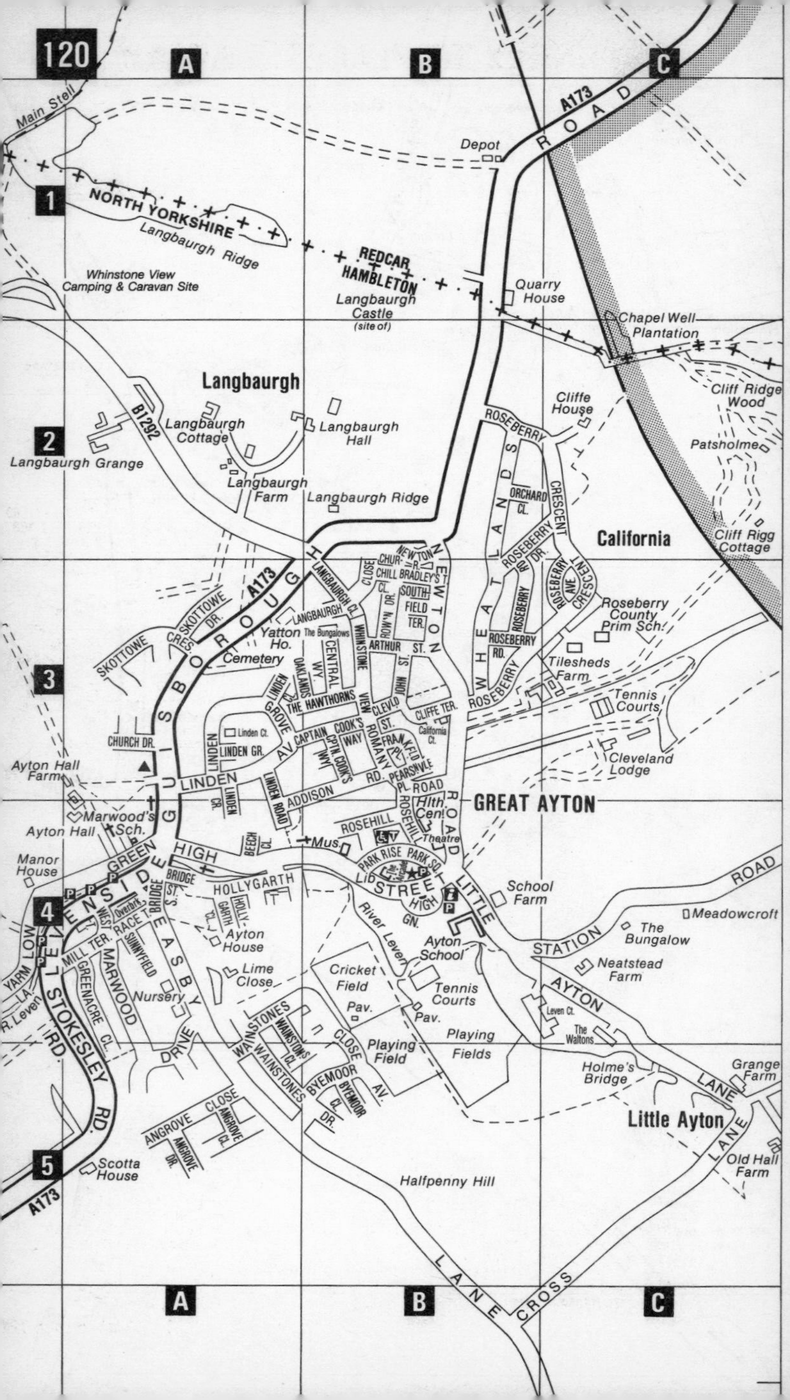

A   **B**   **C**

1

Main Stell

NORTH YORKSHIRE
Langbaurgh Ridge

REDCAR
HAMBLETON

Depot

A173 ROAD

Whinstone View
Camping & Caravan Site

Langbaurgh Castle
(site of)

Quarry
House

Chapel Well
Plantation

2

Langbaurgh

B1292

Langbaurgh Grange

Langbaurgh
Cottage

Langbaurgh
Hall

Langbaurgh
Farm

Langbaurgh Ridge

ROSEBERRY

Cliffe
House

ORCHARD
CL.

ROSEBERRY DR.

ROSEBERRY CRESCENT

Cliff Ridge
Wood

Patsholme

Cliff Rigg
Cottage

California

WHEATLANDS

Roseberry
County
Prim Sch.

3

A173

SKOTTOWE CRES.

SKOTTOWE DR.

LANGBAURGH RD.

Yatton
Ho.

The Bungalows

Langbaurgh
Cemetery

CENTRAL WY.

OAKLANDS

LINDEN GROVE

The Hawthorns

LINDEN CT.

LINDEN GR.

LINDEN AV.

CAPTAIN COOK'S WY.

COOK'S WY.

LINDEN DR.

LINDEN RD.

ADDISON

CHURCHILL DR.

BRADLEY'S CL.

DE LA MOR.

SOUTH
FIELD
TER.

ARTHUR ST.

CLEVELAND VIEW

ROMAN RD.

CLIFFE TER.

California CL.

PEARSDALE

ROSEBERRY RD.

ROSEBERRY
RD.

Tilesheds
Farm

Tennis
Courts

Cleveland
Lodge

Ayton Hall
Farm

CHURCH DR.

LINDEN

GUISBOROUGH

ROSEHILL

Mus.

Hlth Cen.

Theatre

ROAD

GREAT AYTON

4

Manor
House

Marwood's
Sch.

Ayton Hall

GREEN

HIGH

BRIDGE

BEECH

HOLLYGARTH

Smith's
RACE
TERR.

DOWNFIELD

HOLLYGARTH

LEVENSIDE

MILL TER.

GREENACRE CL.

MARWOOD

EASBY

DRIVE

Ayton
House

Nursery

Lime
Close

WAINSTONES

WAINSTONES

WAINSTONES

BYEMOOR
CLOSE

BYEMOOR
AV.

BYEMOOR
DR.

PARK RISE

PARK SQ.

Lib.

STREET

LITTLE

HIGH

GN.

Cricket
Field

Pav.

Playing
Field

River Leven

Ayton
School

Tennis
Courts

Pav.

Playing
Fields

School
Farm

STATION

AYTON

LANE

Leven Ct.

The
Waltons

Meadowcroft

The
Bungalow

Neatstead
Farm

Holme's
Bridge

Little Ayton

Grange
Farm

ROAD

Old Hall
Farm

5

YARM RD.

LOW

R. Leven

STOKESLEY RD.

A173

Scotta
House

Halfpenny Hill

CROSS

LANE

A   **B**   **C**

INDEX TO PLACES & AREAS

Names in this index shown in CAPITAL LETTERS followed by their Postcode District(s), are Postal Addresses.

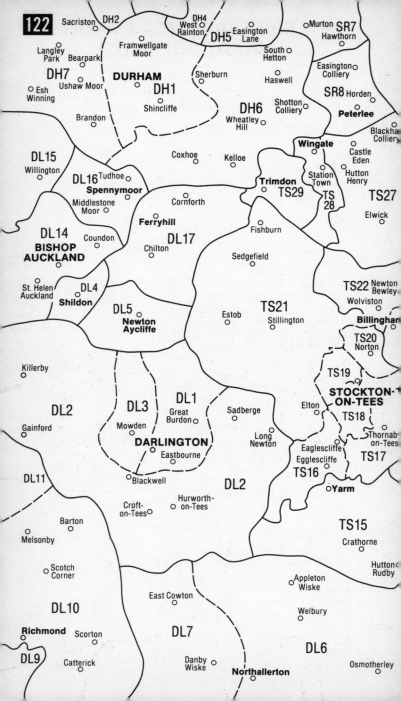

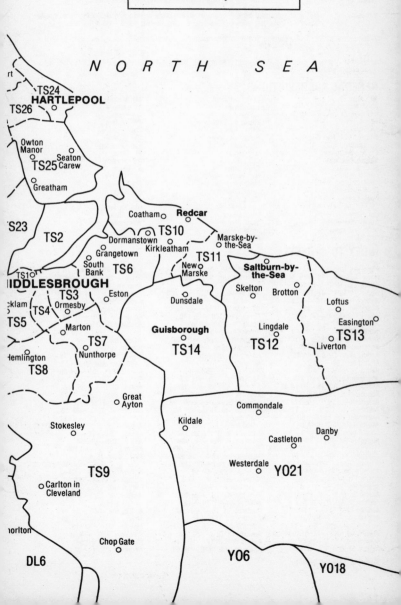

POSTCODE MAP

Posttown Boundary ————
Postcode Boundary – – – –

NORTH SEA

rt
TS24
HARTLEPOOL
TS26

Owton
Manor
TS25 Seaton
Carew
Greatham

S23 TS2
Coatham **Redcar**
TS10
Dormanstown Marske-by-
Grangetown Kirkleatham the-Sea
South TS6 TS11
Bank New **Saltburn-by-**
TS1 Marske **the-Sea**
IDDLESBROUGH
TS3 Eston Skelton Brotton
cklam Dunsdale Loftus
TS4 Ormesby
TS5 Lingdale Easington
Marton TS12 TS13
Hemlington TS7 **Guisborough** Liverton
TS8 Nunthorpe TS14

Great
Ayton Commondale

Stokesley Kildale Danby
Castleton

Westerdale YO21
TS9

Carlton in
Cleveland

norlton

Chop Gate
DL6 YO6
YO18

INDEX TO STREETS

HOW TO USE THIS INDEX

1. Each street name is followed by its Postal District and then by its map reference;
   e.g. Abbey Rd. DL3 —2D **115** is in the Darlington 3 Postal District and is to be found in square 2D on page **115**. The page number being shown in bold type.
   A strict alphabetical order is followed in which Av., Rd., St., etc. (though abbreviated) are read in full and as part of the street name; e.g. Ashbourne Clo. appears after Ash Bank Rd. but before Ashbourne Rd.

2. Streets and a selection of Subsidiary names not shown on the Maps, appear in the index in *Italics* with the thoroughfare to which it is connected shown in brackets; e.g. *Admiral Ho. TS24 —4B 8 (off Warrior Quay)*

3. The Postcode for any Posttown or Postal Locality can be found in the Index to Places on page **121** or the Postcode Map on pages **122** & **123**.

4. With the now general usage of Postcodes for addressing mail, it is not recommended that this index is used for such a purpose.

GENERAL ABBREVIATIONS

All : Alley	Cres : Crescent	M : Mews
App : Approach	Dri : Drive	Mt : Mount
Arc : Arcade	E : East	N : North
Av : Avenue	Embkmt : Embankment	Pal : Palace
Bk : Back	Est : Estate	Pde : Parade
Boulevd : Boulevard	Gdns : Gardens	Pk : Park
Bri : Bridge	Ga : Gate	Pas : Passage
B'way : Broadway	Grn : Green	Pl : Place
Bldgs : Buildings	Gro : Grove	Rd : Road
Bus : Business	Gt : Great	S : South
Cen : Centre	Ho : House	Sq : Square
Chu : Church	Ind : Industrial	Sta : Station
Chyd : Churchyard	Junct : Junction	St : Street
Circ : Circle	La : Lane	Ter : Terrace
Cir : Circus	Lit : Little	Up : Upper
Clo : Close	Lwr : Lower	Vs : Villas
Comn : Common	Mnr : Manor	Wlk : Walk
Cotts : Cottages	Mans : Mansions	W : West
Ct : Court	Mkt : Market	Yd : Yard

INDEX TO STREETS

Abberley Dri. TS8 —4A **90**
Abberston Wlk. TS4 —4B **74**
Abbey Clo. TS19 —4B **46**
Abbey Ct. TS6 —1E **77**
Abbeyfield Dri. TS16 —5C **84**
Abbey Rd. DL3 —2D **115**
Abbey Rd. DL14 —5C **102**
Abbey St. TS12 —5C **64**
Abbey St. TS24 —2D **9**
Abbotsfield Way. DL3 —2C **110**
Abbotsford Rd. TS5 —3C **72**
Abbots Way. TS19 —4A **46**
Abdale Av. TS5 —3C **72**
Abdiel Ct. TS24 —1A **8**
Abercorn Ct. DL3 —2C **110**
Abercrombie Rd. TS10 —1A **42**
Aberdare Rd. TS6 —3F **55**
Aberdeen Rd. DL1 —2E **113**
Aberdeen Rd. TS25 —4E **11**
Aberdovey Dri. TS16 —5D **85**
Aberfalls Rd. TS8 —4A **90**
Abigail Wlk. TS24 —3F **7**
Abingdon Rd. TS1
—5A **52** to 3A **52**
Abingdon Rd. TS13 —1E **67**
Abrams Bldgs. TS13 —4D **67**
Abridge Clo. TS11 —2A **60**
Acacia Rd. DL14 —3D **103**
Acacia Rd. TS19 —3A **48**
Acacia St. DL3 —5E **111**
Acclom St. TS24 —3E **7**
Achilles Clo. TS6 —4C **54**
Acklam Ct. TS5 —4D **73**
Acklam Hall Cotts. TS5 —4E **73**
Acklam Rd. TS5 —5D **51** to 2F **89**
Acklam Rd. TS17 —3E **71**
Acklam St. N. TS2 —1F **51**

Acklam St. S. TS2 —2F **51**
Ackworth Grn. TS3 —5E **53**
Acle Burn. DL5 —1C **106**
Acle Meadows. DL5 —1C **106**
Aclet Clo. DL14 —5C **102**
Acorn Bank. TS17 —3B **86**
Acres, The. TS9 —2E **119**
Acton St. TS1 —5A **52**
Adam Clo. TS10 —3B **42**
Adamson St. DL4 —5D **105**
Adam St. TS18 —4B **70**
Adcott Rd. TS5 —5D **73**
Adderley St. TS18 —2B **70**
Addington Dri. TS3 —5E **53**
Addison Rd. TS5 —1E **73**
Addison Rd. TS9 —3B **120**
Addison Rd. TS24 —4F **7**
Adelaide Bank. DL4 —5F **103**
Adelaide Gro. TS18 —2E **69**
Adelaide Pl. TS11 —4D **45**
Adelaide Rd. TS7 —3D **91**
Adelaide St. DL1 —2B **116**
Adelaide St. DL4 —4C **104**
Adelaide St. DL14 —2D **103**
Adelaide Ter. DL4 —1B **104**
Adelphi Ct. DL1 —2C **116**
Aden St. TS5 —5D **51**
*Admiral Ho. TS24 —4B 8
(off Warrior Quay)*
Admirals Av. TS3 —5E **53**
Admiral Way. TS24 —4B **8**
Adshead Rd. TS10 —1A **42**
Adstock Av. TS4 —4C **74**
Agecroft Gdns. TS5 —2C **72**
Agricola Ct. DL3 —2C **110**
Aidens Wlk. DL17 —1D **101**
Ainderby Gro. TS18 —2B **68**

Ainderby Wlk. TS24 —1A **8**
Ainderby Way. TS4 —3B **74**
Ainsdale Clo. TS11 —2A **60**
Ainsdale Way. TS4 —4B **74**
Ainsford Way. TS7 —3C **76**
Ainsley Gro. DL3 —2C **110**
Ainsley St. TS25 —1B **12**
Ainstable Rd. TS7
—4B **76** to 3C **76**
Ainsty Hunt. DL5 —4A **106**
Ainsworth Way. TS7 —3C **76**
*Ainthorpe Bungalows. TS6 —5A 56
(off Ainthorpe Rd.)*
Ainthorpe Pl. TS6 —5A **56**
Ainthorpe Rd. TS6 —5A **56**
Aintree Ct. DL1 —5F **113**
Aintree Oval. TS5 —1B **72**
Aintree Rd. TS10 —2E **43**
Aintree Rd. TS18 —3A **50**
Airdrie Gro. TS25 —4D **11**
Aireborough Clo. TS19 —3E **47**
Aire St. TS1 —5E **51**
Aire St. TS6 —3A **54**
Airton Pl. DL5 —4C **106**
Airy Hill La. TS12
—5A **80** to 2C **80**
Aiskew Gro. TS19 —1B **68**
Aislaby Ct. TS14 —1D **97**
Aislaby Gro. TS23 —3F **19**
*Aislaby Ho. TS2 —1F 51
(off Dacre St.)*
Aislaby Ho. TS14 —1D **97**
Aislaby Rd. TS16 —3A **94**
Ajax St. DL1 —3D **113**
Ajax Way. TS6 —4B **54**
Alan St. TS6 —2B **54**
Albany Ct. TS26 —4E **7**

Albany Rd. TS7 —2D 91
Albany Rd. TS20 —1D 49
Albany St. TS1 —4F 51
Albatross Way. DL1 —2E 117
Albert Hill. DL14 —3D 103
Albert M. TS1 —3A 52
Alberto St. TS18 —4B 48
Albert Rd. DL1 —5A 112
Albert Rd. TS1 —3A 52
Albert Rd. TS6 —1E 77
Albert Rd. TS16 —3D 85
Albert Rd. TS18 —5B 48
Albert Rd. TS19 —5C 46
Albert St. DL1 —2B 116
Albert St. DL4 —2D 105
Albert St. TS2 —2A 52
Albert St. TS10 —4D 29
Albert St. TS24 —5A 8
Albert Ter. TS1 —5F 51
Albery Pl. DL1 —2C 116
Albion Av. DL4 —2B 104
Albion Ho. TS2 —1A 52
(off Dacre St.)
Albion Pl. TS13 —1B 66
Albion St. DL16 —5A 98
Albion St. TS12 —5C 80
Albion St. TS18 —1B 70
Albion Ter. DL14 —3D 103
Albion Ter. TS12 —1D 63 & 2D 63
Albion Ter. TS14 —2E 97
Albion Ter. TS24 —3D 9
Albourne Grn. TS4 —4C 74
(in two parts)
Albury Way. TS3 —1A 76
Alconbury Way. TS3 —1A 76
Aldam St. DL1 —4A 112
Aldbrough Clo. TS19 —5C 46
Aldbrough Wlk. DL1 —4D 117
Aldburgh Clo. TS25 —2C 14
Aidenham Rd. TS14 —5C 96
Aldergrove Dri. TS4 —4C 74
Alderlea. TS7 —2A 92
Alderney Wlk. TS14 —4C 96
Alder Rd. TS19 —3A 48
Alderson St. DL14 —3D 103
Alderson St. TS26 —5E 7
Alderwood. TS8 —3C 90
Alderwood Clo. DL1 —3E 113
Alderwood Clo. TS7 —4C 76
Alderwood Clo. TS27 —3A 4
Aldfrid Pl. DL5 —4D 107
Aldgrove Way. DL3 —4F 111
Aldhun Clo. DL14 —5D 103
Aldridge Rd. TS3 —3E 75
Aldwark Clo. TS20 —3D 89
Aldwych Clo. TS6 —3D 77
Aldwyn Wlk. DL5 —4F 107
Alexander St. DL1 —5D 113
Alexander Ter. TS3 —5F 53
Alexandra Gdns. DL4 —2D 105
Alexandra Rd. TS6 —3E 55
Alexandra St. DL4 —2D 105
Alexandra St. TS18 —1A 70
Alford Gro. TS25 —4E 11
Alford La. TS19 —3E 47
Alford Rd. TS12 —5C 64
Alfred St. DL1 —4B 112
Alfred St. TS10 —4E 29
Alfred St. TS24 —2D 9
Alfriston Clo. TS17 —5C 86
Alice Row. TS18 —1A 70
Alice St. TS20 —5C 32
Alington Rd. DL5 —5D 107
Allan St. DL1 —5C 112
Allan Wlk. DL5 —5E 107
Allen Ct. TS9 —4D 119
Allendale Ho. TS7 —3C 76

Allendale Rd. TS7 —3B 76
Allendale Rd. TS18 —4F 47
Allendale Rd. TS23 —2D 33
Allendale St. TS25 —5C 12
Allendale Ter. TS11 —2A 60
Allen Gro. TS9 —3D 119
Allensway. TS17 —1F 87
Allerford Clo. TS17 —5A 86
Allerton Balk. TS15 —5B 94
Allerton Pk. TS7 —3B 92
Alliance Ind. Est. DL1 —5C 112
Alliance St. DL3 —4A 112
Alliance St. TS18 —1A 70
Alliance St. TS24 —1D 9
Allington Dri. TS23 —4E 19
Allington Wlk. TS23 —4E 19
Allington Way. DL1 —2F 117
Allinson St. TS3 —4D 53
Allison Av. TS17 —4B 86
Allison Pl. TS24 —2C 8
Allison St. TS14 —3D 97
Allison St. TS18 —5B 48
Alloa Gro. TS25 —4E 11
Alloway Gro. TS8 —4A 90
All Saints Ind. Est. DL4 —5E 105
All Saints Rd. DL4 —5D 105
Alma Ho. TS2 —2A 52
(off Cleveland St.)
Alma Pde. TS10 —4D 29
Alma Rd. DL4 —4C 104
(in two parts)
Alma St. TS18 —5B 48
Alma St. TS26 —4E 7
(in two parts)
Almond Ct. DL4 —4E 105
Almond Ct. TS4 —3A 74
Almond Gro. TS11 —5D 45
Almond Gro. TS19 —5D 47
Alness Gro. TS25 —4E 11
Ainport Rd. TS18 —4D 49
Alnwick Clo. DL14 —3B 102
Alnwick Clo. DL17 —3E 101
Alnwick Clo. TS10 —1F 43
Alnwick Clo. TS27 —5B 4
Alnwick Ct. TS4 —2B 74
Alnwick Gro. DL5 —3E 107
Alnwick Gro. TS20 —4B 32
Alnwick Ho. TS4 —2C 74
Alnwick Pl. DL1 —3D 113
Alpha Gro. TS20 —2C 48
Alphonsus St. TS3 —4C 52
Alston Cres. DL5 —5A 106
Alston Grn. TS3 —5E 53
Alston Moor Clo. DL1 —4E 117
Alston St. TS26 —1F 11
Alston Wlk. DL5 —5A 106
Althorpe Clo. TS3 —2A 76
Alton Rd. TS5 —1C 72
Alum Way. TS12 —5F 63
Alva Gro. TS25 —4E 11
Alverstone Av. TS25 —2F 11
Alverton Clo. TS3 —1A 76
Alverton Ct. DL5 —4B 106
Alverton Dri. DL3 —2C 110
Alverton Gro. TS3 —1A 76
Alvingham Ter. TS3 —2A 76
Alvis Clo. TS23 —1C 34
Alvis Ct. TS23 —1C 34
Alwent Clo. DL3 —2A 114
Alwent Rd. TS1 —4F 51
Alwin Clo. TS17 —4A 86
Alwinton Ct. TS7 —4B 76
Alwyn Rd. DL3 —1B 112
Amberley Clo. TS18 —2D 69
Amberley Grn. TS3 —5E 53
Amberley Gro. DL3 —2C 110
Amberley Way. TS16 —5B 84

Amber St. TS1 —4F 51
Amber St. TS12 —1D 63
Amberton Rd. TS24 —2F 7
Amberwood Clo. TS27 —3A 4
Amberwood Wlk. TS27 —3A 4
(off Amberwood Clo.)
Amble Clo. TS26 —4B 6
Amble Ct. TS25 —1C 10
Ambleside Av. TS10 —1D 43
Ambleside Gro. TS5 —4D 73
Ambleside Rd. TS6 —2D 77
Ambleside Rd. TS23 —5F 33
Amble View. TS20 —1D 49
Ambrose Rd. TS6 —2F 77
Amersham Rd. TS3 —3E 75
Amesbury Cres. TS8 —4A 90
Amiens Clo. DL3 —3C 110
Ammerston Rd. TS1 —3E 51
Ampleforth Av. TS6 —1E 77
Ampleforth Clo. TS12 —1E 81
Ampleforth Rd. TS3 —2D 75
Ampleforth Rd. TS23 —1A 34
Ampleforth Way. DL3 —4B 110
Amroth Grn. TS3 —5E 53
Anchorage M. TS17 —1D 71
Anchor Ct. TS24 —2D 9
Anchor Ho. TS24 —4B 8
(off Warrior Quay)
Ancroft Dri. TS7 —4B 76
Ancroft Gdns. TS20 —1C 48
Anderson Rd. TS17 —2E 71
Anderson St. TS17 —2E 71
Andover Way. TS8 —4F 89
Andrew Pl. TS24 —5F 7
Andrew St. TS24 —5A 8
Androssan Ct. TS25 —4E 11
Anfield Ct. DL1 —5F 113
Angle Ct. TS4 —5B 52
Anglesey Av. TS3 —3F 75
Anglesey Gro. TS26 —2C 6
Anglesey Wlk. TS14 —4D 97
(off Hutton La.)
Angle St. TS4 —5B 52
Angling Grn. TS13 —2B 66
Angram Pl. DL5 —5A 106
Angrove Clo. TS9 —5A 120
Angrove Clo. TS15 —4F 95
Angrove Dri. TS9 —5A 120
Angus St. TS26 —4E 7
Anlaby Clo. TS23 —3F 19
Annandale. DL1 —2F 113
Annandale Cres. TS24 —5D 5
Annan Rd. TS23 —4F 19
Ann Crooks Way. TS24 —2D 9
Anne Swyft Rd. DL5 —2E 109
Annfield Clo. TS23 —4E 19
Ann's Ter. DL1 —4A 112
Ann St. TS6 —3B 54
Ansdale Rd. TS3 —5B 54
Anson Ho. TS17 —5E 71
Anstruther Dri. DL1 —2C 112
Antrim Av. TS19 —4B 46
Appleby Av. TS3 —5E 53
Appleby Clo. TS11 —2F 59
Appleby Gro. TS24 —2F 7
Appleby Ho. TS17 —1E 87
Appleby Rd. TS23 —5F 19
Appleby St. DL14 —4E 103
Applegarth. TS8 —5C 90
Applegarth, The. TS14 —2F 97
Apple Orchard Bank. TS12 —4F 61
Appleton Clo. DL3 —4A 112
Appleton Rd. TS5 —3C 72
Appleton Rd. TS19 —3A 48
Applewood Clo. TS27 —3A 4
Appley Clo. TS16 —1E 85
Apsley St. TS1 —5A 52

Aquinas Ct. DL3 —3B **112**
Arabella Clo. TS24 —1C **8**
Arabella St. TS24 —1C **8**
Arbroath Gro. TS25 —4D **11**
Arcade, The. TS9 —4B **120**
Arcadia Ct. DL1 —2A **116**
Arch Ct. TS24 —1A **8**
Archdeacon Cres. DL3 —4C **110**
Archer Av. DL14 —5B **102**
Archer Clo. TS4 —4B **74**
Archer St. DL3 —1A **116**
Archer St. TS17 —2D **71**
Archer St. TS24 —5A **8**
Archibald St. TS5 —5D **51**
Arden Clo. TS14 —5D **97**
Arden Ct. TS10 —2C **42**
Arden Gro. TS19 —1C **68**
Ardmore Dri. DL1 —2E **113**
Ardrossan Rd. TS25 —4E **11**
Argory, The. TS17 —5C **86**
Argyle St. TS6 —2E **55**
Argyll Clo. DL1 —2E **113**
Argyll Rd. TS7 —3D **91**
Argyll Rd. TS25 —4E **11**
Arisaig Clo. TS16 —5D **85**
Arkendale. TS8 —5E **89**
Arkendale St. DL1 —4B **112**
Arken Ter. TS20 —2C **48**
Arkle Cres. DL1 —5A **116**
Arkley Cres. TS24 —5E **5**
Ark Royal St. TS25 —4B **12**
Arlington Ct. TS18 —2B **70**
Arlington Rd. TS5 —3F **73**
Arlington St. TS13 —4D **67**
Arlington St. TS18 —2A **70**
  (in two parts)
*Armada Ho. TS24 —4B **8***
  (off Warrior Quay)
Armadale Clo. TS19 —4A **46**
Armadale Gro. TS25 —4D **11**
Armitage Rd. TS10 —2F **41**
Armoury St. DL16 —2C **98**
Armstrong. DL5 —4F **107**
Armstrong Ct. DL3 —5E **111**
Arncliffe Av. TS18 —3A **70**
Arncliffe Gdns. TS26 —1E **11**
Arncliffe Gro. DL3 —2A **114**
Arncliffe Pl. DL5 —5C **106**
  (in two parts)
Arncliffe Rd. TS5 —5C **50**
Arnold Gro. TS25 —3C **10**
  (in two parts)
Arnold Rd. DL1 —1C **116**
Arnside Av. TS3 —5E **53**
Arran Clo. TS17 —2D **87**
Arrandale. TS8 —5E **89**
Arran Gro. TS25 —4E **11**
Arran Wlk. DL1 —2E **113**
Arran Wlk. TS14 —4D **97**
Arrathorne Rd. TS18 —3B **68**
Arrowsmith Sq. TS5 —5F **107**
Arthur St. DL3 —5A **112**
Arthur St. TS9 —3B **120**
Arthur St. TS10 —3C **28**
Arthur Ter. DL14 —4C **102**
Arthur Ter. DL17 —4E **101**
Arthur Ter. TS11 —2B **60**
Arundel Clo. DL14 —3B **102**
Arundel Dri. DL3 —3B **110**
Arundel Grn. TS3 —5E **53**
Arundel Rd. TS6 —4F **55**
Arundel Rd. TS23 —5E **19**
Arundel St. TS10 —3C **28**
Ascot Av. TS5 —2C **72**
Ascot Ct. DL1 —3A **50**
Ascot Rd. TS10 —2E **43**
Ascot View. DL1 —5F **113**

Ash Bank Rd. TS14 —5D **97**
Ashbourne Clo. TS6 —1A **78**
Ashbourne Rd. TS19 —3B **48**
Ashburn St. TS25 —5C **12**
Ashburton Clo. TS8 —1C **90**
Ashby Gro. TS25 —1C **14**
Ashby Rd. TS23 —5E **19**
Ashcombe Clo. TS22 —5B **18**
Ashcroft Gdns. DL14 —3D **103**
Ashcroft St. DL3 —3E **115**
Ashdale. TS8 —5E **89**
Ashdown Clo. TS17 —2D **87**
Ashdown Way. TS23 —4B **20**
Ashfield. DL5 —1C **108**
Ashfield Av. TS4 —2A **74**
Ashfield Clo. TS25 —4C **14**
Ashford Av. TS19 —5B **72**
Ashford Clo. TS14 —5D **97**
Ash Grn. TS8 —5C **90**
Ash Gro. DL4 —3D **105**
Ash Gro. DL16 —4B **98**
Ash Gro. TS6 —4C **54**
Ash Gro. TS13 —4C **66**
Ashgrove Av. TS25 —2F **11**
Ashgrove Pl. TS25 —2F **11**
Ash Hill. TS8 —4D **91**
Ashkirk Rd. TS6 —1D **77**
Ashley Gdns. TS24 —3D **7**
Ashling Way. TS5 —5D **51**
Ashridge Clo. TS11 —2A **60**
Ashridge Clo. TS17 —4D **87**
Ash Rd. TS14 —2D **97**
Ashton Rd. TS20 —5F **31**
Ashtree Clo. DL14 —1C **114**
Ashvale Caravan Site. TS27 —3A **4**
Ashville Av. TS16 —3D **85**
Ashville Av. TS20 —4A **32**
Ashwood Clo. TS7 —4C **76**
Ashwood Clo. TS27 —4A **4**
Ashwood Dri. TS9 —2F **119**
Askern Rd. TS5 —5F **73**
Aske Rd. TS1 —4F **51**
Aske Rd. TS10 —5E **29**
Askewdale TS14 —4A **96**
Askrigg Clo. DL1 —4B **112**
Askrigg Clo. DL5 —4C **106**
Askrigg Rd. TS18 —5F **47**
Askrigg St. DL1 —4B **112**
Askrigg Wlk. TS3 —2D **75**
Askwith Rd. TS5 —2E **73**
Aspen Ct. DL4 —4D **105**
Aspen Dri. TS5 —2A **74**
Aspen Rd. TS16 —5C **84**
Association Ct. DL4 —2C **104**
Association St. DL4 —2C **104**
Astbury. TS7 —5F **91**
Aster Clo. TS7 —2C **90**
Asterley Dri. TS5 —4B **72**
Astley Clo. TS19 —5C **46**
Aston Av. TS3 —4F **53**
Astonbury Grn. TS4 —4C **74**
Aston Dri. TS17 —2C **86**
Aston Rd. TS22 —5C **18**
Aston Ter. DL3 —5D **111**
Atherstone Dri. TS14 —4E **97**
Atherstone Way. DL3 —3A **110**
  (in two parts)
Atherton Clo. DL16 —4C **98**
Atherton Ter. DL14 —4F **103**
Atherton Way. TS15 —5B **94**
Athol Gro. TS10 —5B **28**
Atholl Clo. DL1 —2D **113**
Atholl Gro. TS25 —4E **11**
Athol St. TS1 —5F **51**
Atkinson Gdns. DL5 —5F **109**
Atkinson St. TS18 —5B **48**

Atlas Wynd. TS15 —3D **95**
Attingham Clo. TS8 —4A **90**
Attlee Rd. TS6 —4F **55**
Attlow Wlk. TS3 —1A **76**
Atwater Clo. TS15 —4E **95**
Atwick Clo. TS23 —2F **19**
Aubrey St. TS1 —5A **52**
Auckland Av. DL3 —4D **111**
Auckland Av. TS7 —3F **91**
*Auckland Ho. TS2 —2A **52***
  (off Durham St.)
Auckland M. DL5 —5F **107**
Auckland Oval. DL3 —4E **111**
Auckland Pl. DL5 —5F **107**
Auckland Rd. DL14 —4F **103**
Auckland Rd. DL17 —2E **101**
Auckland Rd. TS23 —3B **20**
Auckland St. TS14 —2E **97**
Auckland Ter. DL4 —4D **105**
Auckland Way. TS18 —2C **68**
Auckland Way. TS26 —1A **10**
Auckland Wynd. DL4 —2B **104**
Audrey Gro. DL1 —3E **117**
Audrey Gro. TS18 —2D **69**
Augusta Clo. DL1 —3E **113**
Aurora Ct. TS2 —1D **51**
Austin Av. TS18 —2A **70**
Autumn Gro. TS19 —5D **47**
Avalon Ct. TS8 —4A **90**
Avebury Clo. TS17 —5D **87**
Avens Way. TS17 —4C **86**
Avenue Pl. TS14 —2E **97**
Avenue Rd. TS24 —5F **7**
Avenue, The. TS5 —1E **89**
  (Brookfield)
Avenue, The. TS5 —2F **73**
  (Linthorpe)
Avenue, The. TS6 —5D **55**
Avenue, The. TS7 —3B **92**
Avenue, The. TS9 —3F **119**
Avenue, The. TS10 —4E **29**
Avenue, The. TS12 —4C **64**
Avenue, The. TS14 —4B **96**
Avenue, The. TS16 —3D **85**
Avenue, The. TS17 —3E **71**
Avenue, The. TS19 —5C **46**
Aviemore Ct. DL1 —5F **113**
Aviemore Rd. TS8 —4A **90**
Avill Gro. TS17 —4A **86**
Avoca Ct. TS10 —3C **28**
Avon Clo. TS12 —2D **63**
  (Saltburn)
Avon Clo. TS12 —5D **63**
  (Skelton)
Avon Clo. TS17 —4E **71**
Avon Ct. DL5 —4C **106**
Avon Ct. TS12 —5F **81**
Avondale Clo. TS6 —4E **55**
Avondale Gdns. TS24 —3E **7**
Avon Dri. TS14 —4C **96**
Avon Gro. TS22 —5B **18**
Avon Rd. TS10 —1B **42**
Avon Rd. TS20 —1D **49**
Avon St. TS12 —2D **63**
Avon Way. DL1 —5B **116**
Avro Clo. TS11 —4B **44**
Avro Clo. TS18 —5F **69**
Axbridge Ct. TS2 —1D **51**
Axminster Rd. TS8 —4A **90**
Axton Clo. TS17 —2C **86**
Aycliffe Clo. TS19 —5B **46**
Aycliffe Ind. Est. DL5 —3D **109**
Aycliffe Rd. TS7 —3D **91**
Aylmer Gro. DL5 —5D **107**
Aylsham Clo. TS17 —5D **87**
Aylton Dri. TS5 —2D **89**
Ayresome Grange Rd. TS5 —5D **51**

Ayresome Grn. La. TS5
        —5D **51** to 1E **73**
Ayresome Pk. Rd. TS5 —5E **51**
Ayresome Rd. TS5 —4C **50**
Ayresome St. TS1 —5D **51**
Ayresome Way. DL1 —5E **113**
Ayr Gro. TS25 —4E **11**
Aysgarth Clo. DL5 —5C **106**
Aysgarth Ho. TS19 —3F **47**
Aysgarth Rd. DL1 —4C **116**
Aysgarth Rd. TS5 —2D **73**
Aysgarth Rd. TS18 —5E **47**
Ayton Ct. TS14 —1D **97**
Ayton Cres. TS6 —2F **77**
Ayton Dri. DL3 —4D **115**
Ayton Dri. TS10 —2C **42**
Ayton Pl. TS20 —3C **48**
Ayton Rd. TS9 —3F **119**
Ayton Rd. TS17 —4D **71**
Azalia Rd. TS19 —3B **48**

Babbacombe Dri. DL17 —3F **101**
Bk. Cheapside. DL4 —2D **105**
Bk. Eldon Ter. DL17 —4F **101**
Bk. Garnet St. TS12 —1D **63**
Backhouse Wlk. DL5 —1F **109**
Back La. TS12 —2A **80**
Back La. TS16 —1D **95**
Back La. TS21 —4B **68**
  (in two parts)
Back La. Cotts. TS12 —2B **80**
Bk. South Chu. Rd. DL14 —2D **103**
Bk. Throston St. TS24 —2D 9
  (off Throston St.)
Bacon Wlk. TS17 —4B **10**
Baden St. TS26 —1E **11**
Bader Av. TS17 —2C **86**
Badger La. TS17 —4D **87**
Badminton Clo. DL1 —5F **113**
Badminton Gro. DL5 —3F **107**
Badsworth Clo. TS14 —5D **97**
Baffin Ct. TS17 —1E **87**
Baff St. DL16 —3C **98**
Bailey Gro. TS3 —5D **53**
Bailey St. TS26 —1F **11**
Bainton Clo. TS23 —2F **19**
Bakehouse Hill. DL1 —2A **116**
Bakehouse Wall. DL14 —1D 10
  (off Market Pl.)
Bakehouse Sq. TS14 —3E **97**
Baker Clo. TS27 —4B **4**
Bakers Ct. DL3 —1F **115**
Baker St. TS1 —3E **51**
Bakery Dri. TS19 —3E **47**
Bakery St. TS18 —5B **48**
Bakewell Pl. DL5 —4C **106**
Balaclava St. TS18 —5B **48**
Balcary Ct. TS25 —5D **11**
Balcary Gro. TS25 —5D **11**
Balder Rd. TS20 —5B **32**
Balfour Ter. TS5 —3C **72**
Baliol Grn. DL5 —1E **109**
Baliol Rd. DL5 —1E **109**
Ballarat, The. DL5 —3D **107**
Ballater Gro. TS25 —5E **11**
Balliol Ct. DL1 —3B **112**
Balmoral Av. TS17 —3E **71**
Balmoral Av. TS23 —5F **19**
Balmoral Ct. TS25 —5E **11**
Balmoral Dri. TS4 —2B **74**
Balmoral Gro. DL14 —3C **102**
Balmoral Rd. DL1 —2D **113**
Balmoral Rd. DL17 —1E **101**
Balmoral Rd. TS3 —3F **75**
Balmoral Rd. TS25 —5D **11**

Balmoral Ter. TS12 —1D 63
  (off Windsor Rd.)
Balmoral Ter. TS18 —2A **70**
Balmor Rd. TS6 —1D **77**
Baltic Clo. TS18 —4C **48**
Baltic Rd. TS18 —4C **48**
Baltic St. TS25 —2A **12**
Baltimore Way. DL1 —3C **112**
Bamburgh Av. DL14 —3B **102**
Bamburgh Clo. TS10 —1F **43**
Bamburgh Ct. TS27 —4B **4**
Bamburgh Cres. DL5 —3E **107**
Bamburgh Dri. TS7 —4B **76**
Bamburgh Ho. TS4 —2C **74**
Bamburgh Pde. DL16 —3D **99**
Bamburgh Pl. DL1 —4D **113**
Bamburgh Rd. DL17 —1E **101**
Bamburgh Rd. TS27 —5B **4**
Bamford Rd. TS17 —4D **71**
Bamletts Wharf Ind. Est. TS23
        —5D **35**
Bamletts Wharf Rd. TS23 —5C **34**
Bampton M. DL1 —2F **113**
Banbury Gro. TS5 —5C **72**
Banff Gro. TS25 —5E **11**
Bangor Clo. TS6 —4F **55**
Bangor Gro. DL1 —4F **113**
Bangor St. TS26 —1E **11**
Bankfields Ct. TS6 —3E **77**
Bankfields Rd. TS6 —3E **77**
Banklands Ct. DL3 —5E **111**
Banklands Rd. DL3 —5E **111**
Bank La. TS6 —2A **78**
Bank Rd. TS23 —4E **33**
Bank Sands. TS5 —2C **8ʀ**
Bankside. DL14 —3C **102**
Bankside. TS15 —3F **95**
Bankside Ct. TS6 —2A **78**
Banks Rd. DL1 —1E **117**
Bankston Clo. TS26 —3A **6**
Bank St. TS10 —4D **29**
Bank St. TS14 —3E **97**
Bank Top M. DL1 —3B **116**
Bannockburn Way. TS23 —4A **20**
Baptist St. TS24 —3D **9**
Barbara Mann Ct. TS26 —5E **7**
Barberry. TS8 —5E **91**
  (in two parts)
Barberry Clo. TS17 —3D **87**
Barden Moor Rd. DL1 —5D **117**
Barden Rd. TS3 —1D **75**
Bardsey Wlk. TS14 —4C **96**
Bardsley Clo. TS16 —1E **85**
Barford Clo. TS10 —3C **42**
Barford Clo. TS20 —5F **31**
Barford Clo. TS25 —2C **14**
Bargate. TS3 —4C **52**
Barholm Clo. TS3 —2A **76**
Barker Rd. TS5 —2D **73**
Barker Rd. TS17 —3E **71**
Barkers Pl. TS24 —3D 9
  (off Town Wall)
Barkston Av. TS17 —2C **86**
Barkstone Clo. TS22 —4C **18**
Barlborough Av. TS19 —3E **47**
Barle Clo. TS17 —4B **86**
Barley Hill Clo. TS6 —3F **77**
Barlow Clo. TS14 —4D **97**
Barlow Ct. TS23 —4F **19**
Barlow St. DL3 —1E **115**
Barmet Ind. Est. TS12 —5A **82**
Barmoor Gro. TS20 —4B **32**
Barmouth Rd. TS6 —5F **55**
Barmpton La. DL1
       —3F **113** to 1F **113**
Barmpton Rd. TS23 —3F **19**
Barnaby Av. TS5 —5D **51**

Barnaby Clo. TS11 —5E **45**
Barnaby Cres. TS6 —2F **77**
Barnaby Pl. TS14 —2C **96**
Barnaby Rd. TS7 —2C **92**
Barnack Av. TS7 —2F **91**
Barnard Av. DL14 —3C **102**
Barnard Av. TS19 —1D **69**
Barnard Clo. DL5 —3F **107**
Barnard Clo. DL16 —1D **99**
Barnard Clo. TS17 —2D **71**
Barnard Ct. TS4 —2B **74**
Barnard Gro. TS10 —1F **43**
Barnard Gro. TS24 —3B **4**
Barnard Rd. DL17 —2E **101**
  (in two parts)
Barnard Rd. TS13 —1E **67**
Barnard Rd. TS23 —1F **33**
Barnard St. DL3 —2F **115**
  (in two parts)
Barnes Clo. DL3 —1B **114**
Barnes Ct. TS24 —4C **4**
Barnes Rd. DL3 —1B **114**
Barnes Rd. TS6 —3D **55**
Barnes Wlk. DL5 —4E **107**
Barnes Wallis Way. TS11 —4B **44**
Barnet Way. TS23 —3B **20**
Barnfield Rd. DL16 —2D **99**
Barnford Wlk. TS3 —3E **75**
Barningham St. DL3 —5F **111**
Barnstaple Clo. TS8 —1C **90**
Baronport Grn. TS18 —4D **49**
Barra Gro. TS25 —5E **11**
Barras Ter. TS19 —2B **46**
Barrett Rd. DL3 —2C **114**
Barrhead Clo. TS19 —4A **46**
Barrington Av. TS19 —4D **47**
Barrington Cres. TS3 —5A **54**
Barrington Rd. DL5 —1C **108**
Barrington Ter. DL17 —3B **100**
Barritt St. TS1 —4F **51**
Barron St. DL3 —5F **111**
Barrowburn Grn. TS17 —4A **86**
Barsby Grn. TS3 —1D **75** & 2E **75**
Barsford Rd. TS3 —5A **54**
Bartlett St. DL3 —5A **112**
Barton Av. TS25 —2E **11**
Barton Clo. DL5 —3C **106**
Barton Clo. TS17 —2C **86**
Barton Cres. TS22 —5C **18**
Barton Rd. TS2 —1D **51**
Barton St. DL3 —1C **112**
Barwick Clo. TS17 —4C **86**
Barwick Fields. TS17 —4C **86**
Barwick La. TS17 —4A **86** to 5B **86**
Barwick View. TS17 —4C **86**
Barwick Way. TS17 —5C **86**
Basildon Grn. TS3 —5E **53**
Basil St. TS3 —4C **52**
Bassenthwaite. TS5 —2C **88**
Bassleton Ct. Shopping Cen. TS17
  (off Bader Av.)   —2D **87**
Bassleton La. TS17
       —2B **86** to 1D **87**
Bates Av. DL3 —4C **110**
Bates Clo. DL5 —4C **106**
Bathgate Ter. TS24 —1F **11**
Bath La. TS18 —5C **48**
Bath Pl. TS18 —5C **48**
Bath Rd. TS6 —1F **77**
Bath St. TS10 —4D **29**
Bath St. TS12 —1D **63**
Bath Ter. TS24 —2E **9**
Battersby Clo. TS15 —3F **95**
Batts Ter. DL14 —1D **103**
Baydale Rd. DL3 —3B **114**
Baysdale Clo. DL14 —4A **102**
Baysdale Clo. TS14 —3F **97**

Baysdale Ct. TS12 —5E **63**
Baysdale Gdns. DL4 —3E **105**
Baysdale Gro. TS10 —2A **42**
Baysdale Rd. TS17 —5E **71**
Baysdale Wlk. TS5 —5F **73**
Baysdale Wlk. TS6 —5A **56**
Bay St. TS18 —5C **48**
Baytree Rd. DL1 —1B **112**
Beachfield Dri. TS25 —3E **11**
Beacon Av. TS21 —4C **118**
Beacon Dri. TS11 —2B **60**
Beacon La. TS21 —1C **118**
Beaconsfield Rd. TS20 —4C **32**
Beaconsfield Sq. TS24 —2D **9**
Beaconsfield St. DL3 —5F **111**
Beaconsfield St. TS24 —2D **9**
Beacon St. TS24 —2D **9**
Beadlam Av. TS7 —2C **92**
Beadnall Ho. TS2 —2A 52
(off East St.)
Beadnell Clo. TS17 —5D **87**
Beadnell Way. TS10 —2A **44**
Beadon Gro. TS5 —1C **72**
Beale Clo. TS17 —4D **87**
Beamish Rd. TS23 —5A **20**
Beardmore Av. TS11 —3C **44**
Beath Gro. TS25 —5E **11**
Beaufort Clo. TS14 —5D **97**
Beaufort St. TS1 —3F **51**
Beauly Dri. DL1 —2D **113**
Beauly Gro. TS25 —5E **11**
Beaumaris Dri. TS16 —5D **85**
Beaumont Clo. DL5 —3E **107**
Beaumont Ct. TS21 —4C **118**
Beaumont Pk. TS23 —1B **34**
Beaumont Rd. TS3 —4D **53**
Beaumont St. DL1 —2A **116**
Beaumont St. DL14 —4C **102**
Beaumont St. DL17 —2B **100**
Beaumont St. W. DL1 —2A **116**
Beaumont View. TS20 —1D **49**
Beaumont Way. DL5 —4D **109**
Beaver Clo. TS17 —4D **87**
Beaver Ct. TS6 —3B **54**
Beccles Clo. TS19 —3C **46**
Beckenham Gdns. TS8 —4A **90**
Beckett Clo. DL14 —3A **102**
Beckfields Av. TS17 —5D **87**
Beckfields Cen. TS17 —5D **87**
Beck Rd. DL1 —1A **116**
Beckston Clo. TS26 —4A **6**
Beckwith Rd. TS15 —5C **94**
Bedale Av. TS23 —4E **33**
Bedale Gro. TS19 —1B **68**
Bedale Hunt. DL5 —4A **106**
Bedburn Dri. DL3 —2A **114**
Bedburn Dri. DL14 —4A **102**
Bede Clo. TS19 —2E **47**
Bede Cres. TS1 —1E **109**
Bede Gro. TS25 —2D **11**
Bede Rd. DL3 —2B **114**
Bede Ter. DL17 —3D **101**
Bedford Pl. DL14 —4D **103**
Bedford Rd. TS7 —3B **92**
Bedford St. DL1 —3A **116**
Bedford St. TS1 —3F **51**
Bedford St. TS19 —4A **48**
Bedford St. TS24 —3D **9**
Bedford Ter. TS23 —2F **33**
Bedlington Wlk. TS23 —3E **19**
(in two parts)
Beech Av. DL16 —4B **98**
Beech Av. TS10 —4F **29**
Beech Clo. TS9 —4A **120**
Beech Cres. DL17 —3D **101**
Beechers Gro. DL5 —2E **107**
Beeches Rise. TS7 —2F **91**

Beechfield. DL5 —1C **108**
Beechfield. TS8 —5C **90**
(in two parts)
Beech Gro. DL17 —3D **101**
Beech Gro. TS6 —4C **54**
Beech Gro. TS12 —3B **64**
Beech Gro. TS13 —4C **66**
Beech Gro. Rd. TS5 —2F **73**
Beech Oval. TS21 —3C **118**
Beech Rd. DL1 —2F **113**
Beech Rd. DL14 —3D **103**
Beech Rd. TS13 —1B **66**
Beech Rd. TS14 —2E **97**
Beech St. TS1 —3A **52**
Beech Ter. TS2 —5F **51**
Beechtree Ct. TS15 —2C **94**
Beechwood Av. DL3 —3F **115**
Beechwood Av. TS4 —2B **74**
Beechwood Av. TS9 —2F **119**
Beechwood Av. TS12 —2D **63**
Beechwood Dri. DL14 —4D **103**
Beechwood Rd. TS16 —2D **85**
Beechwood Rd. TS17 —4D **71**
Beeford Clo. TS23 —2F **19**
Beeford Dri. TS5 —5F **73**
Bek Rd. DL5 —5F **107**
Belaise Ct. TS23 —2B **34**
Belasis Av. TS23 —4F **33** to 3E **35**
Belasis Bus. Cen. TS23 —3B **34**
Belasis Hall Technology Pk. TS23
—2C **34**
Belford Clo. TS19 —4D **47**
Belford Gdns. DL1 —3D **113**
Belford Way. DL5 —5A **106**
Belgrave Dri. TS6 —4D **77**
Belgrave St. DL1 —3C **116**
Belk Clo. TS6 —3E **55**
Belk St. TS1 —5F **51**
Belk St. TS24 —4F **7**
Bellamy Ct. TS3 —5E **53**
Bellasis Clo. DL5 —4E **107**
Bellasis Gro. TS27 —4B **4**
Bellburn La. DL3 —4E **111**
Bell Clo. TS18 —1A **70**
Bellerby Rd. TS18 —2C **68**
Belle Vue Ct. TS20 —3C **48**
Belle Vue Gro. TS4 —2B **74**
Belle Vue Ho. TS20 —2C **48**
Belle Vue Rd. TS5 —1E **73**
Belle Vue St. DL16 —4B **98**
Belle Vue Ter. TS13 —2A **66**
Belle Vue Vs. DL16 —4B **98**
Belle Vue Way. TS25
—4F **11** to 1F **11**
Bell's Pl. DL3 —2A **116**
Belmont St. DL14 —4C **102**
Belsay Clo. TS5 —5D **51**
Bell St. TS20 —3C **48**
Bell Wlk. DL5 —1F **109**
Bellwood Av. TS12 —5E **81**
Belmangate. TS14 —3E **97**
Belmont Av. TS5 —3E **89**
Belmont Av. TS6 —5C **54**
Belmont Av. TS19 —3A **48**
Belmont Av. TS22 —5D **19**
Belmont Gdns. TS26 —1D **11**
Belmont St. TS6 —1A **78**
Belmont Ter. TS14 —3E **97**
Belsay Clo. DL17 —2E **101**
Belsay Gro. TS19 —4D **47**
Belsay Ct. TS21 —3B **118**
Belsay Wlk. DL1 —4D **113**
Belshaw Ho. TS2 —2F 51
(off Silver St.)
Belton Dri. TS5 —5F **73**
Belvedere Rd. DL1 —3B **116**
Belvedere Rd. TS4 —2B **74**

Belvedere Rd. TS17 —3E **71**
Belvoir Gro. DL14 —3B **102**
Benedict St. TS3 —4C **52**
Beningborough Gdns. TS17
—5C **86**
Benmore Rd. TS25 —5D **11**
Bennett Rd. TS25 —3C **10**
Bennison Cres. TS10 —1A **42**
Bennison St. TS14 —2E **97**
Benridge Clo. TS5 —1C **88**
Bensham Rd. DL1 —2B **112**
Benson St. TS5 —1E **73**
Benson St. TS20 —1C **48**
Benson St. TS26 —5E **7**
Bentick St. TS26 —4E **7**
Bentinck Av. TS5 —3F **73**
Bentinck Rd. TS19 —1C **68**
Bentley Av. TS23 —5C **20**
Bentley St. TS26 —5E **7**
Bentley Wynd. TS15 —3C **94**
Benton Clo. TS23 —3F **19**
Benton Rd. TS5 —4F **73**
Benwell Clo. TS19 —4D **47**
Berberis Gro. TS19 —5D **47**
Beresford Bldgs. TS3 —5A **54**
Beresford Cres. TS3 —5A **54**
Beresford St. DL4 —5C **104**
Berkeley Av. TS25 —1E **15**
Berkeley Clo. TS23 —5E **19**
Berkeley Dri. DL14 —3B **102**
Berkeley Rd. DL1 —4A **116**
Berkley Dri. TS10 —2F **43**
Berkley Dri. TS14 —4E **97**
Berkshire Ho. TS6 —5F **55**
Berkshire Pl. DL14 —4D **103**
Berkshire Rd. TS20 —1D **49**
Bernaldby Av. TS14 —4C **96**
Bernera Ct. DL1 —2E **113**
Berner St. TS5 —1E **73**
Bernica Gro. TS17 —3A **86**
Berriedale Dri. DL1 —2C **112**
Berrington Gdns. TS17 —5C **86**
Berrybank Crest. DL3 —4C **110**
Bertha St. DL17 —3D **101**
Bertha St. TS24 —1A **12**
Bertie Rd. DL5 —5D **107**
Berwick Gro. TS20 —4B **32**
Berwick Hills Av. TS3
—5F **53** & 5A **54**
Berwick Rd. DL3 —4B **110**
Berwick St. TS25 —5C **12**
Berwick Wlk. TS10 —1F **43**
Bessemer Ct. TS6 —2E **55**
Bessemer St. DL17 —3B **100**
Bethune Rd. TS5 —1C **72**
Betjeman Clo. TS23 —2E **19**
Bevanlee Rd. TS6 —3C **54**
Beveridge Arc. DL5 —5D **107**
Beveridge Way. DL5 —5D **107**
Beverley Rd. TS4 —4A **74**
Beverley Rd. TS7 —2C **92**
Beverley Rd. TS10 —2A **44**
Beverley Rd. TS23 —3A **20**
Bewholme Clo. TS23 —2F **19**
Bewick Cres. DL5 —1D **109**
Bewley Gro. TS5 —5D **73**
Bexley Clo. TS4 —5C **74**
Bexley Dri. TS6 —4D **77**
Bexley Dri. TS25 —3F **11**
Bickersteth Clo. TS18 —2B **70**
Bickersteth Wlk. TS18 —2B **70**
Bickford Ter. DL5 —5E **109**
Bickley Clo. TS22 —1B **32**
Bickley Way. TS8 —4C **90**
Biddick Clo. TS19 —4D **47**
Bielby Av. TS23 —2F **19**
Biggin Clo. TS5 —5F **73**

Bigland Ter. DL14 —5F **103**
Billingham Bank. TS23 —5E **33**
Billingham Bottoms Interchange.
           TS20 —5D **33**
Billingham Ind. Est. TS23 —1C **34**
Billingham Reach Ind. Est. TS23
           —1C **50**
Billingham Rd. TS20
         —5C **32** & 5D **33**
Billingham Rd. Bri. TS20 —5D **33**
Bilsdale Av. TS10 —1B **42**
Bilsdale Rd. TS4 —2E **7**
Bilsdale Rd. TS19 —4F **47**
Bilsdale Rd. TS25 —1B **16**
Binchester Croft. DL5 —2A **108**
Bingfield Ct. TS23 —3F **19**
Binks St. TS5 —1F **73**
Birch Av. DL4 —3D **105**
Birch Av. DL14 —5C **102**
Birches, The. TS6 —1D **77**
Birches, The. TS8 —5C **90**
Birchfield Clo. TS16 —5C **84**
Birchfield Dri. TS16 —4C **84**
Birchgate Rd. TS5 —3E **73**
Birch Gro. TS19 —2F **47**
Birchill Gdns. TS26 —3C **6**
Birchington Av. TS6
        —2F **55** to 5A **56**
Birchmere. DL16 —1B **98**
Birch Rd. DL1 —1B **112**
Birch Tree Clo. TS7 —4C **76**
Birch Wlk. TS24 —2E **7**
Birchwood Av. TS4 —2B **74**
Birchwood Rd. TS7 —2A **92**
Birdsall Brow. TS20 —5A **32**
Birdsall Ho. TS3 —5E 53
(off Bodmin Clo.)
Birdsall Row. TS10 —4D **29**
Biretta Clo. TS19 —4B **46**
Birkdale Clo. TS27 —4A **4**
Birkdale Dri. TS6 —2F **77**
Birkdale Rd. DL3 —1C **114**
Birkdale Rd. TS11 —2A **60**
Birkdale Rd. TS18 —2C **68**
Birkhall Rd. TS3 —1A **76**
Birkley Rd. TS20 —2C **48**
Birtley Av. TS5 —1D **89**
Biscop Cres. DL5 —5E **107**
Bisham Av. TS5 —2D **73**
Bishop Auckland By-Pass. DL14
        —5D **103**
Bishop Clo. DL1 —4E **113**
Bishop's Clo. DL16 —3C **98**
Bishopsgarth Cotts. TS19 —3B **46**
Bishop St. DL14 —2C **102**
Bishop St. TS5 —5C **50**
Bishop St. TS18 —5C **48**
Bishops Way. TS19 —4B **46**
Bishopton Av. TS19 —4E **47**
Bishopton Ct. TS19 —5C **46**
Bishopton La. TS18 —5B **48**
  (in two parts)
Bishopton Rd. TS4 —2A **74**
Bishopton Rd. TS18 & TS19
        —4F **47**
Bishopton Rd. W. TS19
        —4A **46** to 4E **47**
Bisley Ct. DL1 —5F **113**
Blackburn Clo. TS19 —5D **47**
Blackburn Gro. TS11 —4B **44**
Blackbush Wlk. TS17 —3D **87**
Blackett Av. TS20 —2D **49**
Blackett Rd. DL1 —5D **113**
Blackett St. DL14 —2D **103**
Blackfriars. TS15 —4D **95**
Blackhall Sands. TS5 —2C **88**
Blackhouse Wlk. DL5 —1F **109**

Blackmore Clo. TS14 —4E **97**
Blackmore Wlk. TS25 —3B **10**
Black Path. TS11 —5C **44**
Black Path, The. TS20 & TS18
        —4C **48**
Blacksail Clo. TS19 —5A **48**
Blackthorn. TS8 —5D **91**
Blackthorn Gro. TS19 —5D **47**
Blackton Clo. DL5 —5A **106**
Blackwell. DL3 —5D **115**
Blackwell Clo. DL3 —5D **115**
Blackwell Clo. TS23 —5B **20**
Blackwellgate. DL1 —2A **116**
Blackwellgate Arc. DL1 —2A **116**
Blackwell Gro. DL3 —5D **115**
Blackwell La. DL3 —4E **115**
Blackwell Roundabout. DL2
        —5C **114**
Blackwell Scar. DL3 —4D **115**
Blackwood Clo. TS27 —3A **4**
Bladon Dri. TS11 —3D **45**
Blagden Gro. DL14 —5A **102**
Blair Av. TS17 —3A **86**
Blairgowrie. TS8 —4F **91**
  (in two parts)
Blairgowrie Gro. TS25 —5D **11**
Blair Gro. DL14 —3C **102**
Blairmore Gdns. TS16 —5D **85**
Blaise Garden Village. TS26 —4B **6**
Blake Clo. TS23 —2F **19**
Blakelock Gdns. TS25 —1E **11**
Blakelock Rd. TS25 —2D **11**
Blakeston Ct. TS19 —4E **31**
Blakeston La. TS21 & TS19
        —1A **30** to 4E **31**
Blakeston Rd. TS23 —5A **20**
Blake St. DL4 —4C **104**
Blake St. TS26 —4E **7**
Blake Wlk. TS26 —4E **7**
Blakey Clo. TS10 —3D **43**
Blakey Wlk. TS24 —5A **56**
Blakiston Ct. DL5 —2C **106**
Blanchland Grn. DL3 —4B **110**
Blanchland Rd. TS3 —3F **75**
Blandford St. DL17 —3B **100**
Bland Wlk. DL5 —5F **107**
Blankney Clo. TS14 —4D **97**
Blantyre Gro. TS25 —5E **11**
Blantyre Rd. TS6 —1D **77**
Blatchford Rd. TS6 —3A **54**
Blayberry Clo. TS10 —3D **43**
Blenavon Ct. TS15 —2C **94**
Blenheim Av. TS11 —4D **45**
Blenheim Clo. TS11 —4D **45**
Blenheim M. TS10 —4B **28**
Blenheim Rd. TS4 —4B **52**
Blenheim Rd. S. TS4 —5B **52**
Blenheim Ter. TS10 —4C **28**
Bletchley Clo. TS19 —4D **47**
Bloomfield Rd. DL3 —5E **111**
Bluebell Clo. DL5 —4C **106**
Blue Bell Gro. TS5 —2F **89**
Blue Bell Gro. TS19 —5D **47**
Blue Bell Interchange. TS8 —2F **89**
Bluebell Meadow. DL5 —4B **106**
Bluebell Way. DL5 —4B **106**
Bluebell Way. TS12 —2F **81**
Blue Ho. Point Rd. TS18 —4F **49**
  (in two parts)
Blue Post Yd. TS18 —1B **70**
Blythport Clo. TS18 —4D **49**
Boagey Wlk. TS24 —5E **5**
Board St. DL16 —3C **98**
Boar La. TS17 —4D **87**
Boathouse La. TS18 —1C **70**
Bob Hardisty Dri. DL14 —1C **102**
Bodiam Dri. TS10 —2F **43**

Bodmin Gro. TS26 —3B **6**
Boeing Way. TS18 —4A **70**
Bolam Gro. TS23 —4F **19**
Bolckow Cen. TS7 —4B **76**
Bolckow Rd. TS6 —2E **55**
Bolckow Rd. Ind. Est. TS6 —2E 55
(off Laing Clo.)
Bolckow St. TS1 —3F **51**
Bolckow St. TS6 —2A **78**
Bolckow St. TS12 —2F **81**
Bolckow St. TS14 —2D **97**
Boldron Clo. TS18 —3B **68**
Bollihope Gro. DL14 —4A **102**
Bollington Rd. TS4 —4C **74**
Bolsover Rd. TS20 —2C **48**
Boltby Clo. TS5 —4F **73**
Boltby Ct. TS10 —2C **42**
Boltby Way. TS16 —3C **84**
Bolton Clo. DL3 —4C **110**
Bolton Clo. TS10 —2F **43**
Bolton Ct. TS4 —2B **74**
Bolton Ct. TS12 —5E **63**
Bolton Gro. DL14 —4C **102**
Bolton Gro. TS25 —4C **12** & 5C **12**
Bolton Way. TS14 —3F **97**
Bondene Gro. TS19 —3B **46**
Bondfield Rd. TS6 —5E **55**
Bondgate. DL3 —1F **115** & 2A **116**
Bond St. TS24 —2D **9**
Bonemill Bank. DL14 —4F **103**
Bone St. TS18 —4C **48**
Bon Lea Trading Est. TS17 —2E **71**
Bonny Gro. TS8 —5A **92**
Bonny Gro. Way. TS8 —5D **91**
Bonnyrigg Clo. TS17 —4A **86**
Bonnyrigg Wlk. TS25 —5D **11**
Boosbeck Rd. TS12 —2C **80**
  (in two parts)
Booth Wlk. DL5 —4C **106**
Boraston Ho. TS3 —5E 53
(off Bodmin Clo.)
Bordesley Grn. TS3 —5E **53**
Borough Rd. DL1 —2B **116**
Borough Rd. TS1 & TS3 —4F **51**
Borough Rd. TS10 —1E **43**
Borough Rd. Ind. Est. DL1
        —1B **116**
Borrowby Ct. TS14 —1D **97**
Borrowdale Gro. TS5 —4D **73**
Borrowdale Gro. TS10 —1D **95**
Borrowdale Rd. TS6 —4A **56**
Borrowdale St. TS25 —2F **11**
Borrowdale Wlk. TS6 —4A **56**
Borton Wlk. TS19 —4A **48**
Boscombe Gdns. TS8 —4A **90**
Boston Clo. DL1 —3C **112**
Boston Clo. TS25 —1D **15**
Boston Dri. TS7 —3E **91**
Boston Wlk. TS20 —1D **49**
Boswell Gro. TS25 —3C **10**
Boswell St. TS1 —4A **52**
Bosworth Way. TS23 —4A **20**
Botany Way. TS7 —3B **92**
Bothal Dri. TS19 —3B **46**
Bothal Wlk. TS19 —2B **46**
Botham Gro. DL3 —1A **112**
Bottomley Mall. TS1 —3F **51**
Bouch St. DL4 —5D **105**
Boulby Dri. TS13 —5D **67**
Boulby Rd. TS10 —1A **42**
Boulby Rd. TS13 —2A **66**
Boulby Wlk. TS6 —5A **56**
Boundary Rd. TS1 —2F **51**
Boundary Rd. TS6 —3D **77**
Boundary View. DL3 —5C **110**
Bournemouth Av. TS3 —3A **76**
Bournemouth Dri. TS24 —3B **4**

Bourton Ct. TS3 —4E **75**
Bousdale Cotts. TS14 —5A **96**
Bousfield Cres. DL5 —4E **107**
Bowden Ct. DL5 —1F **109**
Bowen Rd. DL3 —4D **111**
Bowesfield Cres. TS18 —4B **70**
Bowesfield Ind. Est. TS18 —4B **70**
Bowesfield La. TS18 —4B **70**
Bowesfield N. Ind. Est. TS18
—3B **70**
Bowes Grn. TS24 —3B **4**
Bowes Gro. DL14 —4B **102**
Bowes Gro. DL16 —1C **98**
Bowesmoor Clo. DL1 —4E **117**
Bowes Rd. DL5 —1D **109**
Bowes Rd. TS2 —1E **51**
Bowes Rd. TS23 —4E **19**
Bowfell Clo. TS16 —4C **84**
Bowfell Rd. TS3 —1D **75**
Bowhill Way. TS23 —3B **20**
Bowland Clo. TS7 —3A **92**
Bowley Clo. TS6 —2C **76**
Bowley Wlk. TS1 —4E **51**
Bowman St. DL3 —2B **112**
Bowness Clo. TS25 —3F **11**
Bowness Gro. DL17 —3C **100**
Bowness Gro. TS10 —1D **43**
Bowron St. TS20 —4C **48**
Bowser St. DL14 —3C **102**
Bowser St. TS24 —1A **12**
Bow St. TS1 —4E **51**
Bow St. TS14 —2E **97**
Boxer Ct. TS6 —3B **54**
Box, The. TS7 —3C **92**
Boyes Hill Gro. DL3 —1D **115**
Boyne Ct. TS21 —4B **118**
Boyne St. DL3 —3F **111**
Boynston Gro. TS21 —4C **118**
Boynton Rd. TS4 —1B **74**
Brabazon Dri. TS11 —4C **44**
Brabourn Gdns. TS8 —4A **90**
Brackenberry Cres. TS10 —2F **43**
Brackenbury Wlk. TS6 —5A **56**
Bracken Cres. TS14 —4B **96**
Brackenfield Ct. TS7 —3F **77**
Brackenhill Clo. TS7 —5B **92**
Bracken Rd. DL3 —1E **115**
Bracken Rd. TS19 —2F **47**
Brackenthwaite. TS5 —2C **88**
Bracknell St. TS17 —4F **71**
Brack's Rd. DL14 —3F **103**
Bradbury Rd. DL5 —3D **109**
Bradbury Rd. TS20 —4C **32**
Bradford Clo. DL5 —2E **109**
Bradhope Rd. TS3 —1C **74**
Bradley Ct. TS23 —5A **20**
Bradley's Ter. TS9 —3B **120**
Bradshaw Ct. TS24 —5D **5**
Braehead. TS16 —4D **85**
Braemar Ct. DL1 —2E **113**
Braemar Gro. TS6 —5C **54**
Braemar Rd. TS5 —3C **72**
Braemar Rd. TS23
—5D **19** & 5E **19**
Braemar Rd. TS25 —5E **11**
Brafferton Clo. DL5 —3E **107**
Brafferton Dri. TS23 —3A **20**
Brafferton St. TS26 —4D **7**
Brafferton Wlk. TS5 —1D **89**
Braid Cres. TS23 —2E **33**
Braidwood Rd. TS6 —2D **77**
Braithwaite St. DL4 —4B **104**
Braithwaite St. DL14 —2C **102**
Bramall La. DL1 —5F **113**

Bramble Rd. TS19 —2F **47**
Bramcote Way. TS17 —3D **87**
Bramham Chase. DL5 —4A **106**
Bramham Down. TS14 —4E **97**
Bramley Ct. TS25 —5E **11**
Bramley Gro. TS7 —2F **91**
Bramley Pde. TS18 —2B **70**
Brampton Side. TS8 —3F **89**
Bramwith Av. TS3 —3E **75**
Brancepeth Av. TS3 —3D **75**
Brancepeth Clo. DL5 —3E **107**
Brancepeth Gro. DL14 —3B **102**
Brancepeth Rd. DL17 —2D **101**
Brancepeth Wlk. TS24 —4D **5**
Brandon Clo. TS14 —2E **19**
Brandon Clo. TS25 —2B **14**
Brandon Rd. TS3 —1A **76**
Brankin Dri. DL1 —5C **116**
Brankin Rd. DL1 —5C **116**
Branklyn Gdns. TS17 —5C **86**
Branksome Av. TS5 —3F **73**
Branksome Grn. DL3 —4A **110**
Branksome Gro. TS18 —3D **69**
Branksome Hall. DL3 —4B **110**
Branksome Hall Dri. DL3 —4B **110**
Branksome Lodge. DL3 —4B **110**
Branksome Ter. DL3 —1F **115**
Bransdale. DL16 —2B **98**
Bransdale. TS14 —4A **96**
Bransdale Clo. TS19 —4F **47**
Bransdale Gro. TS10 —1A **42**
Bransdale Gro. TS25 —5B **12**
Bransdale Rd. TS3 —1D **75**
Brantwood Clo. TS17 —5D **87**
Brass Castle La. TS8 & TS7 —5A **92**
Brass Wynd. TS7 —4A **92**
Brawton Gro. DL3 —4F **111**
Braygate Mill La. TS13 —1F **83**
Brechin Dri. TS17 —3E **87**
Brechin Gro. TS25 —5E **11**
Breckland Wlk. TS3 —2E **75**
Breckon Hill Rd. TS4 —4B **52**
Breck Rd. DL3 —2D **115**
Brecon Dri. TS10 —2B **42**
Brecon Side. DL1 —4F **113**
Breen Clo. TS3 —4C **52**
Brenda Rd. TS25 —2F **11** to 4C **16**
Brendon Cres. TS23 —2F **33**
Brendon Gro. TS17 —4B **86**
Brenkley Clo. TS20 —5F **31**
Brent Ct. TS3 —3D **33**
Brentford Ct. TS12 —5D **65**
Brentford Rd. TS20 —3C **48**
Brentnall St. TS1 —3F **51**
Brereton Rd. TS4 —3B **74**
Bretby Clo. TS4 —3B **74**
Brettenham Av. TS4 —5C **74**
(in two parts)
Breward Wlk. TS24 —3F **7**
Brewer St. DL14 —3D **103**
Brewery St. TS24 —1F **11**
Brewery Ter. TS9 —3E **119**
Brewery Yd. TS15 —2C **94**
Brewery Yd. TS9 —4E **119**
Brewsdale Rd. TS3 —3D **53**
Brian Rd. DL1 —2B **112**
Briar Clo. DL3 —5D **115**
Briar Clo. DL16 —5A **98**
Briardene Av. TS5 —4F **73**
Briardene Ct. TS19 —2B **46**
Briardene M. TS25 —3F **11**
Briardene Wlk. TS19 —1B **46**
Briar Gro. TS10 —5D **29**
Briarhill Gdns. TS26 —3C **6**
Briar Rd. TS17 —5D **71**
Briarvale Av. TS5 —3E **73**

Briar Wlk. DL3 —5D **115**
Briar Wlk. TS18 —2F **69**
Briar Wlk. TS26 —4E **7**
Brickton Rd. TS5 —1C **72**
Bridge Ct. TS6 —2D **77**
Bridge Ct. TS15 —2C **94**
Bridge Ho. Est. DL17 —3C **100**
Bridgend Clo. TS6 —3F **55**
Bridge Rd. DL3 —5C **114**
Bridge Rd. DL14 —1B **102**
Bridge Rd. TS9 —4E **119**
Bridge Rd. TS10 —4B **28**
Bridge Rd. TS18 —1C **70** & 2C **70**
Bridge St. DL14 —1C **102**
Bridge St. TS9 —4A **120**
Bridge St. TS15 —2C **94**
Bridge St. TS17 —2D **71**
Bridge St. TS20 —3C **48**
Bridge St. TS24 —5B **8**
Bridge St. E. TS2 —2A **52**
Bridge St. W. TS2 —2F **51**
Bridge Ter. DL1 —2B **116**
Bridle, The. DL5 —2D **107**
Bridnor Rd. TS3 —3D **75**
Bridport Clo. TS18 —4E **49**
Bridport Gro. TS8 —4A **90**
Brierley Grn. TS7 —3F **91**
(in two parts)
Brierley Ho. TS3 —5E 53
(off Bodmin Clo.)
Brierton La. TS22 & TS25
—4A **10** to 4E **11**
Brierville Rd. TS19 —3A **48**
Brigandine Clo. TS25 —5B **12**
(in two parts)
Briggs Av. TS6 —4B **54**
Brigham Rd. TS3 —2C **74**
Brighouse Bus. Village. TS2
—5D **35**
Brighouse Ct. DL5 —3E **109**
Brighouse Rd. TS2 —5D **35**
Brighton Clo. TS17 —1C **86**
Brighton Rd. DL1 —3C **116**
Bright St. DL1 —2C **116**
Bright St. TS1 —3B **52**
Bright St. TS18 —5B **48**
Bright St. TS26 —4D **7**
Brignall Moor Cres. DL1 —3E **117**
Brignall Rd. TS18 —3A **70**
Brignell Rd. TS2 —1E **51**
Brig Open. TS24 —2D **9**
Brimham Clo. TS17 —5D **87**
Brimston Clo. TS26 —4B **6**
Brindle Clo. TS7 —3F **91**
Brindle Ho. TS2 —2A 52
(off East St.)
Brine St. TS4 —4B **52**
Brinewells Grn. TS4 —5C **52**
Brinkburn Av. DL3 —4E **111**
Brinkburn Clo. DL14 —4A **102**
Brinkburn Dri. DL3 —4E **111**
Brinkburn Rd. DL3 —5D **111**
Brinkburn Rd. TS20 —2B **48**
Brinkburn Rd. TS25 —1E **11**
Brisbane Cres. TS17 —1D **87**
Brisbane Gro. TS18 —2E **69**
Briscoe Way. TS8 —4D **89**
Bristol Av. TS12 —1D **63**
Bristol Wlk. TS26 —2C **6**
Bristow Rd. TS4 —2C **74**
Bristow St. TS3 —4D **73**
Britain Av. TS5 —3D **73**
Britannia Ct. TS2 —1E **51**
Britannia Pl. TS10 —1F **41**
Britannia Rd. TS19 —5B **48**
Britannia Ter. TS12 —4C **64**
British School Yd. DL3 —2A **116**

Broadbent St. TS12 —5C **64**
Broad Clo. TS8 —5C **88**
Broadfield Rd. TS24 —2D **19**
Broadgate Gdns. TS5 —3D **73**
Broadgate Rd. TS5 —3D **73**
Broadhaven Clo. TS6 —5F **55**
Broadmeadows. DL3 —2C **114**
Broadstone. TS8 —5F **91**
Broad Wlk. DL14 —1D **103**
Broadway. TS6 —3F **55**
Broadway E. TS10 —1F **41**
Broadway S. DL1 —2E **117**
Broadway, The. DL1
　　　　—1E **117** & 2E **117**
Broadway W. TS10 —2E **41**
Broadwell Rd. TS4 —5C **74**
Brockett Clo. DL5 —4D **107**
Brocklesby Rd. TS14 —5E **97**
Brockrigg Ct. TS14 —1D **97**
Brockwell Clo. DL5 —3D **107**
Brodick Gro. TS25 —5E **11**
Brogden Grn. TS3 —2D **75**
Broken Banks. DL14 —1C **102**
Bromley Hill Clo. TS7 —5B **92**
Bromley Rd. TS18 —2E **69**
Brompton Gro. TS18 —3D **69**
Brompton Rd. TS5 —1E **73**
Brompton St. TS5 —5E **51**
Brompton Wlk. DL3 —2D **115**
Brompton Wlk. TS25 —1B **16**
Brook Clo. DL5 —3E **107**
Brookdale Rd. TS7 —3E **91**
Brookes, The. TS15 —4D **95**
Brookfield Rd. TS19 —5B **46**
Brook Ho. TS2 —2A 52
(off Cleveland St.)
Brooklands. DL14 —5C **102**
Brooksbank Av. TS10 —5D **29**
Brooksbank Clo. TS14 —1C **92**
Brooksbank Rd. TS7 —1C **92**
Brookside. TS12 —4C **80**
Brookside Av. TS4 —3A **74**
Brookside Vs. DL14 —4E **103**
Brook St. DL16 —2C **98**
Brook St. TS2 —2A **52**
Brook St. TS26 —4E **7**
Brook Ter. DL3 —5A **112**
Brookwood Way. TS16 —5D **85**
Broom Cotts. DL17 —3D 10
(off Gordon Ter.)
Broomfield Av. TS16 —5C **84**
Broomhill Gdns. TS26 —3C **6**
Broomlee Clo. DL5 —5A **106**
Broomlee Clo. TS17 —4A **86**
Broom Rd. DL17 —2D **101**
Broomside. DL17 —3D **101**
Broom St. DL16 —2F **99**
Broom, The. DL17 —1E **101**
Brotton Rd. TS12 & TS13 —4E **65**
Brotton Rd. TS17 —4E **71**
Brougham St. DL3 —3A **112**
Brougham St. TS2 —2F **51**
Brougham St. TS18 —1C **70**
Brougham Ter. TS4 —3F **7**
Brough Clo. TS17 —1F **87**
Brough Ct. TS4 —2B **74**
Brough St. TS27 —5B **4**
Brough Gro. DL14 —4B **102**
Brough Rd. TS23 —5F **19**
Broughton Av. TS4 —5C **74**
Broughton Grn. TS10 —2C **42**
Broughton Rd. TS9 —4F **119**
Broughton Rd. TS22 —1C **32**
Browning Av. TS25 —2C **10**
Brownsea Ct. TS17 —5C **86**
Brown St. DL4 —3C **104**
Broxa Clo. TS10 —4C **42**

Bruce Av. TS5 —2C **72**
Bruce Cres. TS24 —5E **5**
Bruce Rd. DL5 —1D **109**
Brummer Ho. TS3 —2E **75**
Brundall Clo. TS19 —3C **46**
Brunel Clo. TS24 —1A **8**
Brunel Rd. TS6 —3A **54**
Brunel St. DL17 —3A **100**
Brunel Way. DL1 —2C **116**
Brunner Ho. TS3 —2E **75**
Brunner Rd. TS23 —5F **33**
Brunswick Av. TS6 —4C **54**
Brunswick Gro. TS24 —5A **8**
Brunswick St. DL1 —2B **116**
Brunswick St. TS1 —2A **52**
Brunswick St. TS18 —1B **70**
Brunswick St. TS24 —5A **8**
Brunswick St. N. DL1 —2B 11
(off Brunswick St.)
Bruntoft Av. TS24 —4D **5**
Bruntons Mnr. Ct. TS3 —1F **75**
Brunton St. DL1 —3C **116**
Brunton Wlk. DL5 —1C **108**
Brus Corner. TS24 —5E **5**
Brus Ho. TS17 —1E **87**
Brusselton Clo. TS5 —1D **89**
Brusselton Cotts. DL4 —5A **104**
Bryan St. DL16 —2D **99**
Brylston Rd. TS3 —5A **54**
Bryony Ct. TS14 —4B **96**
Bryony Gro. TS7 —2D **91**
Buccleuch Clo. TS14 —5E **97**
Buchanan St. TS18 —1B **70**
Buckfast Rd. TS12 —1E **81**
Buckie Gro. TS25 —5E **11**
Buckingham Ct. DL1 —3F **115**
Buckingham Dri. TS6 —4D **77**
Buckingham Rd. TS10 —4D **29**
Buckingham Rd. TS18 —1A **70**
Buckland Clo. TS17 —5D **87**
Buck St. TS2 —1F **51**
Buckton's Yd. DL1 —2A **116**
Buckton's Yd. DL3 —2A 11
(off Skinnergate)
Buddle Wlk. DL5 —1D **109**
Budworth Clo. TS23 —2A **20**
Bull Wynd. DL1 —2A **116**
Bulmer Clo. DL5 —5F **107**
Bulmer Clo. TS15 —4E **95**
Bulmer Ct. TS6 —2E **77**
Bulmer Pl. TS24 —1D **7**
Bulmer's Bldgs. TS14 —2D 97
(off Park La.)
Bulmer Sq. DL3 —4A **112**
Bulmer Way. TS1 —3E **51**
Bungalows, The. TS6 —3F **55**
(in two parts)
Bungalows, The. TS7 —4B 76
(off Henry Taylor Ct.)
Bungalows, The. TS9 —3B 12
(off Central Way)
Bungalows, The. TS21 —5B **68**
Bunting Clo. TS17 —5C **86**
Burbank Ct. TS24 —5A **8**
Burbank St. TS24 —1A **12**
Burdon Clo. DL5 —5D **107**
Burdon Clo. TS19 —4D **47**
Burford Av. TS18 —3A **90**
Burgess St. TS18 —5B **48**
Burghley Ct. TS8 —4A **90**
Burghley M. DL5 —3F **107**
Burke Pl. TS24 —1C **8**
Burke St. DL4 —3C **104**
Burlam Rd. TS5 —1D **73**
Burleigh Pl. DL3 —2F **115**
Burlesdon Ho. TS3 —5E 53
(off Bordesley Grn.)

Burnaby Clo. TS25 —3F **11**
Burneston Ct. DL3 —2A **114**
Burneston Gro. TS18 —2B **68**
Burnet Clo. TS17 —3C **87**
Burnhill Way. DL5
　　　　—1A **108** to 3D **107**
Burnholme Av. TS3 —5F **53**
Burnhope. DL5 —5B **106**
Burnie Gdns. DL4 —3C **104**
Burniston Dri. TS17 —2C **86**
Burniston Dri. TS22 —5C **18**
Burniston Ho. TS3 —5E 53
(off Basildon Grn.)
Burn La. DL5 —3C **106** to 5E **107**
Burnmere. DL16 —1B **98**
Burnmoor Clo. TS10 —3D **43**
Burnmoor Dri. TS16 —4C **84**
Burn Rd. TS25 —1F **11**
Burnsall Rd. TS3 —1C **74**
Burns Av. TS25 —2C **10**
Burnside Ct. TS18 —1F **69**
Burnside Gro. TS18 —1F **69**
Burnside Rd. DL1 —4E **117**
Burns Rd. TS6 —5D **55**
Burnston Clo. TS26 —4B **6**
Burnsville Rd. TS6 —3E **55**
Burn Ter. DL16 —2D **99**
Burn Valley App. TS26 —1E **11**
Burn Valley Gro. TS25 —1E **11**
Burn Valley Rd. TS26 —1E **11**
Burnynghill Clo. DL5 —2A **108**
Burringham Rd. TS20 —5A **32**
Burtonport Way. TS18 —4D 49
(off Alnport Rd.)
Burton Ter. TS12 —1D **63**
Burtree La. DL3 —1A **112**
Burtree Pk. TS25 —4C **12**
Burtree Rd. DL5 —3E **109**
Burwell Dri. TS19 —4B **46**
Burwell Rd. TS3 —2A **76**
Burwell Wlk. TS25 —2C **14**
Bury Rd. DL5 —1F **109**
Burythorpe Clo. TS4 —1B **74**
Bushel Hill Ct. DL3 —1C **114**
Bushel Hill Dri. DL3 —1C **114**
Bushmead Ter. TS3 —3F **75**
Bush St. TS5 —5E **51**
Bushton Clo. TS26 —4B **6**
Busty Ter. DL4 —1B **104**
Butchers Race. DL16 —1F **99**
Bute Av. TS25 —2E **11**
Bute Clo. TS17 —2D **87**
Bute St. TS18 —5B **48**
Butler Rd. DL5 —1D **109**
Butler St. TS20 —2C **48**
Butterby Grange. DL16 —2D **99**
Butterfield Clo. TS16 —5C **84**
Butterfield Dri. TS16 —5C **84**
Butterfield Gro. TS16 —5C **84**
Buttermere. DL16 —1B **98**
Buttermere Av. TS5 —4D **73**
Buttermere Rd. TS6 —4A **56**
Buttermere Rd. TS10 —1C **42**
Buttermere Rd. TS18 —5F **47**
Butterwick Ct. DL5 —4E **107**
Butterwick Rd. TS21 —4C **118**
Butterwick Rd. TS24 —4C **4**
Butt La. TS14 —3F **97**
Buttsfield Way. TS23 —3F **19**
Butts La. TS16 —1C **94**
Buxton Av. TS7 —4E **91**
Buxton Gdns. TS22 —1D **33**
Buxton Moor Cres. DL1 —4D **117**
Buxton Rd. TS14 —4C **48**
Bydales Dri. TS11 —4E **45**
Byelands St. TS4 —5B **52**

Byemoor Av. TS9 —5B **120**
Byemoor Clo. TS9 —5B **120**
Byerley Rd. DL4 —3B **104**
Byers Ho. TS2 —1A 52
(off Dacre St.)
Byford Ho. TS3 —5E 53
(off Bodmin Clo.)
Byland Clo. TS10 —3C **42**
Byland Clo. TS14 —3F **97**
Byland Gro. TS25 —5C **12**
Byland Rd. TS7 —3C **92**
Byland Rd. TS12 —1E **81**
Bylands Gro. TS19 —1C **68**
Bylands Rd. TS6 —1E **77**
Bylands Way. DL3 —4B **110**
Byland Way. TS23 —2B **34**
By-Pass Rd. TS23 —4E **33**
Byrneside Av. TS4 —2A **74**
Byron Av. DL14 —3C **102**
Byron Clo. TS23 —2F **19**
Byron Ct. TS12 —3C **64**
Byron Rd. DL1 —1C **116**
Byron St. TS26 —4D **7**
Byway, The. DL1 —2E **117**
Bywell Gro. TS7 —4B **76**

Cabot Ct. TS17 —1E **87**
Cadogan Sq. DL5 —5D **107**
Cadogan St. TS1 —4E **51**
Cadogan St. TS3 —4D **53**
Cadwell Clo. TS3 —2A **76**
Caedmon Cres. DL3 —3C **114**
Caernarvon Clo. TS6 —4D **55**
Caernarvon Gro. TS26 —3B **6**
Cairn Ct. TS2 —1E **51**
Cairngorm Dri. DL1 —3C **112**
Cairn Rd. TS25 —1D **15**
Cairnston Rd. TS26 —4A **6**
Caistor Dri. TS25 —2D **15**
Caithness Rd. TS6 —5C **54**
Caithness Rd. TS25 —1D **15**
Caithness Way. DL1 —2F **113**
Calcott Clo. TS19 —4E **47**
Calder Clo. DL14 —4A **102**
Calder Clo. TS22 —5B **18**
Calder Gro. TS4 —4C **74**
Calder Gro. TS10 —1C **42**
Calder Gro. TS25 —5D **11**
Caldermere. DL16 —1B **98**
Caldicot Clo. TS6 —4F **55**
Caldwell Clo. TS8 —4F **89**
Caldwell Grn. DL1 —3D **117**
Caledonian Rd. TS25 —2E **11**
Caledonian Way. DL1 —2E **113**
Calf Fallow La. TS20 —3A **32**
California Ct. TS9 —3D **119**
California Rd. TS6 —1A **78**
California St. TS18 —5B **48**
Callander Rd. TS25 —5D **11**
Callerton Rise. DL5 —3D **107**
Calluna Gro. TS7 —2D **91**
Calthorpe Clo. TS1 —3E **51**
Calverley Rd. TS4 —1A **76**
Calvert Clo. TS3 —4C **52**
Calvert's La. TS18 —5C **48**
Camborne Ho. TS3 —5E **53**
Camborne Ho. TS3 —5E 53
(off Cottingham Dri.)
Cambourne Clo. TS8 —4F **89**
Cambrian Av. TS10 —3B **42**
Cambrian Rd. TS23 —1D **33**
Cambridge Av. TS5 —3D **73**
Cambridge Av. TS7 —3E **91**
Cambridge Rd. TS3 —3D **53**
Cambridge Rd. TS5 —3C **72**
Cambridge Rd. TS17 —3D **71**

Cambridge St. DL16 —3C **98**
Cambridge St. TS12 —1D **63**
Cambridge St. Ind. Est. DL16
—3C **98**
Cambridge Ter. TS2 —4F **35**
Camden St. TS1 —4B **52**
Camden St. TS18 —2A **70**
Camelon St. TS17 —3E **71**
Cameron Rd. TS24 —4F **7**
Cameron St. TS20 —5B **32**
Campbell Ct. TS18 —4E **49**
Campbell Rd. TS25 —5D **11**
Campion Clo. TS17 —3C **86**
Campion Ct. DL5 —2E **107**
Campion Dri. TS14 —4B **96**
Campion Gro. TS7 —2D **91**
Campion Rd. DL1 —3B **112**
Campion St. TS26 —5E **7**
Canberra Gro. TS18 —2E **69**
Canberra Rd. TS7 —2E **91**
Canney Hill By-Pass. DL14
—3F **103**
Cannobie Clo. DL3 —3D **115**
Cannock Rd. TS3 —2D **75**
Cannon Pk. Clo. TS1 —3E **51**
Cannon Pk. Ind. Est. TS1 —3E **51**
Cannon Pk. Rd. TS1 —3E **51**
Cannon Pk. Way. TS1 —3E **51**
Cannon St. TS1 —4D **51**
Cannon St. TS5 —4C **50**
Canon Gro. TS15 —4E **95**
Canterbury Clo. DL16 —1B **98**
Canterbury Gro. DL1 —4F **113**
Canterbury Gro. TS5 —1F **73**
Canterbury Rd. TS10 —1A **44**
Canterbury Rd. TS12 —4D **65**
Canton Gdns. TS5 —2E **89**
Canvey Wlk. TS14 —4D **97**
Captain Cook's Cres. TS7 —3F **91**
Captain Cook's Way. TS9 —3B **120**
Captain's Wlk. TS24 —4B 8
(off Maritime Av.)
Carburt Rd. TS19 —1C **46**
Carcut Rd. TS3 —3D **53**
Cardigan Clo. TS6 —4F **55**
Cardigan Gro. TS26 —2C **6**
Cardinal Gdns. DL3 —2C **114**
Cardinal Gro. TS19 —4A **46**
Cardwell Wlk. TS17 —3D 71
(off Walker St.)
Carew Clo. TS15 —5C **94**
Carey Clo. TS1 —4E **51**
Cargo Fleet La. TS3
—3E **53** to 3B **76**
Cargo Fleet Rd. TS1 & TS3
—3B **52**
Carileph Clo. DL5 —1D **109**
Carisbrooke Av. TS3 —1A **76**
Carisbrooke Cres. DL14 —3A **102**
Carisbrooke Rd. TS26 —5B **6**
Carisbrooke Way. TS10 —2F **43**
Carisbrook Wlk. DL3 —2B **114**
Carlbury Av. TS5 —1C **88**
Carlbury Cres. DL3 —2B **114**
Carlbury Rd. DL5 —4E **109**
Carleton Dri. DL3 —1B **114**
Carleton Gro. DL3 —1C **114**
Carleton Ter. TS15 —2C **94**
Carlile Wlk. TS20 —3C **48**
Carlisle Gro. DL14 —3B **102**
Carlisle St. TS25 —5C **12**
Carlow St. TS14 —4E **97**
Carlow St. TS1 —5D **51**
Carlton Av. TS22 —5C **18**
Carlton Clo. TS18 —5B **48**
Carlton Ct. DL1 —2C **116**
Carlton Dri. TS17 —2C **86**

Carlton Moor Cres. DL1 —4E **117**
Carlton St. DL1 —2C **116**
Carlton St. DL17 —5F **101**
Carlton St. TS26 —5E **7**
Carlyle Rd. TS6 —5E **55**
Carmarthen Rd. TS3 —3F **75**
Carmel Gdns. DL3 —3D **115**
Carmel Gdns. TS5 —2E **89**
Carmel Gdns. TS7 —2C **92**
Carmel Gdns. TS14 —2D **97**
Carmel Gdns. TS20 —1D **49**
Carmel Gro. DL3 —4D **115**
Carmel Rd. N. DL3 —1D **115**
(in two parts)
Carmel Rd. S. DL3 —4D **115**
Carnaby Rd. DL1 —3E **117**
Carnaby Wlk. TS5 —4F **73**
Carney St. TS12 —4C **80**
Carnoustie Dri. TS16 —4D **85**
Carnoustie Gro. DL1 —2D **113**
Carnoustie Gro. TS27 —4A **4**
Carnoustie Rd. TS11 —2B **60**
Carnoustie Way. TS8 —4F **91**
Caroline St. DL14 —4D **103**
Caroline St. TS26 —1F **11**
Carpenter Clo. TS15 —5F **95**
Carradale Clo. TS16 —5D **85**
Carrick Ct. TS2 —5E **35**
Carrick Ho. TS2 —1F 51
(off Stockton St.)
Carrick St. TS24 —5D **5**
Carrick's Yd. TS12 —1C **80**
Carr La. DL16 —1B **98**
Carroll Rd. DL3 —2C **114**
Carroll Wlk. TS25 —4B **10**
Carrol St. TS18 —5C **48**
Carron Gro. TS6 —2D **77**
Carr Pl. DL5 —5F **107**
Carside. DL3 —3A **112**
Carrsides La. DL17 —1F **107**
Carr St. DL16 —2B **98**
Carr St. TS18 —1A **70**
Carr St. TS26 —4E **7**
Carthorpe Dri. TS23 —4F **19**
Cartington Clo. DL5 —3E **107**
Cartmel Clo. DL16 —1B **98**
Cartmell Ter. DL3 —4F **111**
Cartmel Rd. TS10 —2D **43**
Carvers St. TS12 —5D **65**
Carville Ct. TS19 —2C **46**
Carwardine Clo. DL5 —2D **107**
Casebourne Rd. TS25 —2A **12**
Casper Ct. TS16 —4D **85**
Cass Ho. Rd. TS8 —5E **89**
Casson Ct. TS23 —4E **19**
Casson Way. TS23 —4E **19**
Cassop Gro. TS5 —5C **72**
Cassop Wlk. TS19 —2C **46**
Castlebay Ct. DL1 —2E **113**
Castle Cen. TS18 —1C **70**
Castle Ct. TS12 —5C **80**
Castle Clo. TS19 —4D **47**
Castle Dyke Wynd. TS15 —2D **95**
Castle Eden Walkway. TS21
—1A **30**
Castle Howard Clo. TS27 —5B **4**
Castlereagh Clo. DL5 —1D **109**
Castlereagh Clo. TS21 —5B **68**
Castlereagh Rd. TS19 —4A **48**
Castle Rd. TS10 —1F **43**
Castleton Av. TS5 —3C **72**
Castleton Dri. TS22 —1C **32**
Castleton Rd. TS6 —5A **56**
Castleton Rd. TS18 —2A **70**
Castleton Rd. TS25 —5C **12**
Castleton Wlk. TS17 —1D **87**

Castle Way. TS4 —2B **74**
Castle Way. TS18 —1C **70**
Castlewood. TS3 —2A **76**
Castle Wynd. TS7 —4B **92**
Catcote Rd. TS25 —2C **10** to 2C **14**
Caterton Clo. TS15 —4F **95**
Cat Flatt La. TS11 —4A **44** & 4B **44**
Cathedral Dri. TS19 —4B **46**
Cathedral Gdns. TS2 —2F **51**
Catherine Clo. DL16 —3D **99**
Catherine Gro. TS24 —5A **8**
Catherine Rd. TS24 —5B **8**
Catherine St. TS12 —5F **81**
Catherine St. TS24 —3E **9**
Catkin Way. DL14 —5A **102**
Catterall Ho. TS3 —5E **53**
Catterall Ho. TS3 —5E 53
(off Cottingham Dri.)
Cattersty Way. TS12 —3C **64**
Cattistock Clo. TS14 —4F **97**
Caudwell Clo. TS19 —1B **46**
Causeway, The. DL1 —2D **117**
Causeway, The. TS23 —1F **33**
Cavendish Clo. DL1 —3B **112**
Cavendish Ct. DL17 —3B **100**
Cavendish Dri. DL1 —3B **112**
Cavendish Rd. TS4 —3B **74**
(in two parts)
Caversham Rd. TS4 —4C **74**
Cawdor Clo. TS11 —2F **59**
Cawood Dri. TS5 —4F **73**
Cawthorne Clo. TS8 —4D **89**
Caxton Gro. TS25 —2C **10**
Caxton St. TS5 —5F **51**
Cayton Clo. TS10 —3C **42**
Cayton Dri. TS5 —4F **73**
Cayton Dri. TS17 —2C **86**
Cayton Dri. TS22 —5C **18**
Cecil Ho. TS5 —4F **11**
Cecil St. TS18 —2B **70**
Cedar Clo. TS6 —1D **77**
Cedar Ct. TS17 —4D **71**
Cedars Cres. TS16 —2E **85**
Cedar Gro. DL4 —3D **105**
Cedar Gro. TS10 —5F **29**
Cedar Gro. TS12 —4B **64**
Cedar Gro. TS13 —4C **66**
Cedar Gro. TS17 —3D **71**
Cedar Rd. DL3 —5E **111**
Cedar Rd. DL14 —3D **103**
Cedar Rd. TS7 —2A **92**
(Marton)
Cedar Rd. TS7 —4C **76**
(Ormesby)
Cedars, The. DL3 —1E **115**
Cedar St. TS18 —5C **48**
Cedar Wlk. TS24 —2E **7**
Cedarwood Av. TS9 —2F **119**
Cedarwood Glade. TS8 —5D **89**
Celandine Clo. TS7 —1D **91**
Cemetery La. DL3 —3C **114**
Cemetery Roundabout. TS14
—1F **97**
Centenary Cres. TS20 —1B **48**
Central Arc. TS15 —2D **95**
Central Av. DL5 —5E **107**
Central Av. TS5 —1C **72**
Central Av. TS23 —3E **33**
Central M. TS1 —3A **52**
Central Pde. DL4 —3C **104**
Central Rd. TS24 —1B **8** & 3B **8**
(in two parts)
Central St. TS15 —2D **95**
Central Ter. TS10 —4D **29**
Central Way. TS9 —3B **120**
Centre Ct. TS5 —2D **89**

Centre Mall. TS1 —3F **51**
Cestria Way. DL5 —4B **106**
Ceylon Sq. TS16 —3B **84**
Chadburn Grn. TS4 —3A **74**
Chadburn Rd. TS20 —2B **48**
Chadderton Clo. TS12 —4C **80**
Chadderton Dri. TS17 —5F **71**
Chadwell Av. TS3 —2E **75**
Chadwick Clo. TS6 —3D **55**
Chalcot Wlk. TS3 —5F **53**
Chalfield Clo. TS17 —5D **87**
Chalford Oaks. TS5 —4B **72**
Chalk Clo. TS18 —2B **70**
Chalk Wlk. TS18 —2B 70
(off Chalk Clo.)
Challacombe Cres. TS17 —4A **86**
Challoner Rd. TS15 —4C **94**
Challoner Rd. TS24 —2D **7**
Challoner Sq. TS24 —2D **7**
Chaloner M. TS14 —3E **97**
Chaloner St. TS14 —3E **97**
Chancel Way. TS6 —1F **77**
Chancery La. DL1 —2A **116**
Chandler Clo. DL5 —4E **107**
Chandlers Clo. TS24 —5B **8**
Chandlers Ridge. TS7 —4B **92**
Chandlers Wharf Shopping Cen.
TS18 —1C **70**
Chandos St. DL3 —5F **111**
Chantilly Av. DL1 —3E **113**
Chantry Clo. TS3 —3D **75**
Chantry Clo. TS20 —5B **32**
Chapelbeck Bungalows. TS14
—2D **97**
Chapel Clo. TS3 —3A **76**
Chapel Clo. TS11 —5D **45**
Chapel Ct. TS23 —4E **33**
Chapelgarth. TS8 —4D **89**
Chapelhope Clo. DL1 —2C **112**
Chapel Rd. TS23 —4E **33**
Chapel Row. DL17 —4F **101**
Chapel Row. TS13 —4D **67**
Chapel St. DL4 —4C **104**
Chapel St. TS6 —4D **57**
Chapel St. TS11 —5D **45**
Chapel St. TS12 —4D **65**
Chapel St. TS13 —1B **66**
Chapel St. TS14 —3E **97**
Chapel St. TS17 —2D **71**
Chapel Ter. DL17 —2C **100**
Chapel Yd. TS15 —2C **94**
Chapman Clo. DL5 —4E **107**
Chapman Ct. TS3 —1F **75**
Chapman St. TS20 —1C **48**
Chards Cotts. TS12 —3D **63**
Chard Wlk. TS3 —2D **75**
Charlbury Rd. TS3 —5E **53**
Charles St. DL1 —4A **112**
Charles St. DL4 —5C **104**
Charles St. DL16 —3C **98**
Charles St. TS10 —4E **29**
Charles St. TS11 —2B **60**
Charles St. TS17 —3D **71**
Charles St. TS24 —5A **8**
Charles St. TS25 —5C **12**
Charlotte Grange. TS25 —1E **11**
Charlotte St. TS2 —2F **51**
Charlotte St. TS10 —4E **29**
Charlotte St. TS12 —1E **81**
Charlotte St. TS26 —1E **11**
Charlton Rd. TS10 —1A **42**
Charltons Garth. TS14 —2D **97**
Charnley Grn. TS4 —4B **74**
Charnwood Clo. TS11 —5D **45**
Charnwood Dri. TS17 —1C **92**
Charrington Av. TS17 —2C **86**
Charterhouse St. TS25 —2E **11**

Chart Ho. TS24 —4B **8**
(off Warrior Quay)
Chartwell Clo. TS11 —4C **44**
Chartwell Clo. TS17 —5D **87**
Charwood. TS3 —1A **76**
Chase Clo. DL3 —5B **110**
Chase, The. DL5 —4A **106**
Chase, The. TS10 —5E **29**
Chase, The. TS19 —5C **46**
Chatfield Ho. TS3 —4E 53
(off Northfleet Av.)
Chatham Gdns. TS24 —2E **7**
Chatham Rd. TS16 —4A **84**
Chatham Rd. TS24 —3D **7**
Chatham Sq. TS24 —3E **7**
Chathill Wlk. TS7 —4B **76**
Chatsworth Av. DL14 —4C **102**
Chatsworth Ct. TS19 —3E **47**
Chatsworth Gdns. TS22 —5D **19**
Chatsworth Ho. TS3 —5E 53
(off Cottingham Dri.)
Chatsworth Ter. DL1 —3A **116**
Chatton Clo. TS3 —3E **75**
Chaucer Av. TS3 —5A **54**
Chaucer Av. TS25 —2C **10**
Chaucer Rd. DL1 —4B **112**
Chaytor Ct. DL3 —2F **111**
Chaytor Lee. TS15 —4D **95**
Cheadle Wlk. TS3 —2E **75**
Cheam Av. TS3 —5E **53**
Cheapside. DL4 —2C **104**
Cheapside. DL16 —3C **98**
Cheddar Clo. TS6 —4F **55**
Cheesmond Av. DL14 —5B **102**
Cheetham St. TS6 —2E **55**
Chelmsford Av. TS18 —1D **69**
Chelmsford Rd. TS5 —1F **73**
Chelmsford St. DL3 —1F **115**
Chelmsford St. TS17 —2D **71**
Chelmsford Wlk. TS5 —2F **73**
Chelsea Ct. DL1 —3F **115**
Chelsea Gdns. TS20 —4F **31**
Chelston Clo. TS26 —3A **6**
Cheltenham Av. TS7 —4E **91**
Cheltenham Av. TS17 —3E **71**
Cheltenham Clo. TS5 —1A **74**
Cheltenham Rd. TS18 —3A **50**
Chepstow Clo. TS23 —5E **19**
Chepstow Clo. DL1 —5F **113**
Chepstow Wlk. TS26 —2C **6**
Cheriton Grn. TS3 —5E **53**
Cherry Ct. TS19 —3B **48**
Cherry Tree Clo. TS7 —4C **76**
Cherry Tree Cotts. TS12 —5D **81**
Cherry Tree Dri. TS21 —4B **118**
Cherry Tree Gdns. TS20 —1D **49**
Cherry Trees. TS10 —4C **28**
Cherry Wlk. TS24 —2E **7**
Cherrywood Av. TS9 —2F **119**
Cherrywood Ct. TS5 —2F **89**
Chertsey Av. TS3 —5E **53**
Cherwell Ter. TS3 —4F **53**
(in two parts)
Chesham Clo. TS20 —5C **32**
Chesham Gro. TS20 —5D **33**
Chesham Rd. TS20 —5D **33**
Chesham St. TS5 —1F **73**
Cheshire Pl. DL14 —4D **103**
Cheshire Rd. TS20 —2D **49**
Chesneywood. TS3 —1A **76**
Chesnut Clo. DL1 —1A **116**
Chester Gro. DL3 —1B **114**
Chester Rd. TS10 —1A **44**
Chester Rd. TS26 & TS24 —3D **7**
Chester St. DL14 —2D **103**
Chester St. TS1 —5E **51**
Chesterton Av. TS17 —1C **86**

Chesterton Ct. TS20 —1C **48**
Chesterton Rd. TS25 —3C **10**
Chestnut Av. DL16 —4B **98**
Chestnut Av. DL17 —2D **101**
Chestnut Av. TS10 —5F **29**
Chestnut Clo. DL4 —3D **105**
Chestnut Clo. TS6 —4D **57**
Chestnut Clo. TS12 —2B **62**
Chestnut Dri. TS7 —2F **91**
Chestnut Gro. TS12 —4B **64**
Chestnut Gro. TS17 —4D **71**
Chestnut Rd. TS16 —2E **85**
Chestnut Rd. TS21 —4C **118**
Chestnut Sq. TS19 —3A **48**
Chetwode Ter. TS3 —3F 75
(off Carmarthen Rd.)
Chevil. TS8 —5D **91**
Chevin Wlk. TS3 —2D **75**
Cheviot Ct. DL1 —3C **112**
Cheviot Cres. TS23 —2E **33**
Cheviot Dri. TS12 —5D **63**
Cheviot Pl. TS4 —4B **106**
Chez Nous Av. TS25 —2F **11**
Chichester Clo. TS25 —2D **15**
Chichester Wlk. DL1 —3F **113**
Chilcroft Clo. TS22 —5B **18**
Childeray St. TS18 —1A **70**
Child St. TS12 —4C **64**
Child St. TS14 —3D **97**
Chillingham Ct. TS23 —3F **19**
Chillingham Gro. DL5 —3E **107**
Chiltern Av. TS10 —2B **42**
Chilton Clo. DL3 —2C **114**
Chilton Clo. DL5 —3E **107**
Chilton Clo. TS5 —5D **73**
Chilton Clo. TS19 —1B **46**
Chilton La. DL17 —4F **101**
Chiltons Av. TS23 —4F **33**
China St. DL3 —3B **112**
Chine, The. TS12 —1C **62**
Chingford Av. TS3 —2A **76**
Chingford Gro. TS19 —4E **47**
Chipchase Rd. TS5 —1E **73**
Chippenham Rd. TS4 —4B **74**
Chopwell Clo. TS19 —2C **46**
Christchurch Clo. DL1 —3B **112**
Christchurch Dri. TS18 —2C **68**
Christopher St. TS20 —3C **48**
Christopher St. TS26 —4E **7**
Christopher Wlk. DL5 —5D **107**
Church Clo. DL5 —5E **107**
Church Clo. DL17 —2C **100**
Church Clo. TS7 —4B **76**
Church Clo. TS8 —5D **89**
Church Clo. TS11 —4E **45**
Church Clo. TS13 —4D **67**
Church Clo. TS16 —2D **95**
Church Clo. TS17 —3C **70**
Church Clo. TS24 —2D **9**
Church Dri. DL14 —4E **103**
Church Dri. TS9 —3A **120**
Church Dri. TS12 —5D **81**
Churchend Clo. TS23 —4E **33**
Church Howle Cres. TS11 —4F **45**
Churchill Clo. TS6 —5F **55**
Churchill Clo. TS9 —3B **120**
Churchill Dri. TS11 —4C **44**
Churchill Ho. DL5 —5D **107**
Churchill Rd. TS6 —1F **77**
Church La. DL5 —5F **109**
Church La. DL17 —2C **100**
Church La. TS5 —5D **73**
Church La. TS6 —3E **55** to 1F **77**
Church La. TS7 —5C **92**
(Nunthorpe)
Church La. TS7 —4A **76** & 5B **76**
(Ormesby)

Church La. TS11 —4D **45**
Church La. TS12 —1B **80**
Church La. TS14 —1E **97**
Church Mt. TS16 —1F **77**
Church Rd. DL17 —2C **100**
Church Rd. TS16 —2D **95**
Church Rd. TS18 —5C **48** to 4D **49**
Church Rd. TS23 —4E **33**
Church Row. DL1 —2A **116**
Church Row. TS13 —4D **67**
Church Row. TS22 —3D **19**
Church Row. TS24 —1F **11**
Church Sq. TS24 —5A **8**
Church St. DL4 —3C **104**
Church St. DL16 —3C **98**
Church St. DL17 —5F **101**
Church St. TS10 —4B **28**
Church St. TS11 —4D **45**
Church St. TS14 —2E **97**
Church St. TS24 —4A **8**
Church St. TS25 —5C **12**
Church St. S. TS11 —4D **45**
Church View. TS21 —5B **68**
(Long Newton)
Church View. TS21 —4B **118**
(Sedgefield)
Church Wlk. TS3 —5A **54**
Church Wlk. TS14 —2E **97**
Church Wlk. TS24 —3D **9**
Churchyard Link Rd. TS18 —1B **70**
Cinderwood. TS3 —1A **76**
Clairville Ct. TS4 —5B **52**
Clairville Rd. TS4 —5B **52**
Clanny Rd. DL5 —2F **109**
Clapham Grn. TS3 —1C **74**
Clapham Rd. TS15 —4C **94**
Clare Av. DL3 —2C **114**
Claremont Ct. TS17 —1D **71**
Claremont Dri. TS7 —4F **91**
Claremont Dri. TS26 —1D **11**
Claremont Gdns. TS19 —5C **46**
Claremont Gro. TS21 —5A **118**
Claremont Pk. TS26 —1D **11**
Claremont Rd. TS4 —4C **116**
Clarence Chare. DL5 —2E **109**
Clarence Clo. DL5 —2E **109**
Clarence Corner. DL5 —2E **109**
Clarence Gdns. DL14 —2C **102**
Clarence Grn. DL5 —2E **109**
Clarence Ho. DL16 —3C **98**
Clarence Rd. TS7 —3C **92**
Clarence Rd. TS16 —4D **85**
Clarence Rd. TS24 —4F **7**
Clarence Row. TS18 —4C **48**
Clarence St. DL14 —2C **102**
Clarence St. DL16 —3C **98**
Clarence St. TS18 —4C **48**
Clarence St. TS23 —4E **35**
Clarence St. TS24 —2D **9**
Clarence, The. DL14 —2C **102**
Clarendon Rd. DL1 —3F **113**
Clarendon Rd. TS1
　　　　　　　—4F **51** & 4A **52**
Clarendon Rd. TS17 —5E **71**
Clarendon Rd. TS20 —2B **48**
Clarendon St. TS10 —4E **29**
Clareville Rd. DL3 —2D **115**
Clark St. TS24 —1A **12**
Clark's Yd. DL3 —2A 11
(off Skinnergate)
Claude Av. TS3 —3E **73**
Clavering Rd. TS27 —4A **4**
Claxton Av. DL3 —1C **114**
Claxton Clo. TS19 —1B **46**
Claxton Ct. DL5 —4A **106**
Claydon Gro. TS17 —5C **86**
Claygate. TS23 —4E **19**

Claymond Ct. TS20 —5B **32**
Claymore Rd. TS25 —1D **15**
Clayton Ct. DL14 —1D **103**
Clayton St. DL14 —1D **103**
Claytons Yd. DL1 —2B **116**
Cleadon Av. TS23 —3F **19**
Cleadon Wlk. TS19 —2C **46**
Clearpool Clo. TS24 —1A **8**
Cleasby View. DL3 —4C **110**
Cleasby Way. TS16 —2C **84**
Cleatlam Clo. TS19 —2C **46**
Cleator Dri. TS14 —5D **97**
Clee Ter. TS23 —2F **33**
Clements Rise. TS20 —5A **32**
Clepstone Av. TS5 —3D **73**
Clevegate. TS7 —3A **92**
Cleveland Av. DL3 —1E **115**
Cleveland Av. DL4 —3E **105**
Cleveland Av. DL14 —3C **102**
Cleveland Av. TS5 —3E **73**
Cleveland Av. TS9 —2F **119**
Cleveland Av. TS20 —1C **48**
Cleveland Bus. Cen. TS1 —3A **52**
Cleveland Cen. TS1 —3A **52**
Cleveland Clo. TS7 —5B **76**
Cleveland Ct. DL17 —4F **101**
Cleveland Ct. TS6 —2C **54**
Cleveland Dri. TS7 —5B **76**
Cleveland Gdns. TS16 —5C **84**
Cleveland Pl. TS10 —2E **41**
Cleveland Pl. TS14 —2E **97**
Cleveland Rd. TS24 —1A **8**
Cleveland Sq. TS1 —3A 52
(off Cleveland Cen.)
Cleveland St. DL1 —5B **112**
Cleveland St. TS2 —2A **52**
Cleveland St. TS6 —1A **78**
(Eston)
Cleveland St. TS6 —2E **77**
(Normanby)
Cleveland St. TS9 —3B **120**
Cleveland St. TS10 —3D **29**
Cleveland St. TS13 —5B **66**
(Liverton Mines)
Cleveland St. TS13 —4D **67**
(Loftus)
Cleveland St. TS14 —2D **97**
Cleveland St. TS24 —2D **9**
Cleveland Ter. DL3 —3D **115**
Cleveland Trading Est. DL1
　　　　　　　　　　—4B **112**
Cleveland View. TS3 —1F **75**
Cleveland View. TS11 —4B **44**
Cleveland View. TS12 —2B **80**
Cleveland Way. TS12 —4A **80**
Cleves Av. DL17 —3F **101**
Cleves Clo. DL17 —2E **101**
Cleves Cotts. DL17 —3E **101**
Cleves Ct. DL17 —2E **101**
Cleves Cross Grange. DL17
　　　　　　　　　　—2E **101**
Cliff Cotts. TS5 —2D **73**
Cliff Cotts. TS11 —3D **45**
Cliff Cres. TS13 —4B **66**
Cliffden Ct. TS12 —2E **63**
Cliffe Av. TS13 —5F **65**
Cliffe Ct. TS25 —4C **12**
Cliffe St. TS12 —4C **64**
Cliffe Way. DL1 —4D **117**
Clifford Av. DL14 —4D **103**
Clifford Clo. TS24 —5D **5**
Clifford St. TS10 —4C **28**
Cliffport Ct. TS18 —4D **49**
Cliff St. TS11 —2B **60**
Cliff Ter. TS11 —3D **45**
Cliff Ter. TS13 —5B **66**
(Loftus)

Cliff Ter. TS13 —1B **66**
(Skinningrove)
Cliff Ter. TS24 —2E **9**
Cliff, The. TS25 —4C **12** & 5C **12**
Cliffwood Clo. TS6 —2A **78**
Clifton Av. DL1 —4B **116**
Clifton Av. TS16 —3E **85**
Clifton Av. TS18 —3A **70**
Clifton Av. TS22 —5C **18**
Clifton Av. TS26 —5D **7**
Clifton Gdns. TS16 —3E **85**
Clifton Ho. TS19 —3F **47**
Clifton Pl. TS6 —2E **77**
Clifton Rd. DL1 —3A **116** & 4A **116**
Clifton St. TS1 —4F **51**
Clinton Ho. TS25 —1F **15**
Clive Cres. TS20 —2B **48**
Clive Rd. TS5 —1E **73**
Clive Rd. TS6 —2E **77**
Clive St. DL17 —4F **101**
Clockwood Gdns. TS15 —3E **95**
Cloisters, The. TS19 —4B **46**
Close St. DL1 —4B **112**
Close, The. DL16 —1D **99**
Close, The. TS4 —2B **74**
Close, The. TS13 —1F **67**
Close, The. TS21 —5A **68**
Clover Ct. DL5 —2E **107**
Cloverdale. DL1 —2F **113**
Cloverdale Ct. DL5 —4B **106**
Cloverwood Clo. TS7 —2A **92**
Clyde Gdns. TS22 —5B **18**
Clyde Pl. TS24 —1B **8**
Clyde Ter. DL16 —4B **98**
Clynes Rd. TS6 —4F **55**
Coach Ho. M. TS6 —3D **77**
Coach Rd. TS12 —3B **64**
Coal La. TS22 —1A **18** to 2D **19**
(in three parts)
Coast Rd. TS10 & TS11
—5F **29** to 3D **45**
Coast Rd. TS27 —2A **4**
Coate Clo. TS8 —4E **89**
Coatham Av. DL5 —3D **109**
Coatham Bay Caravan Site. TS10
—4A **28**
Coatham Clo. TS8 —4F **89**
Coatham Cres. DL1 —2C **112**
Coatham Dri. TS10 —1B **10**
Coatham Gro. TS23 —3A **20**
Coatham Lodge. TS10 —4B **28**
Coatham Rd. TS10 —4B **28**
Coatham Rd. TS19 —2C **46**
Coatham Vale. TS16 —5B **84**
Coatsay Clo. TS19 —2C **46**
Cobble Carr. TS14 —3D **97**
Cobb Wlk. TS24 —2C **8**
Cobden Ct. DL1 —3D **117**
Cobden Cl. DL1 —2D **117**
Cobden St. TS17 —2E **71**
Cobden St. TS18 —5B **48**
Cobden St. TS26 —4D **7**
Cobham St. TS1 —5F **51**
Coburg St. DL1 —2B **116**
Cobwood. DL3 —1A **76**
Cochrane Ter. DL17 —5F **101**
Cockburn St. TS12 —5F **81**
Cocken Rd. TS19 —2C **46**
Cockerton Grn. DL3 —5C **110**
Cockerton Wlk. TS19 —2C **46**
Cockfield Av. TS23 —3A **20**
Cockton Hill Rd. DL14 —4D **103**
Cohen Ct. TS20 —5A **32**
Colburn Av. DL5 —4A **106**
Colburn Wlk. TS6 —5A **56**
Colchester Rd. TS13 —1F **67**
Colchester Rd. TS20 —5C **32**

Coleby Av. TS4 —4B **74**
Coledale Rd. TS3 —2D **75**
Colenso St. TS26 —1E **11**
Coleridge Av. TS25 —2F **11**
Coleridge Gdns. DL1 —5A **116**
Coleridge Rd. TS23 —2F **19**
Coleshill Clo. TS23 —5F **19**
Coleton Gdns. TS17 —5C **86**
College Ct. DL3 —2E **115**
College Ct. TS3 —5A **54**
College Ct. TS9 —3E **119**
College Rd. TS3 —5F **53**
College Sq. TS9 —3E **119**
College St. DL4 —2B **104**
Colleton Wlk. TS3 —2E **75**
Colliers Grn. TS4 —5C **52**
Collin Av. TS4 —3A **74**
Colling Wlk. DL5 —1D **109**
Collingwood Chase. TS12 —3C **64**
Collingwood Ct. TS2 —1D **51**
Collingwood Rd. TS23 —5E **33**
Collingwood Rd. TS26 —4E **7**
Collingwood Wlk. TS26 —4E **7**
Collins Av. TS20 —1D **49**
Collinson Av. TS5 —3B **72**
Colmans Nook. TS23 —3C **34**
Colmore Av. TS3 —5A **54**
Colorado Gro. DL1 —3C **112**
Colpitt Clo. TS20 —5B **32**
Colsterdale Clo. TS23 —4F **19**
Coltman St. TS3 —4D **53**
Columbia Dri. TS17 —1C **70**
Columbia St. DL3 —5F **111**
Columbine Clo. TS7 —2D **91**
Colville St. TS1 —4E **51**
Colwell Cl. DL5 —5A **106**
Colwyn Clo. TS10 —3E **43**
Colwyn Rd. TS20 —5D **33**
Colwyn Rd. TS26 —1E **11** & 1F **11**
(in four parts)
Comfrey. TS8 —5D **91**
Commerce Way. TS6 —4B **54**
Commercial St. DL3 —2A **116**
Commercial St. DL17 —5F **101**
Commercial St. TS2 —1A **52**
Commercial St. TS18 —5C **48**
Commercial St. TS24 —2C **8**
Commercial St. TS24 —3B **8**
Commondale Av. TS19 —3F **47**
Commondale Dri. TS25 —1B **16**
Commondale Gro. TS10 —1B **42**
Compass Ho. TS24 —4B 8
(off Warrior Quay)
Compton Clo. TS20 —3C **48**
Compton Gro. DL3 —1D **115**
Compton Gro. DL14 —3C **102**
Compton Ho. TS3 —5E 53
(off Cottingham Dri.)
Compton Rd. TS25 —3B **10**
Comrie Rd. TS25 —1D **15**
Concorde Way. TS18
—5F **69** & 5A **70**
Coney Av. DL14 —5B **102**
Coney Clo. TS17 —4D **87**
Congreve Ter. DL5 —5E **109**
Conifer Av. TS21 —3B **118**
Conifer Clo. TS7 —4C **76**
Conifer Cres. TS23 —3D **33**
Conifer Dri. TS19 —2F **47**
Conifer Gro. TS23 —3D **33**
Conisborough Dri. TS19 —2F **43**
Conisbrough Rd. TS3
—3A **114** to 2F **115**
Coniscliffe Rd. TS19 —2C **46**
Coniscliffe Rd. TS26 —5A **6**
Coniston Av. TS10 —1D **43**
Coniston Gro. TS5 —4D **73**

Coniston Rd. DL17 —3C **100**
Coniston Rd. TS6 —4A **56**
Coniston Rd. TS12 —5C **62**
Coniston Rd. TS18 —4E **47**
Coniston Rd. TS25 —3A **12**
Coniston St. DL3 —5E **111**
Connaught Clo. TS7 —3C **92**
Connaught Rd. TS5 —5C **50**
Connaught Rd. TS7 —3B **92**
Conningsby Clo. TS25 —2C **14**
Conrad Wlk. TS6 —3B **10**
Consett Clo. TS19 —2C **46**
Constance St. TS3 —4C **52**
Convalescent St. TS12 —1D **63**
Conway Av. TS23 —1F **33**
Conway Dri. TS3 —1F **75**
(in two parts)
Conway Rd. DL14 —3C **102**
Conway Rd. TS10 —1E **43**
Conway Wlk. TS26 —2C **6**
Conyers Av. DL3 —1B **114**
Conyers Clo. DL3 —1B **114**
Conyers Clo. TS15 —4C **94**
Conyers Ct. TS12 —4D **65**
Conyers Gro. DL3 —1B **114**
Conyers Pl. DL5 —5E **107**
Conyers Ter. DL17 —3D **101**
Cook Cres. TS20 —1B **48**
Cookgate. TS7 —3A **92**
Cook's Ct. TS7 —4C **76**
Coombe Dri. DL1
—5E **113** & 5F **113**
Coombe Hill. TS11 —2B **60**
Coombe Way. TS18 —2B **68**
Co-operative Clo. TS13 —4B **66**
Co-operative St. DL4 —2B **104**
Co-operative Ter. TS13 —4C **66**
Cooper Clo. TS6 —1F **77**
Copeland Ct. TS2 —1E **51**
Copgrove Clo. TS3 —1C **74**
(in two parts)
Copley Clo. TS19 —2C **46**
Copley Ho. DL1 —4C **116**
Copley Wlk. TS3 —3E **75**
Copnor Wlk. TS3 —3E **75**
Copperwood. TS3 —2A **76**
Copperwood Clo. TS27 —3A **4**
Coppice Rd. TS4 —2B **74**
Coppice, The. TS8 —3A **90**
(in two parts)
Coppice Wlk. DL3 —5B **110**
Copse Clo. TS17 —4C **86**
Copse La. TS17 —4C **86**
Copse Side. DL3 —2B **114**
Copse, The. DL14 —2C **102**
Copse, The. TS24 —3E **7**
Copsewood Wlk. TS9 —2F **119**
Coquet Clo. TS10 —3A **44**
Coquet Clo. TS17 —4A **86**
Coral St. TS1 —4F **51**
Coral St. TS12 —1D **63**
Coral Way. TS10 —2F **43**
Corbridge Clo. TS8 —4F **89**
Corbridge Clo. TS19 —2C **46**
Corbridge Cres. DL1 —3D **113**
Corby Av. TS5 —4B **72**
Corby Ho. TS4 —2C **74**
Corder Rd. TS5 —5C **50**
Corfe Cres. TS23 —5E **19**
Coris Clo. TS7 —1D **91**
Cormland Clo. TS20 —1D **49**
Cormorant Dri. TS10 —3F **43**
Corncroft M. TS6 —2F **55**
Cornfield Av. TS3 —4A **54**
Cornfield Rd. TS5 —2F **73**
Cornfield Rd. TS17 —3C **70**
Cornfield Rd. TS19 —5B **46**

Cornfields Ho. TS6 —3F **77**
Cornforth Av. TS3 —3E **75**
Cornforth Clo. TS19 —2C **46**
Cornforth Gro. TS23 —3A **20**
Corngrave Clo. TS11 —4E **45**
Cornhill Wlk. TS7 —4B **76**
Cornmill Cen. DL1 —2A **116**
Cornriggs Wlk. TS19 —2C **46**
Cornsay Clo. TS5 —5C **72**
Cornsay Clo. TS19 —2C **46**
Cornwall Av. DL1 —5C **112**
Cornwall Clo. TS7 —3B **92**
Cornwall Cres. TS23 —2A **34**
Cornwall Gro. TS20 —2D **49**
Cornwall Pl. DL14 —4D **103**
(in two parts)
Cornwall Rd. TS14 —4C **96**
Cornwall St. TS25 —2E **11**
Coronation Av. DL4 —3D **105**
Coronation Ct. TS6 —2E **77**
Coronation Cres. TS15 —4C **94**
Coronation Dri. TS25 —1B **12**
Coronation Grn. TS3 —3A **76**
Coronation Rd. TS13 —4B **66**
Coronation St. DL3 —4F **111**
Coronation St. TS3 —4D **53**
Coronation St. TS13 —5F **65**
Coronation Ter. TS14 —2E **97**
Corporation Ho. TS1 —3A 52
(off Albert Rd.)
Corporation Rd. DL3 —5F **111**
Corporation Rd. TS1 —3A **52**
Corporation Rd. TS10 —5B **28**
Corporation Rd. TS24 —2C **8**
Corporation St. TS18 —5B **48**
Corsham Wlk. TS3 —3E **75**
Cortland Rd. TS7 —3D **93**
Coryton Wlk. TS3 —3E **75**
Cosgrove Av. DL14 —5C **102**
Cosin Clo. DL5 —1F **109**
Cosin Ho. TS24 —2D 9
(off Throston St.)
Costain Gro. TS20 —5D **33**
Costa St. TS1 —5E **51**
Costa St. TS6 —2A **54**
Cotgarth Way. TS19 —2B **46**
Cotherstone Dri. TS5 —2D **89**
Cotherstone Moor Dri. DL1
—4E **117**
Cotherstone Rd. TS18 —3A **70**
Cotswold Av. TS3 —5E **53**
Cotswold Cres. TS23 —2E **33**
Cotswold Dri. TS10 —1B **42**
Cotswold Dri. TS12 —5D **63**
Cottage Farm Clo. TS18 —1E **69**
Cottage Rd. DL4 —3B **104**
Cottersloe Rd. TS20 —4C **32**
Cottingham Ct. DL3 —4C **110**
Cottingham Dri. TS3 —5E **53**
Cottonwood. TS3 —1A **76**
Coulby Farm Way. TS8 —5C **90**
Coulby Mnr. Farm. TS8 —3B **90**
(in three parts)
Coulby Mnr. Way. TS8 —3A **90**
Coulson Clo. TS15 —5C **94**
Coulson St. DL16 —3E **99**
(in two parts)
Coulthard Ct. TS6 —2B **54**
Coulton Gro. TS22 —1B **32**
Coundon Grn. TS19 —2C **46**
Countisbury Rd. TS20 —4F **31**
Courageous Clo. TS25 —4B **12**
Courtlands Rd. TS12 —5E **111**
Courtney Wlk. TS3 —5F **53**
Court Rd. TS4 —2B **74**
Covent Clo. TS6 —4D **77**
Coverdale. TS8 —5E **89**

Coverdale Bldgs. TS12 —4D **65**
Coverdale Rd. TS19 —1D **69**
Covert, The. DL5 —4A **106**
Covert, The. TS8 —5D **91**
Cowbridge La. TS23 —4C **20**
Cowdray Clo. TS14 —4F **97**
Cowley Clo. TS16 —1E **85**
Cowley Clo. TS25 —3C **12**
Cowley Rd. TS5 —5E **73**
Cowpen Bewley Rd. TS23 —5D **21**
Cowpen Cres. TS19 —2C **46**
Cowpen La. TS23 —3F **33** to 5C **20**
Cowper Gro. TS25 —3B **10**
Cowper Rd. TS20 —3D **49**
Cowscote Cres. TS13 —3B **66**
Cowshill Grn. TS19 —2C **46**
Cowton Way. TS16 —3C **84**
Coxgreen Clo. TS19 —2C **46**
Coxhoe Rd. TS23 —1A **34**
Coxmoor Way. TS11 —2A **60**
Coxwold Clo. TS5 —4F **73**
Coxwold Dri. DL1 —4C **116**
Coxwold Ho. DL1 —4C **116**
Coxwold Rd. TS18 —1E **69**
Coxwold Way. TS23 —3C **34**
Crabtree Wlk. TS7 —5E **77**
Craddock St. DL14 —3D **103**
Craddock St. DL16 —4B **98**
Cradley Dri. TS5 —2D **89**
Cragdale Rd. TS3 —1D **75**
Craggs St. TS4 —3B **52**
Craggs St. TS19 —4B **48**
Cragside. TS21 —5B **118**
Cragside Ct. TS17 —5C **86**
Cragston Clo. TS26 —4B **6**
Cragwellside. DL1 —3C **112**
Craigearn Rd. TS6 —1D **77**
Craigside Clo. DL16 —4C **98**
Craig St. DL3 —5E **111**
Craigweil Cres. TS19 —3A **48**
Crail Gdns. DL1 —2C **112**
Crail Wlk. TS25 —5D **11**
Craister Rd. TS20 —4D **49**
Cramlington Clo. TS8 —4F **89**
Cramond Clo. DL3 —2B **114**
Cranage Clo. TS5 —3C **72**
Cranberry. TS8 —5E **91**
Cranbourne Ter. TS18 —2A **70**
Cranbrook. TS7 —4F **91**
Cranfield Av. TS3 —4A **54** to 5A **54**
Cranford Av. TS6 —4C **54**
Cranford Clo. TS6 —4C **54**
Cranford Gdns. TS5 —4C **72**
Cranleigh Rd. TS18 —1F **69**
Cranmore Rd. TS3 —5D **53**
Cranstock Clo. TS22 —5B **18**
Cranswick Clo. TS23 —2A **20**
Cranswick Dri. TS5 —5F **73**
Cranwell Gro. TS17 —3E **87**
Cranwell Rd. TS25 —1B **14**
Cranworth Grn. TS17 —2E **71**
Cranworth St. TS17 —2D **71**
Crathorne Cres. TS5 —1C **72**
Crathorne Pk. TS6 —2D **77**
Crathorne Rd. TS20 —5C **32**
Craven St. TS1 —5E **51**
Craven Vale. TS14 —4D **97**
Crawcrook Wlk. TS19 —2C **46**
Crawford Clo. DL14 —5C **102**
Crawford Rd. DL5 —1E **109**
Crawford St. TS25 —5C **12**
Crawley Rd. TS17 —4F **71**
Crayke Rd. TS18 —2E **69**
Creighton Rd. DL5 —5F **107**
Cremorne Clo. TS7 —1D **91**
Crescent Av. TS23 —5F **33**
Crescent Rd. TS1 —5E **51**

Crescent, The. TS5 —2E **73**
Crescent, The. TS7 —3D **93**
(Nunthorpe)
Crescent, The. TS7 —4A **76**
(Ormesby)
Crescent, The. TS10 —5F **29**
Crescent, The. TS11 —4D **45**
Crescent, The. TS12 —2D **63**
Crescent, The. TS16 —1C **94**
Crescent, The. TS17 —4D **71**
Crescent, The. TS20 —4D **7**
Cresswell Clo. TS8 —4F **89**
Cresswell Ct. TS26 —4B **6**
Cresswell Dri. TS26 —4B **6**
Cresswell Rd. TS6 —2F **55**
Cresswell Rd. TS26 —4B **6**
Crest, The. TS26 —4B **6**
Crestwood. TS3 —1A **76**
Crestwood. TS10 —4E **43**
Crewe Rd. DL5 —1E **109**
Cricketfield Row. DL3 —4A **112**
Cricket La. TS6 —3D **77**
Crieff Wlk. TS25 —5D **11**
Crimdon Clo. TS8 —4F **89**
Crimdon Wlk. TS19 —1B **46**
Cringle Ct. TS10 —2C **42**
Cringlemoor Cres. DL1 —4E **117**
Crinkle Av. TS3 —3E **75**
Crinklewood. TS3 —1A **76**
Crispin Ct. TS12 —5D **65**
Crispin Ct. TS21 —4C **118**
Crisp St. TS20 —3C **48**
Croat Way. DL5 —3E **109**
Croft Av. TS5 —4C **72**
Croft Dri. TS7 —4C **92**
Croft Gdns. DL17 —4F **101**
Crofton Av. TS4 —2A **74**
Crofton Ct. TS18 —4E **49**
Crofton Rd. TS18 —4E **49**
Croft Rd. DL2 —5E **115**
Croft Rd. TS16 —5C **84**
Croft St. TS20 —4C **48**
Croft Ter. TS24 —3D **9**
(in two parts)
Croft, The. DL5 —2F **107**
Croft, The. TS7 —3F **91**
Cromarty Clo. DL1 —2F **113**
Cromer Ct. TS16 —1D **95**
Cromer St. TS4 —4B **52**
Cromer Wlk. TS25 —1C **14**
Cromore Clo. TS17 —2D **87**
Crompton Clo. DL17 —3B **100**
Cromwell Av. TS13 —4D **67**
Cromwell Av. TS18 —5C **48**
Cromwell Grn. TS18 —5C **48**
Cromwell Rd. TS6 —3B **54**
Cromwell St. TS3 —4C **52**
Cromwell St. TS24 —1A **12**
Cromwell Ter. TS17 —3D **71**
Crookers Hill Clo. TS7 —5B **92**
Crookhall Wlk. TS19 —2C **46**
Crooks Barn La. TS20 —4B **32**
Crook St. TS20 —4B **32**
Cropton Clo. TS10 —3C **42**
Cropton Way. TS8 —4C **90**
Crosby Ct. TS16 —4E **85**
Crosby Ho. TS3 —5E 53
(off Cottingham Dri.)
Crosby Rd. DL5 —1C **108**
Crosby Rd. DL3 —2A **112**
Crosby St. TS20 —3C **48**
Crosby St. TS17 —2D **71**
Crosby Ter. TS2 —1B **52**
Crosby Wlk. TS17 —2D **71**
Crossbeck Ter. TS6 —2E **77**
Crossbeck Way. TS7 —4C **76**
Crosscliff. TS8 —4F **89**
Cross Fell. TS10 —1C **42**

Crossfell Rd. TS3 —2D **75**
Crossfield Rd. DL3 —4D **111**
Crossfields. TS8 —5C **90**
Cross Ho. TS2 —1A 52
(off Silver St.)
Cross La. TS9 —5C **120**
Cross La. TS13 —2C **66**
Cross Row. TS12 —4C **80**
Cross St. DL3 —4A **112**
Cross St. DL4 —4C **104**
Cross St. TS6 —1A **78**
Cross St. TS14 —3D **97**
Cross St. TS20 —1C **48**
Cross St. TS21 —4C **118**
Cross St. TS23 —4E **35**
Crossway, The. DL1 —2D **117**
Crosthwaite Av. TS4 —2A **74**
Crowhurst Clo. TS14 —4D **97**
Crowland Av. TS3 —2A **76**
Crowland Rd. TS25 —2B **14**
Crow La. TS6 —5B **56**
Crowley Pl. DL5 —4E **107**
Crown St. DL1 —2A **116**
Crown St. DL14 —4F **103**
Crowood Av. TS9 —2F **119**
Croxdale DL14 —5A **102**
Croxdale Gro. TS19 —1C **68**
Croxdale Rd. TS23 —5F **19**
Croxden Gro. TS3 —3F **75**
Croxton Av. TS25 —2D **15**
Croxton Clo. TS19 —5B **46**
Croydon Rd. TS1 —5B **52**
Crummock Rd. TS10 —1D **43**
Culgaith Av. TS3 —1D **75**
Cullen Clo. DL1 —2D **113**
Cullen Rd. TS25 —5D **11**
Culloden Way. TS23 —4B **20**
Culross Gro. TS19 —5A **46**
Cumberland Cres. TS23 —3E **33**
Cumberland Gro. TS20 —4A **32**
Cumberland Ho. TS5 —1F 73
(off Chelmsford Rd.)
Cumberland Rd. TS5 —1F **73**
Cumberland St. DL3 —3A **112**
Cumbernauld Rd. TS17 —4F **71**
Cumbie Way. DL5 —4D **109**
Cumbria Pl. DL14 —4D **103**
Cumbria Wlk. TS25 —2F **11**
Cumby Rd. DL5 —1C **108**
Cumnor Wlk. TS3 —5E **53**
Cundall Rd. TS26 —4D **7**
Cunningham Clo. TS12 —3C **64**
Cunningham Dri. TS17 —3E **87**
Cunningham St. TS5 —5D **51**
Curlew La. TS20 —4B **32**
Curran Av. TS5 —2C **72**
Curson St. TS6 —1A **78**
Curthwaite. TS5 —2C **88**
Cuthbert Clo. TS17 —3D **71**
Cuthbert St. DL16 —1D **99**
Cutler Clo. TS7 —2F **91**
Cyclamen Gro. DL1 —2C **116**
Cypress Ct. TS19 —3B **48**
Cypress St. TS7 —1F **91**
Cypress Rd. TS10 —1F **43**

Dacre Clo. TS17 —5D **71**
Daimler Dri. TS23 —1C **34**
Dalby Clo. TS10 —4C **42**
Dalby Clo. TS22 —1B **32**
Dalby View. TS8 —4C **90**
Dalby Way. TS8 —4C **90**
Dalcross Ct. TS8 —4F **89**
(in two parts)
Dale Clo. TS19 —2B **46**

Dale Garth. TS11 —5E **45**
Dale Gro. TS19 —1C **68**
Dale Rd. DL3 —1E **115**
Dale Rd. DL4 —5D **105**
Dale Rd. Ind. Est. DL4 —5E **105**
Dales Pk. Rd. TS8 —5E **89**
Daleston Av. TS5 —3E **73**
Daleston Clo. TS26 —3A **6**
Dale St. TS1 —3F **51**
Dale St. TS11 —1B **60**
Daleville Clo. TS4 —3A **74**
Dalewood Wlk. TS9 —2F **119**
Dalkeith Clo. DL3 —2B **114**
Dalkeith Cres. TS8 —3F **89**
Dalkeith Rd. TS25 —4C **10**
Dallas Ct. TS8 —4F **89** & 5F **89**
Dallas Rd. TS25 —4C **10**
Dalmuir Clo. TS16 —5D **85**
Dalry Gro. TS25 —5C **10**
Dalston Ct. TS7 —4C **76**
Dalton Bk. La. TS22 —3A **14**
Dalton Cotts. DL4 —5D **105**
Dalton Cres. DL4 —5D **105**
Dalton Gro. TS20 —2B **48**
Dalton Gro. TS23 —3F **19**
Dalton St. DL1 —2B **116**
Dalton St. TS26 —5E **7**
Dalton Way. DL5 —5D **107**
Daltry Clo. TS15 —4F **95**
Dalwood Ct. TS8 —4F **89**
Damson Clo. DL3 —5F **111**
Dam St. TS13 —4D **67**
Danby Ct. TS20 —3C **48**
Danby Dale Av. TS10 —1B **42**
Danby Gro. TS17 —3E **71**
Danby Gro. TS25 —5C **12**
Danby Ho. TS2 —2F 51
(off Suffield St.)
Danby Rd. TS6 —5A **56**
Danby Rd. TS20 —3C **48**
Danby Wlk. TS23 —5D **19**
Danby Wynd. TS15 —2C **94**
Danes Brook Ct. TS17 —4B **86**
Danesfort Av. TS14 —3C **96**
Danesmoor Cres. DL3 —2D **115**
Daniels Ct. TS4 —5B **52**
Dante Rd. TS7 —1C **90**
Daphne Rd. TS19 —3B **48**
Darcy Clo. TS15 —5C **94**
Darenth Cres. TS3 —2E **75**
(in two parts)
Darlington Bk. La. TS21 & TS19
—4A **46**
Darlington By-Pass. DL2
—5E **115** to 5F **117**
Darlington La. TS19 & TS20
—3C **46** to 5B **32**
Darlington Retail Pk. DL1 —3F **117**
Darlington Rd. DL4 —5D **105**
Darlington Rd. DL17 —2C **100**
Darlington Rd. TS21 —5A **68**
(Long Newton)
Darlington Rd. TS21 & TS18
(Stockton-on-Tees) —4A **68**
Darlington St. TS17 —2D **71**
Darlington St. TS24 —2D **9**
Darnall Grn. TS4 —5C **74**
Darnbrook Way. TS7 —4A **92**
Darnton Dri. TS4 —5C **74**
Darras Wlk. TS3 —5E **53**
Darrowby Dri. DL3 —4F **111**
Dartford Clo. TS19 —2A **48**
Dartmouth Gro. TS10 —3E **43**
Dartmouth Ho. TS3 —5E 53
(off Admirals Av.)
Darvel Rd. TS25 —4C **10**
Darwen Ct. TS8 —4F **89**

Darwin Gro. DL1 —4D **117**
Darwin Gro. TS25 —3B **10**
Daryngton Clo. DL1 —3D **113**
Dauntless Clo. TS25 —4C **12**
Davenport Rd. TS15 —5C **94**
Daventry Av. TS19 —2F **47**
David Rd. TS20 —2D **49**
David Ter. DL14 —5F **103**
Davison Dri. TS24 —5D **5**
Davison Rd. DL1 —2C **112**
Davison St. TS1 —3F **51**
Davison St. TS12 —5F **81**
Davy Rd. TS6 —4A **54**
Davy St. DL17 —2B **100**
Dawdon Clo. TS19 —1C **46**
Dawley Clo. TS17 —4F **71**
Dawlish Dri. TS25 —1E **15**
Dawlish Grn. TS4 —5C **74**
Dawn Clo. TS20 —4B **32**
Dawson Sq. TS5 —1C **72**
Daylesford Gro. DL3 —2C **110**
Daylight Bakery Ho. TS19 —3F **47**
Daylight Rd. TS19 —3F **47**
Days Ter. TS12 —4C **64**
Day St. TS12 —5C **64**
Deacon St. TS3 —4D **53**
Deal Clo. TS19 —2F **47**
Deal Ct. TS4 —2B **74**
Deal Rd. TS10 —3F **43**
Deal Rd. TS23 —5E **19**
Dean & Chapter Ind. Est. DL17
—2B **100**
Dean Clo. DL4 —2C **104**
Dean Ct. Grange. DL17 —3B **100**
Dean Gdns. DL4 —2C **104**
Dean Rd. DL17 —3C **100**
Deansgate. TS6 —1B **78**
Dean St. DL4 —2C **104**
Dean St. TS18 —1B **70**
De Brus Ct. TS12 —1D **63**
Debruse Av. TS15 —5B **94**
De Brus Way. TS14 —1E **97**
Deepdale. TS14 —4A **96**
Deepdale Av. TS4
—3B **74** to 2B **74**
Deepdale Av. TS6 —4A **56**
Deepdale La. TS13 —2B **66**
Deepdale Rd. TS13 —4B **66**
Deepdale Way. DL1 —5F **113**
Deepgrove Wlk. TS6 —5A **56**
Deerness Rd. DL14 —3C **102**
Dee Rd. TS6 —5E **55**
Deerpool Clo. TS24 —1A **8**
Defoe Cres. DL5 —4E **107**
De Havilland Av. TS18 —4A **70**
De Havilland Dri. TS11 —3B **44**
Deighton Gro. TS23 —4E **19**
Deighton Rd. TS4 —5C **74**
De La Mare Dri. TS23 —2E **19**
Delamere Dri. TS11 —5C **44**
Delamere Rd. TS3 —3E **75**
Delarden Rd. TS3 —5E **53**
Delaval Rd. TS23 —1A **34**
Deleval Clo. DL5 —3D **107**
Dell Bank. DL14 —1E **103**
Dell Clo. TS3 —3D **91**
Dellfield Clo. TS3 —3D **75**
Dell, The. DL14 —1E **103**
Del Strother Av. TS19 —4F **47**
Denbigh Clo. TS19 —2A **48**
Denbigh Rd. TS23 —5F **19**
Dene Clo. TS17 —4F **71**
Dene Gro. DL3 —5E **111**
Dene Gro. DL14 —3D **103**
Dene Gro. TS10 —4E **29**
Dene Hall Dri. DL14 —3B **102**
Dene Rd. TS4 —2B **74**

Deneside. DL14 —3D **103**
Dene Side. DL16 —2C **98**
Deneside Clo. TS15 —4E **95**
Deneside Rd. DL3 —5D **111**
Denevale. TS15 —3E **95**
Dene Wlk. TS11 —5C **44**
Denham Grn. TS3 —5E **53**
(in two parts)
Denham Pl. DL5 —5F **107**
Denholme Av. TS18 —3A **70**
Denmark St. DL3 —4A **112**
Denmark St. TS2 & TS1 —2E **51**
Dennison St. TS18 —2A **70**
Dennison Ter. DL17 —4F **101**
Denshaw Clo. TS19 —5B **46**
Dentdale Clo. TS13 —5D **95**
Denton Av. DL5 —5D **109**
Denton Clo. DL3 —4C **110**
Denton Clo. TS5 —1C **88**
Denton Clo. TS19 —1C **46**
Dent St. DL4 —2D **105**
Dent St. TS26 —4F **7**
Dent Wlk. DL5 —5D **107**
Deorna Ct. DL1 —3C **112**
Depot Rd. TS2 —1F **51**
Derby Av. TS5 —2B **72**
Derby Clo. TS17 —3E **71**
Derby Rd. TS14 —4D **97**
Derby St. DL3 —4A **112**
Derby St. TS18 —5B **48**
Derby St. TS25 —2F **11**
Derby Ter. TS17 —2E **71**
Derby, The. TS7 —2D **91**
Dere Av. DL14 —5B **102**
Derwent Av. TS14 —4C **96**
Derwent Ct. DL16 —2D **99**
Derwent Ho. TS23 —4B **20**
Derwent M. DL16 —2D **99**
Derwent Pk. TS13 —4E **67**
Derwent Pl. DL5 —5A **106**
Derwent Rd. DL17 —3C **100**
Derwent Rd. TS10 —5B **28**
Derwent Rd. TS12 —5C **62**
Derwent Rd. TS17 —5E **71**
Derwent St. DL3 —1A **116**
Derwent St. TS1 —4E **51**
Derwent St. TS3 —4D **53**
Derwent St. TS20 —2B **48**
Derwent St. TS26 —4F **7**
Derwent Ter. DL16 —2D **99**
Derwentwater Av. TS5 —4D **73**
Derwentwater Rd. TS6 —4A **56**
Desford Grn. TS5 —1E **75**
Deuchars Ct. DL3 —2A **116**
Deva Clo. TS4 —2C **74**
Devon Clo. TS10 —1C **42**
Devon Cres. TS12 —1B **80**
Devon Cres. TS23 —2A **34**
Devon Pl. DL14 —4D **103**
Devonport Rd. TS5 —2A **74**
Devonport Rd. TS18 —4D **49**
Devon Rd. TS6 —4F **55**
Devon Rd. TS14 —4C **96**
Devonshire Rd. DL1 —5D **113**
Devonshire Rd. TS5 —1E **73**
Devonshire St. TS18 —3A **70**
Devon St. TS25 —2F **11**
Dewberry. TS8 —5E **91**
Dew La. TS7 —4B **76**
Dewsbury Clo. TS19 —2A **48**
Dial Stob Hill. DL14 —1D **103**
Diamond Rd. TS1 —4F **51**
Diamond Rd. TS17 —3E **71**
Diamond St. DL4 —4B **104**
Diamond St. TS12 —1D **63**
Dickens Gro. TS25 —2D **11**
Dickens St. DL16 —3C **98**

Dickens St. TS24 —5D **5**
Dickinson St. DL1 —2C **116**
Didcot Clo. DL3 —2C **110**
Dillside. TS19 —4D **47**
Dingleside. TS19 —4D **47**
Dinsdale Av. TS5 —5D **73**
Dinsdale Ct. TS23 —5A **20**
Dinsdale Cres. DL1 —2C **116**
Dinsdale Dri. TS16 —5E **85**
Dinsdale Rd. TS19 —1C **46**
Diomed Ct. TS7 —1D **91**
Dionysia Rd. TS3 —5D **53**
Dipton Grn. TS4 —5C **74**
Dipton Rd. TS19 —1C **46**
Dishforth Clo. TS17 —3F **87**
Dixon Gro. TS3 —5D **53**
Dixon Rd. DL5 —2D **109**
Dixons Bank. TS7 —3F **91** to 5C **92**
Dixon St. TS12 —4C **64**
(Brotton)
Dixon St. TS12 —5D **63**
(Skelton)
Dixon St. TS13 —3A **66**
Dixon St. TS18 —5B **48**
Dobson Pl. TS24 —4C **4**
Dobson Ter. TS10 —4E **29**
Dockside Rd. TS3 & TS6
—2A **52** to 1B **54**
Dock St. TS2 —2A **52**
Dock St. TS24 —2C **8**
Dodd's St. DL3 —1F **115**
Dodford Rd. TS8 —4F **89**
Dodsworth St. DL1 —5C **112**
Dodsworth Wlk. TS27 —4B **4**
Doncaster Cres. TS19 —2A **48**
Donegal Ter. TS1 —5D **51**
Donington Grn. TS3 —2B **76**
Dorchester Clo. TS8 —2C **90**
Dorchester Clo. TS19 —2A **48**
Dorchester Ct. DL1 —3F **115**
Dorchester Dri. TS24 —4B **4**
Doric Ho. TS21 —4B **118**
Doris Clo. TS7 —1D **91**
Dorlcote Pl. TS20 —2C **48**
Dorman Rd. TS6 —1F **77**
Dorman's Cres. TS10 —1A **42**
Dormanstown Ind. Est. TS10
—1E **41**
Dormor Way. TS6 —3F **53**
Dornoch Sands. TS5 —2C **88**
Dorothy St. TS3 —4D **53**
Dorrien Cres. TS3 —5D **53**
Dorset Clo. TS5 —1E **73**
Dorset Clo. TS10 —2C **42**
Dorset Cres. TS23 —2A **34**
Dorset Dri. DL1 —5D **113**
Dorset Pl. DL14 —4D **103**
Dorset Rd. TS12 —1B **80**
Dorset Rd. TS14 —4C **96**
Dorset Rd. TS20 —2D **49**
Dorset St. TS25 —2F **11**
Double Row. DL14 —1D **105**
Douglas Clo. TS18 —4A **70**
Douglas Cres. DL14 —3F **103**
Douglass Ter. DL14 —1C **104**
Douglas St. TS4 —4B **52**
(in two parts)
Douglas Ter. TS6 —2E **77**
Douthwaite Rd. DL14 —5B **102**
Dovecote Clo. TS11 —4D **45**
Dovecot Hill. DL14 —5D **103**
Dovecot Rd. TS18 —1B **70**
Dovedale Av. TS6 —4A **56**
Dovedale Clo. TS20 —1D **49**
Dovedale Rd. TS20 —1D **49**
Dover Clo. TS10 —3E **43**

Dover Clo. TS23 —5D **19**
Dover Rd. TS19 —2A **48**
Dover St. TS24 —5A **8**
Downe St. DL3 —4B **66**
Downfield Way. TS11 —2A **60**
Downham Av. TS3 —3D **75**
Downham Gro. TS25 —1C **14**
Downholme Gro. TS18 —3D **69**
Downing Ct. DL1 —3C **112**
Downside Rd. TS5 —3B **72**
Dowson Rd. TS24 —4D **5**
Doxford Clo. DL5 —1C **108**
Doxford Wlk. TS8 —4F **89**
Doyle Wlk. TS25 —3B **10**
Doyle Way. TS19 —4B **46**
Dragon Ct. TS20 —5C **32**
Drake Clo. TS11 —5F **45**
Drake Ct. TS2 —2D **51**
Drake Rd. TS20 —1C **48**
Drake St. DL16 —3C **98**
Draycote Cres. DL3 —4E **115**
Draycott Av. TS5 —2E **89**
Draycott Clo. TS10 —4C **42**
Draycott Clo. TS20 —5F **31**
Drayton Rd. TS25 —3B **10**
Driffield Way. TS23 —3A **20**
Driftwell Dri. TS19 —4B **46**
Drinkfield Cres. DL3 —2A **112**
Drive, The. TS8 —5D **89**
Drive, The. TS11 —5C **44**
Drive, The. TS17 —1D **87**
Drive, The. TS25 —4C **14**
Droitwich Av. TS19 —2F **47**
Drummond Clo. DL1 —2F **113**
Druridge Gro. TS10 —3F **43**
Drury St. DL3 —5A **112**
Drybourne Av. DL4 —3C **104**
Drybourne Pk. DL4 —3B **104**
Dryburgh View. DL3 —5C **110**
Dryburn Rd. TS19 —1B **46**
Dryden Clo. TS23 —2F **19**
Dryden Rd. TS25 —3C **10**
Dublin St. DL3 —3B **112**
Duchy Rd. TS26 —5A **6**
Duddon Sands. TS5 —2C **88**
Duddon Wlk. TS19 —5A **48**
Dudley Dri. DL5 —2E **107**
Dudley Gro. DL14 —3B **102**
Dudley Rd. TS23 —5E **19**
Dudley Wlk. TS10 —2F **43**
(off Carisbrooke Way)
Dufton Rd. TS5 —1D **73**
Dugdale St. TS18 —4D **49**
Dukeport Ct. TS18 —4D **49**
(off Alnport Rd.)
Duke St. DL3 —2F **115**
Duke St. DL14 —3D **103**
Duke St. TS26 —4D **7**
Dukesway. TS17 —4E **87**
Dulverton Clo. TS17 —5A **86**
Dulverton Way. TS14 —4F **97**
Dumbarton Av. TS19 —2A **48**
Dumfries Rd. TS25 —5D **11**
Dumfries St. DL1 —1B **116**
Dunbar Av. TS4 —5C **74**
Dunbar St. TS13 —1F **67**
Dunbar Dri. TS16 —1D **95**
Dunbar Rd. TS23 —5E **19**
Dunbar Rd. TS25 —4C **10** & 4D **11**
Duncan Av. TS10 —5B **28**
Duncan Pl. TS13 —4C **66**
Duncan St. TS25 —4C **10**
Duncombe Clo. DL16 —4A **98**
Duncombe Ter. DL17 —3E **101**
Dundas Arc. TS1 —3A **52**
(off Dundas St.)
Dundas M. TS1 —3A **52**

Dundas St. DL16 —3C **98**
Dundas St. TS1 —3A **52**
(in two parts)
Dundas St. TS10 —4D **29**
Dundas St. TS11 —2B **60**
Dundas St. TS13 —4C **66**
Dundas St. TS19 —4A **48**
Dundas St. E. TS12 —1D **63**
Dundas St. W. TS12 —1D **63**
Dundas Ter. TS11 —5D **45**
(Marske)
Dundas Ter. TS11 —2B **60**
(New Marske)
Dundee Av. TS19 —2A **48**
Dundee Rd. TS25 —5D **11**
Dundee St. DL1 —1B **116**
Dunedin Av. TS19 —2C **68**
Dunelm Ct. DL16 —1B **98**
Dunelm Ct. TS21 —5B **118**
Dunelm Gro. DL4 —2B **104**
Dunelm Rd. TS19 —3D **47**
Dunelm Ter. DL17 —2D **10**
(off Broom Rd.)
Dunelm Wlk. DL1 —4E **113**
Duneside. TS19 —3D **47**
Dunford Clo. TS19 —1C **46**
Dunhallow Clo. TS14 —4D **97**
Dunholm Av. TS3 —3B **76**
Dunkeld Clo. TS19 —1C **46**
Dunkerque Mall. TS1 —3F **51**
Dunkery Clo. TS17 —4A **86**
Dunlane Clo. TS5 —5C **50**
Dunlin Clo. TS20 —3C **32**
Dunmail Clo. TS10 —1C **42**
Dunmail Rd. TS19 —5A **48**
Dunmoor Gro. TS17 —4A **86**
Dunmow Av. TS3 —3F **75**
Dunnet Clo. TS10 —4D **43**
Dunning Rd. DL17 —2C **100**
Dunning Rd. TS1 —3A **52**
(in two parts)
Dunning St. TS1 —3A **52**
Dunoon Clo. TS19 —2A **48**
Dunoon Rd. TS25 —5C **10**
Dunottar Av. TS16 —3D **85**
Dunrobin Clo. DL1 —2E **113**
Dunsdale Clo. TS6 —2F **77**
Dunsdale Clo. TS11 —4E **45**
Dunsley Clo. TS3 —1C **74**
Dunsley Ct. TS14 —2D **97**
Dunsley Dri. TS23 —4F **19**
Dunsop Av. TS4 —5C **74**
Dunstable Clo. TS19 —2F **47**
Dunstable Rd. TS5 —5C **50**
Dunster Clo. DL3 —4A **110**
Dunster Ho. TS3 —2E **75**
Dunster Rd. TS23 —5F **19**
Dunston Clo. TS14 —5D **97**
Dunston Rd. TS19 —1C **46**
Dunston Rd. TS26 —4B **6**
Durham Chare. DL14 —1D **103**
(in two parts)
Durham Ho. TS4 —2C **74**
Durham La. TS21 & TS16
               —3B **68** to 5C **84**
Durham Rd. DL5 —4F **109**
Durham Rd. DL14 —1D **103**
Durham Rd. DL16 —2D **99**
Durham Rd. DL17 —2C **100**
Durham Rd. TS6 —5F **55**
Durham Rd. TS10 —1A **44** & 2A **44**
Durham Rd. TS12 —4D **65**
Durham Rd. TS21 —1B **118**
(Sedgefield, in two parts)
Durham Rd. TS21 & TS19
               —2A **30** to 4B **48**
(Stockton-on-Tees)

Durham Rd. TS22 —3D **19**
Durham St. DL14 —2C **102**
Durham St. DL16 —5A **98**
Durham St. TS2 —2A **52**
Durham St. TS18 —5B **48**
Durham St. TS24 —1C **8**
Durham Way. DL5 —4E **109**
Durham Way N. DL5 —3E **109**
Durham Way S. DL5 —4E **109**
Durness Gro. TS25 —4C **10**
Durnford Rd. TS3 —2A **76**
Duxford Gro. DL3 —2C **110**
Dykes Wlk. DL5 —1F **109**

Eagle Ct. TS18 —5A **70**
Eagle Pk. TS7 —4A **92**
Eaglescliffe Clo. TS11 —2A **60**
Eaglescliffe Ind. Est. TS16 —3C **84**
Eaglesfield Rd. TS25 —4B **10**
Eamont Gdns. TS26 —1E **11**
Eamont Rd. DL17 —2C **100**
Eamont Rd. TS20 —1B **48**
Earl Clo. DL1 —2C **112**
Earle Clo. TS15 —4F **95**
Earls Ct. Rd. TS8 —5F **89**
Earlsdon Av. TS5 —1C **88**
Earlsferry Rd. TS25 —4B **10**
Earls Nook. TS23 —2B **34**
Earlston Wlk. TS25 —4B **10**
Earl St. TS24 —1B **8**
Earlsway. TS17 —4F **87**
Earn Wlk. TS25 —4B **10**
Earsdon Clo. TS20 —5F **31**
Easby Av. TS5 —3F **73**
Easby Clo. DL14 —4A **102**
Easby Clo. TS6 —5B **56**
Easby Clo. TS10 —2C **42**
Easby Clo. TS14 —3F **97**
Easby Ct. TS12 —5E **63**
Easby Gro. TS6 —1E **77**
Easby Gro. TS17 —4E **71**
Easby La. TS9 —4A **120**
Easby Pl. DL3 —4B **110**
Easby Rd. TS23 —2F **33**
Easdale Wlk. TS5 —3F **73**
Easington Rd. TS19 —5C **30**
Easington Rd. TS24 & TS27
               —3A **4** to 2E **7**
Easson Rd. DL3 —1A **116**
Easson Rd. TS10 —5D **29**
Easson St. TS4 —1B **74**
East Av. TS23 —4E **33**
Eastbank Rd. TS7 —5C **76**
Eastbourne Av. TS16 —1D **95**
Eastbourne Gdns. TS3 —3A **76**
Eastbourne Rd. DL1 —3C **116**
Eastbourne Rd. TS5 —2F **73**
Eastbourne Rd. TS19 —3B **48**
Eastbury Clo. TS17 —5D **87**
East Cres. TS5 —2C **72**
East Cres. TS13 —4D **67**
Eastcroft. TS3 —1D **75**
Eastcroft Rd. TS6 —2F **55**
East End. TS9 —3E **119**
East End. TS21 —4C **118**
Easterside Rd. TS4 —5C **74**
Eastfield Rd. TS11 —4C **44**
Eastfields. TS9 —3E **119**
Eastfields Rd. DL5 —3A **108**
Eastgate Rd. TS5 —3D **73**
Eastham Sands. TS5 —2C **88**
Eastland Av. TS26 —1D **11**
Eastland View. TS3 —5F **53**
Eastlea Av. DL14 —3D **103**
Eastleigh. TS17 —5F **71**
E. Lodge. TS5 —5A **52**

E. Lodge Gdns. TS11 —4C **42**
Eastlowthian St. TS2 —5A **36**
E. Meadows. TS11 —5E **45**
E. Middlesbrough Ind. Est. TS3
               —4E **53** & 3F **53**
E. Mount Rd. DL1 —5B **112**
Easton St. TS17 —3E **71**
East Pde. DL14 —2D **103**
East Pde. TS12 —1B **80**
East Pde. TS21 —4C **118**
East Pde. TS24 —1B **8**
Eastport Rd. TS18 —4D **49**
E. Precinct. TS23 —1E **33**
E. Raby St. DL3 —2F **115**
East Row. DL1 —2A **116**
East Row. DL5 —5F **109**
East Row. TS5 —2C **72**
East Row. TS6 —1A **78**
East Scar. TS10 —2F **43**
East St. DL1 —2A **116**
East St. TS2 —2A **52**
East St. TS11 —5D **45**
East St. TS13 —4D **67**
East St. TS18 —5B **48**
East Ter. TS12 —1B **80**
East View. DL17 —2D **101**
E. View Ter. DL4 —2B **104**
E. View Ter. TS4 —1B **74**
E. View Ter. TS25 —4C **12**
E. Well Clo. TS17 —5F **87**
Eastwood Rd. TS3 —1B **76**
Ebba Clo. DL5 —1D **109**
Ebchester Clo. TS19 —5C **30**
Eccleston Wlk. TS4 —5B **74**
Eckert Av. TS5 —2B **72**
Eckford Wlk. TS25 —4C **10**
Eddison Way. TS8 —5F **89**
(in three parts)
Eddleston Wlk. TS25 —4B **10**
Eden Cres. DL1 —5A **116**
Eden Dri. TS21 —5C **118**
Edenhall Gro. TS10 —3D **43**
Eden Rd. DL5 —5F **107**
Eden Rd. DL16 —4C **98**
Eden Rd. TS4 —1A **74**
Eden Rd. TS12 —5D **63**
Eden St. TS12 —1D **63**
Eden St. TS24 —5F **7**
Eden Way. TS22 —4B **18**
Eder Rd. TS20 —2C **48**
Edgar Gro. DL14 —1C **102**
Edgar St. TS20 —2C **48**
Edgar St. TS25 —2A **12**
Edgecombe Dri. DL3 —5B **110**
Edgecombe Gro. DL3 —5B **110**
Edge Hill. DL14 —1C **102**
Edgehill Way. TS23 —4B **20**
Edgemoor Rd. DL1 —5D **117**
Edgeworth Ct. TS8 —5A **90**
Edgley Rd. TS18 —2C **68**
Edinburgh Av. TS5 —3E **73**
Edinburgh Clo. TS7 —3B **92**
Edinburgh Dri. DL3 —3B **114**
Edinburgh Gro. TS25 —5A **12**
Ediscum Garth. DL14 —3A **102**
Edmondbyers Rd. TS19 —5C **30**
Edmondsley Wlk. TS19 —5D **31**
Edmundsbury Rd. TS5 —1A **74**
Edmund St. DL1 —4B **112**
Ednam Gro. TS25 —4C **10**
Edridge Grn. TS5 —5F **53**
Edwards St. TS6 —2A **78**
Edwards St. TS18 —2B **70**
Edward St. DL1 —5B **112**
Edward St. DL14 —1C **102**
Edward St. DL16 —3B **98**
Edward St. TS3 —4D **53**

Edward St. TS6 —3B **54**
Edward St. Ind. Est. DL1 —5B 11
  (off Cleveland St.)
Edzell Wlk. TS25 —4B **10**
Egerton Clo. TS20 —4F **31**
Egerton Gro. DL5 —3E **107**
Egerton Rd. TS26 —5A **6**
Egerton St. TS1 —5A **52**
Egerton Ter. TS25 —4C **14**
Egglescliffe Bank. TS16 —1C **94**
Egglescliffe Clo. TS19 —5D **31**
Eggleston Ct. TS2 —1D **51**
Eggleston Ct. TS12 —1E **81**
Eggleston Ter. TS18 —1A **70**
Eggleston Rd. TS10 —4D **43**
Eggleston View. TS4 —4A **110**
Eglington Rd. TS6 —2F **55**
Eglinton Av. TS14 —4E **97**
Egmont Rd. TS4 —5B **52**
Egton Av. TS7 —4A **92**
Egton Clo. TS10 —4D **43**
Egton Dri. TS25 —1B **16**
Egton Rd. TS20 —3C **48**
Egton Way. DL1 —2E **113**
Eider Clo. TS17 —5C **86**
Elcho St. TS26 —4E **7**
Elcoat Rd. TS20 —5C **32**
Elder Ct. TS1 —3A **52**
Elder Gro. TS19 —2F **47**
Elderslie Wlk. TS25 —4B **10**
Elderwood. DL3 —4A **112**
Elderwood Ct. TS4 —3A **74**
Eldon Bank. DL14 —1D **105**
Eldon Bank Top. DL4 —2C **104**
Eldon Clo. DL5 —5E **107**
Eldon Gro. TS20 —5C **32**
Eldon Pl. DL3 —3A **112**
Eldon Rd. DL5 —2D **109**
Eldon St. DL3 —3A **112**
Eldon St. TS17 —2E **71**
Eldon Ter. DL17 —4F **101**
Eldon Wlk. TS17 —2E 71
  (off Cobden St.)
Eleanor Pl. TS18 —2B **70**
Elemere Ct. TS23 —5F **19**
Elemore Pl. DL5 —3D **107**
Elgin Av. TS3 —3B **75**
Elgin Av. TS6 —3D **55**
Elgin Ct. DL1 —2F **113**
Elgin Rd. TS17 —3E **87**
Elgin Rd. TS25 —4C **10**
Elishaw Grn. TS17 —4A **86**
Elizabeth Barrett Wlk. DL5 —1E **109**
Elizabeth Pl. DL1 —4B **112**
Elizabeth St. TS17 —3E **71**
Elizabeth Ter. TS4 —4C **52**
Elizabeth Way. TS25 —5B **12**
Elkington Wlk. TS3 —2B **76**
Elland Av. TS4 —5C **74**
Elland Ct. DL1 —5F **113**
Ellary Wlk. TS25 —4B **10**
Ellen Av. TS18 —2A **70**
Ellenport Ct. TS18 —4D **49**
Ellerbeck Ct. TS9 —5F **119**
Ellerbeck Way. TS7 —3C **76**
Ellerbeck Way. TS9 —5F **119**
Ellerburne St. TS17 —3E **71**
Ellerby Clo. TS10 —2C **42**
Ellerby Gro. TS3 —1D **75**
Ellerby Rd. TS6 —5A **56**
Ellerton Clo. DL3 —4A **110**
Ellerton Clo. TS5 —5F **73**
Ellerton Rd. TS18 —2C **68**
Ellesmere. DL16 —1B **98**
Ellesmere Wlk. TS3 —5F **53**
Ellett Ct. TS24 —5D **5**

Ellicott Wlk. TS18 —2B 70
  (off Parliament St.)
Elliot St. TS1 —3A **52**
Elliot St. TS10 —4C **28**
Elliot St. TS12 —2C **80**
Elliott St. TS26 —4E **7**
Elliott Wlk. TS18 —2B **70**
Ellis Gdns. TS8 —5F **89**
Ellison St. TS26 —1E **11**
Elm Av. TS21 —4C **118**
Elm Clo. TS6 —5C **54**
Elm Clo. TS12 —2B **62**
Elm Dri. DL4 —2B **104**
Elm Dri. TS7 —2E **91**
Elmfield Pl. DL5 —1B **108**
Elmfield Ter. DL3 —1A **116**
Elmfield Ter. DL4 —2B **104**
Elm Gro. TS17 —4D **71**
Elm Gro. TS26 —4C **6**
Elmhurst Gdns. TS8
  —4F **89** & 5F **89**
Elm Rd. DL4 —2B **104**
Elm Rd. DL17 —3D **101**
Elm Rd. TS10 —4F **29**
Elm Rd. TS14 —2D **97**
Elms Rd. DL3 —1F **115**
Elmstone Gdns. TS8 —4F **89**
  (in three parts)
Elm St. TS1 —3A **52**
Elm St. TS6 —2B **54**
Elm Ter. DL14 —3D **103**
Elm Tree Av. TS19 —3C **46**
Elm Tree Cen. TS19 —3D **47**
Elmtree Dri. DL3 —3F **111**
Elm Wlk. TS13 —4C **66**
Elmwood. TS8 —3C **90**
Elmwood Av. TS5 —1C **72**
Elmwood Clo. TS9 —2F **119**
Elmwood Gro. TS19 —4F **47**
Elmwood Pl. TS26 —3C **6**
Elmwood Rd. TS16 —2D **85**
Elmwood Rd. TS26 —3C **6**
Elphin Wlk. TS25 —4B **10**
Elsdon St. TS18 —1A **70**
Elstob Clo. DL5 —4E **107**
Elstob Clo. TS19 —5C **30**
Elstob Rd. DL5 —4E **109**
Elterwater Clo. TS10 —1C **42**
Eltham Cres. TS17 —4D **87**
Eltisley Grn. TS3 —5F **53**
Elton Clo. TS19 —5D **31**
Elton Gro. DL3 —2E **115**
Elton Gro. TS19 —1B **68**
Elton Interchange. TS21 —3B **68**
Elton La. TS16 —5C **84**
Elton Pde. DL3 —3E **115**
Elton Rd. DL3 —2E **115**
Elton Rd. TS22 —5C **18**
Elton St. TS10 —4D **29**
Eltringham Rd. TS26 —5E **7**
Elvan Gro. TS25 —4C **10**
Elvet Pl. DL3 —4C **110**
Elvington Clo. TS23 —2A **20**
Elvington Grn. TS3 —1F **75**
Elwick Av. DL5 —3A **106**
Elwick Clo. TS5 —5D **73**
Elwick Clo. TS19 —5C **30**
Elwick Ct. TS25 —1E **11**
Elwick Gdns. TS19 —5C **30**
Elwick Rd. TS26 & TS24
  —4A **6** to 1F **11**
Ely Clo. DL1 —4F **113**
Ely Cres. TS10 —1A **44**
Ely Cres. TS12 —4D **65**
Ely St. TS4 —4B **52**
Embles La. DL5 —5F **109**

Embleton Av. TS5 —4D **73**
Embleton Clo. TS19 —5C **30**
Embleton Ct. TS10 —3E **43**
Embleton Rd. TS22 —5C **18**
Embleton Wlk. TS19 —5C **30**
Embsay Clo. TS4 —3B **74**
Embsay Clo. TS17 —4B **86**
Emerald St. TS1 —4F **51**
Emerald St. TS12 —1D **63**
Emerson Av. TS5 —3F **73**
Emerson Ct. TS24 —5D **5**
Emerson Way. DL5 —1D **109**
Emily St. TS1 —4A **52**
Emley Moor Rd. DL1 —4D **117**
Emmanuel Clo. DL1 —3B **112**
Emma Simpson Ct. TS18 —3D **69**
Emmerson St. TS5 —1F **73**
Emmetts Garden. TS17 —5C **86**
Emsworth Dri. TS16 —5B **84**
Encombe Ter. DL17 —5F **101**
Endeavour Clo. TS25 —4C **12**
Endeavour Dri. TS7 —4C **76**
Endeavour, The. TS7 —3B **92**
Enderby Gdns. TS8 —5F **89**
Endeston Rd. TS3 —3F **75**
Endrick Rd. TS3 —3F **75**
Endsleigh Dri. TS5 —3B **72**
Enfield Chase. TS10 —4D **97**
Enfield Gro. TS6 —4D **77**
Enfield Shopping Cen. TS14
  —4E **97**
Enfield St. TS1 —4E **51**
Engine Houses. DL4 —5A **104**
Ennerdale Av. TS5 —4D **73**
Ennerdale Cres. TS12 —5C **62**
Ennerdale Rd. DL1 —4C **116**
Ennerdale Rd. TS18 —5E **47**
Ennis Rd. TS10 —1F **41**
Ennis Sq. TS10 —1F **41**
Ensign Ct. TS24 —5B **8**
Enterpen Clo. TS15 —3F **95**
Enterprise Way. DL16 —1F **99**
Epping Av. TS3 —3E **75**
Epping Clo. TS11 —5D **45**
Epping Clo. TS17 —2D **87**
Eppleby Way. DL1 —3D **117**
Epsom Av. TS4 —5C **74**
Epsom Ct. DL1 —5F **113**
Epsom Rd. TS10 —2E **43**
Epsom Rd. TS18 —3A **50**
Epworth Grn. TS3 —1F **75**
Erica Gro. TS7 —1D **91**
Eric Av. TS17 —3E **71**
Eridge Rd. TS14 —4E **97**
Eriskay Wlk. TS25 —4B **10**
Eris Rd. TS18 —5F **69**
Erith Gro. TS4 —5C **74**
Ernest St. TS26 —4E **7**
Ernest Wlk. TS26 —4E **7**
Errington Garth. TS11 —5F 45
  (off Hambleton Cres.)
Errington St. TS12 —5C **64**
Errol St. TS1 —5A **52**
Errol St. TS24 —4F **7**
Erskine Rd. TS25 —4C **10**
Escomb Clo. DL5 —4F **107**
Escomb Clo. TS19 —5C **30**
Escombe Av. TS4 —5C **74**
Escombe Rd. TS23 —3F **19**
Escomb Ho. TS4 —2C **74**
Escomb Rd. DL14 —3C **102**
Esher Av. TS6 —4D **77**
Esher Rd. TS1 —4B **52**
Eshwood Sq. TS1 —3F **51**
Esk Clo. TS14 —4C **96**
Eskdale. TS8 —5E **89**
Eskdale Clo. TS15 —5C **94**

Eskdale Ct. TS25 —5B **10**
Eskdale Gdns. DL4 —3E **105**
Eskdale Pl. DL5 —1B **108**
Eskdale Rd. TS10 —1A **42**
Eskdale Rd. TS25 —5B **10**
Eskdale St. DL3 —2F **115**
Eskdale Ter. TS12 —5F **81**
Eskdale Ter. TS14 —2E **97**
  (off Bolckow St.)
Esk Grn. TS16 —1C **94**
Esk Gro. TS25 —4C **10**
Esk Rd. DL1 —5B **116**
Esk Rd. TS20 —1B **48**
Esk St. TS3 —4D **53**
Esk Ter. TS13 —4E **67**
  (off Whitby Rd.)
Espin Wlk. DL5 —4E **107**
Esplanade. TS10 —3D **29**
Essex Av. TS6 —3E **55**
Essex Clo. TS10 —2C **42**
Essex Cres. TS23 —2A **34**
Essex Gro. TS20 —1D **49**
Essexport Rd. TS18 —4D **49**
Essex St. TS1 —5E **51**
Essex Way. DL1 —5D **113**
Eston Clo. TS17 —4E **71**
Eston Ho. TS6 —1A **78**
Eston Moor Cres. DL1 —5E **117**
Eston Rd. TS6 —2D **55**
  (Grangetown)
Eston Rd. TS6 —1B **78** to 4D **57**
  (Lazenby, in two parts)
Eston View. TS3 —2E **75**
Estoril Rd. DL1 —3E **117**
Estoril Rd. S. DL1 —3E **117**
Ethel St. DL1 —2C **116**
Etherley Clo. TS19 —5C **30**
Etherley La. DL14 —3A **102**
Etherley Wlk. TS19 —5D **31**
  (in two parts)
Eton Rd. TS18 —2D **73**
Eton Rd. TS18 —2A **70**
Eton St. TS25 —4C **10**
Ettersgill Dri. DL3 —2A **114**
Ettington Av. TS3 —3E **75**
Etton Rd. TS23 —2A **20**
Ettrick Wlk. TS25 —4B **10**
Evans St. TS6 —3E **55**
Evendale. TS14 —4A **96**
Evenwood Clo. TS19 —5C **30**
Evenwood Gdns. TS5 —2E **89**
Everett St. TS26 —3D **7**
Evergreen Wlk. TS4 —3A **74**
Everingham Rd. TS15
  —5B **94** to 4C **94**
Eversham Rd. TS6 —2F **55**
Eversley Wlk. TS3 —3E **75**
Evesham Rd. TS3 —3E **75**
Evesham Way. TS23 —3B **20**
Ewbank Clo. DL5 —4E **107**
Ewbank Dri. TS18 —1A **70**
Ewbank Gdns. TS18 —1A **70**
Exchange Pl. TS1 —2A **52**
Exchange Sq. TS1 —2A **52**
Exeter Dri. DL1 —4F **113**
Exeter Rd. TS5 —1A **74**
Exeter Rd. TS6 —1F **77**
Exeter St. TS12 —1D **63**
Exeter St. TS24 —5A **8**
Exford Clo. TS17 —5A **86**
Exmoor Gro. TS26 —3C **6**
Ezard St. TS19 —4B **48**

Faber Clo. DL5 —4E **107**
Fabian Ct. Shopping Cen. TS6
  —5F **55**

Fabian Rd. TS6 —5D **55** to 5F **55**
Faceby Pl. TS20 —3C **48**
Faceby Wlk. TS3 —2D **75**
Fagg St. TS18 —5B **48**
Fairbank Ho. TS19 —3F **47**
Fairbridge St. TS1 —3F **51**
Fairburn Clo. TS19 —5B **46**
Fairburn Rd. TS6 —2D **77**
Fairdene Av. TS19 —5B **46**
Fairfax Ct. TS8 —5F **89**
Fairfax St. TS15 —2C **94**
Fairfield Av. TS5 —2C **72**
Fairfield Av. TS7 —5B **76**
Fairfield Clo. TS10 —2D **43**
Fairfield Clo. TS19 —5C **46**
Fairfield Rd. TS4 —2A **74**
Fairfield Rd. TS9 —3D **119**
Fairfield Rd. TS19 —5C **46**
Fairfield St. DL3 —5F **111**
Fairholme Clo. TS8 —5F **89**
Fairmead. TS10 —3B **42**
Fairmead. TS15 —4B **94**
Fairstone Av. TS19 —4B **46**
Fairthorn Av. TS19 —5B **46**
Fairview. TS21 —5B **68**
Fairview Dri. DL16 —3D **99**
Fairville Rd. TS19 —5B **46**
Fairway, The. DL1 —2D **117**
Fairway, The. TS8 —4F **91**
Fairway, The. TS12 —3C **62**
Fairway, The. TS16 —5D **85**
Fairwell Rd. TS19 —3C **46**
Fairwood Pk. TS8 —4F **91**
Fairy Cove Ter. TS24 —1D **9**
  (off Moor Pde.)
Fairy Cove Wlk. TS24 —1D **9**
Fairy Dell. TS7 —3D **91**
Fakenham Av. TS5 —3C **72**
Falcon La. TS20 —3B **32**
Falcon Rd. TS19 —5C **46**
Falcon Rd. DL1 —2E **117**
Falcon Rd. TS3 —4F **53**
Falcon Way. TS14 —3A **96**
Falkirk Rd. TS25 —5C **10**
Falkirk St. TS17 —3E **71**
Falklands Clo. TS11 —4C **44**
Falkland St. TS1 —4E **51**
Fallow Clo. TS17 —4C **86**
Fallow Rd. DL5 —2E **107**
Fallows Ct. TS1 —4E **51**
  (in two parts)
Fall Way. TS6 —4D **77**
Falmer Rd. DL1 —3C **116**
Falmouth Gro. TS26 —2C **6**
Falmouth St. TS1 —5A **52**
Falstaff Ct. DL1 —2B **116**
Falston Clo. TS23 —4D **19**
Falstone St. DL1 —3D **113**
Fanacurt Rd. TS14 —4B **96**
Fane Clo. TS19 —5C **46**
Fane Gro. TS5 —5D **73**
Faraday St. DL17 —3A **100**
Faraday St. TS1 —4E **51**
Fareham Clo. TS25 —2D **15**
Farfields Clo. TS21 —5B **68**
Farington Dri. TS7 —3A **92**
Farleigh Clo. TS23 —5F **19**
Farley Dri. TS5 —4B **72**
Farmbank Rd. TS7 —1C **92**
Farm Clo. DL14 —5C **102**
Farmcote Ct. TS8 —5E **89**
Farm La. TS17 —4C **86**
Farm La. TS18 —1E **69**
Farnborough Av. TS5 —3D **73**
Farndale. DL16 —1B **98**
Farndale Ct. TS4 —2B **74**
Farndale Cres. DL3 —1C **114**
Farndale Cres. TS4 —2B **74**

Farndale Dri. TS14 —4A **96**
Farndale Gdns. DL4 —3E **105**
Farndale Gdns. TS12 —5F **81**
Farndale Grn. TS19 —3F **47**
Farndale Rd. TS4 —2B **74**
Farndale Rd. TS7 —2C **92**
Farndale Rd. TS25 —5C **12**
Farndale Sq. DL14 —5A **102**
Farndale Sq. TS10 —1A **42**
Farndale Wlk. TS6 —5A **56**
Farne Ct. TS17 —5C **86**
Farnell Gro. TS25 —4C **10**
Farne Wlk. TS14 —4D **97**
  (off Hutton La.)
Farnham Clo. DL5 —3E **107**
Farnham Clo. TS16 —5B **84**
Farnham Wlk. TS3 —3D **75**
Farrer St. DL3 —5A **112**
Farrer St. TS18 —4B **48**
Farrholme. DL3 —5D **115**
Farrier Clo. TS17 —4C **86**
Farr Wlk. TS25 —5C **10**
Fastnet Gro. TS24 —5A **8**
Fauconberg Clo. TS23 —2C **34**
Fauconberg Way. TS15 —5B **94**
Faulder Wlk. TS25 —3F **11**
Faulkner Rd. DL5 —5D **107**
Faverdale. DL3 —3D **111**
Faverdale Av. TS5 —2C **88**
Faverdale Black Path. DL3
  —3D **111** to 3F **111**
Faverdale Clo. TS1 —3F **51**
Faverdale Clo. TS19 —3D **47**
Faverdale Ct. DL3 —2D **111**
Faverdale E. DL3 —3E **111**
Faverdale Ind. Est. DL3 —3D **111**
Faverdale N. DL3 —3E **111**
Faverdale Rd. DL3 —3D **111**
Faverdale W. DL3 —3D **111**
Fawcett Av. TS8 —5D **89**
Fawcett Clo. DL14 —5B **102**
Fawcett Rd. TS17 —1E **87**
Fawcett Way. TS17 —1E **87**
Fawcus Ct. TS10 —1A **42**
  (in two parts)
Fawn Clo. DL5 —2F **107**
Faygate Ct. TS8 —5E **89**
Fearby Rd. TS18 —3C **68**
Fearnhead. TS8 —5F **91**
Feetham Av. DL1 —4E **113**
Feethams. DL1 —2A **116**
Feethams S. DL1 —3A **116**
Felbrigg La. TS17 —5C **86**
Felby Av. TS3 —4E **75**
Felixstowe Clo. TS25 —2C **14**
Fell Briggs Dri. TS11 —4D **45**
Fellston Clo. TS26 —4B **6**
Felton Clo. DL5 —4F **107**
Felton La. TS19 —3B **46**
Fenby Av. DL1 —4C **116**
Fencote Gdns. TS19 —5C **46**
Fenhall Grn. DL5 —3D **107**
Fenmoor Clo. TS8 —4D **89**
Fenner Clo. TS11 —5F **45**
Fens Cres. TS25 —1D **15**
Fenton Clo. TS6 —2B **54**
Fenton Clo. TS17 —5C **86**
Fenton Ct. TS12 —5C **80**
Fenton Rd. TS25 —1B **14**
Fenton St. TS12 —4C **80**
Fenwick St. DL16 —2F **99**
Fenwick St. TS18 —4C **48**
Ferens Ter. DL4 —5D **105**
Ferndale. TS19 —3D **47**
Ferndale Av. TS3 —4F **53** to 5A **54**
Ferndale Clo. TS11 —2B **60**
Ferndale Ct. TS3 —5A **54**

Fern Gro. DL16 —5A **98**
Fernhill Rd. TS6 —2A **78**
Fernie Rd. TS14 —5E **97**
Fernie Rd. TS20 —4C **32**
Fernlea Ct. DL1 —4C **116**
Fern St. TS1 —4A **52**
Fernwood. TS10 —3E **43**
Fernwood Av. TS25 —3E **11**
Ferry Rd. TS2 —1A **52**
Ferry Rd. TS24 —3C **8**
Festival Wlk. DL16 —3C **98**
Festival Wlk. La. DL16 —3C **98**
Feversham St. TS2 —2A **52**
Feversham Ter. DL17 —5F **101**
Fewston Clo. DL5 —5A **106**
Fewston Clo. TS3 —1D **75**
Fidler St. TS1 —3B **52**
Field Clo. TS17 —4F **71**
Fieldfare La. TS20 —4C **32**
Field Head. TS10 —1C **42**
Field St. DL1 —4B **112**
Fieldview Clo. TS2 —4F **35**
Fife Gro. TS25 —5B **10**
Fife Rd. DL3 —2F **115**
Fife Rd. TS20 —4B **32**
Fife St. TS1 —4B **52**
Filey Clo. TS10 —2F **43**
Finchale Av. TS23 —5E **19**
Finchale Cres. DL3 —4B **110**
Finchale Rd. DL5 —2D **109**
Fincham Clo. TS20 —5F **31**
Finchdale Av. TS3 —3F **75**
Finchfield Clo. TS16 —4C **84**
Finchley Rd. TS20 —4C **32**
Findlay Gro. TS25 —5C **10**
Finkle St. DL14 —1D **103**
Finkle St. TS18 —1C **70**
Finsbury St. TS1 —4E **51**
Firbeck Wlk. TS17 —3D **87**
Firby Clo. TS20 —5F **31**
Firby Clo. TS24 —1A **8**
Fir Gro. TS10 —3B **42**
Fir Gro. TS17 —4D **71**
Firlands, The. TS11 —3E **45**
Fir Rigg Dri. TS11 —4D **45**
Firsby Ct. TS8 —5F **89**
(in two parts)
Firsby Wlk. TS3 —1E **75**
Firs, The. DL1 —2E **113**
Firthmoor Cres. DL1 —4E **117**
Firtree. DL4 —3D **105**
Firtree Av. TS6 —3D **77**
Firtree Dri. TS6 —3D **77**
Firtree Rd. TS19 —3F **47**
Firwood Ter. DL17 —5F **101**
Fishermans Sq. TS10 —4E **29**
Fishponds Rd. TS11 —1C **58**
Fiske Ct. TS5 —2D **89**
Fitzwilliam Clo. TS11 —5E **45**
Fitzwilliam Dri. DL1 —3B **112**
Fitzwilliam St. TS10 —5E **29**
Flambard Wlk. DL5 —1E **109**
Flamborough Ho. TS4 —2C **74**
Flamingo Clo. DL1 —2E **117**
Flatts La. TS6 & TS7
                             —3E **77** to 2F **93**
Flatts La. TS7 —5D **77**
Flatts La. Dri. TS6 —3E **77**
*Flaxton Ho. TS3 —2E **75***
(off Langridge Cres.)
Flaxton St. TS26 —1E **11**
Fleck Way. TS17 —4E **87**
Fleet Av. TS24 —4B **8**
Fleet Bri. Rd. TS20 & TS23 —1D **49**
Fleetham Gro. TS18 —2C **68**
Fleetham Pl. TS1 —3E **51**
Fleetham St. TS1 —4F **51**

Fleet Ho. TS3 —1A **76**
*Fleet Ho. TS24 —4B **8***
(off Warrior Quay)
Fleet St. DL14 —3D **103**
Fleet St. TS3 —4D **53**
Fleet, The. TS10 —2F **41**
Fleet, The. TS17 —4A **72**
Fleming Rd. TS6 —4B **54**
Fleming St. TS10 —3C **28**
Fletcher Wlk. TS25 —3B **10**
Flexley Av. TS3 —3A **76**
Flintoff St. DL14 —2D **103**
Flint Wlk. TS26 —3B **6** to 2C **6**
Flixton Gro. TS22 —1C **32**
Flodden Way. TS23 —4B **20**
Flora Av. DL3 —3E **115**
Flora St. DL16 —3B **98**
Flora St. TS6 —1E **77**
Florence Ct. TS17 —5C **86**
Florence St. DL1 —2C **116**
Florence St. TS2 —2F **51**
Florida Gdns. TS5 —4E **73**
*Flotilla Ho. TS24 —4B **8***
(off Warrior Quay)
Flounders Rd. TS15 —5C **94**
Folkestone Clo. TS8 —5F **89**
Folland Dri. TS11 —4C **44**
Fonteyn Clo. TS8 —5E **89**
Fonteyn Ct. TS8 —5F **89**
Fontwell Clo. TS19 —4B **46**
Forber Rd. TS4 —4A **74**
Forbes Av. TS5 —2C **72**
(in two parts)
Forcett Clo. TS5 —1D **89**
Forcett St. DL3 —5D **111**
*Fordham Ho. TS24 —2D **9***
(off Throston St.)
Fordon Pl. TS4 —4B **74**
Ford Pl. TS18 —4B **48**
Ford St. TS18 —4B **48**
Ford Way. DL14 —5C **102**
Fordwell Rd. TS19 —4B **46**
Fordyce Rd. TS8 —5E **89**
Fordyce Rd. TS25 —5B **10**
Fordy Gro. TS17 —4D **71**
Fore Bondgate. DL14 —1D **103**
Foreland Point. TS17 —4A **86**
Forest Dri. TS7 —1C **92**
Forester Clo. TS25 —4B **12**
Foresters Path. DL5 —2A **108**
Forest M. TS17 —1E **87**
Forest Moor Rd. DL1 —5E **117**
Forfar Av. TS4 —5C **74**
Forfar Clo. DL1 —2E **113**
Forfar Rd. TS25 —5B **10**
Forge Way. DL1 —5B **112**
Formby Clo. TS27 —4B **4**
Formby Grn. TS4 —4B **74**
Formby Wlk. TS16 —4D **85**
Forres Wlk. TS25 —5C **10**
Forster Ho. TS1 —3A **52**
Forster Dri. DL3 —1A **116**
Forth Gro. TS25 —5C **10**
Forth Rd. TS10 —5B **28**
Fortrose Clo. TS16 —5D **85**
Forty Foot Rd. TS2 —2E **51**
Forum Ct. TS3 —4C **52**
Fosdyke Grn. TS3 —2B **76**
Fossfeld. TS19 —3B **46**
Foster St. TS12 —5B **64**
Foston Clo. TS20 —5A **32**
Fotheringhay Dri. DL1 —2F **113**
Founders St. TS25 —4C **14**
Foundry St. DL4 —2C **104**
Fountain Ct. TS1 —3A **52**
Fountains Av. TS17 —5D **87**
Fountains Clo. TS14 —3E **97**

Fountains Ct. TS12 —1E **81**
Fountains Cres. TS6 —1E **77**
Fountains Dri. TS5 —4E **73**
Fountains Meadow. DL16 —3D **99**
Fountains Pl. TS14 —3E **97**
Fountain St. TS14 —3E **97**
Fountains View. TS5 —3B **110**
Four Riggs. DL3 —1A **116**
Four Winds Ct. TS26 —5B **6**
Fowler Clo. TS15 —4F **95**
Fowler Rd. DL5 —5F **107**
Fox Almshouses. TS20 —5C **32**
Foxberry Av. TS5 —2C **88**
Fox Clo. TS17 —4D **87**
Foxgloves. TS8 —5D **91**
Foxheads Ct. TS1 —3E **51**
Fox Howe. TS8 —3C **90**
(in two parts)
Fox Pl. DL5 —4D **107**
Foxrush Clo. TS10 —4D **43**
Fox St. TS20 —1C **48**
Foxton Clo. DL5 —4E **107**
Foxton Clo. TS15 —3F **95**
Foxton Dri. TS23 —3F **19**
Foxwood Dri. TS19 —3D **47**
Frampton Grn. TS3 —3E **75**
Frances Ter. DL14 —4C **102**
France St. TS10 —4D **29**
*Francis Wlk. TS17 —3D **71***
(off Gilmour St.)
Frankfield Pl. TS9 —3B **120**
Franklin Clo. TS18 —2C **68**
Franklin Ct. TS17 —1E **87**
Fransham Rd. TS3 —1E **75**
Fraser Ct. TS25 —5B **10**
Fraser Gro. TS25 —5B **10**
(in two parts)
Fraser Rd. TS18 —3E **69**
Frederick St. TS3 —4D **53**
Frederick St. TS17 —2D **71**
Frederick St. TS18 —4B **48**
Frederic St. TS24 —1C **8**
Fredric Ter. TS23 —3E **35**
Freeman's Pl. DL1 —1B **116**
Freemantle Gro. TS25 —5F **11**
Fremantle Cres. TS4 —3A **74**
Fremington Wlk. TS4 —5C **74**
Frensham Dri. TS25 —3F **11**
Freville Gro. DL3 —1B **114**
Freville St. DL4 —3B **104**
Freville St. TS24 —1A **12**
Friarage Gdns. TS24 —2D **9**
Friar St. TS24 —2D **9**
Friarswood Clo. TS15 —4F **95**
Friar Ter. TS24 —2D **9**
Friendship La. TS24 —2D **9**
Friends School Yd. DL3 —2A **116**
Frimley Av. TS3 —1E **75**
Frobisher Clo. TS11 —5F **45**
Frobisher Rd. TS17 —1E **87**
Frome Ho. TS4 —3A **74**
Frome Rd. TS20 —2C **48**
*Front Chapel Row. DL17 —4F **10***
(off Chilton La.)
Front Row. DL14 —1D **105**
Front St. DL14 —3A **102**
Front St. DL16 —3D **99**
(Merrington Lane)
Front St. DL16 —1E **99**
(Tudhoe Grange)
Front St. TS13 —2A **66**
Front St. TS21 —4C **118**
Front St. TS25 —4C **14**
Front, The. TS25 —5D **13**
(in two parts)
Frosterley Gro. TS23 —3A **20**
Fryer Cres. DL1 —4E **113**

Fryer St. DL4 —3C **104**
Fry St. TS1 —3A **52**
Fryup Cres. TS14 —5D **97**
Fuchsia Gro. TS19 —5D **47**
Fudan Way. TS17 —1D **71**
Fulbeck Ct. TS23 —1A **34**
Fulbeck Ho. TS3 —2B **76**
Fulbeck Rd. DL5 —3D **109**
Fulbeck Rd. TS3 —2B **76**
Fulford Gro. TS11 —2A **60**
Fulford Pl. DL3 —2A **112**
Fulford Way. TS7 —4F **91**
Fuller Cres. TS20 —5A **32**
Fullerton Ho. TS3 —5F 53
(off Northfleet Av.)
Fulmar Head. TS14 —3B **96**
Fulmar Rd. TS20 —3B **32**
Fulmerton Cres. TS10 —4D **43**
Fulthorp Av. TS24 —4C **4**
Fulthorpe Av. DL3 —1B **114**
Fulthorpe Clo. DL3 —1C **114**
Fulthorpe Gro. DL3 —1B **114**
Fulthorpe Rd. TS20 —5A **32**
Fulton Ct. DL4 —2C **104**
Fulwood Av. TS4 —3B **74**
Furlongs, The. TS10 —5E **29**
Furnace Ind. Est. DL4 —4B **104**
Furness Clo. DL14 —4A **102**
Furness St. DL1 —3C **112**
Furness St. TS24 —4F **7**

Gables, The. DL14 —2C **102**
Gables, The. TS7 —3E **91**
Gables, The. TS21 —3B **118**
Gainford St. TS3 —3F **73**
Gainford Rd. TS19 —1D **69**
Gainford Rd. TS23 —1A **34**
Gainford St. DL1 —1A **116**
Gainford St. TS26 —5F **7**
Gainsborough Ct. DL1 —4B **116**
Gainsborough Ct. DL14 —1C 10
(off Grainger St.)
Gainsborough Rd. TS7 —2D **91**
Gaisgill Clo. TS7 —4C **76**
Galgate Clo. TS7 —3F **91**
Galleys Field Ct. TS24 —2D **9**
Galloway. DL1 —1F **113**
Galloway Sands. TS5 —2C **88**
Galsworthy Rd. TS25 —3B **10**
Ganstead Way. TS23 —2A **20**
Ganton Clo. TS11 —2B **60**
Ganton Clo. TS22 —5B **18**
Garburn Pl. DL5 —5B **106**
Garbutt Clo. DL4 —3B **104**
Garbutt Sq. DL1 —3B **116**
Garbutt St. DL4 —3B **104**
Garbutt St. TS18 —4C **48**
Garden Clo. TS17 —3C **70**
Gardener Ho. TS25 —4B **10**
Garden Pl. TS6 —2E **77**
Gardens, The. TS4 —3B **74**
Garden St. DL1 —1A **116**
Garden Ter. DL14 —2D **103**
Garnet Rd. TS17 —4E **71**
Garnet St. TS1 —4F **51**
Garnet St. TS12 —1D **63**
Garrett Wlk. TS1 —4E **51**
Garrick Ct. DL1 —2C 11
(off King William St.)
Garrick Gro. TS25 —3C **10**
Garrowby Rd. TS3 —1D **75**
Garsbeck Way. TS7 —3C **76**
Garsdale Clo. TS15 —5C **94**
Garsdale Grn. TS3 —1E **75**
Garsdale Ho. TS3 —2E 75
(off Langridge Cres.)

Garstang Clo. TS7 —2A **92**
Garston Gro. TS25 —5F **11**
Garthlands Rd. DL3 —5D **111**
Garthorne Av. DL3 —2B **114**
Garth, The. DL5 —3A **108**
Garth, The. DL16 —2E **99**
Garth, The. DL17 —2C **100**
Garth, The. TS8 —5C **90**
Garth, The. TS9 —3E **119**
Garth, The. TS11 —4D **45**
Garth, The. TS12 —4D **65**
Garth, The. TS20 —5B **32**
Garth, The. TS21 —4B **118**
Garth Wlk. TS3 —2D **75**
Garton Clo. TS20 —4A **32**
Garvin Clo. TS3 —2D **75**
Gascoyne Clo. TS7 —2F **91**
Gaskell La. TS13 —5C **66**
Gate Ho. Clo. DL1 —3F **113**
Gatenby Dri. TS5 —2D **89**
Gatesgarth Clo. TS24 —2F **7**
Gateway, The. DL1 —2B **112**
Gatley Wlk. TS16 —1E **85**
Gatwick Grn. TS3 —1E **75**
Gaunless Ter. DL14 —4F **103**
Gayle Moor Clo. TS17 —4A **86**
Gayles Ho. DL1 —3D **117**
Gayton Sands. TS5 —2C **88**
Gedney Av. TS3 —4E **75**
Geltsdale. TS5 —2D **89**
General Boucher Ct. DL14
—3D **103**
Geneva Cres. DL1 —5B **116**
Geneva Dri. DL1 —4C **116**
(in two parts)
Geneva Dri. TS10 —1D **43**
Geneva Gdns. DL1 —5B **116**
Geneva La. DL1 —4C **116**
Geneva Rd. DL1 —4C **116**
Geneva Ter. DL1 —4B **116**
Gent Rd. DL14 —4D **103**
George Reynolds Ind. Est. DL4
—5D **105**
George Short Clo. DL1 —5A **112**
George St. DL1 —3A **116**
George St. DL4 —3B **104**
George St. DL14 —1D **103**
George St. DL17 —5F **101**
George St. TS10 —5E **29**
George St. TS14 —2D **97**
George St. TS17 —2D **71**
George St. TS24 —5A **8**
George Ter. TS12 —5B **64**
Georgiana Clo. TS17 —2D **71**
Gerard St. DL16 —2D **99**
Gerrie St. TS12 —5C **80**
Gervaulx Ct. DL16 —1B **98**
Gibbon St. DL14 —1D **103**
Gibbon St. DL16 —5A **98**
Gibb Sq. TS24 —2D **9**
Gibralter Rd. TS16 —3A **84**
Gibson Gro. TS24 —4C **4**
Gibson St. TS3 —4D **53**
Gifford St. TS5 —1F **73**
Gilberti Pl. TS24 —5D **5**
Gilkes St. TS1 —3F **51**
(in two parts)
Gillercomb. TS10 —4D **43**
Gilling Cres. DL1 —4D **117**
Gilling Cres. DL16 —2D **99**
(in two parts)
Gilling Rd. TS19 —5C **46**
Gilling Wlk. TS1 —1D **75**
Gilling Way. TS10 —2F **43**
Gillpark Gro. TS25 —5B **12**
Gill St. TS12 —2C **62**
Gill St. TS14 —2E **97**

Gill St. TS26 —5F **7**
Gilmonby Rd. TS3 —4E **75**
Gilmour St. TS17 —3D **71**
Gilpin Ct. DL5 —1F **109**
Gilpin Rd. DL5 —1F **109**
Gilpin Rd. TS17 —4D **71**
Gilpin Sq. TS19 —3A **48**
Gilside Rd. TS23 —1A **34**
Gilsland Clo. TS5 —2C **88**
Gilsland Cres. DL1 —3D **113**
Gilsland Gro. TS6 —2E **77**
Girrick Clo. TS8 —4D **89**
Girton Av. TS3 —4E **75**
Girton Wlk. DL1 —3B **112**
Gisborne Gro. TS18 —2D **69**
Gisburn Av. TS3 —3E **75**
Gisburn Rd. TS23 —1A **34**
Gladesfield Rd. TS20 —2C **48**
Gladstone Ind. Est. TS17 —2D **71**
Gladstone St. DL3 —1A **116**
Gladstone St. TS6 —1A **78**
Gladstone St. TS12 —5B **64**
Gladstone St. TS13 —5F **65**
(Carlin How)
Gladstone St. TS13 —4D **67**
(Loftus)
Gladstone Ter. TS17 —2D **71**
Gladstone Ter. TS18 —2B **70**
Gladstone St. TS24 —2D **9**
Gladstone Ter. DL17 —4E **101**
Gladstone Vs. DL17 —4E **101**
Glaisdale. DL16 —2B **98**
Glaisdale Av. TS5 —4F **73**
Glaisdale Av. TS10 —1A **42**
Glaisdale Av. TS19 —4F **47**
Glaisdale Clo. TS6 —5B **56**
Glaisdale Gdns. DL4 —3E **105**
Glaisdale Gro. TS25 —5C **12**
Glaisdale Rd. TS6 —5B **56**
Glaisdale Rd. TS15 —3F **95**
Glamis Gro. TS4 —2B **74**
Glamis Rd. DL1 —2D **113**
Glamis Rd. TS23 —5D **19**
Glamis Wlk. TS25 —5C **10**
Glamorgan Gro. TS26 —2B **6**
Glasgow St. TS17 —2D **71**
Glastonbury Av. TS6 —1F **77**
Glastonbury Clo. DL16 —1B **98**
Glastonbury Ho. TS3 —3F **75**
Glastonbury Rd. TS12 —1E **81**
Glastonbury Wlk. TS26 —2C **6**
Gleaston Cres. TS4 —4B **74**
Gleaston Wlk. TS4 —4B **74**
Glebe Gdns. TS13 —1F **67**
Glebe Ho. DL17 —2C **100**
Glebe Rd. DL1 —1B **112**
Glebe Rd. TS1 —4E **51**
Glebe Rd. TS9 —4F **119**
Glebe, The. TS20 —5A **32**
Glencairn Gro. TS25 —5B **10**
Glendale. TS14 —4A **96**
Glendale Av. TS26 —5D **7**
Glendale Dri. DL3 —4E **115**
Glendale Rd. TS5 —4F **73**
Glendue Clo. TS7 —4B **92**
Gleneagles Clo. TS22 —5B **18**
Gleneagles Ct. TS4 —4B **74**
Gleneagles Rd. DL1 —2E **113**
Gleneagles Rd. TS4 —4A **74**
Gleneagles Rd. TS11 —2B **60**
Gleneagles Rd. TS27 —4A **4**
Glenfall Clo. TS22 —5B **18**
Glenfield Clo. TS19 —5C **46**
Glenfield Dri. TS19 —5C **46**
Glenfield Rd. DL3 —4E **115**
Glenfield Rd. TS19 —5B **46**
Glenfield Ter. TS13 —4E **67**

Glenhow Gdns. TS12 —2D **63**
Glenluce Clo. TS16 —4D **85**
Glenmere. DL16 —1B **98**
Glenmor Gro. TS6 —1D **77**
Glenn Cres. TS7 —3E **91**
Glenside. TS12 —1D **63**
Glenston Clo. TS26 —3A **6**
Glen, The. TS16 —1D **95**
Glentower Gro. TS25 —5B **12**
Glentworth Av. TS3 —2B **76**
Glentworth Ho. TS3 —2B **76**
Globe Clo. TS7 —3C **116**
Gloucester Clo. TS7 —3B **92**
Gloucester Pl. DL1 —5D **113**
Gloucester Rd. TS14 —4C **96**
Gloucester St. TS25 —2E **11**
Gloucester Ter. TS24 —2A **34**
Goathland Dri. TS25 —5B **12**
Goathland Gro. TS14 —5D **97**
Goathland Rd. TS6 —5A **56**
Gofton Pl. TS6 —4E **55**
Goldcrest. TS14 —3B **96**
Goldcrest Clo. TS17 —4C **86**
Golden Flatts. TS25 —1F **15**
Golden Lion M. TS9 —4E **119**
Goldsmith Av. TS24 —4C **4**
Gomer Ter. DL14 —1C **102**
Gonville Ct. DL1 —3B **112**
Goodison Way. DL1 —5F **113**
Goodwin Clo. TS10 —4C **42**
Goodwin Wlk. TS24 —5A **8**
Goodwood Rd. TS10 —2E **43**
Goodwood Sq. TS17 —2A **72**
Goosepastures. TS15 —3D **95**
Gooseport Rd. TS18 —4D **49**
Gordon Clo. DL1 —2F **113**
Gordon Cres. TS6 —3F **55**
Gordon Rd. TS10 —5B **28**
Gordon St. TS24 —4D **7**
Gordon Ter. DL14 —1D **103**
Gordon Ter. DL17 —3D **101**
Gore Sands. TS5 —2B **88**
Gorman Rd. TS5 —1E **73**
Gorscombe Clo. DL17 —3F **101**
Gorsefields Ct. TS6 —2F **77**
Gorton Clo. TS23 —4D **19**
Gort Rd. DL5 —5D **107**
Gosford M. TS2 —2F **51**
Gosford Rd. TS20 —2B **48**
Gosford St. TS2 —2A **52**
Gosforth Av. TS10 —4E **29**
Gough Clo. TS1 —4E **51**
Gouldsmith Gdns. DL1 —3F **113**
Goulton Clo. TS15 —3F **95**
Gower Clo. TS1 —4E **51**
Gower Wlk. TS26 —2C **6**
Grace Clo. TS25 —1C **16**
Graffenberg St. TS10 —4E **29**
Grafton Clo. TS14 —4E **97**
Graham Ct. DL1 —2C **116**
Graham Ho. TS2 —2A 52
  (off East St.)
Graham St. TS13 —5B **66**
Graham St. TS24 —2C **8**
Graham Wlk. TS25 —5C **10**
Grainger St. DL1 —4B **116**
Grainger St. DL16 —3E **99**
Grainger St. TS24 —3F **7**
Grammar School La. TS15 —3D **95**
Grampian Rd. TS12 —5D **63**
Grampian Rd. TS23 —2E **33**
Grange Av. DL14 —3F **103**
Grange Av. TS18 —4E **47**
Grange Av. TS23 —5F **33**
Grange Av. TS26 —4D **7**
Grange Bungalows, The. TS6
  —3F **55**

Grange Bus. Cen., The. TS23
  —3A **34**
Grange Clo. TS6 —3F **55**
Grange Clo. TS26 —5C **6**
Grange Ct. DL5 —3E **107**
Grange Cres. TS7 —3E **91**
Grange Est. TS6 —4D **57**
Grange Dri. TS9 —3E **119**
Grange Farm. TS8 —3C **90**
Grange Farm Rd. TS6 —3F **55**
Grangefield. TS12 —4B **64**
Grangefield Rd. TS18 —5F **47**
Grange La. TS13 —2F **67**
Grange Pk. TS19 —3E **47**
Grange Rd. DL1
  —5E **115** to 2A **116**
Grange Rd. TS1 & TS4
  —3F **51** to 3B **52**
Grange Rd. TS17 —3D **71**
Grange Rd. TS20 —1C **48**
Grange Rd. TS26 —5D **7**
Grangeside. DL3 —5E **115**
Grange, The. DL5 —2D **107**
Grangetown By-Pass. TS6 —2C **54**
Grange View. TS22 —3D **19**
Grangeville Av. TS19 —5B **46**
Grange Wood. TS8 —3A **90**
Grantham Av. TS26 —5D **7**
Grantham Grn. TS4 —5C **74**
  (in two parts)
Grantham Rd. TS20 —4A **32**
Grantley Av. TS3 —5B **54**
Granton Clo. DL3 —2B **114**
Grant St. TS10 —4D **29**
Granville Av. DL4 —3B **104**
Granville Av. TS26 —4D **7**
Granville Clo. DL4 —3B **104**
Granville Gro. TS20 —2C **48**
Granville Pl. TS26 —5D **7**
Granville Rd. DL14 —3B **102**
Granville Rd. TS1 —5F **51**
Granville Rd. TS6 —3E **55**
Granville Ter. TS10 —4E **29**
Granwood Rd. TS6 —2A **78**
Grasby Clo. TS3 —2B **76**
Grasmere. DL16 —1B **98**
Grasmere Av. TS5 —4D **73**
Grasmere Cres. TS12 —1C **80**
Grasmere Dri. TS6 —1D **77**
Grasmere Rd. DL1 —3C **116**
Grasmere Rd. DL17 —3C **100**
Grasmere Rd. TS10 —5D **29**
Grasmere Rd. TS18 —5F **47**
Grasmere St. TS26 —1E **11**
Grass Croft. TS21 —5B **68**
Grassholme. DL1 —4C **116**
Grassholme Av. TS5 —1C **72**
Grassholme Pl. DL5 —5B **106**
Grassholm Rd. TS20 —1C **48**
Grassington Grn. TS17 —4A **86**
Grassington Rd. TS4 —3B **74**
Grass St. DL1 —4B **112**
Graygarth Rd. TS3 —1D **75**
Grayson Grange. DL16 —5A **98**
Grayson Rd. DL16 —5A **98**
Gray's Rd. TS18 —5F **47**
Gray St. TS2 —2A **52**
Gray St. TS24 —2F **7**
Graythorp Ind. Est. TS25 —5A **16**
Graythorp Rd. TS25 —4A **16**
Gt. Auk. TS14 —3B **96**
Gt. Gth. TS14 —3D **97**
Gt. Gates. DL14 —1D **103**
Greatham Clo. TS5 —1E **89**
Greatham St. TS25 —2A **12**
Greathead Cres. DL5 —1F **109**
Gt. North Rd. DL1 —1B **112**

Gt. North Rd. DL5 & DL17
  —3F **109** to 1F **107**
Greear Garth. TS14 —3D **97**
Greenacre Clo. TS9 —4A **120**
Greenacre Clo. TS11 —4D **45**
Greenacres. TS8 —5C **88**
Greenbank Av. TS5 —1C **72**
Green Bank Clo. TS12 —4C **80**
Greenbank Ct. TS26 —4C **6**
Greenbank Rd. DL3 —5F **111**
Greenbank Ter. TS12 —4C **80**
Green Clo. TS7 —3B **92**
Greencroft. TS10 —3B **42**
Greencroft Clo. DL3 —3E **115**
Greencroft Ct. DL3 —3E **115**
Greencroft Wlk. TS3 —3F **75**
Green Dragon Yd. TS18 —1C **70**
Greenfield Dri. TS16 —4C **84**
Greenfields. DL17 —2D **101**
Greenfields Rd. DL14 —5A **102**
Greenfields Rd. Ind. Est. DL14
  —5A **102**
Greenfields Way. TS18 —1B **68**
Greenfield Way. DL5 —5A **106**
Greenford Wlk. TS3 —2B **76**
Greenham Clo. TS3 —1B **76**
Greenhead Clo. TS8 —3F **89**
Greenhow Gro. TS25 —5C **12**
Greenhow Rd. TS3 —1D **75**
Greenhow Wlk. TS10 —2C **42**
Greenland Av. TS5 —2B **72**
Greenland Rd. TS24 —2A **8**
Greenland Rd. Ind. Pk. TS24
  —2A **8**
Greenlands Rd. TS10 —5E **29**
Green La. DL1 —1C **112**
Green La. DL4 & DL14 —1C **104**
Green La. DL14 —2C 10
  (off Prince's St.)
Green La. DL16 —2F **99**
Green La. TS5 —3D **73**
Green La. TS10 & TS11 —3A **44**
Green La. TS12 —1C **80**
Green La. TS15 —5C **94** to 4F **95**
Green La. TS17 —5C **70**
Green La. TS19 —2F **47** to 4A **48**
Green La. Ind. Est. DL16 —1F **99**
Greenlee Clo. TS17 —4A **86**
Greenlee Garth. DL5 —4A **106**
Greenmount Rd. DL3 —3E **115**
Greenock Clo. TS11 —2A **60**
Greenock Rd. TS25 —5C **10**
Green Rd. TS12 —1B **80**
Green's Beck Rd. TS18 —2D **69**
Green's Gro. TS18 —2D **69**
Greenside. TS6 —4D **77**
Greenside. TS17 —4C **86**
Greenside. TS25 —4C **14**
Green's La. TS18 —1D **69**
Greenstones Rd. TS10 —3E **43**
Green St. DL1 —2C **116**
Green St. TS24 —1F **11**
Greens Valley Dri. TS18 —2D **68**
Green Ter. TS25 —5C **12**
Green, The. DL1 —3F **113**
Green, The. DL5 —5F **109**
Green, The. TS4 —3B **74**
Green, The. TS10 —1F **41**
Green, The. TS11 —5C **44**
Green, The. TS12 —3C **62**
Green, The. TS15 —2D **95**
Green, The. TS17 —1D **87**
Green, The. TS20 —5B **32**
Green, The. TS21 —5A **68**
Green, The. TS22 —3D **19**
Green, The. TS23 —4E **33**
  (Billingham)

Green, The. TS23 —5D **21**
(Cowpen Bewley)
Green, The. TS25 —4C **14**
(Greatham)
Green, The. TS25 —4C **12**
(Seaton Carew)
Green Vale Gro. TS19 —1B **68**
Greenway. TS6 —1F **77**
Green Way. TS7 —4B **92**
Greenway. TS17 —4C **86**
Greenway Ct. TS3 —5A **54**
Greenway, The. TS3
—5A **54** to 2A **76**
Greenwell Rd. DL5 —5D **107**
Greenwell St. DL1 —3A **116**
Greenwich Ho. TS3 —5E 53
(off Byfleet Av.)
Greenwood Av. TS5 —3E **73**
Greenwood Rd. TS18 —2E **69**
Greenwood Rd. TS23 —2A **34**
Greenwood Rd. TS24 —4F **7**
Gregory Ct. DL5 —2E **109**
Gregory Ter. DL17 —3D **101**
Grendale Clo. TS13 —5D **67**
Grendon Wlk. TS3 —4E **75**
Grenville Clo. TS11 —5F **45**
Grenville Rd. TS17 —1E **87**
Gresham Clo. DL1 —3B **112**
Gresham Rd. TS1 —4E **51**
Greta Av. TS25 —3E **11**
Greta Rd. TS10 —5B **28**
Greta Rd. TS12 —5D **63**
Greta Rd. TS20 —1B **48**
Greta St. TS1 —4E **51**
Greta St. TS12 —2D **63**
Gretton Av. TS4 —5C **74**
Greville Way. DL5 —1E **109**
Grewgrass La. TS10 & TS11
—4E **43** to 3A **60**
Greyfriars Clo. DL3 —2A **114**
Greylands Av. TS20 —1C **48**
Greymouth Clo. TS18 —2D **69**
Greys Ct. TS17 —5C **86**
Greystoke Ct. TS5 —4D **73**
Greystoke Gro. TS10 —3D **43**
Greystoke Rd. TS10 —3D **43**
Greystoke Wlk. TS10 —3D **43**
Greystone Rd. TS6 —2A **56**
Greystones Roundabout. TS8
—3D **89**
Grey St. DL1 —5C **112**
Grey St. DL14 —2D **103**
Grey St. TS20 —2C **48**
Grey Ter. DL17 —4F **101**
Grey Towers Dri. TS7 —4B **92**
Grey Towers Farm Cotts. TS7
—5C **92**
Greywood Clo. TS27 —3A **4**
Gribdale Rd. TS3 —1E **75**
Griffin Rd. TS4 —1B **74**
Griffiths Clo. TS15 —5C **94**
Griffiths Rd. TS6 —4F **55**
Grimston Wlk. TS3 —1C **74**
Grimwood Av. TS3 —5F **53**
Grindon Ct. DL5 —3E **107**
Grindon Way. DL3 —5D **109**
Grinkle Av. TS3 —3E **75**
Grinkle Ct. TS14 —1E **97**
Grinkle La. TS13 —2F **67**
Grinkle Rd. TS10 —1A **42**
Grinton Pk. Way. DL14 —4C **116**
Grinton Rd. TS18 —3C **68**
Grisedale Clo. TS5 —2D **89**
Grisedale Cres. TS6 —4A **56**
Grisedale Cres. TS16 —1D **95**
Gritten Sq. TS24 —1A **8**
Groat Av. DL5 —2E **109**

Groat Dri. DL5 —2E **109**
Groat Rd. DL5 —2E **109**
Groat Way. DL5 —3E **109**
Grosmont Clo. TS10 —4D **43**
Grosmont Dri. TS23 —1D **33**
Grosmont Pl. TS6 —5A **56**
Grosmont Rd. TS6 —5A **56**
Grosmont Rd. TS25 —5C **12**
Grosvenor Ct. TS17 —3A **86**
Grosvenor Gdns. TS6 —2E **77**
Grosvenor Gdns. TS26 —4E **7**
Grosvenor Pl. TS14 —3D **97**
Grosvenor Rd. TS5 —2D **73**
Grosvenor Rd. TS19 —1D **69**
Grosvenor Rd. TS22 —5C **18**
Grosvenor Sq. TS14 —2D **97**
Grosvenor St. DL1 —3B **116**
Grosvenor St. TS26 —4E **7** & 5E **7**
Grosvenor Ter. TS13 —2A 66
(off Queen St.)
Grove Clo. TS26 —5D **7**
Grove Hill. TS13 —2B **66**
Grove Rd. DL14 —3C **102**
Grove Rd. TS3 —4C **52**
Grove Rd. TS10 —4D **29**
Grove Rd. TS13 —2B **66**
Groves St. TS24 —2D **9**
Groves, The. TS18 —2A **70**
Grove St. TS18 —2A **70**
Grove Ter. TS20 —2C **48**
Grove, The. TS5 —2E **89**
Grove, The. TS7 —1F **91**
Grove, The. TS14 —5B **96**
Grove, The. TS15 —4D **95**
Grove, The. TS25 —4C **14**
Grove, The. TS26 —5D **7**
Grundales Dri. TS11 —4D **45**
Guardian Ct. DL3 —3E **115**
Gudmunsen Av. DL14 —5B **102**
Guernsey Wlk. TS14 —4C **96**
Guildford Clo. DL1 —4F **113**
Guildford Ct. TS6 —4E **77**
Guildford Rd. TS6 —4D **77**
Guildford Rd. TS23 —5D **19**
Guisborough Ct. TS6 —1A **78**
Guisborough Ho. TS4 —2C **74**
Guisborough La. TS12 —1A **80**
Guisborough Rd. TS7
—4B **92** to 2E **93**
Guisborough Rd. TS9 —3A **120**
Guisborough Rd. TS12 —2C **62**
Guisborough Rd. TS17 —3E **71**
Guisborough St. TS6 —2A **78**
Guiseley Way. TS16 —3C **84**
Gulliver Rd. TS25 —3B **10**
Gunnergate Clo. TS12 —2B **62**
Gunnergate La. TS8 & TS7 —4D **91**
Gunnerside Rd. TS19 —5B **46**
Gunn La. DL5 —1F **109**
Gurney Ho. TS1 —3A **52**
Gurney St. DL1 —4B **112**
Gurney St. TS1 —3A **52**
Gurney St. TS11 —1B **60**
Gurney Way. DL5 —3D **109**
Guthrie Av. TS5 —3B **72**
Guthrum Pl. DL5
—3D **107** & 4D **107**
Gwynn Clo. TS19 —4B **46**
Gypsy La. TS7 —3F **91** to 2D **93**

Hackforth Rd. TS18 —3C **68**
Hackness Wlk. TS5 —4F **73**
Hackworth Clo. DL4 —4D **105**
Hackworth Clo. DL5 —1E **109**
Hackworth Clo. DL17 —3B **100**
Hackworth Ct. TS18 —4B **48**

Hackworth Ind. Pk. DL4 —5B **104**
Hackworth Rd. DL4 —4B 10
(off Shildon By-Pass)
Hackworth Rd. DL4 —3C 10
(off St John's Rd.)
Hackworth St. DL4 —4C **104**
Hackworth St. DL17 —3B **100**
Hadasia Gdns. TS19 —5D **47**
Haddon Rd. TS23 —5E **19**
Haddon St. TS1 —5A **52**
Hadleigh Clo. TS21 —5B **118**
Hadleigh Cres. TS4 —2B **74**
Hadlow Wlk. TS3 —1E 75
(off Homerton Rd.)
Hadnall Clo. TS5 —4B **72**
Hadrian Ct. DL3 —3F **115**
Haffron Av. TS4 —4C **48**
Haig St. DL3 —3A **112**
Haig St. DL17 —4F **101**
Haig Ter. DL17 —3B **100**
Hailsham Av. TS17 —5E **87**
Haldane Gro. TS25 —5C **10**
Hale Rd. TS23 —5F **19**
Half Moon Clo. DL16
—3E **99** & 2F **99**
Halidon Way. TS23 —4A **20**
Halifax Clo. TS11 —4C **44**
Halifax Rd. TS17 —2C **87**
Hall Clo. TS11 —4D **45**
Hall Clo., The. TS7 —4B **76**
Hallcroft Clo. TS23 —5E **33**
Hall Dri. TS5 —5D **73**
Hallgarth Clo. TS15 —2D **89**
Hallgarth Ter. DL17 —2D **101**
Hallgate Clo. TS18 —3C **68**
Hall Grounds. TS13 —4C **66**
Hallifield St. TS20 —2C **48**
Hallington Head. DL5 —5A **106**
Hall Lea. TS21 —4B **118**
Hall View Gro. DL3 —5B **110**
Halnaby Av. DL3 —2A **114**
Halton Clo. TS23 —3F **19**
Halton Ct. TS3 —5A **54**
Halton Ct. TS23 —3F **19**
Hambledon Cres. TS12 —5D **63**
Hambledon Rd. TS5 —2C **72**
Hambleton Av. TS10 —3B **42**
Hambleton Ct. DL5 —4A **106**
Hambleton Cres. TS11 —5F **45**
Hambleton Ga. TS9 —4F **119**
Hambleton Gro. DL1 —3D **113**
Hambleton Rd. TS7 —2C **92**
Hambleton Sq. TS23 —1D **33**
Hamilton Dri. DL1 —2C **112**
Hamilton Gro. TS6 —5C **54**
Hamilton Rd. TS19 —3A **48**
Hamilton Rd. TS25 —5C **10**
Hammond Dri. DL1 —5A **116**
Hampden St. TS6 —3B **54**
Hampden Way. TS17 —2C **87**
Hampshire Grn. TS20 —2D **49**
Hampshire Pl. DL14 —5D **103**
Hampstead Gro. TS6 —4D **77**
Hampstead Rd. TS6 —3D **77**
Hampstead, The. TS10 —2F **43**
Hampton Clo. TS7 —2B **92**
Hampton Gro. TS10 —1F **43**
Hampton Rd. TS18 —2F **69**
Hamsterley Rd. DL5 —3C **106**
Hamsterley Rd. TS19 —2D **47**
Hamsterley St. DL3 —5E **111**
Hanbury Clo. TS17 —5C **86**
Handale Clo. TS14 —3F **97**
Handley Clo. TS18 —1A **86**
Hankin Rd. TS3 —4C **52**
Hanover Clo. DL3 —2B **114**
Hanover Ct. DL14 —3E **103**

Hanover Ct. TS20 —5A **32**
Hanover Gdns. DL14 —3E **103**
Hanover Gdns. TS5 —2D **73**
Hanover Pde. TS20 —5A **32**
Hanover Point. TS20 —5A **32**
Hansard Clo. DL5 —3A **108**
Hanson Ct. TS10 —4D **29**
Hanson St. TS10 —4D **29**
Harborne Gdns. TS5 —2E **89**
Harcourt Rd. TS6 —3A **54**
Harcourt St. DL3 —5F **111**
Harcourt St. TS26 —4D **7**
Hardale Gro. TS10 —1B **42**
Hardinge Rd. DL5 —4E **107**
Harding Row. TS20 —1C **48**
Harding Ter. DL3 —5E **111**
Hardisty Cres. DL14 —4C **102**
Hardknott Gro. TS10 —1C **42**
Hardwick Av. TS5 —4D **73**
Hardwick Clo. DL1 —3E **113**
Hardwick Ct. DL5 —4E **107**
Hardwick Rd. TS26 —1A **10**
Hardwick Rd. TS6 —2B **54**
Hardwick Rd. TS19 —1D **47**
Hardwick Rd. TS21 —4B **118**
Hardwick Rd. TS23 —5A **20**
Harebell Clo. TS12 —1F **81**
Harebell Clo. TS17 —4C **86**
Harebell Meadows, DL5 —2E **107**
Harehills Rd. TS5 —2C **72**
Haresfield Way. TS17 —5C **86**
Hareson Rd. DL5 —4B **106**
Harewood Gro. DL3 —3F **115**
Harewood Hill. DL3 —3F **115**
Harewood Ho. TS4 —2C **74**
Harewood Rd. TS17 —2E **71**
Harewood St. TS1 —5F **51**
Harewood Ter. DL3 —3F **115**
Harewood Way. TS10 —2F **43**
Harford St. TS1 —5E **51**
Hargreave Ter. DL1 —3B **116**
Harker Clo. TS15 —5C **94**
Harker St. DL4 —3B **104**
Harland Pl. TS20 —1C **48**
Harlech Clo. TS6 —5F **55**
Harlech Gro. TS11 —2B **60**
Harlech Wlk. TS26 —2C **6**
Harley Gro. DL1 —3F **113**
Harlow Cres. TS17 —4F **71**
Harlsey Cres. TS18 —3D **69**
Harlsey Gro. TS18 —3D **69**
Harlsey Rd. TS18 —3D **69**
Harpenden Wlk. TS3 —1E **75**
Harper Pde. TS18 —2E **69**
Harper Ter. TS18 —2E **69**
Harringay Cres. DL1 —5E **113**
Harris Gro. TS25 —5C **10**
Harrison Clo. DL4 —5C **104**
Harrison Cres. DL14 —5B **102**
Harrison Pl. TS24 —1D **7**
Harrison St. TS3 —4D **53**
Harrison Ter. DL3 —4F **111**
Harris St. DL1 —3D **117**
Harris St. TS1 —3F **51**
Harris Wlk. TS14 —4C **96**
(off Hutton La.)
Harrogate Cres. TS5 —1F **73**
Harrowgate La. TS19 —3B **46**
Harrow St. TS5 —3D **73**
Harrow Rd. TS18 —1A **70**
Harrow St. TS25 —2E **11**
Harry St. DL3 —4A **112**
Harsley Wlk. TS3 —1E **75**
(in two parts)
Hart Av. TS26 —3C **6**
Hartburn Av. TS18 —1F **69**
Hartburn Ct. TS5 —1D **89**

Hartburn La. TS18 —2F **69**
Hartburn Village. TS18 —3E **69**
Hart Clo. TS19 —2E **47**
Harter Clo. TS7 —4B **92**
Hartford Rd. DL3 —3E **115**
Hartforth Av. TS5 —1D **89**
Harthope Gro. DL14 —4A **102**
Hartington Clo. TS17 —3D **71**
Hartington Rd. TS1 —3F **51**
Hartington Rd. TS18 —1B **70**
Hartington St. TS13 —4B **66**
Hartington St. TS17 —3D **71**
Hartington Way. DL3 —4F **111**
Hartland Gro. TS3 —3F **75**
(in two parts)
Hart La. TS27 & TS26
    —1A **6** to 4E **7**
Hart La. Cotts. TS24 —4D **7**
Hartlepool Clo. TS19 —2E **47**
Hartlepool Ind. Est. TS24 —1E **7**
Hartley Clo. TS26 —4E **7**
Hartley Rd. DL5 —5D **107**
Hartley Ter. DL16 —2D **99**
Hartoft Ct. TS10 —3C **42**
Harton Av. TS22 —5C **18**
Hartsbourne Cres. TS11 —2A **60**
Hartside Gro. TS19 —2F **47**
Hartville Rd. TS24 —3A **4**
Hartwith Dri. TS19 —5C **30**
Harvard Av. TS17 —1D **71**
Harvester Ct. TS7 —1C **90**
Harvey Ct. TS10 —1A **42**
Harvey Wlk. TS25 —3B **10**
Harwal Rd. TS10 —4B **28**
Harwell Clo. TS4 —3B **74**
Harwell Dri. TS19 —3C **46**
Harwich Clo. TS10 —3A **44**
Harwich Gro. TS25 —5F **11**
Harwood Ct. TS2 —1E **51**
Harwood St. TS24 —3E **7**
Haselrigg Clo. DL5 —3A **108**
Haselwood Rd. DL5 —2C **106**
Hasledon Gro. TS21 —5A **118**
Hastings Clo. TS7 —3B **92**
Hastings Clo. TS17 —3D **87**
Hastings Ho. TS3 —3E **75**
Hastings Pl. TS24 —1D **7**
Hastings Way. TS23 —4B **20**
Haswell Av. TS25 —3F **11**
Haswell Ct. TS20 —3C **48**
Hatfield Av. TS5 —3D **73**
Hatfield Clo. TS16 —5B **84**
Hatfield Rd. DL5 —5E **107**
Hatfield Rd. TS23 —1A **34**
Hatfield Way. DL14 —5E **103**
Haughton Grn. DL1 —4E **113**
Haughton Rd. DL1 —1B **116**
Hauxley Clo. TS10 —2A **44**
Hauxwell's Yd. TS15 —2C **94**
Havelock Clo. DL5 —1E **109**
Havelock St. DL1 —4A **112**
Havelock St. TS17 —3D **71**
Havelock St. TS24 —1B **12**
Haven Gro. TS24 —1B **8**
Haven Wlk. TS24 —1B **8**
Haverthwaite. TS5 —2C **88**
Haverton Hill Rd. TS18 —3A **50**
Haverton Hill Rd. TS23
    —2B **50** to 4E **35**
Haverton Hill Shipyard Ind. Pk. TS23
    —4E **35**
Havilland St. TS17 —2E **87**
Hawbeck Way. TS7 —4C **76**
Hawes Pl. DL5 —5C **106**
Haweswater Rd. TS10 —1C **42**
Hawford Clo. TS17 —5D **87**
Hawkesbury Clo. TS18 —2D **69**

Hawkesbury M. DL3 —1F **115**
Hawkins Clo. TS11 —5F **45**
Hawkridge Clo. TS26 —4E **7**
Hawk Rd. TS3 —4E **53**
Hawkshead Clo. DL5 —5B **106**
Hawkshead Pl. DL5 —5B **106**
Hawkshead Rd. TS10 —1D **43**
Hawksridge Clo. TS17 —4B **86**
(in two parts)
Hawkstone. TS8 —5F **91**
Hawkstone Clo. TS14 —4D **97**
Hawkstone Clo. TS22 —5B **18**
Hawnby Clo. TS19 —5B **46**
Hawnby Ct. TS10 —2C **42**
Hawnby Rd. TS5 —3F **73**
Hawthorn Av. TS17 —5D **71**
Hawthorn Av. TS23 —4E **33**
Hawthorn Cres. TS7 —1F **91**
Hawthorn Dri. TS12 —4B **64**
Hawthorn Dri. TS14 —3B **96**
Hawthorne Av. TS4 —2A **74**
Hawthorne Gro. TS15 —4E **95**
Hawthorne Rd. TS19 —3A **48**
Hawthorn Gro. TS15 —4E **95**
Hawthorn Pl. TS15 —2D **95**
Hawthorn Rd. DL14 —3D **103**
Hawthorn Rd. DL16 —4A **98**
Hawthorn Rd. TS10 —5D **29**
Hawthorn Rd. TS21 —4B **118**
Hawthorns, The. DL3 —1E **115**
Hawthorns, The. TS9 —3B **120**
Hawthorn St. DL1 —4B **116**
Hawthorn Ter. TS6 —3A **54**
(off Old Middlesbrough Rd.)
Hawthorn Wlk. TS24 —2E **7**
Haxby Clo. TS5 —5F **73**
Haxby Wlk. TS24 —1A **8**
Hayburn Clo. TS10 —3F **43**
Hayburn Clo. TS17 —5D **87**
Hayling Gro. TS10 —3E **43**
Hayling Way. TS18 —1B **68**
Haymore St. TS5 —1F **73**
Hayston Rd. TS26 —4A **6**
Hazel Av. DL3 —5E **111**
Hazelbank. TS8 —3C **90**
Hazel Ct. TS1 —3A **52**
Hazel Ct. TS20 —1C **48**
Hazel Ct. TS24 —2E **7**
Hazeldale Av. DL4 —3E **105**
Hazeldene Av. TS18 —3F **69**
Hazel Gdns. TS12 —4B **64**
Hazel Gro. DL14 —2C **102**
Hazel Gro. TS7 —2A **92**
Hazel Gro. TS10 —5F **29**
Hazel Gro. TS17 —4D **71**
Hazel Gro. TS24 —2E **7**
Hazelmere. DL16 —1B **98**
Hazelmere Clo. TS22 —5B **18**
Hazelrigg Clo. DL5 —3A **108**
Hazel Rd. TS19 —3A **48**
Hazel Slade. TS16 —4D **85**
Hazel Wlk. TS13 —4D **67**
Hazelwood Ct. TS5 —2F **89**
Hazelwood Rise. TS24 —2D **9**
Headingley Cres. DL1 —5F **113**
Headingly Ct. TS25 —1C **16**
Headlam Ct. TS20 —3C **48**
Headlam Rd. DL1 —4C **116**
Headlam Rd. TS20 —3C **48**
Headlam Rd. TS23 —5A **20**
Headlam Ter. TS16 —1C **94**
Headland Promenade. TS24 —1B **8**
Headlands, The. DL3 —2C **114**
Headlands, The. TS11 —3E **45**
Head St. TS1 —3F **51**
Healaugh Pk. TS15 —5E **95**
Heatherburn Ct. DL5 —4D **107**

Heather Clo. TS19 —1F **47**
Heather Dri. TS5 —4D **73**
Heatherfields Rd. TS6 —3F **77**
Heather Gro. DL16 —5A **98**
Heather Gro. TS12 —1F **81**
Heather Gro. TS24 —2D **7**
Heatherwood Gro. DL3 —1D **115**
Heathfield Clo. TS16 —4C **84**
Heathfield Dri. TS25 —2E **11**
Heath Rd. DL16 —5A **98**
Heath Rd. TS3 —3C **52**
Heathrow. TS17 —4F **71**
Heaton Rd. TS23 —3E **19**
Hebburn Rd. TS19 —2D **47**
Hebrides Wlk. DL1 —2E **113**
Hebron Rd. TS5 —2A **74**
Hebron Rd. TS9 —4D **119**
Heddon Gro. TS17 —4A **86**
Hedingham Clo. TS4 —2B **74**
Hedley Clo. DL5 —4C **106**
Hedley Clo. TS15 —5C **94**
Hedley Ct. TS15 —5C **94**
Hedleyhope Wlk. TS19 —2D **47**
Hedley St. TS14 —2E **97**
Heighington Clo. TS19 —2D **47**
Heighington La. DL5 —5A **108**
Heighington La. Bus. Pk. DL5
—5D **109**
Heighington La. Ind. Est. DL5
—5D **109**
Heighington St. DL5 —5E **109**
Heild Clo. DL5 —5E **107**
Helena Ter. DL14 —4C **102**
Helmington Grn. TS19 —2E **47**
Helmsdale Clo. DL1 —2D **113**
Helmsley Clo. TS17 —3E **101**
Helmsley Clo. TS5 —4F **73**
Helmsley Ct. DL5 —3E **107**
Helmsley Dri. TS14 —2D **97**
Helmsley Lawn. TS10 —2F **43**
(off Ludlow Cres.)
Helmsley Moor Way. DL1 —4E **117**
Helmsley St. TS24 —3E **7**
Helston Ct. TS17 —5A **72**
Hemel Clo. TS17 —4F **71**
Hemingford Gdns. TS15 —4E **95**
Hemlington Hall Rd. TS8 —4D **89**
Hemlington La. TS8 —3F **89**
Hemlington Rd. TS8 —5D **89**
Hemlington Rd. TS9 —1E **119**
Hemlington Village Rd. TS8
—4B **90**
Hempstead Clo. TS17 —4F **71**
Henderson Gro. TS24 —4F **7**
Henderson Ho. TS2 —2F **51**
(off Silver St.)
Henderson Rd. DL5 —1E **109**
Henderson St. DL1 —4A **116**
Hendren Clo. DL3 —2A **112**
Henley Gro. TS17 —3D **71**
Henley Rd. TS5 —2D **73**
Henrietta Clo. TS17 —2D **71**
Henrietta St. TS24 —1C **8**
Henry Smith's Ter. TS24 —2D **9**
Henry St. DL1 —4B **112**
Henry St. DL4 —3B **104**
Henry St. TS3 —5D **53**
Henry St. TS6 —2C **54**
Henry St. TS10 —3C **28**
Henry Taylor Ct. TS7 —4B **76**
Hensford Gro. DL3 —4F **111**
Henshaw Dri. TS17 —3A **86**
Hensley St. TS20 —4F **31**
Henson Gro. DL5 —4D **107**
Heortnesse Rd. TS24 —1A **8**
Hepple Clo. TS23 —3E **19**
Herbert St. DL1 —3B **116**

Herbert St. TS3 —4D **53**
Herbert Wlk. TS24 —3F **7**
Hercules St. DL1 —3D **113**
Hereford Clo. TS5 —1F **73**
Hereford Rd. TS14 —4D **97**
Hereford St. TS25 —2F **11**
Hereford Ter. TS23 —3A **34**
Heriot Gro. TS25 —5C **10**
Hermitage Pl. TS20 —4B **32**
Heron Ct. TS18 —1A **70**
Heron Dri. DL1 —2E **117**
Heron Ga. TS14 —3B **96**
Heronspool Clo. TS24 —1A **8**
Herrington Ct. DL5 —4E **107**
Herrington Rd. TS23 —3F **19**
Herriot Ct. DL1 —2F **113**
Herschell St. TS10 —4D **29**
Hershall Dri. TS3 —1F **75**
Hesketh Av. TS4 —5C **74**
Hesleden Av. TS5 —1C **88**
Hesledon Clo. TS19 —2E **47**
Heslop Dri. DL1 —4A **116**
Heslop St. TS17 —3E **71**
Hestobel Ct. DL14 —4C **102**
Heswall Rd. TS23 —1A **34**
Hetton Clo. TS23 —4E **19**
Heugh Chare. TS24 —3E **9**
Hewitson Rd. DL1 —3E **117**
Hewitson Rd. S. DL1 —3E **117**
Hewitt's Bldgs. TS14 —2E **97**
Hewley St. TS6 —2E **77**
Heworth Dri. TS20 —5F **31**
Hexham Dri. TS16 —1F **77**
Hexham Grn. TS3 —3A **76**
Hexham St. DL14 —1C **102**
Hexham Wlk. TS23 —5E **19**
Hexham Way. DL3 —4A **110**
Heysham Gro. TS10 —3F **43**
Heythrop Dri. TS6 —4C **54**
Heythrop Dri. TS14 —4E **97**
Heywood St. TS5 —5D **51**
Hibernian Gro. TS25 —5C **10**
Hickling Gro. TS19 —3C **46**
Hickstead Ct. DL1 —5F **113**
Hickstead Rise. DL5 —2F **107**
Hidcote Gdns. TS17 —5C **86**
Highbank Rd. TS7 —5C **76**
High Barn Rd. DL5 —3A **108**
High Bondgate. DL14 —1C **102**
Highbury Av. TS5 —4F **73**
Highbury Rd. DL3 —1D **115**
High Chu. M. TS15 —2C **94**
High Chu. Wynd. TS15 —2C **94**
Highcliffe Gro. TS11 —2B **60**
Highcliffe Ter. DL17 —2D **101**
Highcliffe View. TS14 —3D **97**
Highcroft. DL16 —5A **98**
High Durham St. DL14 —2C **102**
High Farm View. TS6 —5C **54**
High Fell. TS10 —1C **42**
Highfield Clo. TS16 —4D **85**
Highfield Cres. TS18 —2D **69**
Highfield Dri. TS16 —4D **85**
Highfield Gdns. TS16 —4D **85**
Highfield Rd. DL3 —3C **110**
Highfield Rd. TS4 —1B **74**
Highfield Rd. TS6 —1F **77**
Highfield Rd. TS11 —4B **44**
Highfield Rd. TS18 —2D **69**
High Force Rd. TS2 —1D **51**
Highgate. TS6 —1B **78**
High Gill Rd. TS7 —2B **92**
High Godfalter Hill. TS7 —1D **93**
High Grange Av. TS23 —5E **19**
High Grange Ho. TS23 —4E **19**
High Grange Rd. DL16 —2C **98**
High Grn. DL3 —5C **110**

High Grn. DL5 —2E **107**
High Grn. TS9 —4B **120**
Highland Gdns. DL4 —2B **104**
Highland Rd. TS25 —5C **10**
Highland Ter. DL17 —2D **101**
Highlight, The. TS24 —3A **8**
Highmead Wlk. TS3 —4E **75**
High Melbourne St. DL14 —4D **103**
Highmoor Rd. DL1 —4E **117**
High Newham Ct. TS19 —1D **47**
High Newham Rd. TS19 —1C **46**
High Northgate. DL1 —5A **112**
High Peak. TS14 —4F **97**
High Rifts. TS8 —4C **88**
High Row. DL3 —2A **116**
High Row. DL5 —5F **109**
High Row. TS13 —4B **66**
High Stone Clo. TS10 —2F **43**
High St. Aycliffe, DL5 —5F **109**
High St. Boosbeck, TS12 —4C **80**
High St. Brotton, TS12 —4C **64**
High St. E. TS10 —4E **29**
High St. Eldon Lane, DL14
—1C **104**
High St. Eston, TS6 —1F **77**
High St. Ferryhill, DL17 —4F **101**
High St. Great Ayton, TS9
—4A **120**
High St. Greatham, TS25 —3C **14**
High St. Hartlepool, TS24 —3D **9**
High St. Lackenby, TS6 —5B **56**
High St. Lazenby, TS6 —4D **57**
High St. Lingdale, TS12 —5E **81**
High St. Loftus, TS13 —4D **67**
High St. Marske-by-the-Sea, TS11
—3D **45** to 5D **45**
High St. Normanby, TS6 —2E **77**
High St. Norton, TS20 —5C **32**
High St. Ormesby, TS7 —4A **76**
High St. Port Clarence, TS2
—5A **36**
High St. Redcar, TS10 —4D **29**
High St. Sedgefield, TS21 —4B **118**
High St. Skelton, TS12 —1C **80**
High St. Skinningrove, TS13
—1B **66**
High St. Spennymoor, DL16
—3C **98**
High St. Stockton-on-Tees, TS18
—5C **48**
High St. Stokesley, TS9 —1E **119**
High St. W. TS10 —4B **28**
High St. Wolviston, TS22 —3D **19**
High St. Yarm, TS15 —2C **94**
High Tunstall Cotts. TS26 —5A **6**
Hilda Pl. TS12 —1D **63**
Hilda St. DL1 —1B **116**
Hilda Wlk. TS24 —5A **8**
Hilderthorpe. TS7 —3A **92**
Hildon Dri. DL1 —5C **116**
Hildyard Clo. TS9 —2E **119**
Hillbeck St. DL14 —4E **103**
Hill Clo. TS12 —1C **80**
Hill Clo. Av. DL3 —2B **114**
Hill Cres. TS10 —1F **41**
Hillcrest Av. TS18 —1D **69**
Hillcrest Dri. TS7 —1C **92**
Hillcrest Dri. TS13 —5C **66**
Hillel Wlk. TS5 —2E **89**
Hillfields. DL5 —3A **108**
Hill Garth. DL3 —5D **111**
Hil Ho. Farm. TS20 —2C **48**
Hillingdon Rd. TS3 —4E **75**
Hill Rd. TS23 —4E **33**
Hillside Av. TS4 —3A **74**
(in two parts)
Hillside Clo. TS11 —3A **60**

Hillside Rd. DL3 —3E **115**
Hillside Rd. TS20 —5C **32**
Hills, The. TS12 —1C **80**
Hillston Clo. TS26 —4A **6**
Hill St. TS10 —4C **28**
Hill St. E. TS18 —5D **49**
Hill St. Shopping Cen. TS1 —3F **51**
Hills View Rd. TS6 —1A **78**
Hillview. TS3 —3E 75
(off Delamere Rd.)
Hill View. TS25 —5D **15**
Hill View Ter. TS11 —2B **60**
Hilsdon Dri. DL4 —4E **105**
Hilton Ho. DL3 —3A **112**
Hilton La. TS17 —5B **86**
Hilton Rd. DL5 —2E **109**
Hilton Rd. DL14 —3E **103**
Hind Ct. DL5 —2E **107**
Hinderwell Av. TS10 —1B **42**
Hindhead. TS16 —4D **85**
Hindpool Clo. TS24 —1A **8**
Hind St. TS18 —2A **70**
Hinton Av. TS5 —1C **72**
Hinton Ct. TS14 —2E **97**
Hirdman Gro. TS24 —3C **4**
Hird Rd. TS15 —4C **94**
Hird St. DL1 —2B **116**
Hirst Ct. DL16 —5A **98**
Hirst Gro. DL1 —3E **117**
Hobdale Ter. TS12 —3C **80**
Hob Hill Clo. TS12 —3C **62**
Hob Hill Cres. TS12 —2C **62**
Hob Hill La. TS11 & TS12 —3F **61**
Hobson Av. TS10 —2E **41**
Hodges Ho. TS1 —3A **52**
Hodgson Ct. TS6 —2A **78**
Hoe, The. TS24 —4B **8**
Holbeck Av. TS5 —2E **89**
Holbeck Wlk. TS17 —2F **87**
Holborn. DL16 —2C **98**
Holburn Pk. TS19 —2E **47**
Holdenby Dri. TS3 —4E **75**
Holden Clo. TS6 —2E **55**
Holderness. DL5 —5A **106**
Holder St. TS10 —4D **29**
Holdforth Clo. TS24 —1D **7**
Holdforth Ct. TS24 —1D **7**
Holdforth Crest. DL14 —3E **103**
Holdforth Dri. DL14 —3D **103**
Holdforth Rd. TS24 —1D **7**
Holey Clo. TS8 —4E **89**
Holgate Moor Grn. DL1 —4D **117**
Holindale. DL16 —4C **98**
Holland Rd. TS25 —2C **14**
Hollies, The. TS10 —5F **29**
Hollies, The. TS23 —4E **33**
Hollinside Clo. TS19 —2E **47**
Hollinside Rd. TS23 —5A **20**
Hollins La. TS5 —2D **73**
Hollin Way. DL5 —5D **109**
Hollis Ct. TS8 —3C **90**
Hollowfield. TS8 —3B **90**
(in three parts)
Hollowfield Sq. TS8 —3B **90**
Hollybush Av. TS17 —4D **87**
Hollybush Est. TS12 —5E **63**
Hollygarth. TS9 —4A **120**
Hollygarth Clo. TS9 —4A **120**
Holly Hill. DL4 —3D **105**
Hollyhurst Av. TS4 —3A **74**
Hollyhurst Rd. DL3 —1E **115**
Holly La. TS8 —5D **89**
Hollymead Dri. TS14 —2D **97**
Hollymount. TS23 —4E **33**
Hollystone Ct. TS23 —3F **19**
Holly St. DL3 —1A **116**
Holly St. TS1 —4A **52**

Holly St. TS20 —1C **48**
Holly Ter. TS2 —5F **35**
Hollywalk Av. TS6 —3D **77**
Hollywalk Clo. TS6 —3D **77**
Hollywalk Dri. TS6 —2D **77**
Holmbeck Rd. TS12 —1F **81**
Holme Ct. TS3 —4A **75**
Holmefields Rd. TS6 —3E **77**
Holme Ho. Rd. TS18 —3F **49**
Holmes Clo. TS17 —5C **70**
Holmeside Gro. TS23 —3A **20**
Holmlands Rd. DL3 —5E **111**
Holmside Wlk. TS19 —2E **47**
Holmwood Av. TS4 —3A **74**
Holmwood Gro. DL1 —1B **112**
Holnest Av. TS3 —2E **75**
Holnicote Clo. TS17 —5A **86**
Holtby Wlk. TS3 —4E **75**
Holt St. TS24 —1F **11**
Holt, The. TS8 —3A **90**
Holwick Rd. DL1 —3B **112**
Holwick Rd. TS2 —2D **51**
Holyhead Dri. TS10 —3F **43**
Holyoake St. DL17 —3B **100**
Holyrood Av. DL3 —2B **114**
Holyrood Clo. TS17 —3E **71**
Holy Rood Ct. TS4 —1B **74**
(in two parts)
Holyrood La. TS4 —1B **74**
Holyrood Wlk. TS25 —5C **10**
Holystone Dri. TS17 —3A **86**
Holywell Grn. TS16 —5D **85**
Holywell Rd. DL14 —5A **102**
Homebryth Ho. TS21 —4B **118**
Homerell Clo. TS10 —3F **43**
Homer Gro. TS25 —3C **10**
Homerton Ct. DL1 —3B **112**
Homerton Rd. TS3 —1E **75**
Honeypot La. DL3 —4E **111**
Honeywood Gdns. DL3 —4E **111**
Honister Clo. TS19 —5A **48**
Honister Gro. TS5 —5C **72**
Honister Pl. DL5 —5B **106**
Honister Rd. TS10 —1C **42**
Honister Wlk. TS16 —1D **95**
Honiton Way. TS25 —5D **15**
Hood Clo. DL5 —4B **106**
Hood Dri. TS6 —3C **54**
Hoode Clo. TS24 —4C **4**
Hoope Clo. TS15 —5C **94**
Hopemoor Pl. DL1 —4E **117**
Hope St. TS18 —2A **70**
Hope St. TS23 —3E **35**
Hope St. TS24 —5A **8**
Hopetown La. DL3 —5A **112**
Hopper Rd. DL5 —2D **109**
Hopps St. TS26 —4E **7**
Horden Rd. TS23 —5A **20**
Hornbeam Clo. TS7 —4C **76**
Hornbeam Wlk. TS19 —1F **47**
Hornby Av. TS21 —5B **118**
Hornby Clo. TS1 —3F **51**
Hornby Clo. TS25 —3C **12**
Hornby Ho. DL1 —4C **116**
Horndale Av. TS6 —2C **108**
Hornleigh Gro. TS10 —4B **28**
Hornsea Clo. TS23 —2A **20**
Hornsea Gro. TS10 —4B **28**
Horsefield St. TS4 —3B **52**
Horse Mkt. DL1 —2A **116**
Horsley Gro. DL14 —5A **102**
Horsley Pl. TS24 —1D **7**
Horsley Way. TS23 —3F **19**
Horswell Gdns. DL16 —4A **98**
Hoskins Way. TS3 —1F **75**
Hospital Clo. TS25 —4C **14**
Hoton Clo. DL5 —5F **109**

Hough Cres. TS17 —4D **71**
Houghton Grn. TS19 —2E **47**
Houghton St. TS24 —1F **11**
Houndgate. DL1 —2A **116**
Houndgate M. DL1 —2A **116**
Hoveton Clo. TS19 —3D **47**
Hovingham St. TS4 —4D **53**
Howard Clo. DL14 —5B **102**
Howard Clo. TS4 —2B **74**
Howard Dri. TS11 —5F **45**
Howard St. TS1 —4E **51**
Howard St. TS24 —1B **8**
Howard Wlk. TS23 —5E **33**
Howbeck La. TS24 —1E **7**
Howcroft Av. TS10 —2F **41**
Howden Dyke. TS15 —5E **95**
Howden Rd. DL5 —3F **109**
Howden Rd. TS24 —4C **4**
Howden Wlk. TS18 —5B **48**
Howe St. TS1 —5F **51**
Howgill Wlk. TS3 —1D **75**
Howlbeck Rd. TS14 —2D **97**
Howson Cres. DL5 —3E **107**
Hoylake Clo. TS11 —2B **60**
Hoylake Rd. TS4 —4A **74**
(in two parts)
Hoylake Way. TS16 —5D **85**
Hucklehoven Way. TS24 —5A **8**
Hudson Ho. TS17 —5E **71**
Hudson St. DL17 —3C **100**
Hudson St. TS2 —2A **52**
Hudswell Gro. TS18 —2D **69**
Hugill Clo. TS15 —5E **95**
Hullock Rd. DL5 —5D **107**
Hulton Clo. TS7 —3A **92**
Humber Clo. TS13 —5E **71**
Humber Gro. TS22 —5B **18**
Humber Pl. DL1 —5A **116**
Humber Rd. TS17 —4E **71**
Humbledon Rd. TS19 —2E **47**
Hume Ho. TS18 —4B **48**
Hume St. TS18 —4B **48** & 4C **48**
(in two parts)
Humewood Gro. TS20 —3D **33**
Hummersea Clo. TS12 —4C **64**
Hummersea La. TS13 —4D **67**
Hummershill La. TS11 —4E **45**
Hummersknott Av. DL3 —3C **114**
Humphrey Clo. DL5 —5C **106**
Hundale Cres. TS10 —3F **43**
Hundens La. DL1 —2C **116**
Hunky Hall Golf Club. TS15
—2D **65**
Hunley Av. TS12 —3C **64**
Hunley Clo. TS12 —3C **64**
Hunstanton Gro. TS11 —2A **60**
Hunstanworth Rd. DL3 —4C **110**
Huntcliffe Av. TS10 —1B **42**
Huntcliffe Dri. TS12 —3B **64**
Hunter Houses Ind. Est. TS25
—3B **16**
Hunter Rd. DL5 —1E **109**
Huntersgate. TS6 —1B **78**
Hunters Grn. DL5 —4A **106**
Huntershaw Way. DL3 —2A **112**
Huntingdon Grn. TS20 —1D **49**
Huntley Clo. TS3 —4F **75**
Huntley Rd. TS25 —5C **10**
Huntley St. DL1 —3B **116**
Hunwick Clo. TS5 —1C **88**
Hunwick Wlk. TS19 —3D **47**
Hurn Wlk. TS17 —5F **71**
Huron Clo. TS4 —1B **74**
Hurst Pk. TS10 —2E **43**
Hurworth Clo. TS19 —5B **46**
Hurworth Hunt. DL5 —5A **106**
Hurworth Rd. DL5 —3C **108**

148 A-Z Middlesbrough

Hurworth Rd. TS4 —3B **74**
Hurworth Rd. TS23 —3B **20**
Hurworth St. DL14 —3D **103**
Hurworth St. TS24 —3E **7**
Hury Rd. TS20 —1B **48**
Hustler Rd. TS5 —3D **89**
Hutchinson St. DL14 —2C **102**
Hutchinson St. TS12 —4C **64**
Hutchinson St. TS18 —5B **48**
Hutchinson Wlk. DL5 —4F **107**
Hutone Pl. TS24 —4C **4**
Hutton Av. DL1 —3D **113**
Hutton Av. TS26 —5D **7**
Hutton Clo. DL14 —5E **103**
Hutton Clo. TS17 —4D **71**
Hutton Ct. TS26 —5E **7**
Hutton Gro. TS10 —2F **41**
Hutton Gro. TS18 —2E **69**
Hutton La. TS14 —5B **96**
Hutton Pl. DL5 —3D **107**
Hutton Rd. TS4 —5C **52**
Hutton Rd. TS6 —5B **56**
Hutton St. TS13 —1B **66**
Hutton St. TS24 —1A **8**
Hutton Village Rd. TS14 —5B **96**
Huxley Gro. DL1 —4D **117**
Huxley Wlk. TS25 —3C **10**
Hylton Clo. DL5 —4F **107**
Hylton Gro. TS20 —3B **48**
Hylton Rd. DL17 —2E **101**
Hylton Rd. TS23 —5A **20**
Hylton Rd. TS26 —1B **10**
Hythe Clo. TS10 —3A **44**

Ian Gro. TS25 —1C **14**
I'Anson Sq. DL1 —1A **116**
I'Anson St. DL3 —3A **112**
Ian St. TS17 —3E **71**
Ibbetson St. TS24 —2D **9**
Iber Gro. TS25 —1C **14**
Ibrox Gro. TS25 —1D **15**
Ibstone Wlk. TS19 —5D **31**
Ickworth Ct. TS17 —3A **86**
Idaho Gdns. DL1 —3C **112**
Ida Pl. DL5 —3D **107**
Ida Rd. TS3 —5C **52**
Ida St. TS20 —2B **48**
Ilam Ct. TS17 —5C **86**
Ilford Rd. TS19 —1D **47**
Ilford Way. TS3 —3E **75**
Ilfracombe Clo. TS8 —2C **90**
Ilkeston Wlk. TS19 —5D **31**
Ilkley Clo. TS14 —5D **97**
Ilkley Gro. TS25 —5F **11**
Ilston Grn. TS3 —3E **75**
Imeson St. TS6 —2A **78**
Imperial Av. TS17 —3E **71**
Imperial Av. TS20 —2C **48**
Imperial Cen. DL1 —2A **116**
Imperial Cres. TS20 —2C **48**
Imperial Rd. TS23 —5E **33**
Inchcape Rd. TS25 —1C **14**
Inch Gro. TS25 —1C **14**
Ingham Gro. TS3 —5F **53**
Ingleborough La. TS17 —4B **86**
Ingleby Clo. TS6 —5B **56**
Ingleby Ct. TS6 —5B **56**
Ingleby Gro. TS18 —2E **69**
Ingleby Ho. TS4 —2C **74**
Ingleby Moor Cres. DL1 —4E **117**
Ingleby Rd. TS4 —5C **52**
Ingleby Rd. TS25 —1C **16**
Ingleby Way. TS17 —5C **86**
*Ingledew Ho. TS2 —2F **51***
(off Suffield St.)
Inglesgarth Ct. DL16 —4B **98**

Ingleton Rd. TS19 —1D **47**
Inglewood Av. TS11 —5D **45**
Inglewood Clo. DL1 —3C **112**
Inglewood Clo. TS3 —1B **76**
Ingoldsby Rd. TS3 —2B **76**
Ingram Gro. TS17 —3A **86**
Ingram Rd. TS3 —1D **75**
Ingrove Clo. TS19 —1D **47**
Ings Av. TS3 —5F **53**
Ings La. TS12 —4D **65** to 2E **65**
Ings La. TS15 —4B **94**
Ings M. TS10 —5E **29**
Ings Rd. TS10 —5E **29**
Inkerman St. TS18 —5B **48**
Innes Rd. TS25 —1C **14**
Innes St. TS2 —1F **51**
Inskip Wlk. TS19 —1D **47**
Institute Ter. TS6 —2E **55**
Instow Clo. TS19 —1D **47**
Inverary Clo. DL1 —2E **113**
Inverness Rd. TS25 —1C **14**
Ipswich Av. TS3 —3E **75**
Irene St. TS13 —2A **66**
Irstead Wlk. TS19 —1D **47**
Irthing Clo. TS17 —4A **86**
Irvin Av. DL14 —4B **102**
Irvin Av. TS12 —1B **62**
Irvine Rd. TS3 —5D **53**
Irvine Rd. TS25 —1C **14**
Isherwood Clo. DL5 —1D **109**
Islay Gro. TS25 —1C **14**
Islington Wlk. TS4 —5C **74**
Italy St. TS2 —2F **51**
Ivanhoe Cres. TS25 —1C **14**
Iveston Gro. TS22 —1C **32**
Iveston Wlk. TS19 —1D **47**
Ivy Clo. DL16 —4C **98**
Ivy Cotts. TS15 —2D **95**
Ivy Gro. TS24 —2D **7**
Ivywood Ct. DL3 —4E **111**

Jack Hatfield Sq. TS1 —3A **52**
(off Fry St.)
Jacklin Wlk. TS16 —4D **85**
Jackson Dri. TS9 —2E **119**
Jackson Pl. DL5 —5F **107**
Jackson's Landing. TS24 —3A **8**
Jackson St. DL16 —3C **98**
Jackson St. TS12 —5C **64**
Jackson St. TS13 —5E **67**
Jackson St. TS25 —2E **11**
Jacques Ct. TS24 —2D **9**
*James Ho. TS2 —2A **52***
(off Garbutt St.)
Jameson Rd. TS20 —4B **32**
Jameson Rd. TS25 —5B **10**
James St. DL1 —4B **112**
James St. DL14 —3D **103**
James St. DL16 —3C **98**
James St. TS3 —4C **52**
James St. TS24 —5B **8**
James Ter. DL14 —5F **103**
Jane Wlk. TS20 —3D **49**
Jarvis Wlk. TS25 —5B **10** & 5C **10**
Jasmine Av. DL4 —3D **105**
Jasmine Gro. TS7 —2D **91**
Jasmine Rd. TS19 —3A **48**
Jay Av. TS17 —5F **87**
Jaywood Clo. TS27 —3A **4**
Jedburgh Dri. DL3 —3A **110**
Jedburgh Rd. TS25 —5B **10**
Jedburgh St. TS1 —4A **52**
Jefferson St. TS3 —4D **53**
Jenison Clo. DL5 —3A **108**
Jenkins Dri. DL14 —5C **102**
Jennings Av. DL4 —3C **104**

Jennings, The. TS6 —2E **77**
Jersey St. TS24 —5A **8**
Jersey Wlk. TS14 —4C **96**
Jervaulx Rd. TS12 —1E **81**
Jervis Ho. TS3 —4F **53**
(off Purfleet Av.)
Jesmond Av. TS5 —3D **73**
Jesmond Ct. DL5 —4A **106**
Jesmond Gdns. TS24 —2D **7**
Jesmond Gro. TS18 —3D **69**
Jesmond M. TS26 —4E **7**
Jesmond Rd. DL1 —3F **113**
Jesmond Rd. TS26 —3D **7**
Jesmond Sq. TS24 —3D **7**
Jobson St. TS26 —4E **7**
John Boyle Clo. TS6 —2C **54**
John Dixon La. DL1 —1C **116**
John Dobbin Rd. DL1 —1A **116**
John F. Kennedy Ho. TS17 —4F **71**
John Howe Gdns. TS24 —5C **4**
Johnson Gro. TS20 —1A **48**
Johnson St. TS1 —3F **51**
Johnson St. TS26 —5F **7**
Johnston Av. TS12 —1C **62**
John St. DL1 —5A **112**
John St. DL4 —3C **104**
John St. TS9 —3B **120**
John St. TS12 —1D **81**
John St. TS13 —4D **67**
John St. TS18 —5B **48**
John St. TS24 —4A **8**
John Ter. DL14 —5F **103**
John Walker Sq. TS18 —1C **70**
Joicey Ct. TS26 —4E **7**
Joicey Pl. DL5 —5F **107**
Jones Rd. TS6 —2C **54**
Jones Rd. TS24 —1D **7**
Joppa Gro. TS25 —5C **10**
Joseph Patterson Cres., The. DL17
　　　　　　　　　—3A **100**
Jowitt Rd. TS24 —1D **7**
Joyce St. TS24 —4C **4**
Jubilee Bank. TS7 —4B **76**
Jubilee Cotts. DL3 —3A **114**
Jubilee Ct. TS6 —2A **78**
Jubilee Cres. DL4 —3D **105**
Jubilee Gro. TS22 —1D **33**
Jubilee Homes. TS25 —1E **11**
Jubilee Rd. DL4 —3D **105**
Jubilee Rd. TS6 —2A **78**
Jubilee St. TS3 —4D **53**
Jubilee St. S. TS3 —4D **53**
Junction Rd. TS19 & TS20
　　　　　　　—5D **31** to 4B **32**
Juniper Gro. TS7 —2A **92**
Juniper Wlk. TS25 —5B **10**
Jupiter Ct. TS3 —5E **53**
Jura Dri. DL1 —2E **113**
Jura Gro. TS25 —5C **10**
Jute Gro. TS25 —5B **10**
Jutland Rd. TS25 —5F **11**

Kader Av. TS5 —5C **72**
Kader Cotts. TS5 —1D **89**
Kader Farm Av. TS5 —1E **89**
Katherine St. DL1 —4A **112**
Kathleen St. TS25 —2F **11**
Kay Gro. DL1 —3D **117**
Kearsley Clo. TS16 —1E **85**
Keasdon Clo. TS3 —1C **74**
Keats Ct. DL1 —3D **117**
Keats Rd. TS6 —2E **77**
Keay St. TS5 —5D **51**
Kebock Wlk. TS25 —5B **10**
Kedleston Clo. TS19 —4E **47**
Kedlestone Pk. TS8 —5F **91**

Kedward Av. TS3 —5F **53**
Keepers La. TS17 —5C **86**
Keighley Clo. TS7 —1C **90**
Keilder Clo. TS10 —3C **42**
Keilder Rise. TS8 —3A **90**
Keir Hardie Clo. TS6 —2C **54**
Keir Hardie Cres. TS6 —3C **54**
Keithlands Av. TS20 —1C **48**
Keith Rd. TS4 —3A **74**
Keith Rd. TS25 —5E **11**
Keithwood Clo. TS4 —3A **74**
Kelbrook Wlk. TS3 —1F **75**
Keld Clo. TS17 —4B **86**
Keld Gro. TS19 —1B **68**
Keldmere. DL16 —1B **98**
Keld Rd. DL5 —5C **106**
Kelfield Av. TS3 —1F **75**
Kelgate Ter. TS8 —5C **88**
Kellawe Pl. DL5 —5F **107**
Kellaw Rd. DL1 —2F **117**
Kelling Clo. TS23 —4F **19**
Kelloe Clo. TS19 —1D **47**
Kells Gro. TS25 —5B **10**
Kelsall Clo. TS3 —3F **75**
Kelso Clo. TS3 —2D **75**
Kelso Gro. TS25 —5B **10**
Kelso Wlk. DL3 —4A **110**
Kelsterne Clo. TS15 —4F **95**
Kelvin Gro. TS3 —2E **75**
Kelvin Gro. TS25 —5B **10**
Kelvin St. DL17 —2B **100**
Kemble Grn. E. DL5 —5F **10**
(off Vane Rd.)
Kemble Grn. N. DL5 —5F **10**
(off Vane Rd.)
Kemble Grn. S. DL5 —5F **10**
(off Vane Rd.)
Kemplah Ho. M. TS14 —3D **97**
Kempston Way. TS20 —5F **31**
Kempthorne Ho. TS3 —4F **53**
(off Purfleet Av.)
Kempton Ct. DL1 —5F **113**
Kendal Clo. DL1 —4F **115**
Kendal Ct. TS4 —2B **74**
Kendal Gro. TS10 —1D **43**
Kendal Rd. TS18 —4F **47**
Kendal Rd. TS25 —2F **11**
Kendrew Clo. DL5 —4E **107**
Kendrew St. DL3 —1A **116**
Kenilworth Av. DL14 —3B **102**
Kenilworth Av. TS3 —3F **75**
Kenilworth Ct. DL5 —3F **107**
Kenilworth Dri. DL3 —4C **110**
Kenilworth Dri. DL14 —3B **102**
Kenilworth Flats. TS23 —1F **33**
Kenilworth Rd. TS23 —1F **33**
Kenilworth Way. TS10 —2A **44**
Kenley Gdns. TS20 —4F **31**
Kenmir Ct. DL16 —3D **99**
Kenmore Rd. TS3 —2B **76**
Kennedy Cres. TS13 —2A **66**
Kennedy Gdns. TS23 —1F **33**
Kennedy Gro. TS20 —1A **48**
Kennel La. DL1 —4E **113**
Kennythorpe. TS7 —3A **92**
Kenny Wlk. DL5 —1F **109**
Kensington. DL14 —4D 10
(off Seymour St.)
Kensington Av. TS6 —3E **77**
Kensington Ct. TS24 —1D **7**
Kensington Gdns. DL1 —3D **117**
Kensington Gdns. DL17 —2C **100**
Kensington Rd. TS5 —5E **51**
Kensington Rd. TS18 —2A **70**
Kensington S. DL14 —4D 10
(off Seymour St.)

Kent Av. TS25 —2F **11**
Kent Clo. DL3 —1A **112**
Kent Clo. TS7 —3C **92**
Kent Clo. TS10 —2C **42**
Kent Clo. TS18 —3D **69**
Kent Gro. TS20 —1D **49**
Kentmere. DL16 —1B **98**
Kentmere Rd. TS3 —2D **75**
Kenton Clo. TS18 —3D **69**
Kentport Ct. TS18 —4D **49**
Kent Rd. TS14 —4C **96**
Kenville Gro. TS19 —4B **46**
Kepier Clo. TS19 —1D **47**
Kepple Av. TS3 —2D **75**
Kepwick Clo. TS5 —5F **73**
Kepwick Clo. TS10 —3C **42**
Kerr Cres. TS21 —3B **118**
Kerr Rd. TS25 —5B **10**
Kerridge Clo. TS11 —4D **45**
Kesteven Rd. TS4 —1C **90**
Kesteven Rd. TS25 —1B **14**
Kestrel Av. TS3 —4E **53**
Kestrel Clo. DL1 —2E **117**
Kestrel Clo. TS20 —3C **32**
Kestrel Hide. TS14 —3A **96**
Keswick Dri. DL16 —2E **99**
Keswick Gro. TS5 —5D **73**
Keswick Rd. TS6 —1D **77**
Keswick Rd. TS10 —1D **43**
Keswick Rd. TS23 —5F **33**
Keswick St. TS26 —1E **11**
Kettleness Av. TS10 —1A **42**
Kettlewell Clo. TS23 —4F **19**
Ketton Av. DL3 —1A **112**
Ketton Rd. TS19 —2E **47**
Ketton Row. TS1 —3E **51**
Ketton Way. DL5 —5D **109**
Keverstone Clo. TS19 —2E **47**
Keverstone Gro. TS23 —3A **20**
Kew Gdns. TS20 —4F **31**
Kew Rise. DL3 —1C **114**
Kew Rise. TS6 —4D **77**
Kexwith Moor Clo. DL1 —5E **117**
Keynes Clo. TS6 —3D **55**
Keynsham Av. TS3 —3F **75**
Kielder Clo. TS22 —1B **32**
Kielder Dri. DL1 —4D **113**
Kilbride Clo. TS17 —4F **71**
Kilbride Clo. TS11 —2B **60**
Kilburn Ho. DL1 —4C **116**
Kilburn Rd. TS4 —3B **74**
Kilburn Rd. TS18 —2E **69**
Kilburn St. DL4 —5D **105**
Kilburns Yd. DL14 —1C **102**
Kildale Gro. TS10 —1B **42**
Kildale Gro. TS19 —1B **68**
Kildale Gro. TS25 —1B **16**
Kildale Ho. TS4 —2C **74**
Kildale Moor Pl. DL1 —4E **117**
Kildale Rd. TS4 —1B **74**
Kildale Rd. TS23 —3E **33**
Kildare St. TS1 —5E **51**
Kildwick Gro. TS3 —3F **75**
Kilkenny Rd. TS14 —4E **97**
Killerby Clo. TS19 —1E **47**
Killhope Gro. DL14 —5A **102**
Killinghall Gro. TS18 —1B **68**
Killinghall St. DL1 —5C **112**
Killin Rd. DL1 —2E **113**
Kilmarnock Rd. DL1 —2E **113**
Kilmarnock Rd. TS25 —5B **10**
Kilmory Wlk. TS25 —5B **10**
Kilnwick Clo. TS23 —3A **20**
Kilsyth Gro. TS25 —5B **10**
Kilton Clo. TS10 —2F **43**
Kilton Clo. TS19 —1E **47**
Kilton Ct. TS4 —2A **74**

Kilton Dri. TS12 —4D **65**
Kilton La. TS12 & TS13
                    —5A **82** to 4D **65**
Kilton Thorpe La. TS12 —3D **83**
Kilwick St. TS24 —1F **11**
Kimberley Dri. TS3 —1E **75**
Kimberley St. TS26 —1E **11**
Kimble Dri. TS17 —1D **87**
Kimblesworth Wlk. DL5 —3D **107**
Kimblesworth Wlk. TS25 —2E **47**
Kimmerton Av. TS5 —1D **89**
Kinbrace Rd. TS25 —5B **10**
Kindersley St. TS3 —4D **53**
Kinderton Gro. TS20 —5F **31**
Kingcraft Rd. TS7 —1C **90**
King Edward's Rd. TS1 —4F **51**
King Edward's Sq. TS1 —4F **51**
King Edward St. DL4 —2D **105**
King Edward Ter. TS11 —4D **45**
Kingfisher Dri. TS14 —3A **96**
King Georges Ter. TS6 —2A **54**
King James St. DL16 —2C **98**
King Oswy Dri. TS24 —3B **4**
Kings Ct. TS20 —5C **32**
Kingsdale Clo. TS15 —5C **94**
Kingsdown Way. TS11 —2B **60**
Kings Ho. DL5 —4D **107**
Kings Ho. TS1 —3A **52**
Kingsley Av. TS25 —3D **11**
Kingsley Clo. TS6 —4F **55**
Kingsley Rd. TS6 —4F **55**
Kingsley Rd. TS18 —1D **69**
Kingsport Clo. TS18 —4E **49**
King's Rd. TS3 —4C **52** to 5D **53**
Kings Rd. TS5 —1E **73**
Kings Rd. TS22 —5D **19**
Kingston Av. TS5 —3E **73**
Kingston Rd. TS20 —3C **48**
Kingston St. DL3 —1F **115**
Kingston St. TS1 —4F **51**
King St. DL3 —1A **116** & 2A **116**
King St. DL16 —2C **98**
King St. TS6 —2B **54**
King St. TS10 —4E **29**
King St. TS17 —2D **71**
King St. TS18 —5C **48**
King St. TS25 —2A **12**
Kingsway. DL1 —2C **112**
Kingsway. DL14 —1D **103**
Kingsway. TS23 —1E **33** & 1F **33**
Kingsway Arc. DL14 —1D **103**
Kingsway Av. TS6 —4C **54**
King William Ct. DL16 —2C 98
(off High Grange Rd.)
King William Grange. DL16 —2C **98**
King William St. DL1 —3C **116**
Kininvie Rd. TS10 —4D **43**
Kininvie Wlk. TS19 —1E **47**
Kinloch Rd. TS6 —1D **77**
Kinloss Clo. TS17 —1F **87**
Kinloss Wlk. TS17 —1F **87**
Kinross Av. TS3 —3F **75**
Kinross Gro. TS25 —5B **10**
Kintra Rd. TS25 —5B **10**
Kintyre Clo. DL1 —2E **113**
Kintyre Dri. TS17 —2D **87**
Kintyre Wlk. TS14 —4C 96
(off Hutton La.)
Kinver Clo. TS3 —2D **75**
Kipling Gro. TS19 —1C **68**
Kipling Rd. TS25 —2C **10**
Kirby Av. TS5 —2C **72**
Kirby Clo. TS6 —5B **56**
Kirby Clo. TS23 —1A **34**
Kirby Ho. DL1 —4D **117**
Kirby Wlk. TS10 —2D **43**
Kirkbright Clo. TS12 —5F **81**

Kirkby Clo. DL1 —5C 112
Kirkdale. DL16 —2B 98
Kirkdale. TS14 —4A 96
Kirkdale Clo. TS19 —4F 47
Kirkdale Way. TS5 —5F 73
Kirkfell Clo. TS16 —4C 84
Kirkfield Rd. DL3 —1A 112
Kirkgate Rd. TS5 —3D 73
Kirkham Clo. DL5 —3E 107
Kirkham Rd. TS7 —2C 92
Kirkham Row. TS4 —3C 74
Kirkham Way. DL14 —3F 103
Kirklands. The. TS11 —4E 45
Kirkland Wlk. TS3 —3E 75
Kirkleatham Av. TS11 —4E 45
Kirkleatham Bus. Pk. TS10 —4B 42
Kirkleatham By-Pass. TS10 —1B 58
Kirkleatham La. TS10
—4B 28 to 1A 58
Kirkleatham St. TS10 —4B 28
Kirklevington Grange. TS15 —5F 95
Kirklevington Wlk. TS19 —1D 47
Kirknewton Clo. TS19 —1E 47
Kirknewton Gro. TS17 —4A 86
Kirknewton Rd. TS6 —2D 77
Kirk Rd. TS15 —4F 95
Kirkstall Av. TS3 —3F 75
Kirkstall Ct. TS12 —1E 81
Kirkstall Cres. DL3 —4C 110
Kirkstone Ct. TS24 —2E 7
Kirkstone Gro. TS10 —1D 43
Kirkstone Gro. TS24 —2D 7
Kirkstone Pl. DL5 —1B 108
Kirkstone Rd. TS3 —2D 75
Kirkview. DL16 —3B 98
Kirkwall Clo. TS19 —4A 46
Kirriemuir Rd. TS25 —5B 10
Kitchen Av. DL14 —5B 102
Kitchener St. DL3 —5F 111
Kitchener Ter. DL17 —3D 101
Kitching Gro. DL3 —2A 112
Knaith Clo. TS15 —5B 94
Knapton Av. TS22 —5B 18
Knaresborough Av. TS7 —4E 91
Knaresborough Clo. TS27 —5B 4
Knayton Gro. TS19 —1B 68
Knighton Ct. TS17 —5F 71
Knightsbridge Av. DL1 —3F 113
Knightsport Rd. TS18 —4D 49
Knitsley Wlk. TS19 —1E 47
Knole Rd. TS23 —5F 19
Knoll Av. DL3 —3D 115
Knotty Hill Golf Cen. TS21
—1A 118
Knowles St. TS18 —5C 48
Kreuger All. TS3 —4C 52
Kyle Av. TS25 —2E 11

Laburnum Av. TS17 —5D 71
Laburnum Ct. TS18 —1A 70
Laburnum Gro. TS2 —5A 36
Laburnum Rd. DL1 —1B 112
Laburnum Rd. DL14 —3D 103
Laburnum Rd. TS6 —5C 54
Laburnum Rd. TS7 —5C 76
Laburnum Rd. TS10 —5F 29
Laburnum Rd. TS12 —4B 64
Laburnum Rd. TS26 —2D 85
Laburnum St. TS26 —4E 7
Lacey Gro. TS26 —3D 7
Lackenby La. TS6 —4A 56 to 5C 56
Lackenby Rd. TS6 —4D 57
Ladgate La. TS5, TS8, TS4 & TS3
—2F 89 to 4A 76
Ladgate View. TS3 —2E 75
Ladybower. DL5 —4A 106

Lady Kathryn Gro. DL3 —4F 111
Ladyport Grn. TS18 —4D 49
Ladysmith Clo. DL14 —2C 102
Ladysmith St. DL14 —2C 102
Ladysmith St. TS25 —2A 12
Lagonda Ct. TS23 —5D 21
Lagonda Rd. TS23 —1C 34
Laindon Av. TS4 —5D 75
Laing Caravan Site. TS10 —4A 28
Laing Clo. TS6 —2E 55
Laing St. DL3 —4D 111
Laing St. TS18 —5B 48
Laird Rd. TS25 —5B 10
Lakes Av. TS10 —5D 29
Lakeside. DL1 —4F 115
Lakeside Ct. DL16 —2E 99
Lakeston Clo. TS26 —4B 6
Lamb Clo. DL5 —4E 107
Lamberd Rd. TS24 —5D 5
Lambert Ter. TS13 —1F 67
Lambeth Rd. TS5 —2E 73
Lamb La. TS17 —3A 86
Lambourne Dri. TS7 —2F 91
Lambton Clo. DL5 —2E 109
Lambton Cres. TS21 —5B 118
(in two parts)
Lambton Dri. DL14 —3B 102
Lambton Lodge. TS21 —4B 118
Lambton Rd. DL17 —3E 101
Lambton Rd. TS4 —1B 74
Lambton Rd. TS19 —4A 48
Lambton Rd. TS23 —5A 20
Lambton St. DL1 —5A 11
(off Progress Way)
Lambton St. DL4 —3B 104
Lambton St. TS6 —2E 77
Lambton St. TS24 —5A 8
Lambton St. Ind. Est. DL4
—4A 104
Lammermuir Clo. DL1 —3D 113
Lammermuir Rd. TS23 —1E 33
Lamonby Clo. TS7 —3A 92
Lamont Gro. TS25 —5A 10
Lamport Clo. TS18 —4E 49
Lamport St. TS1 —4D 51
Lanark Clo. TS19 —4C 46
Lanark Rd. TS25 —5A 10
Lancaster Clo. TS24 —3F 7
Lancaster Dri. TS11 —4C 44
Lancaster Ho. TS6 —4F 55
Lancaster Rd. TS5 —2F 73
Lancaster Rd. TS16 —4A 84
Lancaster Rd. TS24 —2F 7
Lancaster Way. TS17 —2E 87
Lancefield Rd. TS20 —4C 32
Lancelot St. TS26 —4D 7
Lanchester Av. TS23 —4E 19
Lanchester Rd. TS6 —2E 55
Landor Rd. TS3 —5A 54
Lane End Cotts. TS15 —5E 95
Lanehouse Rd. TS17 —3D 71
Lane Pl. TS6 —3E 55
Laneside Rd. TS18 —2E 69
Lane, The. TS21 —4C 118
Lanethorpe Cres. DL1 —3E 117
Lanethorpe Rd. DL1 —4E 117
Langbaurgh Clo. TS9 —3B 120
(in two parts)
Langbaurgh Ct. TS12 —1D 63
(Saltburn)
Langbaurgh Ct. TS12 —1D 81
(Skelton)
Langdale. TS14 —4A 96
Langdale Clo. TS16 —1D 95
Langdale Cres. TS6 —5F 55

Langdale Gro. TS5 —4E 73
Langdale Pl. DL5 —5B 106
Langdale Rd. DL1 —3C 116
Langdale Rd. TS23 —4F 33
Langdale Wlk. DL14 —5A 102
Langdon Sq. TS8 —3C 90
Langham Wlk. TS19 —5B 46
Langholm Cres. DL3 —2F 115
Langleeford Way. TS17 —4A 86
Langley Av. TS17 —3E 71
Langley Clo. TS10 —4D 43
Langley Ct. TS3 —3E 75
Langley Gro. DL14 —3B 102
Langley Ho. TS24 —2D 9
(off Union St.)
Langley Rd. DL5 —5F 107
Langmere. DL16 —1B 98
Langridge Cres. TS3 —2D 75
Langsett Av. TS3 —2D 75
Langthorne Gro. TS18 —2B 68
Langthorpe. TS7 —3A 92
Langthwaite Wlk. TS10 —3D 43
Langton Av. TS22 —1B 32
Langton Clo. TS4 —1A 74
Langton Wlk. DL1 —4C 116
Lanroad Grn. TS4 —1C 74
Lansbury Clo. TS6 —3B 54
Lansbury Gro. TS24 —4F 7
Lansdowne Ct. TS4 —5B 52
Lansdowne Ct. TS26 —5E 7
Lansdowne Rd. TS4 —5B 52
Lansdowne Rd. TS12 —5C 64
Lansdowne Rd. TS15 —3E 95
Lansdowne Rd. TS17 —4F 71
Lansdowne Rd. TS26 —5E 7
Lansdowne St. DL3 —3A 112
Lansdown Way. TS23 —4B 20
Lanshaw Grn. TS4 —1C 74
Lantsbery Dri. TS13 —5B 66
Lanyard, The. TS24 —4A 8
Lapwing La. TS20 —4B 32
Larch Av. DL4 —3E 105
Larch Clo. TS7 —2A 92
Larch Cres. TS16 —2E 85
Larches, The. TS6 —5C 54
Larches, The. TS7 —4C 76
Larches, The. TS10 —1F 43
Larches, The. TS19 —3D 47
Larchfield St. DL3 —2F 115
Larch Gro. TS24 —2E 7
Larch Rd. TS14 —2D 97
Larch Rd. TS19 —3B 48
Larch Ter. TS2 —5A 36
Largo Gdns. DL1 —2D 113
Lark Dri. TS14 —3A 96
Larkhall Sq. TS20 —2C 48
Larkspur Dri. DL1 —2C 116
Larkspur Rd. TS7 —2C 90
Larkswood Rd. TS10 —4D 43
Larun Beat, The. TS15 —4D 95
Larvick Ct. TS13 —1B 66
Lascelles Av. DL5 —4A 106
Lastingham Av. TS6 —1F 77
Latham Rd. TS5 —1E 73
Latimer Clo. TS15 —5B 94
Latimer La. TS14 —4C 96
Latimer Rd. DL1 —4D 113
Lauder Clo. TS19 —4C 46
Lauderdale Dri. TS14 —4E 97
Lauder Ho. TS19 —4C 46
Lauder St. TS24 —4F 7
Laura St. TS1 —5A 52
Laurel Av. TS4 —3B 74
Laurel Av. TS17 —5D 71
Laurel Clo. TS12 —2D 63
Laurel Ct. DL4 —4D 105
Laurel Cres. TS12 —4B 64

Laurel Pk. TS13 —5C **66**
Laurel Rd. TS7 —2E **91**
Laurel Rd. TS10 —1F **43**
Laurel Rd. TS12 —2D **63**
Laurel Rd. TS16 —2E **85**
(in two parts)
Laurel Rd. TS19 —3A **48**
Laurel St. DL3 —5E **111**
Laurel St. TS1 —4A **52**
Laurel Way. DL14 —2D **103**
Lauriston Clo. DL3 —2A **114**
Lavan Sands. TS5 —2C **88**
Lavender Ct. TS11 —5E **45**
Lavender Rd. TS3 —5D **53**
Lavernock Clo. TS10 —3F **43**
Lawns, The. TS24 —2D **9**
Lawnswood Rd. TS3 —1B **76**
Lawrence Rd. TS17
—5C **70** & 5D **71**
Lawrence St. DL1 —2C **116**
Lawrence St. TS10 —5E **29**
Lawrence St. TS18 —1B **70**
Lawson Clo. TS6 —3C **54**
Lawson Ind. Est. TS3 —4D **53**
Lawson Rd. TS25 —4C **12**
Lawson St. TS18 —1B **70**
Lawson Wlk. TS18 —1B **70**
Lawson Way. TS3 —3D **53**
Lax Ter. TS22 —3D **19**
Laxton Clo. TS23 —4E **19**
Laycock St. TS1 —4D **51**
Layland Rd. TS12 —1E **81**
Layton Ct. DL5 —3E **107**
Lazenby Bank Rd. TS6 & TS14
—5D **57** to 2F **79**
Lazenby Clo. DL3 —1C **114**
Lazenby Cres. DL3 —1C **114**
Lazenby Gro. DL3 —1C **114**
Lazenby Rd. TS24 —4C **4**
Leach Gro. DL3 —4D **111**
Leadenhall St. DL1 —4A **112**
Leafield Rd. DL1 —3A **116**
Leahope Ct. TS17 —1F **87**
Lealholm Cres. TS3 —3F **75**
Lealholme Gro. TS19 —1C **68**
Lealholm Wlk. TS6 —5A **56**
Lealholm Way. TS14 —5D **97**
Leamington Dri. TS25 —2F **11**
Leamington Gro. TS3 —3A **76**
Leamington Pde. TS25 —2F **11**
Leam La. TS3 —3B **46**
Leas Gro. TS24 —1B **8**
Leaside. DL5 —2D **109**
Leaside N. DL5 —2D **109**
Leas, The. DL1 —2B **112**
Leas, The. TS10 —2F **43**
Leas, The. TS21 —5B **118**
Leas Wlk. TS24 —1B **8**
Leckfell Clo. TS7 —3A **92**
Ledbury Dri. TS5 —2E **89**
Ledbury Dri. TS17 —1D **87**
Ledbury Way. TS14 —4D **97**
Leeds St. TS18 —5B **48**
Lee Grn. DL5 —1D **109**
Leeholme Rd. TS23 —1A **34**
Leeming Rd. TS5 —2D **73**
Lee Rd. TS6 —2E **55** & 2F **55**
Lees Rd. TS1 —4E **51**
Leicester Gro. DL1 —4F **113**
Leicester Ho. TS6 —4F **55**
Leicester Rd. TS20 —1D **49**
Leicester Way. TS16 —1B **94**
Leighton Rd. TS6 —3F **55**
Leighton Rd. TS18 —3C **68**
Leighton Ter. TS27 —5B **4**
Leinster St. TS1 —5D **51**
Leith Rd. DL3 —2B **114**

Leith Wlk. TS17 —3E **87**
Lenham Clo. TS22 —5B **18**
Lennox Cres. TS23 —2E **33**
Lennox St. TS1 —4A **52**
Lennox Wlk. TS25
—5A **10** & 5B **10**
Leonard Ropner Dri. TS19 —4B **46**
Leonard St. TS18 —3B **116**
Leopold Pl. DL14 —3D **103**
Lerwick Clo. TS19 —5A **46**
Letch La. TS21 & TS19 —5A **30**
Letch Rd. TS20 —5C **32**
Letitia Ind. Est. TS5 —4C **50**
Letitia St. TS5 —4C **50**
Leven Bank. TS17 —5A **86**
Leven Clo. TS9 —4E **119**
Leven Clo. TS16 —1C **94**
Leven Ct. TS9 —4C **120**
Levendale Clo. TS15 —4F **95**
Leven Gdns. DL1 —2C **112**
Leven Gro. TS17 —4E **71**
Leven Gro. TS25 —5B **10**
Leven Rd. TS3 —4D **53**
Leven Rd. TS9 —4D **119**
Leven Rd. TS14 —4C **96**
Leven Rd. TS15 —4D **95**
Leven Rd. TS20 —1B **48**
Levenside. TS9 —4A **120**
(Great Ayton)
Levenside. TS9 —4E **119**
(Stokesley)
Leven St. TS1 —4D **51**
Leven St. TS6 —2B **54**
Leven St. TS12 —1D **63**
Leven St. TS23 —3E **35**
Levens Wlk. TS10 —1D **43**
Leven Wynd. TS9 —4E **119**
Leveret Clo. TS17 —4D **87**
Levick Cres. TS5 —4B **72**
Levick Ho. TS5 —3D **73**
Levington Wynd. TS7 —4B **92**
Levisham Clo. TS5 —4F **73**
Levisham Clo. TS18 —2E **69**
Lewes Rd. DL1 —3C **116**
Lewes Way. TS23 —3B **20**
Lewis Gro. TS25 —3B **10**
Lewis Rd. TS5 —1E **73**
Lewis Wlk. TS14 —4C **96**
Lexden Av. TS5 —4C **72**
Lexington St. TS20 —2C **48**
Leybourne Ter. TS18 —1A **70**
Leyburn Gro. TS18 —3C **68**
Leyburn Rd. DL1 —3B **112**
Leyburn St. TS26 —1E **11**
Lichfield Av. TS6 —5F **55**
Lichfield Av. TS16 —4B **84**
Lichfield Rd. TS5 —2A **74**
Liddell Clo. DL5 —5F **107**
(in two parts)
Lightfoot Cres. TS24 —1D **7**
Lightfoot Gro. TS18 —1B **70**
Lightfoot Rd. DL5 —5D **107**
Lightfoot Ter. DL17 —3B **100**
Light Pipe Hall Rd. TS18 —1A **70**
(in two parts)
Lilac Av. TS17 —5D **71**
Lilac Av. TS21 —4B **118**
Lilac Clo. TS6 —4D **57**
Lilac Clo. TS12 —2B **62**
Lilac Ct. DL4 —4E **105**
Lilac Cres. TS12 —4B **64**
Lilac Gro. TS3 —5F **53**
Lilac Gro. TS10 —5F **29**
Lilac Rd. TS6 —5D **55**
Lilac Rd. TS7 —4B **96**
Lilac Rd. TS16 —2D **85**
Lilac Rd. TS19 —3A **48**

Lilburn Clo. DL4 —3C **104**
Lilburne Cres. DL5 —5D **107**
Lile Gdns. TS21 —5C **118**
Limber Grn. TS3 —2B **76**
Limbrick Av. TS19 —5B **46**
Limbrick Ct. TS19 —5C **46**
Lime Av. DL1 —1B **112**
Lime Clo. TS7 —2E **91**
Lime Cres. TS7 —1D **77**
Lime Cres. TS11 —5E **45**
Lime Cres. TS24 —2E **7**
Lime Gro. DL4 —3E **105**
Lime Gro. DL14 —5C **102**
Lime Gro. TS19 —5D **47**
Limehurst Rd. DL3 —5E **111**
Limeoak Way. TS18 —4D **49**
Limerick Rd. TS10 —1E **41**
Lime Rd. DL17 —2C **100**
Lime Rd. TS6 —5C **54**
Lime Rd. TS10 —4F **29** & 5F **29**
Lime Rd. TS14 —2D **97**
Lime Rd. TS16 —1E **85**
Limes Rd. TS5 —2F **73**
Limetree Ct. TS4 —3A **74**
Limetrees Clo. TS23 —4F **35**
Lime Wlk. TS13 —4C **66**
Limpton Ga. TS15 —5D **95**
Linacre Way. DL1 —3B **112**
Linburn Dri. DL14 —5A **102**
Linby Av. TS3 —3D **75**
Lincoln Clo. DL5 —5D **107**
Lincoln Ct. DL1 —4F **113**
Lincoln Cres. TS23 —2A **34**
Lincoln Gro. TS20 —2D **49**
Lincoln Pl. TS17 —4D **71**
Lincoln Rd. TS10 —2A **44**
Lincoln Rd. TS14 —4D **97**
Lincoln Rd. TS25 —1B **14**
Lincombe Dri. TS5 —3E **89**
Linden Av. DL3 —3D **115**
Linden Av. TS9 —3A **120**
Linden Av. TS18 —3F **69**
Linden Clo. DL4 —4E **105**
Linden Clo. TS9 —3A **120**
Linden Ct. DL16 —3D **99**
Linden Ct. TS9 —3A **120**
Linden Ct. TS17 —4D **71**
Linden Cres. TS7 —3D **91**
Linden Cres. TS9 —3A **120**
Linden Dri. DL3 —3E **115**
Linden Gro. TS5 —2E **73**
Linden Gro. TS9 —3A **120**
Linden Gro. TS17 —4D **71**
Linden Gro. TS26 —5D **7**
Linden Ho. TS1 —4B **64**
Linden Pl. DL5 —1B **108**
Linden Rd. DL14 —3D **103**
Linden Rd. DL17 —3E **101**
Linden Rd. TS9 —3A **120**
Linden Rd. TS12 —4B **64**
Linden Ter. DL17 —5F **101**
Lindisfarne Clo. TS27 —4B **4**
Lindisfarne Ct. DL1 —3E **113**
Lindisfarne Rd. TS3 —3F **75**
Lindrick. TS8 —4F **91**
Lindrick Ct. TS6 —2F **77**
Lindrick Dri. TS27 —4A **4**
Lindrick Rd. TS11 —2A **60**
Lindsay Rd. TS25 —5A **10**
Lindsay St. DL14 —2C **102**
Lindsay St. TS18 —2B **70**
Lindsey Ct. TS12 —5D **65**
Lingard Wlk. DL5 —2F **109**
Lingberry Garth. TS13 —4D **67**
Ling Clo. TS7 —1D **91**
Lingdale Clo. TS19 —4F **47**
Lingdale Dri. TS25 —1B **16**

Lingdale Gro. TS10 —2A **42**
Lingdale Ind. Est. TS12 —5F **81**
Lingdale Rd. TS12 —5D **81**
Lingdale Rd. TS17 —5E **71**
Lingfield Ash. TS8 —5C **90**
Lingfield Clo. DL1 —1F **117**
Lingfield Dri. TS16 —5B **84**
Lingfield Est. DL1 —1F **117**
Lingfield Grn. DL1 —2E **117**
Lingfield Rd. TS15 —3F **95**
Lingfield Rd. TS19 —5C **46**
Lingfield Way. TS8 —5D **91**
Lingford Ct. DL14 —2D **103**
Lingholme. TS10 —2C **42**
Lingmell Rd. TS10 —2D **43**
Link Cen. TS18 —5B **48**
  (off Farrer St.)
Links, The. TS12 —3C **62**
Links, The. TS25 —1C **16**
Link, The. TS3 —3A **76**
Linkway, The. TS23 —1A **34**
Linley Ct. TS20 —3B **32**
Linlithgow Clo. TS14 —4D **97**
Linmoor Av. TS3 —1E **75**
Linnet Ct. TS20 —3C **32**
Linsley Clo. TS3 —4C **52**
Linthorpe M. TS1 —3F **51**
  (in two parts)
Linthorpe Rd. TS5 & TS1
  —1F **73** to 2F **51**
Linton Av. TS7 —3D **91**
Linton Clo. TS19 —3C **46**
Linton Rd. TS6 —2C **76**
Linwood Av. TS9 —2F **119**
Linwood Ct. TS14 —2E **97**
Linwood Gro. DL3 —4D **115**
Lisle Rd. DL5 —4B **106**
Lismore Dri. DL1 —2E **113**
Lister St. TS26 & TS24 —1E **11**
Lithgo Clo. TS25 —3C **12**
Lit. Ayton La. TS9 —4B **120**
Littlebeck Dri. DL1 —3C **112**
Littleboy Dri. TS17 —4F **71**
Lit. Brown St. TS18 —1C **70**
Lit. Crake. TS14 —3B **96**
Lit. Grebe. TS14 —3A **96**
Little La. DL5 —4F **109**
Lit. York St. TS18 —1B **70**
Littondale. TS8 —5E **89**
Littondale Ct. TS17 —4A **86**
Liverton Av. TS5 —5D **51**
Liverton Cres. TS17 —2C **86**
Liverton Cres. TS22 —5C **18**
Liverton Rd. TS13 —5A **66**
  (Liverton, in two parts)
Liverton Rd. TS13 —4C **66**
  (Loftus)
Liverton Ter. TS13 —5B **66**
Liverton Ter. S. TS13 —5B **66**
Liverton Whin. TS12 —1B **62**
Livingstone Rd. TS3 —5D **53**
Lizard Wlk. TS24 —5A **8**
Lloyd St. TS2 —2E **51**
Lobelia Clo. TS7 —4C **76**
Lobster Rd. TS10 —4C **28**
Loch Gro. TS25 —5B **10**
Lockerbie Wlk. TS17 —1D **87**
Locke Rd. TS10 —5C **28**
Lockheed Clo. TS18 —1A **86**
Lock St. DL3 —3A **112**
Lockton Clo. TS8 —4D **89**
Lockton Cres. TS17 —2C **86**
Lockwood Ct. TS6 —2F **77**
Lockyer Clo. DL5 —4B **106**
Locomotive St. DL1 —3C **112**
Lodge Rd. TS6 —1F **77**
Lodge St. DL1 —1B **116**

Lodge St. TS18 —1B **70**
Lodore Gro. TS5 —5C **72**
Loftus Bank. TS13 —3A **66**
Loftus Ho. TS4 —2B **74**
Loftus Rd. TS17 —4E **71**
Logan Dri. TS19 —5D **47**
Logan Gro. TS25 —5B **10**
Lombard Ct. DL1 —4F **115**
Lomond Av. TS23 —2F **33**
Londonderry St. TS24 —3D **9**
Londonderry St. TS24 —3D **9**
Longacre Clo. TS12 —4D **63**
Longbank Rd. TS7 —5C **76**
Longbeck La. TS11 —2D **59**
Longbeck Rd. TS11 —5C **44**
Longbeck Trading Est. TS11
  —4C **44**
Longbeck Way. TS17 —3F **87**
Longcroft Wlk. TS3 —5D **53**
Longfellow Rd. TS23 —4E **19**
Longfellow Wlk. TS25 —4B **10**
Longfield Rd. DL3 —2A **112**
Longfield Rd. DL14 —5E **103**
Longfield View. TS6 —4D **77**
Longford Clo. TS23 —5F **19**
Longford St. TS1 —5D **51**
Longhill Ind. Est. TS25
  (in two parts)   —2A **12** & 3A **12**
Longhirst. TS8 —4D **91**
Longlands Rd. TS4 & TS3 —5C **52**
Long Newton La. TS21 —5B **68**
Longridge. TS7 —4F **91**
Longscar Wlk. TS24 —5A **8**
Longshaw Clo. TS17 —5D **87**
Long Wlk. TS15 —3E **95**
Longworth Way. TS14 —1F **97**
Lonsdale Ct. TS25 —1F **11**
Lonsdale Dri. TS11 —5F **45**
Lonsdale St. TS1 —5E **51**
Loraine Clo. TS11 —5F **45**
Loraine Cres. DL1 —4F **115**
Loraine Wlk. DL5 —4D **107**
Lord Av. TS17 —4E **71**
Lord Nelson's Yd. TS15 —3C **94**
Lord Neville Dri. DL5 —2A **108**
Lord St. TS10 —4D **29**
Lorimer Clo. TS17 —4C **86**
Lorne St. TS1 —4E **51**
Lorne Ter. TS12 —4D **65**
Lorn Wlk. DL1 —2E **113**
Lorrain Gro. TS20 —4D **33**
Lorton Rd. TS10 —2D **43**
Lothian Clo. DL16 —4B **98**
Lothian Gro. TS10 —5B **28**
Lothian Rd. TS4 —5B **52**
Lough Ho. Bank. DL17 —4F **101**
Louisa St. DL1 —2C **116**
Lovaine St. TS1 —4E **51**
Lovaine Ter. DL17 —3E **101**
Lovat Av. TS10 —5B **28**
Lovat Gro. TS25 —5B **10**
Low Chu. Wynd. TS15 —2C **94**
  (in two parts)
Low Cleveland St. TS13 —5B **66**
Lowcross Av. TS14 —4B **96**
Lowdale La. TS24 —3A **4**
Lowell Clo. TS23 —2F **19**
Lwr. Bridge St. DL14 —1C **102**
Lwr. East St. TS2 —2A **52**
Lwr. Feversham St. TS2 —2A **52**
Lwr. Gosford St. TS2 —2A **52**
Lwr. Promenade. TS10 —1D **63**
Lowery Rd. DL5 —1C **108**
Lowe St. DL3 —1A **116**
Loweswater Cres. TS18 —5E **47**
Loweswater Gro. TS10 —5D **29**
Low Farm Dri. TS10 —2C **42**

Lowfield Av. TS3 —5F **53**
Lowfields. DL5 —3A **108**
Lowfields Av. TS17 —4C **86**
Lowfields Grn. TS17 —4C **86**
Lowfields Wlk. TS17 —4D **87**
Low Fold. TS10 —1C **42**
Low Grange Av. TS23
  —2A **20** to 5A **20**
Low Grange Ct. TS23 —4B **20**
Low Grange Rd. DL16 —2D **99**
Low Grn. DL5 —2E **107**
Low Grn. TS9 —4A **120**
Lowick Clo. TS19 —4C **46**
Low La. TS8 & TS5 —5A **88** to 2F **89**
Low La. TS17 —5B **86**
Lowmead Wlk. TS3 —4E **75**
Low Melbourne St. DL14 —4D **103**
Lowmoor Rd. DL11 —4E **117**
Lowood Av. TS7 —3D **91**
Lowson St. DL3 —2A **112**
Lowther Clo. TS22 —5B **18**
Lowther Dri. DL5 —3E **107**
Lowther Rd. DL14 —5B **102**
Lowthian Rd. TS26 & TS24 —4F **7**
Loxley Rd. TS3 —1B **76**
Loyalty Clo. TS25 —4F **11**
Loyalty Ct. TS25 —3F **11**
Loyalty M. TS25 —3F **11**
Loyalty Rd. TS25 —4F **11**
Loy La. TS13 —4E **67**
Lucan St. TS24 —5F **7**
Luccombe Clo. TS17 —5A **86**
Lucerne Ct. TS7 —2D **91**
Lucerne Dri. TS14 —4B **96**
Lucerne Rd. TS10 —1D **43**
Luce Sands. TS5 —2C **88**
Lucia La. TS14 —4C **96**
Lucknow St. DL1 —5C **112**
Ludford Av. TS3 —2E **75**
Ludham Gro. TS19 —3D **47**
Ludlow Cres. TS10 —2F **43**
Ludlow Rd. TS23 —5E **19**
Luff Way. TS10 —2F **43**
Lulsgate. TS17 —1F **87**
Lulworth Gro. TS24 —4B **4**
Lumley Clo. DL5 —1E **109**
Lumley Clo. DL16 —1D **99**
Lumley Cres. DL17 —3E **101**
Lumley Gro. DL14 —4B **102**
Lumley Rd. TS10 —5E **29**
Lumley Rd. TS23 —5F **19**
Lumley Sq. TS24 —2D **9**
Lumley St. TS13 —4B **66**
Lumley Ter. TS14 —2E **97**
Lumpsey Clo. TS12 —4C **64**
Lundy Ct. TS17 —5C **86**
Lundy Wlk. TS14 —4D **97**
  (off Hutton La.)
Lunebeck Wlk. TS17 —3F **87**
Lunedale Av. TS5 —4E **73**
Lunedale Rd. DL3 —5C **110**
Lunedale Rd. TS23 —2E **33**
Lune Rd. TS16 —1C **94**
Lune Rd. TS20 —1B **48**
Lune St. TS12 —2D **63**
Lusby Cres. DL14 —5B **102**
Lustrum Av. TS18 —3A **50**
Lustrum Ind. Est. TS18 —3F **49**
Lutton Cres. TS22 —1B **32**
Luttrell Ho. TS3 —2E **75**
Luttryngton Ct. DL5 —4A **106**
Lycium Clo. TS7 —1D **91**
Lydbrook Rd. TS5 —1C **72**
Lydd Gdns. TS17 —1F **87**
Lyn Clo. TS17 —4B **86**
Lyndale. TS14 —4A **96**
Lyndon Way. TS18 —5B **46**

Lyne Rd. DL16 —5A 98
Lynmouth Clo. TS8 —3D 89
Lynmouth Rd. TS20 —4F 31
Lynmouth Wlk. TS26 —3C 6
Lynnfield Rd. TS26 —4E 7
Lynn St. TS24 —5A 12 & 1A 12
Lynton Ct. TS26 —2C 6
Lynton Gdns. DL1 —3E 117
Lynwood Av. TS5 —4F 73
Lyonette Rd. DL1 —3D 113
Lyon Wlk. DL5 —1D 109
Lysander Clo. TS11 —4C 44
Lytham Rd. DL1 —2B 112
Lytham Wlk. TS16 —5D 85
Lythe Pl. TS4 —3B 74
Lythe Wlk. TS6 —5A 56
Lyttleton Dri. TS18 —2D 69
Lytton St. TS4 —4B 52 & 4C 52

Macaulay Av. TS3 —5F 53
Macaulay Rd. TS25 —3B 10
McAuley Ct. TS5 —1D 75
Mac Bean St. TS3 —4D 53
McClean Av. TS10 —1A 42
McCreton St. TS3 —5D 53
McCullagh Gdns. DL14 —3E 103
McDonald Pl. TS24 —2E 9
(off Cliff Ter.)
McIntyre Ter. DL14 —4D 103
Mackenzie Pl. DL5 —4D 107
Mackie Dri. TS14 —1F 97
Macklin Av. TS23 —1B 34
McLean Rd. TS12 —4D 65
Macmillan Cres. TS6 —3D 55
Macmillan Rd. DL5 —5D 107
Macmillan Rd. TS6 —3D 55
McMullen Rd. TS5 —5E 113
McNay St. DL3 —5A 112
McNay St. TS12 —1D 63
Macrae Rd. TS25 —1A 14
Maddison St. DL4 —4C 104
Madison Sq. TS19 —4C 46
Mafeking Pl. DL4 —4D 105
Magdalene Pl. DL17 —3E 101
Magdalen St. TS3 —4C 52
Magister Rd. TS17 —1D 87
Magnet St. DL4 —4C 104
Magnolia Ct. TS18 —1A 70
Magnolia Way. DL4 —4D 105
Maidstone Dri. TS7 —2F 91
Main Rd. DL14 —1D 105
Mainsforth Dri. TS5 —1E 89
Mainsforth Dri. TS23 —3A 20
Mainsforth Flats. TS24 —5B 8
Mainsforth Front Row. DL17
—5F 101
Mainsforth Rise. DL17 —5F 101
Mainsforth Ter. TS24 & TS25
—4A 8 to 2B 12
Main St. DL4 —3B 104
Main St. DL14 —4E 103
Main St. DL17 —2C 100
Major Cooper Ct. TS25 —5C 12
Major St. DL3 —5F 111
Major St. TS18 —4C 48
Majuba Rd. TS10 —4B 28
Malcolm Dri. TS19 —3B 46
Malcolm Gro. TS10 —1F 43
Malcolm Gro. TS17 —5E 71
Malcolm Rd. TS25 —1B 14
Malden Rd. TS20 —5C 32
Maldon Rd. TS5 —1C 72
Malham Cres. DL5 —5C 106
Malham Gill. TS10 —1C 42
Malham Gro. TS17 —5D 87

Malim Rd. DL1 —2F 117
Maling Grn. DL5 —5F 107
Malin Gro. TS10 —4D 43
Mallaig View. TS19 —4D 47
Mallard Clo. TS14 —3A 96
Mallard Ct. TS10 —1A 42
Mallard La. TS20 —4B 32
Mallard Rd. DL1 —2F 117
Malleable Way. TS18 —4E 49
Malling Rd. TS20 —2C 48
Malling Wlk. TS3 —1E 75
Mallory Clo. TS1 —3E 51
Mallory Ct. DL1 —5F 113
Mallory Rd. TS20 —5B 32
Mallowdale. TS7 —3A 92
Malltreath Sands. TS5 —2B 88
Malta Rd. TS16 —3A 84
Maltby Clo. TS14 —3F 103
Maltby Ho. TS4 —2B 74
Maltby Pl. TS17 —4D 71
Maltby Rd. TS8 —5B 88
Maltby St. TS3 —4D 53
Maltings, The. TS25 —1F 11
Maltkiln La. DL5 —5F 109
Malton Clo. TS17 —4E 71
Malton Dri. TS19 —3B 46
Malton Ter. TS21 —4C 118
Malvern Av. TS10 —2B 42
Malvern Av. TS12 —5D 63
Malvern Clo. TS9 —4D 119
Malvern Cres. DL3 —4A 110
Malvern Dri. TS20 —2D 89
Malvern Dri. TS9 —4D 119
Malvern Rd. TS18 —1A 70
Malvern Rd. TS23 —2E 33
Malvern Way. DL5 —5A 106
Mandale Ho. TS17 —3F 71
Mandale Ind. Est. TS17 —2D 71
Mandale Retail Pk. TS18 —4E 49
Mandale Rd. TS5 —4B 72
Mandale Rd. TS17
—2C 70 to 2E 71
Mandale Roundabout. TS5 —4B 72
Manfield Av. TS5 —2C 72
Manfield Ho. DL1 —4D 117
Manfield St. TS18 —1A 70
Manitoba Gdns. TS4 —5B 52
Manless Ter. TS12 —2C 80
Manners St. TS24 —3D 9
Manning Clo. TS17 —1E 87
Manning Way. TS17 —1E 87
Mannion Ct. TS6 —2C 54
Manor Clo. TS9 —3E 119
Manor Clo. TS22 —3D 19
Manor Ct. DL17 —2C 100
Manor Ct. TS22 —3D 19
Manor Ct. TS26 —4B 6
Manor Farm Way. TS8 —3B 90
Manor Garth Dri. TS26 —4C 6
Manor Ga. TS21 —5B 68
Manor Grn. TS6 —1D 77
Manor Ho. M. TS15 —2C 94
Manor Pl. TS19 —4C 46
Manor Rd. DL3 —3E 115
Manor Rd. TS26 —4B 6
Manorside. TS9 —3E 119
Manor St. TS1 —4E 51
Manor View. DL17 —2D 10
(off Broom Rd.)
Manor Way. TS23 —3C 34
Manor Wood. TS8 —3A 90
Mansepool Clo. TS24 —1F 7
Mansfield Av. TS17 —2E 71
Mansfield Rd. TS6 —2F 77
Mansforth Dri. TS5 —1E 89
Mansley Ct. DL3 —4F 111

Manton Av. TS5 —3C 72
Maple Av. DL4 —3D 105
Maple Av. TS4 —2A 74
Maple Av. TS17 —5D 71
Maple Gro. TS12 —4B 64
Maple Gro. TS21 —4B 118
Maple Rd. DL1 —1B 112
Maple Rd. TS19 —3A 48
Maple Sq. TS10 —4E 29
Maple St. TS1 —4A 52
Maple St. TS3 —3E 53
Mapleton Clo. TS10 —4D 43
Mapleton Cres. TS10 —4C 42
Mapleton Dri. TS8 —3E 89
(in two parts)
Mapleton Dri. TS20 —5A 32
Mapleton Rd. TS24 —3F 7
Maplin View. TS19 —4C 46
Marburn Pl. DL1 —5A 112
Mardale. TS8 —5E 89
Mardale Av. TS25 —1E 15
Mardale Wlk. TS10 —3D 43
Margaret St. TS3 —4C 52
Margaret Ter. DL14 —5F 103
Margill Clo. TS7 —2F 91
Margrove Rd. TS12 —5C 80
Margrove Wlk. TS3 —2E 75
Margrove Way. TS12 —3B 64
Marham Clo. TS3 —3A 76
Maria Dri. TS19 —4B 46
Maria St. TS3 —4D 53
Marigold Ct. DL1 —2C 116
Marina Av. TS10 —4A 28
Marina Rd. DL3 —1B 112
Marina Way. TS24 —4A 8
Marine Ct. TS12 —1D 63
Marine Cres. TS24 —2D 9
Marine Dri. TS24 —1B 8
Marine Pde. TS12 —1D 63
Mariners Ct. TS11 —4D 45
Marine Ter. TS13 —1B 66
Marion Av. TS5 —3D 73
Marion Av. TS16 —5C 84
Maritime Av. TS24 —4A 8
Maritime Clo. TS18 —4C 48
Maritime Clo. TS24 —4B 8
Maritime Ind. Est. TS20 —4C 48
Maritime Rd. TS20 & TS18
—4C 48
Mark Av. TS20 —4B 32
Markby Grn. TS3 —3B 76
Market Pl. DL1 —2A 116
Market Pl. DL4 —2D 105
Market Pl. DL14 —1D 103
Market Pl. DL17 —2C 100
Market Pl. TS3 —4C 52
Market Pl. TS9 —3E 119
Market Pl. TS13 —4D 67
Market Pl. TS14 —2E 97
Market Pl. TS24 —5F 7
Market St. DL17 —2C 100
Market St. TS6 —2B 54
Markham Pl. DL5 —5F 107
Markham Sq. TS19 —4C 46
Marlborough Av. TS11 —3D 45
Marlborough Clo. TS23 —5E 33
Marlborough Dri. DL1 —3F 115
Marlborough Gdns. TS2 —2F 51
Marlborough Ho. TS2 —2F 51
(off Stockton St.)
Marlborough Rd. TS7 —3D 91
Marlborough Rd. TS12 —5D 63
Marlborough Rd. TS18 —2A 70
Marlborough St. TS25 —2E 11
Marley Clo. TS19 —4D 47
Marley Rd. DL5 —1D 109
Marley Wlk. TS27 —4B 4

154 A-Z Middlesbrough

Marlowe Rd. TS25 —3B **10**
Marlsford Gro. TS5 —4D **73**
Marmaduke Pl. TS20 —4B **32**
Marmaduke St. DL16 —2D **99**
Marmion Clo. TS25 —3F **11**
Marquand Rd. TS6 —3C **54**
Marquis Gro. TS20 —4A **32**
Marquis St. TS24 —3D **9**
Marrick Av. DL3 —4A **110**
Marrick Clo. DL5 —5C **106**
Marrick Rd. TS3 —3E **75**
Marrick Rd. TS18 —3C **62**
Marsden Clo. TS4 —3B **74**
Marsden Clo. TS17 —5D **87**
Marsden Wlk. DL3 —2A **112**
Marshall Av. TS3 —5F **53**
Marshall Clo. TS12 —1B **62**
Marshall Clo. TS24 —4C **4**
Marshall Ct. TS3 —4A **54**
Marshall Dri. TS12 —3A **64**
Marshall Gro. TS18 —4F **47**
Marshall Rd. DL5 —5D **107**
Marshall St. DL3 —5F **111**
Marsh Ho. Av. TS23
　　　　—2F **19** to 2A **34**
Marsh Ho. La. TS25 —5D **15**
Marsh La. TS23 —4D **21**
Marsh Rd. TS1 —3E **51** & 2F **51**
Marsh Rd. TS3 —3C **52**
Marsh St. TS1 —3E **51**
Marske By-Pass. TS11
　　　　—4F **43** to 1E **61**
Marske Gro. DL3 —4A **112**
Marske La. TS11 —2E **61**
Marske La. TS12 —4A **62**
Marske La. TS19 —2B **46**
Marske Mill La. TS12
　　　　—2C **62** to 3D **63**
Marske Mill Ter. TS12 —2C **62**
Marske Pde. TS19 —3B **46**
Marske Rd. TS12 —1F **61**
Marske Rd. TS17 —4E **71**
Marske St. TS25 —1F **11**
Marston Gdns. TS24 —3F **7**
Marston Moor Rd. DL1 —4E **117**
Marston Rd. TS12 —5D **65**
Marston Rd. TS18 —4F **49**
Martham Clo. TS19 —3D **47**
Martindale. TS5 —2C **88**
Martindale Gro. TS16 —1D **95**
Martindale Pl. TS6 —4F **55**
Martindale Rd. DL1 —3C **112**
Martindale Rd. TS6 —5F **55**
Martindale Way. TS10 —4D **43**
Martinet Ct. TS17 —1D **87**
Martinet Rd. TS17 —1D **87**
Martin Gro. TS25 —2D **11**
Martinhoe Clo. TS17 —5A **86**
Marton Av. TS4 —4E **75**
Marton Burn Rd. TS4 —2A **74**
Marton Cres. TS6 —2F **77**
Marton Dri. TS22 —1C **32**
Marton Gro. TS12 —1B **62**
Marton Gro. Rd. TS4 —1A **74**
Marton Ho. TS1 —4B **52**
Marton Interchange. TS7 —2E **91**
Marton Moor Rd. TS7 —3C **92**
Marton Rd. TS1 & TS4
　　　　—3A **52** to 5D **75**
Martonside Way. TS4 —3B **74**
Marton St. TS24 —3E **7**
Marton Way. TS4 —3C **74**
Marway Rd. TS12 —3B **64**
Marwood Cres. DL3 —4E **111**
Marwood Dri. TS9 —4A **120**
Marwood Dri. TS12 —3B **64**

Marwood Sq. TS19 —4C **46**
Mary Ann St. TS5 —1F **73**
Mary Ct. DL3 —5C **110**
Mary Jacques Ct. TS4 —1B **74**
Marykirk Rd. TS17 —3E **87**
Maryport Clo. TS18 —4D **49**
Mary St. TS17 —2E **71**
　(off Anderson Rd.)
Mary St. TS18 —1A **70**
Mary St. TS26 —4E **7**
Masefield Rd. TS25 —3B **10**
Masham Gro. TS19 —1C **68**
Masham Moor Way. DL1 —5E **117**
Mason Ho. TS2 —2A **52**
　(off East St.)
Mason St. TS6 —2E **77**
Mason Wlk. TS24 —3F **7**
Massey Rd. TS17 —1D **71**
Master Rd. TS17 —1D **87**
Masterton Dri. TS18 —2D **69**
Mastiles Clo. TS17 —4A **86**
Matfen Av. TS7 —2B **92**
Matfen Ct. TS21 —3B **118**
Matford Av. TS3 —5F **53**
Matlock Av. TS7 —4E **91**
Matlock Gdns. TS22 —5D **19**
Matthew Clo. DL5 —4F **107**
Mattison Av. TS5 —1C **72**
Maude St. DL3 —1F **115**
Maughan St. DL4 —3B **104**
Maxton Rd. TS6 —3B **54**
Maxwell Clo. DL1 —3D **117**
Maxwell Ct. TS25 —1B **14**
Maxwell Pl. TS10 —1F **41**
Maxwell Rd. TS3 —4F **53**
Maxwell Rd. TS25 —1B **14**
Mayberry Gro. TS5 —3F **73**
Maybray King Wlk. TS20 —1C **48**
Mayes Wlk. TS15 —5C **94**
Mayfair Av. TS4 —1B **74**
Mayfair Av. TS6 —4D **77**
Mayfair Rd. DL1 —1B **112**
Mayfair St. TS26 —4E **7**
Mayfield. DL3 —2F **115**
Mayfield Clo. TS16 —5B **84**
Mayfield Cres. TS16 —5B **84**
Mayfield Rd. TS7 —2B **92**
Mayfields. DL16 —1C **98**
Maygate. TS6 —1B **78**
Maynard St. TS13 —2A **66**
May St. DL14 —2C **102**
May St. TS24 —2F **7**
Maze La. TS17 —1F **71**
Mead Cres. TS17 —4F **71**
Meadfoot Rd. TS5 —2D **89**
Meadowbank Rd. TS7 —5C **76**
Meadow Clo. TS7 —5B **76**
Meadow Clo. TS14 —2D **97**
Meadowcroft Rd. TS6 —2C **76**
Meadowdale Clo. TS22 —4F **35**
Meadow Dale Ct. TS12 —5F **81**
Meadow Dri. TS7 —5C **76**
Meadow Dri. TS26 —5B **6**
Meadow End. TS16 —4C **84**
Meadowfield. TS9 —2F **119**
Meadowfield Av. DL16 —1F **99**
Meadowfield Av. TS4 —2A **74**
Meadowfield Ct. TS25 —1C **16**
Meadowfield Dri. TS16 —4C **84**
Meadowfield Dri. DL3 —4C **110**
Meadowfield Way. DL5 —4B **106**
Meadowgate. TS6 —1B **78**
Meadowings, The. TS15 —4C **94**
Meadowlands. TS13 —2F **67**
Meadow Rise. DL3 —2C **114**
Meadow Rd. TS11 —5E **45**

Meadow Rd. TS19 —5D **47**
Meadows, The. TS8 —4D **91**
Meadows, The. TS21 —5B **118**
Meadow, The. TS25 —3E **11**
Mead, The. DL1 —2D **117**
Meadway. TS10 —4C **42**
Measham Clo. TS20 —5A **32**
Meath St. TS1 —5D **51**
Meath Way. TS14 —4D **97**
Meatlesburn Clo. DL5 —3A **108**
Mechanic's Yd. DL3 —2A **116**
Medbourne Clo. TS6 —1A **78**
Medbourne Gdns. TS5 —2E **89**
Medina Clo. TS19 —4C **46**
Medina Gdns. TS5 —2F **89**
Medway Clo. TS12 —4D **63**
Medwin Clo. TS12 —4B **64**
Meet, The. DL5 —5F **107**
Megarth Rd. TS5 —1E **73**
Meggitts Av. TS10 —2F **41**
Meggitts La. TS10 —3F **41**
Melbourne Clo. TS7 —3F **91**
Melbourne St. TS1 —4D **51**
Melbourne St. TS18 —5B **48**
Melbreak Gro. TS5 —5D **73**
Meldon Clo. DL1 —4D **113**
Meldreth Ho. TS12 —2D **63**
Meldrum Sq. TS19 —4C **46**
Meldyke La. TS8 —5D **89**
Meldyke Pl. TS8 —5D **89**
Melford Gro. TS17 —5C **86**
Melgrove Way. TS21 —5B **118**
Melksham Sq. TS19 —4C **46**
Mellanby Cres. DL5 —5F **107**
Melland St. DL1 —2B **116**
Mellor Ct. DL3 —4A **112**
Mellor St. TS19 —4A **48**
Melrose Av. DL3 —1B **112**
Melrose Av. TS5 —3D **73**
Melrose Av. TS23 —5F **19**
Melrose Cres. TS14 —3F **97**
Melrose Ho. TS1 —3A **52**
Melrose St. TS1 —4A **52**
Melrose St. TS25 —2E **11**
Melsonby St. TS3 —3F **75**
Melsonby Ct. TS23 —3B **20**
Melsonby Cres. DL1 —3D **117**
Melsonby Gro. TS18 —2B **68**
Melton Rd. TS19 —4C **46**
Melton Wlk. TS8 —3E **89**
Melville St. DL1 —5A **112**
Melville Wlk. TS20 —3D **49**
Mendip Av. TS12 —5D **63**
Mendip Dri. TS10 —2B **42**
Mendip Gro. DL1 —3D **113**
Mendip Rd. TS23 —2E **33**
Menom Rd. DL5 —5D **109**
Menville Clo. DL5 —2A **108**
Mercia St. DL3 —1F **115**
Meredith Av. TS6 —3D **77**
Mereston Clo. TS26 —3B **6**
Merion Dri. TS11 —2F **59**
Merlay Clo. TS15 —5B **94**
Merlin Clo. TS14 —3A **96**
Merlin Rd. TS3 —4A **53**
Merlin Rd. TS19 —4C **46**
Merriman Grn. TS24 —4C **4**
Merring Clo. TS18 —1B **68**
Merrington Av. TS5 —1C **88**
Merrington La. Ind. Est. DL16
　　　　　　—4E **99**
Merrington Rd. DL17 —3A **100**
Merrington View. DL16 —3C **98**
Merry Weather's Yd. TS14 —2E **97**
Mersehead Sands. TS5 —2C **88**
Mersey Rd. TS10 —5C **28**
Merton Clo. DL1 —3C **112**

Merville Av. TS19 —1D **69**
Meryl Gdns. TS25 —1E **15**
Merz Rd. DL5 —1D **109**
Metcalfe Clo. TS15 —5C **94**
Metcalfe Rd. TS6 —3A **54**
Metz Bri. Caravan Site. TS2
—3D **51**
Metz Bri. Rd. TS2 —2E **51**
Mewburn Ct. DL3 —2F **111**
Mewburn Rd. DL3 —1F **111**
Mews, The. TS7 —4B **76**
Mews, The. TS11 —4D **45**
Mews, The. TS16 —3D **85**
Mexborough Clo. TS19 —3E **47**
Meynell Av. TS14 —4B **96**
Meynell Ho. TS17 —1E **87**
Meynell Rd. DL3 —4A **112**
Meynell Wlk. TS15 —4C **94**
Mickleby Clo. TS7 —4A **92**
Mickledales Dri. TS11 —5D **45**
Micklemire La. TS25 —4D **15**
Mickleton Rd. TS2 —1D **51**
Micklow Clo. TS10 —3D **43**
Micklow La. TS13 —4D **67**
Micklow Ter. TS13 —4E **67**
Midbourne Rd. TS19 —3B **48**
Middle Av. TS23 —5E **33**
Middle Bank Rd. TS7 —5C **76**
Middlefield Rd. TS11 —4B **44**
Middlefield Rd. TS19 —2D **47**
Middlegate. TS24 —2D **9**
Middleham Rd. DL1 —2B **112**
Middleham Rd. TS19 —1D **69**
Middleham Wlk. DL16
—1C **98** & 1D **99**
Middleham Way. DL5 —3F **107**
Middleham Way. TS10 —2D **43**
Middlehaven Development. TS2
—2B **52**
Middlehope Gro. DL14 —4A **102**
Middle Rd. TS10 —3D **43**
Middlesbrough By-Pass. TS1, TS4 &
TS3 —2F **51**
Middlesbrough Rd. TS6 —3A **54**
Middlesbrough Rd. TS7 & TS14
—2E **93**
Middlesbrough Rd. E. TS17 —2E **71**
Middlesbrough Rd. E. TS6
—2B **54** & 2C **54**
Middlesbrough Wharf Trading Est.
TS2 —1F **51**
Middle St. TS18 —5B **48**
Middleton Av. TS5 —3C **72**
Middleton Av. TS17 —2D **87**
Middleton Av. TS24 —5C **18**
Middleton Ct. DL1 —2B **116**
Middleton Ct. TS15 —4D **95**
Middleton Dri. TS14 —4E **97**
Middleton Grange La. TS24 —5F **7**
(in two parts)
Middleton Grange Shopping Cen.
TS24 —5F **7**
Middleton Rd. DL4 —4C **104**
Middleton Rd. TS24 —4F **7** to 3B **8**
Middleton St. DL1 —2B **116**
Middleton Wlk. TS18 —1A **70**
Middleway. TS17 —2D **71**
Middlewood Clo. TS27 —4A **4**
Middridge Drift Ind. Est. DL4
—2F **105**
Middridge Gro. TS23 —3A **20**
Middridge La. DL4 —2D **105**
Middridge La. DL5 —3A **106**
Middridge Rd. DL5 & DL17 —2C **106**
Midfields. DL5 —3A **108**
Midfield View. TS19 —4C **46**
Midhurst Rd. TS3 —1B **76**

Midlothian Rd. TS25 —5A **10**
Midville Wlk. TS3 —2B **76**
Miers Av. TS24 —5D **5**
Milbank Ct. DL3 —1D **115**
Milbank Ct. TS18 —5B **48**
Milbank Cres. DL3 —1E **115**
Milbank Rd. DL3 —1D **115**
Milbank Rd. TS24 —2F **7**
Milbank St. TS18 —5B **48**
Milbank Ter. TS10 —4D **29**
Milbourne Ct. TS21 —3B **118**
Milburn Cres. TS20 —2B **48**
Mildenhall Clo. TS25 —2C **14**
Mildred St. DL3 —5A **112**
Mildred St. TS26 —4E **7**
Miles St. TS6 —2B **54**
Milfoil Clo. TS7 —2C **90**
Milford Ter. DL17 —2D **101**
Milholme Av. TS12 —5E **63**
Milkwood Ct. DL3 —4E **111**
Millbank. TS13 —3A **66**
Millbank La. TS17 —1D **87**
Millbank St. TS6 —2B **54**
Millbank Ter. DL14 —1C **104**
Millbeck. TS20 —5C **32**
Millbeck Way. TS7 —4C **76**
Millbrook Av. TS3 —4A **54** & 5A **54**
Mill Ct. TS23 —5E **33**
Mill Ct. TS25 —3C **14**
Miller Clo. TS15 —4F **95**
Miller Cres. TS24 —4B **4**
Millfield Clo. TS16 —1C **94**
Millfield Clo. TS17 —3F **71**
Millfield Ho. TS17 —3F **71**
Millfield Rd. TS3 —5D **53**
Millfields. DL5 —4F **109**
Millholme Clo. TS12 —5B **64**
Millholme Dri. TS12 —5B **64**
Millholme Ter. TS12 —5B **64**
Millington Clo. TS23 —2A **20**
Mill La. DL1 —4F **113**
Mill La. DL14 —4E **103**
Mill La. TS20 —4C **32**
Mill La. TS21 —5A **68**
Mill La. TS23 —4F **7**
Millpool Clo. TS24 —1A **8**
Millrace Clo. DL1 —3F **113**
Mill Riggs. TS9 —3F **119**
Mills Clo. DL5 —1C **108**
Millston Clo. TS26 —3A **6**
Mill St. DL4 —4C **104**
Mill St. TS1 —4D **51**
Mill St. TS14 —3E **97**
Mill St. TS20 —5C **32**
Mill St. E. TS18 —5C **48**
Mill St. W. TS18 —5B **48**
Mill Ter. TS9 —4A **120**
Mill Ter. TS25 —4C **14**
Mill View. TS13 —5C **66**
Mill Wynd. TS15 —2D **95**
Milner Gro. TS24 —4F **7**
Milner Rd. DL1 —3A **116**
Milner Rd. TS20 —4B **32**
Milne Wlk. TS25 —5A **10**
(in two parts)
Milton Av. DL14 —3C **102**
Milton Clo. TS12 —3B **64**
Milton Ct. TS1 —3E **51**
Milton Rd. TS26 —5E **7**
Milton St. DL1 —3D **117**
Milton St. TS12 —1D **63**
Minch Rd. TS25 —1B **14**
Minerva M. TS1 —2D **95**
Miniott Wlk. TS8 —3B **89**
Minors Cres. DL3 —3B **110**

Minsterley Dri. TS5 —4B **72**
Missenden Gro. TS3 —3A **76**
Mistral Dri. DL1 —1C **112**
Mitchell Av. TS17 —5F **71**
Mitchell St. TS26 —5E **7**
Mitford Clo. TS7 —4C **76**
Mitford Ct. TS21 —3B **118**
Mitford Cres. TS19 —3B **46**
Mizpah Cotts. TS10 —4D **29**
Moat, The. TS23 —2B **34**
Model Pl. DL1 —2B **116**
Moffat Clo. DL1 —2E **113**
Moffat Rd. TS25 —1A **14**
Monach Rd. TS25 —1B **14**
Monarch Grn. DL1 —2C **112**
Monarch Gro. TS7 —2F **91**
Mond Cres. TS23 —5F **33**
Mond Ho. TS3 —2E **75**
Monkland Clo. TS1 —3F **51**
Monkseaton Dri. TS22 —5D **19**
Monks End. DL5 —5F **109**
Monkton Rd. TS25 —1A **14**
Monmouth Dri. TS16 —5D **85**
Monmouth Gro. TS26 —2C **6**
Monmouth Rd. TS6 —4E **55**
Monreith Av. TS16 —5D **85**
Montagu Dri. DL1 —4F **115**
Montague St. TS1 —3B **52**
Montague St. TS24 —1D **9**
Montagu's Harrier. TS14 —3A **96**
Montgomery Gro. TS26 —2C **6**
Montreal Pl. TS4 —1B **74**
Montrose Clo. TS7 —3D **91**
Montrose St. DL1 —1B **116**
Montrose St. TS1 —3A **52**
Montrose St. TS12 —2D **63**
Moorbeck Way. TS7 —4C **76**
Moorcock Clo. TS6 —2F **77**
Moorcock Row. TS12 —5E **81**
Moore La. DL5 —1F **109**
Moore St. TS10 —4E **29**
Moore St. TS24 —3E **7**
Moor Farm Est. DL16 —5B **98**
Moorgate. TS6 —1B **78**
Moor Grn. TS7 —4B **92**
Moorhead Way. DL5 —3F **109**
Moor Ho. TS2 —2A **52**
(off South St.)
Moorhouse St. TS18 —5E **69**
Moorlands Rd. DL3 —5D **111**
Moor La. DL4 & DL5 —1A **106**
Moor Pde. TS24 —2D **9**
Moor Pk. TS7 —4B **92**
Moor Pk. TS16 —5D **85**
Moor Rd. TS3 —3C **52**
Moorsholm Way. TS10 —2D **43**
Moorside. DL16 —5A **98**
Moorston Clo. TS26 —4A **6**
Moor Ter. TS24 —2E **9**
Moortown Rd. TS4 —4B **74**
Moortown Rd. TS11 —2A **60**
Moray Clo. DL1 —2D **113**
Moray Clo. TS4 —2B **74**
Moray Rd. TS20 —1A **48**
Mordales Dri. TS11 —5F **45**
Moreland Av. TS23 —1F **33**
Moreland Clo. TS22 —3D **19**
Moreland St. TS24 —1A **12**
Moresby Clo. TS4 —3C **74**
Morgan Dri. TS14 —3D **97**
Morison Gdns. TS24 —2D **9**
Morland Fell. TS10 —2C **42**
Morland St. DL14 —4C **102**
Mornington La. DL3 —4E **111**
Morpeth Av. DL1 —3D **113**
Morpeth Av. TS4 —1C **90**
Morpeth Clo. DL16 —3D **99**

Morpeth Clo. DL17 —2E **101**
Morpeth Gro. DL14 —4B **102**
Morrison Clo. DL5 —3D **107**
Morrison Rd. TS14 —1E **97**
Morris Rd. TS6 —2F **77**
Mortain Clo. TS15 —4F **95**
Mortimer Dri. TS20 —5A **32**
Morton Carr La. TS7 —3D **93**
Morton Clo. TS14 —4B **96**
Morton St. TS3 —4C **52**
Morton Wlk. DL5 —5E **107**
Morven View. TS19 —4C **46**
Morville Ct. TS17 —5C **86**
Mosbrough Clo. TS19 —4E **47**
Mosedale Rd. TS6 —5F **55**
Moses St. TS3 —4C **52**
Mosman Ter. TS3 —4D **53**
Mossbank Gro. DL1 —3D **113**
Mossdale Gro. TS14 —4A **96**
Moss Gdns. TS8 —3E **89**
Mossmere. DL16 —1B **98**
Mosston Rd. TS19 —4D **47**
Moss Way. TS10 —5F **69**
Mosswood Cres. TS5 —5C **72**
Motherwell Rd. TS25 —1B **14**
Moule Clo. DL5 —2D **109**
Moulton Clo. TS19 —5B **46**
Moulton Way. DL1 —3D **117**
Mountbatten Clo. TS24 —1A **8**
Mount Gro. TS20 —4C **32**
Mt. Leven Rd. TS15 —3F **95**
Mt. Pleasant. TS13 —2A **66**
Mt. Pleasant Av. TS11 —5E **45**
Mt. Pleasant Bungalows. TS19
—5D **31**
Mt. Pleasant Clo. DL16 —2E **99**
Mt. Pleasant Ct. DL16 —2E **99**
Mt. Pleasant Rd. TS20 —2C **48**
Mt. Pleasant View. DL16 —2E **99**
Mt. Pleasant Way. TS8 —5D **91**
Mountston Clo. TS26 —3B **6**
Mount, The. TS6 —3D **77**
Mowbray Dri. TS8 —3E **89**
Mowbray Gro. TS19 —2B **46**
Mowbray Ho. TS4 —3A **74**
Mowbray Rd. TS20 —2C **48**
Mowbray Rd. TS25 —1B **14**
Mowden Clo. TS19 —3E **47**
Mowden Hall Dri. DL3 —5C **110**
Mowden St. DL3 —5A **112**
Mowden Ter. DL3 —5A **112**
Mowden Wlk. DL3 —5B **110**
Moyne Gdns. TS25 —1F **11**
Muirfield. TS7 —4B **92**
Muirfield Clo. TS11 —2B **60**
Muirfield Clo. TS27 —4A **4**
Muirfield Rd. TS16 —5D **85**
Muirfield Wlk. TS27 —4A **4**
Muirfield Way. TS4 —4B **74**
Muir Gro. TS25 —1B **14**
(in two parts)
Muirkirk Gro. DL1 —2D **113**
Muker Gro. TS19 —1B **68**
Mulgrave Ct. DL5 —3E **107**
Mulgrave Ct. TS14 —1E **97**
Mulgrave Rd. TS5 —2F **73**
Mulgrave Rd. TS26 —5D **7**
Mulgrave Wlk. TS5 —5A 56
(off Birchington Av.)
Mulgrave Wlk. TS10 —2C **42**
Mulheim Clo. DL3 —3D **111**
Mullroy Rd. TS25 —5A **10**
Munro Gro. TS25 —1B **14**
Murdock Rd. TS3 —4A **54**
Muriel St. TS1 —5A **52**
Muriel St. TS10 —4E **29**
Muriel St. TS13 —5F **65**

Murphy Cres. DL14 —4B **102**
Murray Av. DL14 —4B **102**
Murrayfield Way. DL1 —5F **113**
Murray St. TS26 —4E **7**
Murray Wlk. DL3 —1B **114**
Murton Clo. DL5 —5F **109**
Murton Clo. TS17 —2C **86**
Murton Gro. TS22 —1C **32**
Murton Scalp Rd. TS12 —5C **80**
Museum Rd. TS24 —4F **7**
Musgrave St. TS24 —5B **8**
Musgrave Ter. TS22 —3D **19**
Musgrave Wlk. TS24 —5A **8**
Muston Clo. TS5 —5F **73**
Myrddin-Baker Rd. TS6 —5F **55**
Myrtle Ct. TS17 —3D **71**
Myrtle Gdns. DL1 —1B **112**
Myrtle Gro. TS17 —3D **71**
Myrtle Rd. TS16 —2D **85**
Myrtle Rd. TS19 —3A **48**
Myrtle St. TS1 —4A **52**
Myton Wlk. TS24 —3E **89**
(in two parts)

Nab Clo. TS6 —2F **77**
Nairn Clo. DL1 —2F **113**
Nairnhead Clo. TS8 —4E **89**
Nantwich Clo. TS8 —4E **89**
Napier Ct. DL17 —3B **100**
Napier St. DL3 —2F **115**
Napier St. TS5 —5F **51**
Napier St. TS6 —2B **54**
Napier St. TS20 —2C **48**
Naseby Ct. TS12 —5D **65**
Naseby Ct. TS23 —4B **20**
Nash Gro. TS25 —3C **10**
Navenby Gro. TS25 —2B **14**
Navigation Ho. TS24 —4B 8
(off Warrior Quay)
Navigation Way. TS17 —1F **71**
Naylor Rd. TS21 —5C **118**
Neale St. DL17 —3B **100**
Neasham Av. TS7 —3E **91**
Neasham Av. TS23 —3A **20**
Neasham Clo. TS18 —5C **48**
Neasham Ct. TS9 —2E **119**
Neasham Dri. DL1 —5C **116**
Neasham La. TS9
—2E **119** & 3E **119**
Neasham Rd. DL1 & DL2 —3C **116**
Nebraska Clo. DL1 —3C **112**
Nederdale Clo. TS15 —5C **94**
Needles Clo. TS10 —4C **42**
Neile Rd. DL5 —4F **107**
Nelson Ct. TS6 —2B **54**
Nelson Sq. TS20 —5C **32**
Nelson St. DL14 —2C **102**
Nelson St. DL17 —4F **101**
Nelson St. TS6 —2A **54**
Nelson St. TS24 —1B **12**
Nelson St. Ind. Est. TS6 —2B **54**
Nelson Ter. DL1 —3B **116**
Nelson Ter. TS10 —4C **28**
Nelson Ter. TS18 —5B **48**
Nesbyt Rd. TS24 —4D **5**
Nesham Av. TS5 —1C **72**
Nesham Rd. TS1 —4D **51**
Nesham Rd. TS24 —2D **9**
Nestfield Ind. Est. DL1 —5C **112**
Nestfield St. DL1 —5C **112**
(in two parts)
Netherby Clo. TS15 —3F **95**
Netherby Ga. TS26 —3C **6**
Netherby Grn. TS3 —3F **75**
Netherby Rise. DL3 —2D **115**
Netherfield Ho. TS3 —2B **76**

Netherfields Cres. TS3 —2B **76**
Netley Gro. TS3 —3A **76**
Nevada Gdns. DL1 —3C **112**
Neville Clo. DL16 —2E **99**
Neville Dri. TS21 —3B **118**
Neville Pde. TS14 —4C **96**
Neville Pde. DL5 —1E **109**
Neville Rd. DL3 —2D **115**
Neville Rd. TS18 —3B **50**
Neville's Ct. TS5 —3E **73**
Newark Av. DL14 —3A **102**
Newark Rd. TS25 —2B **14**
Newark Wlk. TS20 —2D **49**
Newbank Clo. TS7 —5C **76**
Newbiggin Rd. TS23 —3F **19**
Newbridge Ct. TS5 —4F **73**
Newbrook. TS12 —2C **80**
Newburgh Ct. DL16 —1B **98**
Newburgh St. TS23 —2B **34**
Newburn Bri. Ind. Est. TS25
—1B **12**
Newburn Ct. DL5 —5D **107**
Newbury Av. TS5 —2C **72**
Newbury Rd. TS12 —5C **64**
Newbury Way. TS23 —4A **20**
Newby Clo. TS5 —4F **73**
Newby Clo. TS20 —5B **32**
Newby Gro. TS17 —4E **71**
Newby Ho. TS4 —2B **74**
Newcomen Clo. TS10 —3C **28**
Newcomen Grn. TS4 —1B **74**
Newcomen Gro. TS10 —4D **29**
Newcomen Rd. TS6 —4A **54**
Newcomen St. DL17 —2B **100**
Newcomen Ter. TS10 —3C **28**
Newcomen Ter. TS13 —4C **66**
New Company Row. TS13 —1B **66**
New Fenwick St. DL16 —2F **99**
Newfield Cres. TS5 —1C **88**
Newfoundland St. DL3 —5F **111**
Newgate. TS6 —1A **78**
Newgate Cen. DL14 —1D **103**
Newgate St. DL14 —2D **103**
New Gro. Ter. TS13 —1B **66**
Newham Av. TS5 —4E **73**
Newham Cres. TS7 —3E **91**
Newham Grange Av. TS19 —4F **47**
Newham Way. TS8 —3A **90**
Newhaven Clo. TS8 —4E **89**
Newhaven Ct. TS24 —5A **8**
Newholme St. TS14 —2D **97**
Newholm Way. TS10 —2C **42**
(in two parts)
Newick Av. TS3 —1E **75**
Newington Rd. TS4 —3B **74**
Newlands Av. DL4 —4C **104**
Newlands Av. DL14 —3A **102**
Newlands Av. TS20 —1C **48**
Newlands Av. TS26 —1D **11**
Newlands Gro. TS10 —1C **42**
(in three parts)
Newlands Rd. DL3 —5D **111**
Newlands Rd. TS1 —4B **52**
Newlands Rd. TS12 —3B **80**
Newlands Rd. TS16 —1C **94**
New La. DL5 —4A **108**
Newley Ct. TS3 —2B **76**
Newlyn Grn. TS3 —3F **75**
Newmarket Av. TS17 —2A **72**
Newmarket Rd. TS10 —2E **43**
Newport Ct. DL1 —4F **113**
Newport Cres. TS1 —3F **51**
Newport Ind. Est. TS1 —4E **51**
Newport Rd. TS1 —4D **51** to 3F **51**
Newport Rd. TS5 —4C **50**
Newport Way. TS1 —3D **51**
Newquay Clo. TS8 —4E **89**

Newquay Clo. TS26 —3C **6**
New Rd. TS14 —3E **97**
New Rd. TS23 —5E **33**
New Row. DL14 —1D **105**
New Row. TS14 —5E **59**
Newsam Cres. TS16 —5C **84**
Newsam Rd. TS16 —5C **84**
Newstead Av. TS19 —3E **47**
Newstead Farm La. TS14 —3C **96**
Newstead Rd. TS4 —5B **52**
New St. TS17 —2D **71**
Newton Cap Bank. DL14 —1C **102**
Newton Clo. TS6 —2A **78**
Newtondale. TS14 —4A **96**
Newton Dri. TS17 —2D **87**
Newton Gro. TS22 —5C **18**
Newton La. DL2 & DL3
— —1A **110** to 5C **110**
Newton Mall. TS17 —3F **51**
(off Cleveland Cen.)
Newton Rd. TS9 —3B **120**
Newton Rd. TS10 —2C **42**
Newton St. DL17 —2B **100**
Newton Wlk. TS20 —3C **48**
Newtown Av. TS19 —4A **48**
Nicholas Ho. TS2 —2F **51**
(off Suffield St.)
Nicholson Way. TS24 —4C **4**
Nicklaus Dri. TS16 —4D **85**
Nickstream La. DL3 —4C **110**
Nightingale Av. DL1 —3D **113**
Nightingale Rd. TS6 —5E **55**
Nightingale Wlk. TS20 —4B **32**
Nile St. TS2 —2F **51**
Nimbus Clo. TS17 —1D **91**
Ninefields. DL14 —2C **102**
Nolan Ho. TS18 —4B **48**
Nolan Pl. TS18 —4B **48**
Nookston Clo. TS26 —3B **6**
Norbury Rd. TS20 —1A **48**
Norcliffe St. TS3 —4D **53**
Norfolk Clo. TS10 —1C **42**
Norfolk Clo. TS12 —1B **80**
Norfolk Clo. TS25 —2F **11**
Norfolk Cres. TS3 —3A **76**
Norfolk Pl. DL14 —4D **103**
Norfolk Pl. TS3 —1D **75**
Norfolk St. TS18 —1A **70**
Norfolk Ter. TS23 —2A **34**
Norham Wlk. TS7 —4B **76**
Normanby Ter. TS7 —3D **91**
Normanby Hall Pk. TS6 —2D **77**
Normanby Rd. TS6
— —1B **54** to 2E **77**
Normanby Rd. TS7 —3B **76**
Norman Ter. TS6 —2A **54**
N. Albert Rd. TS20 —4B **32**
Northallerton Rd. TS17 —4E **71**
Northampton Ho. TS6 —4F **55**
Northampton Wlk. TS25 —1F **11**
North Av. TS12 —1C **62**
N. Bank Cres. TS7 —5C **76**
N. Bondgate. DL14 —1D **103**
Northbourne Rd. TS19 —3B **48**
Northbrook Ct. TS26 —1C **10**
Northcliffe. DL14 —5F **103**
North Clo. Rd. DL16 —5B **98**
Northcote St. TS18 —2A **70**
Northcote Ter. DL3 —5F **111**
North Cotts. DL5 —3A **108**
Northdale Ct. TS3 —1F **75**
North Dri. DL16 —5A **98**
North Dri. TS7 —4B **76**
North Dri. TS26 —4C **6**
N. Eastern Ter. DL1 —2B **116**
North End. TS21 —4B **118**
N. End Gdns. DL14 —4E **103**

158 A-Z Middlesbrough

Northern Rd. TS5 —1C **72**
Northern Route. TS5 & TS1
— —1C **72** to 3E **51**
Northfen. TS10 —1C **42**
Northfield Clo. TS9 —3E **119**
Northfield Dri. TS9 —3E **119**
Northfield Rd. TS11 —4B **44**
Northfield Rd. TS22 —1D **33**
Northfield Way. DL5 —2C **108**
Northfleet Av. TS3 —5F **53**
Northgate. DL1 —2A **116** & 1A **116**
Northgate. TS14 —2E **97**
Northgate. TS24 —1C **8**
Northgate Ho. DL1 —1A **116**
Northgate Rd. TS5 —3E **73**
North Grn. TS18 —2B **70**
Northiam Clo. TS8 —3E **89**
Northland Av. TS26 —1D **11**
Northleach Dri. TS8 —4E **89**
N. Liverton Ind. Est. TS13 —5B **66**
N. Lodge Roundabout. TS14
— —1F **97**
N. Lodge Ter. DL3 —1A **116**
N. Mt. Pleasant St. TS20 —2C **48**
N. Ormesby By-Pass. TS3 —3C **52**
N. Ormesby Rd. TS4 —3B **52**
Northpark. TS23 —3F **19**
North Pk. Rd. TS21 —4B **118**
Northport Rd. TS18 —4D **49**
North Rise. DL3 —3B **112**
North Rd. DL1 —4A **112** to 1B **112**
North Rd. DL16 —1E **99**
North Rd. TS2 —2E **51**
North Rd. TS9 —4D **119**
North Rd. TS13 —4D **67**
North Rd. TS25 —4C **12**
North Rd. Ind. Est. DL3 —4A **112**
North Row. DL5 —5F **109**
North Row. TS6 —4D **57**
N. Skelton Rd. TS12 —1E **81**
N. Slip Rd. TS9 —3E **15**
North St. DL16 —3C **98**
North St. DL17 —2C **100**
North St. TS2 —1A **52**
North St. TS6 —2B **54**
North St. TS18 —5B **48**
(off Bishopton La.)
N. Tees Ind. Est. TS18 —3B **50**
North Ter. DL4 —2C **104**
North Ter. DL5 —5F **109**
North Ter. TS10 —4D **29**
North Ter. TS12 —1B **80**
North Ter. TS13 —3D **67**
Northumberland Av. DL14
— —3C **102**
Northumberland Gro. TS20 —4A **32**
Northumberland Gro. TS25 —2F **11**
Northumberland Rd. TS17 —4D **71**
Northumberland St. DL3 —2F **111**
Northumberland Wlk. TS25 —2F **11**
North View. TS6 —1A **78**
North View. TS10 —1A **44**
Northwold Clo. TS25 —2C **14**
North Wood. TS5 —4E **73**
Norton Av. TS20 —1A **48**
Norton Ct. TS20 —3C **48**
Norton Dri. TS19 —3B **46**
Norton Junct. TS20 —4D **33**
Norton Junct. Cotts. TS20 —4E **31**
Norton Rd. TS18 & TS20
— —5C **48** to 1C **48**
Norton Rd. TS20 —5D **33**
Norwich Av. TS19 —4C **47**
Norwich Gro. DL1 —4F **113**
Norwich Rd. TS5 —1F **73**
Norwich Rd. TS10 —2A **44**
Norwood Clo. TS19 —4C **46**

Norwood Rd. TS3 —1B **76**
Notre Dame Clo. TS17 —1D **71**
Nottingham Dri. TS10 —1F **43**
Nottingham Wlk. TS25 —1F **11**
Nuffield Ct. DL1 —3C **112**
Nuffield Rd. TS23 —1B **34**
Nugent Av. TS1 —4D **51**
Nuneaton Dri. TS8 —4E **89**
Nunnery Clo. DL3 —1C **114**
Nunnery La. DL3
— —2A **114** to 1D **115**
Nunnington Clo. TS17 —5C **86**
Nuns Clo. DL14 —5E **103**
Nuns St. TS24 —2D **9**
Nunthorpe By-Pass. TS7 —5C **92**
Nursery Gdns. TS15 —5E **95**
Nursery La. TS5 —1D **73**
Nursery La. TS18 —1F **69**
Nutfield Clo. TS8 —4E **89**
Nut La. TS4 —5B **52**
Nutley Rd. TS23 —1A **34**

Oak Av. TS7 —2F **91**
Oakdale. TS7 —3C **76**
Oakdale Rd. TS11 —2A **60**
Oakdene Av. DL3 —3F **115**
Oakdene Av. TS18 —3F **69**
Oakdene Clo. TS6 —2E **77**
Oakenshaw Dri. TS5 —1D **89**
Oakesway. TS24 —1E **7**
Oakfield. DL5 —1C **108**
Oakfield Av. TS16 —4C **84**
Oakfield Clo. TS16 —4C **84**
Oakfield Rd. TS3 —5C **52**
Oak Gro. TS24 —2D **7**
Oakham Grn. TS20 —2D **49**
Oak Hill. TS8 —3D **91**
Oakhurst Clo. TS17 —5D **87**
Oakhurst Rd. DL3 —1E **115**
Oakland Av. TS25 —3E **11**
Oakland Gdns. DL1 —1B **112**
Oaklands. TS9 —3A **120**
Oaklands Av. TS20 —1C **48**
Oaklands Rd. TS6 —3E **77**
Oaklands Ter. DL3 —1F **115**
Oak Lea. DL4 —3E **105**
Oaklea Clo. TS20 —5B **32**
Oaklea Ct. DL1 —3F **115**
Oaklea Ter. DL14 —3D **103**
Oakley Clo. TS8 —3E **89**
Oakley Clo. TS14 —5E **97**
Oakley Gdns. TS24 —3E **7**
Oakley Rd. TS12 —4C **80**
Oakley Wlk. TS6 —2F **77**
Oakridge. TS7 —3C **76**
Oak Rise. TS7 —3C **76**
Oak Rd. TS10 —5F **29**
Oak Rd. TS12 —3B **64**
Oak Rd. TS14 —2D **97**
Oak Rd. TS16 —1E **85**
Oaksham Dri. TS23 —3F **19**
Oaks, The. DL3 —1D **115**
Oaks, The. DL5 —2E **107**
Oaks, The. TS8 —3E **89**
Oak St. TS1 —3A **52**
Oak St. TS3 —3E **53**
Oak St. TS6 —2B **54**
Oak Ter. DL14 —3D **103**
Oak Ter. DL16 —3B **98**
Oak Tree Cres. TS21 —3B **118**
Oaktree Gro. TS18 —3C **68**
Oak Wlk. TS13 —3C **66**
Oakwell Gdns. TS20 —5B **32**
Oakwell Rd. TS20 —5B **32**
Oakwood Clo. TS27 —4A **4**
Oakwood Ct. TS7 —3A **92**

Oakwood Dri. DL1 —2C **112**
Oakworth Grn. TS4 —3B **74**
Oatfields Ct. TS6 —2F **77**
Oatlands Gro. TS13 —2F **67**
Oban Av. TS25 —2E **11**
Oban Ct. DL1 —2E **113**
Oban Rd. TS3 —1E **75**
Oberhausen Mall. TS1 —3F **51**
Occupation Rd. TS6 —2A **78**
Ocean Rd. TS24 —3A **4**
Ochil Ter. TS23 —2F **33**
Offerton Dri. TS8 —3F **89**
Office Row. DL14 —1D **105**
O'Hanlan St. DL16 —2C **98**
Okehampton Dri. TS7 —2D **91**
Oldbury Gro. TS8 —3F **89**
Old Cemetery Rd. TS24 —1A **8**
Old Convent Gdns. TS4 —1B **74**
Old Durham Rd. TS21 —1B **118**
Old Flatts La. TS6 —4E **77**
Oldford Cres. TS5 —5D **73**
Oldgate. TS6 —1B **78**
Oldham Clo. TS12 —4C **80**
Oldham St. TS12 —4C **80**
Old Mkt., The. TS15 —2C **94**
Old Middlesbrough Rd. TS6
—3A **54**
Old Middlesbrough Rd. TS14
—2A **96**
Old Rd. TS23 —5E **33**
Old Row. TS6 —1A **78**
Old Sta. Rd. TS6 —1A **54**
Oldstead Ct. TS8 —3E **89**
Old Stokesley Rd. TS7 —5C **92**
Oliver St. TS5 —1E **73**
Oliver St. TS6 —3B **54**
Oliver St. TS10 —5E **29**
Olive St. TS24 —2D **9**
Olney Wlk. TS3 —3E **75**
Olympic St. DL3 —5E **111**
Ontario Gro. TS10 —1D **43**
Orchard Clo. TS9 —2B **120**
Orchard Clo. TS14 —3E **97**
Orchard Clo. TS21 —4C **118**
Orchard Gro. TS6 —1E **77**
Orchard Rd. DL3 —5E **111**
Orchard Rd. TS5 —2E **73**
Orchard Rd. TS10 —5D **29**
Orchard Rd. TS17 —5C **70**
Orchard Rd. TS19 —5C **46**
Orchard, The. TS17 —4B **86**
Orchard, The. TS21 —4C **118**
(in two parts)
Orchard Way. DL4 —3D **105**
Orchard Way. TS7 —4B **76**
Orde Wingate Way. TS19 —4B **48**
Ordsall Grn. TS3 —3F **75**
Oriel Clo. TS5 —3E **73**
Oriel Ct. DL1 —3C **112**
Orkney Wlk. DL1 —2E **113**
Orkney Wlk. TS14 —4C **96**
Orlands, The. DL5 —5F **109**
Orleans Gro. TS7 —2F **91**
Ormesby Bank. TS7 —5B **76**
Ormesby Rd. TS3 —5D **53** to 4F **75**
Ormesby Rd. TS6 —2D **77**
Ormesby Rd. TS25 —5E **11**
Ormston Av. TS3 —3F **75**
Oronsay Wlk. DL1 —2E **113**
Orpington Rd. TS3 —3F **75**
Orton Gro. TS22 —1C **32**
Orwell Clo. TS12 —5D **63**
Orwell Gdns. TS19 —1C **68**
Orwell St. TS1 —4D **51**
Orwell Wlk. TS25 —3C **10**
Osbert Pl. DL5 —3D **107**
Osborne Clo. DL3 —1D **115**

Osborne Rd. DL16 —4B **98**
Osborne Rd. TS5 —1E **73**
Osborne Rd. TS18 —2A **70**
Osborne Rd. TS26 —5E **7**
Osborne St. DL4 —3B **104**
Osborne Ter. DL17 —3E **101**
Osbourne Clo. TS8 —3E **89**
Osric Pl. DL5 —4D **107**
Ostler Clo. TS17 —4C **86**
Oswald Pl. DL17 —2C **100**
Oswestry Grn. TS4 —1C **90**
Otley Av. TS3 —3F **75**
Otley St. DL4 —4C **104**
Otley Ter. DL3 —4A **112**
Ottawa Rd. TS4 —1B **74**
Otterburn Clo. DL1 —3D **113**
Otterburn Gdns. TS5 —2E **89**
Otterburn Way. TS23 —4A **20**
Otterhill Ct. TS8 —3E **89**
Otterpool Clo. TS24 —1F **7**
Otter Way. TS17 —4D **87**
Oughton Clo. TS15 —4F **95**
Oulston Rd. TS18 —1E **69**
Ouseport Rd. TS18 —4D **49**
Ouston St. TS24 —5F **7**
Outhwaite St. TS5 —5D **51**
Outram St. DL3 —1F **115**
Outram St. TS1 —4E **51**
Outram St. TS18 —1B **70**
Oval Grange. TS26 —4C **6**
Oval, The. DL4 —2C **104**
Oval, The. TS20 —2D **89**
Oval, The. TS26 —5D **7**
Overbrook. TS9 —4A **120**
Overdale. TS14 —4A **96**
Overdale Clo. TS10 —4D **43**
Overdale Rd. TS3 —2D **75**
Overmans Cotts. TS13 —2B **66**
Owens Rd. TS6 —3A **54**
Owen St. DL17 —3B **100**
Owington Gro. TS23 —3B **20**
Owletts Ct. TS17 —3B **86**
Owton Clo. TS25 —5D **11**
Owton Mnr. La. TS25
—5B **10** to 5E **11**
—1E **69** & 5E **47**
Oxbridge Av. TS18
—1E **69**
Oxbridge Ct. TS18 —1E **69**
Oxbridge Ind. Est. TS18 —5A **48**
Oxbridge La. TS19 & TS18
—1D **69** to 1A **70**
Ox Clo. Cotts. TS12 —1B **62**
Ox Clo. Cres. DL16 —2C **98**
Oxclose La. DL3 —4B **110**
Oxfield. TS8 —3C **90**
Oxford Rd. DL16 —3C **98**
Oxford Rd. TS5 —2C **72**
Oxford Rd. TS17 —3D **71**
Oxford Rd. TS25 —2C **10** to 2F **11**
Oxford St. DL1 —1A **116**
Oxford St. DL4 —4C **104**
Oxford St. TS1 —5E **51**
Oxford St. TS6 —2B **54**
Oxford St. TS12 —4C **80**
(Boosbeck)
Oxford St. TS12 —2D **63**
(Saltburn)
Oxford St. TS25 —2F **11** & 2A **12**
Oxford Ter. DL14 —2D **103**
Oxgang Clo. TS10 —4D **43**
Oxley St. TS10 —4E **29**

Paddock, The. DL5 —2E **107**
Paddock, The. TS8 —5C **92**

Paddock, The. TS9 —2E **119**
Paddock, The. TS16 —3D **85**
Paddock Wood. TS8 —3B **90**
Padstow Clo. TS26 —3B **6**
Page Gro. DL16 —4A **98**
Paignton Clo. TS8 —1C **90**
Paignton Dri. TS25 —1D **15**
Palladium Bldgs. TS4 —2A **74**
Pallister Av. TS3 —5F **53**
Pallister Ct. TS3 —4A **54**
Palmer Rd. DL5 —1F **109**
Palmerston Ct. TS17 —3D **71**
Palmerston St. TS18 —5B **48**
Palmer St. TS1 —4F **51**
Palm Gro. TS19 —5C **46**
Palm St. TS1 —4A **52**
Palm Ter. TS2 —5F **35**
Panmore Wlk. TS16 —4D **85**
Pannal Clo. TS11 —2A **60**
Pannal Wlk. TS16 —4D **85**
Pannel Clo. TS27 —4A **4**
Pannell Av. TS5 —3C **72**
Pannell Pl. TS27 —4A **4**
Pannierman La. TS9 —2F **119**
Parade, The. TS26 —5C **6**
Paris Pl. TS7 —1D **91**
Park Av. TS6 —5C **54**
Park Av. TS10 —4E **29**
Park Av. TS17 —3E **71**
Park Av. TS26 —4C **6**
Park Av. N. TS3 —3A **76**
Park Av. S. TS3 —3B **76**
Park Ct. TS10 —1F **41**
Park Cres. DL1 —4B **116**
Parkdale Way. TS16 —4F **73**
Park Dri. TS19 —2E **47**
Park Dri. TS26 —5B **6**
Parker Ter. DL17 —3C **100**
Parkfield Av. TS5 —4E **73**
Parkfield Rd. TS18 —2B **70**
Parkfield Way. TS18 —2B **70**
Parkgate. DL1 —2B **116**
Parkgate. TS6 —1B **78**
Parkgate Chambers. DL1 —2B **116**
Parkinson Ho. TS1 —3A **52**
(off Albert M.)
Parkin St. TS18 —5B **48**
Parkland Dri. DL3 —1B **114**
Parkland Gro. DL3 —1B **114**
Parklands. TS3 —1E **75**
Parklands Av. TS23 —4E **33**
Parklands Clo. TS3 —1E **75**
Parklands, The. TS10 —3D **43**
(in three parts)
Parklands Way. TS26 —5A **6**
Park La. DL1 —3B **116** & 4B **116**
Park La. TS1 —5F **51**
Park La. TS13 —2F **67**
Park La. TS14 —3C **96**
Park M. TS26 —5C **6**
Park Pde. DL16 —2C **98**
Park Pl. DL1 —3B **116**
Park Rise. TS9 —4B **120**
Park Rd. TS5 —5F **51**
Park Rd. TS12 —5B **64**
Park Rd. TS17 —5D **71**
Park Rd. TS18 —2A **70**
Park Rd. TS26 & TS24 —5D **7**
Park Rd. N. TS1 —5F **51**
(in two parts)
Park Rd. S. TS5 & TS4 —1F **73**
Parkside. DL1 —4F **115** to 4C **116**
Parkside. DL16 —2B **98**
Parkside. TS1 —5A **52**
Park Side. TS3 —3F **75**
Parkside. TS14 —2D **97**

Pinfold St. TS18 —4C **48**
Piper Knowle Rd. TS19 —1C **46**
Pipit Clo. TS17 —5C **86**
Pippins, The. TS22 —2D **19**
Pirbright Gro. TS8 —3F **89**
Pirnmill View. TS19 —4C **46**
Planetree Ct. TS7 —2F **91**
Plantation Rd. TS10
 (in two parts) —5B **42** & 5C **42**
Player Ct. TS16 —4D **85**
Playlin Clo. TS15 —4F **95**
Pleasant View. DL3 —2A **112**
Plumer Dri. TS20 —5B **32**
Plymouth Gro. TS26 —2C **6**
Plymouth Wlk. TS26 —2C **6**
Pochin Rd. TS6 —2E **55**
Polam La. DL1 —3F **115** & 3A **116**
Polam Rd. DL1 —3F **115**
Poldon Ter. TS23 —2F **33**
Pollard's Dri. DL14 —3B **102**
Pondfield Clo. DL3 —3C **114**
Pontac Rd. TS11 —1B **60**
Pope Gro. TS25 —2B **10**
Poplar Ct. TS15 —2C **94**
Poplar Gro. TS6 —4C **54**
Poplar Gro. TS10 —5F **29**
Poplar Gro. TS12 —4B **64**
Poplar Gro. TS18 —2A **70**
Poplar Pl. TS14 —2C **96**
Poplar Rd. TS16 —1C **94**
Poplar Rd. TS17 —3D **71**
Poplars Rd. TS5 —2F **73**
Poplars, The. TS5 —1E **73**
Poplars, The. TS8 —5C **88**
Poplars, The. TS22 —2D **19**
Poplar Ter. TS23 —1D **33**
Porlock Rd. TS23 —1D **33**
Porrett Clo. TS24 —4C **4**
Port Clarence Rd. TS2 —4E **35**
Porter Clo. DL5 —4F **107**
Portland Clo. TS7 —3D **91**
Portland Clo. TS10 —4C **42**
Portland Clo. TS16 —1D **95**
Portland Gro. TS24 —4B **4**
Portland Ho. TS3 —4F **53**
Portland Pl. DL3 —2F **115**
Portland Wlk. TS10 —4D **43**
Portmadoc Wlk. TS26 —2B **6**
Portman Rise. TS14 —5E **97**
Portman Rd. TS20 —2B **48**
Portman St. TS1 —4F **51**
Portrack Back La. TS20 —2E **49**
Portrack Grange Clo. TS18 —4A **50**
Portrack Grange Rd. TS18 —4F **49**
Portrack Interchange. TS18
 —2B **50**
Portrack La. TS18 —4C **48** to 3F **49**
Portrack Retail Pk. TS18 —4E **49**
Portrush Clo. DL1 —3E **113**
Portrush Clo. TS4 —4A **74**
Portrush Clo. TS11 —2A **60**
Portsmouth Pl. DL1 —4F **113**
Portsmouth Rd. TS16 —4A **84**
Post Horn, The. DL5 —4A **106**
Post Ho. Wynd. DL3 —2A **116**
Potter Wlk. TS24 —3F **7**
Pottery St. TS17 —3C **70**
Potto Clo. TS15 —3F **95**
Pounder Pl. TS24 —1D **7**
Powburn Clo. TS19 —3B **46**
Powell St. TS26 —1E **11**
Powlett Rd. TS24 —2E **7**
 (in two parts)
Powlett St. DL3 —2F **115**
Prebend Row. DL1 —2A **116**
Preen Dri. TS5 —4C **72**
Premier Pde. TS19 —1B **68**

Premier Rd. TS3 —1E **75**
Premier Rd. TS7 —5B **76**
Premier Rd. TS19 —5D **47**
Prescot Rd. TS3 —3A **76**
Prescott St. DL1 —5C **112**
Preston Farm Bus. Pk. TS18
 —4A **70**
Preston Farm Ind. Est. TS18
 —5F **69**
Preston La. TS18 —5E **69** & 1A **85**
Preston Rd. DL5 —3C **108**
Preston Rd. TS18 —1D **69**
Preston St. TS26 —4E **7**
Preston Way. TS9 —2E **119**
Prestwick Clo. TS4 —4B **74**
Prestwick Ct. TS16 —5D **85**
Preswick Clo. TS11 —3A **60**
Price Av. DL14 —5B **102**
Price Av. TS5 —3C **72**
Price Rd. TS10 —2F **41**
Priestcrofts. TS11 —4F **45**
Priestfield Av. TS3 —4F **75**
Priestgate. DL1 —2A **116**
Priestman Rd. DL5 —5C **106**
Primitive St. DL4 —3C **104**
Primrose Clo. TS14 —3B **96**
Primrose Cotts. TS12 —2D **63**
Primrose Hill. DL14 —3A **102**
Primrose Hill. TS13 —2B **66**
Primrose St. DL3 —2F **115**
Primrose St. TS19 —4A **48**
Prince Pl. TS10 —4D **29**
Princeport Rd. TS18 —4D **49**
Prince Regent St. TS18 —1B **70**
Princes Rd. TS1 —4E **51**
Princes Rd. TS12 —2D **63**
Princess Av. TS18
 —4C **48** & 5C **48**
Princess Ct. DL16 —3B **98**
Princes Sq. TS17 —3E **87**
Princess Rd. DL3 —1A **112**
Princess St. DL1 —3B **116**
Princess St. DL16 —3B **98**
Princess St. TS2 —2F **51**
Princess St. TS17 —2D **71**
Princess St. TS24 —2E **9**
Princes St. DL4 —3B **104**
Prince's St. TS14 —2C **102**
Princeton Dri. TS17 —1D **71**
Prior Ct. TS23 —4B **20**
Prior Dene. DL3 —5D **111**
Priors Path. DL17 —2D **101**
Prior St. DL3 —5D **111**
Priorwood Gdns. TS17 —5D **87**
Priory Ct. TS14 —2E **97**
Priory Ct. TS20 —5C **32**
Priory Ct. TS24 —1A **8**
Priory Dri. TS8 —5D **89**
Priory Gdns. TS20 —5C **32**
Priory Gro. DL14 —4F **103**
Priory Gro. TS10 —4B **28**
Priory Pl. TS1 —3F **51**
Priory Rd. TS5 —3B **72**
Priory St. TS1 —3F **51**
Prissick Farm Cotts. TS4 —5D **75**
Prissick St. TS24 —3D **9**
Pritchett Rd. TS3 —3A **76**
Proctor's Ct. TS25 —5D **13**
Progress Way. DL1 —5A **112**
Promenade. TS24 —3E **9**
Prospect Pl. DL3 —3F **111**
Prospect Pl. TS12 —5F **81**
 (Lingdale)
Prospect Pl. TS12 —2B **80**
 (Skelton)
Prospect Pl. TS14 —3D **97**

Prospect Pl. TS20 —2C **48**
Prospect Ter. TS6 —1A **78**
Prospect Ter. TS11 —4D **45**
Prospect Ter. TS12 —5F **81**
Prospect, The. TS5 —3F **73**
Prospect Way. TS25 —5F **11**
Protear Gro. TS20 —3D **33**
Proudfoot St. DL14 —5C **102**
Providence St. TS14 —3D **97**
Puddlers Rd. TS6 —2B **54**
Pudsey Ho. TS24 —2D **9**
 (off Union St.)
Pudsey Wlk. DL5 —2F **109**
Pulford Rd. TS20 —1A **48**
Punch Bowl Yd. DL3 —2A **11**
 (off Skinnergate)
Punch St. TS1 —4D **51**
Purfleet Av. TS3 —4F **53**
Pursglove Ter. TS14 —2E **97**
Pym St. TS6 —3B **54**
Pytchley Rd. TS14 —4E **97**

Quaker La. DL1 —3A **116**
Quantock Clo. DL1 —3C **112**
Quarry Bank Rd. TS11 —4D **61**
Quarry Clo. DL17 —3E **101**
Quarry Dri. TS8 —5D **89**
Quarry La. TS11 —2E **61**
Quarry Rd. TS16 —2E **85**
Quarry St. DL4 —3C **104**
Quayside. TS24 —4B **8**
Quebec Gro. TS4 —1B **74**
Quebec Gro. TS23 —4F **19**
Quebec Rd. TS18 —3E **69**
Quebec St. DL1 —2A **116**
Queen Anne Ter. TS18 —2E **69**
Queens Av. TS17 —2D **71**
Queensbury Av. TS26 —1D **11**
Queensbury Clo. TS10 —4B **42**
Queens Dri. TS9 —3F **119**
Queens Dri. TS21 —5A **118**
Queens Dri. TS22 —5D **19**
Queensland Av. TS10 —5E **29**
Queensland Gro. TS18 —2E **69**
Queensland Rd. TS25 —5E **11**
Queensport Clo. TS18 —4E **49**
Queen's Rd. DL14 —2E **103**
Queens Rd. TS5 —1E **73**
Queens Rd. TS13 —4B **66**
Queens Sq. TS3 —2A **52**
Queen's Ter. TS2 —2A **52**
 (Middlesbrough)
Queen's Ter. TS2 —5A **36**
 (Port Clarence)
Queen St. DL3 —2A **116**
Queen St. DL4 —2C **104**
Queen St. TS6 —4D **57**
 (Lazenby)
Queen St. TS6 —3B **54**
 (South Bank)
Queen St. TS10 —4C **28**
Queen St. TS12 —4C **80**
 (in two parts)
Queen St. TS13 —2A **66**
Queen St. TS18 —5C **48**
Queen St. TS24 —2E **9**
 (Croft on Heugh)
Queen St. TS24 —1A **12**
 (Hartlepool)
Queen St. TS24 —3B **8**
 (Middleton)
Queen St. TS25 —4C **12**
Queen's Wlk. TS18 —5C **48**
Queensway. DL4 —3E **105**
Queensway. TS3 —4F **53**
Queensway. TS12 —2B **62**

Queensway. TS23 —1E **33**
(in two parts)
Queensway. TS25 —4C **14**
Queen Ter. TS25 —5C **12**
Quenby Rd. TS23 —5F **19**
Quorn Clo. TS14 —4E **97**

Raby Dri. DL5 —3E **107**
Raby Gdns. DL4 —3C **104**
Raby Gdns. DL14 —3D **103**
Raby Gdns. TS24 —3D 7 to 2E **7**
Raby Rd. DL17 —2D **101**
Raby Rd. TS10 —1F **43**
Raby Rd. TS18 —1E **69**
Raby Rd. TS24 —2E 7 to 5F **7**
Raby Sq. TS24 —3E **7**
Raby St. DL3 —2F **115**
Raby St. TS24 —3D **9**
Raby Ter. DL3 —2A **116**
Race Ter. TS9 —4A **120**
Radcliffe Av. TS19 —1F **47**
Radcliffe Cres. TS17 —1D **71**
Radcliffe Ter. TS24 —2E **9**
Radford Clo. TS19 —5E **31**
Radlett Av. TS19 —1F **47**
Radnor Clo. TS19 —1F **47**
Radnor Grn. TS3 —3F **75**
Radnor Gro. TS26 —2B **6**
Radstock Av. TS19 —1F **47**
Radyr Clo. TS19 —5D **31**
Raeburn St. TS26 —4D **7**
Rafton Dri. TS27 —4B **4**
Raglan Clo. TS19 —5D **31**
Raglan Ter. TS23 —1F **33**
Ragpath La. TS19 —5E **31**
Ragworth Pl. TS20 —5B **32**
Ragworth Rd. TS20 —5B **32**
Railway Cotts. DL17 —4E **101**
Railway Cotts. TS7 —3C **92**
Railway Cotts. TS11 —5C **44**
Railway Cotts. TS12 —4D **63**
Railway Cotts. TS13 —5F **65**
(Carlin How)
Railway Cotts. TS13 —5E **67**
(Loftus)
Railway Cotts. TS13 —2B **66**
(Skinningrove)
Railway Cotts. TS16 —1C **94**
Railway Pl. TS6 —3E **55**
Railway St. DL14 —2D **103**
Railway St. TS18 —4C **48**
Railway Ter. DL4 —4C **104**
Railway Ter. TS10 —4D **29**
(in two parts)
Railway Ter. TS12 —5C **64**
(Brotton)
Railway Ter. TS12 —1A **82**
(Skelton)
Railway Ter. TS13 —5E **67**
(East Loftus)
Railway Ter. TS13 —4C **66**
(Loftus)
Railway Ter. TS16 —3D **85**
Railway Ter. TS17 —2D **71**
Raincliffe Ct. TS8 —4C **90**
Raine St. DL14 —1C **102**
Raine Wlk. DL5 —1E **109**
Rainford Av. TS19 —1F **47**
Rainham Clo. TS3 —5B **54**
Rainham Clo. TS17 —3B **86**
Rainsford Cres. TS3 —5B **54**
Rainton Av. TS5 —5D **73**
Rainton Dri. TS17 —2D **87**
Rainton Gro. TS18 —2B **68**
Raisbeck Clo. DL14 —4D **45**
Raisby Clo. TS5 —1C **88**

Raisdale Clo. TS17 —5E **71**
Raisegill Clo. TS3 —1C **74**
Raithwaite Clo. TS14 —2D **97**
Raithwaite Ho. TS14 —2D **97**
Rake Av. TS19 —5E **31**
Raleigh Clo. TS11 —5F **45**
Raleigh Ct. TS2 —2D **51**
Raleigh Rd. TS20 —2B **48**
Raleigh Wlk. TS20 —2B **48**
Ralfland Way. TS7 —4B **92**
Ralph Sq. TS19 —3E **47**
Rampside Av. TS19 —5E **31**
Ramsay Wlk. DL1 —4D **113**
Ramsbury Av. TS19 —5E **31**
Ramsey Cres. DL14 —5A **102**
Ramsey Cres. TS15 —5C **94**
Ramsey Dri. DL17 —3A **100**
Ramsey Pl. DL5 —5F **107**
Ramsey Rd. TS10 —1A **42**
Ramsey View. TS20 —1D **49**
*Ramsey Wlk. TS14 —4D **97***
(off Hutton La.)
Ramsgate. TS18 —1B **70**
Ramsgill. DL1 —4C **116**
Ramsgill Ho. DL1 —4C **116**
Randolph St. TS12 —2D **63**
Ranulf Ct. DL5 —4A **106**
Raskelf Av. TS19 —1E **47**
Rathnew Av. TS19 —5D **31**
Ratten La. TS6 —4C **56**
Raunds Av. TS19 —1E **47**
Raven Clo. TS14 —3A **96**
Ravendale Rd. TS3 —2A **76**
Raven La. TS20 —4B **32**
Ravenscar Cres. TS19 —2A **48**
Ravenscroft Av. TS3 —3F **73**
Ravensdale. TS5 —2C **88**
Ravensdale Rd. DL3 —4E **115**
Ravensdale Wlk. DL3 —4E **115**
Ravensworth Av. DL14 —4C **102**
Ravensworth Av. TS6 —1D **77**
Ravensworth Cres. TS24 —3B **4**
Ravensworth Gro. TS18 —2B **68**
Ravensworth Rd. DL17 —2E **101**
Ravensworth Rd. TS23 —1F **33**
Ravenwood Clo. TS27 —4A **4**
Rawcliffe Av. TS5 —2D **89**
Rawley Dri. TS10 —3B **42**
Rawlings Ct. TS24 —1E **7**
Rawlinson Av. TS7 —4F **33**
Rawlinson St. TS13 —2A **66**
Raydale. TS8 —5E **89**
Raylton Av. TS7 —3E **91**
Reading Rd. TS20 —2B **48**
Rear W. La. DL14 —5B **102**
Rectory Av. TS14 —3D **97**
Rectory Clo. TS14 —3D **97**
Rectory La. TS21 —5B **68**
Rectory La. Ind. Est. TS14 —4D **97**
Rectory Row. TS21 —5B **118**
Red Barnes Way. DL1 —5E **113**
Redbrook Av. TS19 —5F **31**
Redcar Av. TS11 —4C **44**
Redcar Av. TS19 —1F **47**
Redcar Clo. TS25 —1E **11**
Redcar La. TS10 —4E 29 to 4E **43**
Redcar Retail Pk. TS10 —5D **29**
Redcar Rd. TS6 —2B **54**
Redcar Rd. TS10 & TS11
—4F 43 to 4D **45**
Redcar Rd. TS14 —5D **59**
(Dunsdale)
Redcar Rd. TS14 —2E **97**
(Guisborough)
Redcar Rd. TS17 —4D 71 & 4E **71**
Redcar Rd. E. TS6 —2C **54**
Redcar St. TS2 —2A **52**

Redditch Av. TS19 —1F **47**
Rede Ho. TS1 —3A **52**
Redesdale Clo. TS2 —5E **35**
Redesdale Gro. TS17 —3A **86**
Red Hall Dri. DL1 —5E **113**
Redhill Rd. TS19 —1E **47**
Redland Clo. TS18 —1B **68**
Red Lion St. TS10 —4D **29**
Redmarshall Rd. TS21 —4A **46**
Redmayne Clo. TS23 —4F **19**
Redmire Clo. DL1 —4B **112**
Redmire Rd. TS18 —1F **69**
Redruth Av. TS19 —1F **47**
Redwing La. TS20 —4C **32**
Redwing Rising. TS14 —3B **96**
Redwood Clo. TS27 —3A **4**
Redwood Clo. TS7 —1F **91**
Redwood Dri. TS12 —2B **62**
Redworth Gro. DL14 —2F **103**
Redworth Rd. DL3 —4C **110**
Redworth Rd. DL4 —4C **104**
Redworth Rd. TS23 —1A **34**
Redworth St. TS24 —1A **12**
Redworth Wlk. TS24 —5A **8**
Redworth Way. DL5 —3D **109**
Reed Clo. TS20 —1D **49**
Reedston Rd. TS26 —3A **6**
Reed St. TS17 —2D **71**
Reed St. TS24 —5A **8**
Reepham Clo. TS19 —1D **47**
Reethmoor Clo. DL1 —3E **117**
Reeth Pl. DL5 —4C **106**
Reeth Rd. TS5 —3D **73**
Reeth Rd. TS18 —3D **69**
Regal Clo. TS25 —1D **17**
Regal Dri. DL1 —2C **112**
Regency Av. TS6 —3E **77**
Regency Dri. TS25 —4F **11**
*Regency Ho. TS18 —1B **70***
(off West Row)
Regency Pk. TS17 —4B **86**
*Regency W. Mall. TS18 —1B **70***
(off West Row)
Regent Ct. TS6 —4F **55**
Regent M. TS18 —1B **70**
Regent Rd. TS4 —2B **74**
Regent Sq. TS24 —3D **9**
Regent St. DL4 —1D **103**
Regent St. DL14 —1D **103**
Regent St. TS10 —4D **29**
Regent St. TS18 —5B **48**
Regent St. TS24 —3D **9**
Reid St. DL3 —5F **111**
Reid Ter. TS14 —2E **97**
Reigate Av. TS5 —3F **73**
Reigate Clo. TS19 —5E **31**
Rembrandt Way. DL5 —4E **109**
Renfrew Rd. TS20 —5C **32**
Rennie Clo. DL1 —2C **116**
Rennie Rd. TS6 —4A **54**
Rennie St. DL17 —3B **100**
Rennie Wlk. DL1 —2C **116**
Renown Wlk. TS6 —4C **54**
Renvyle Av. TS19 —5D **31**
Repton Av. TS19 —1E **47**
Repton Rd. TS3 —5B **54**
Resolution, The. TS7 —3B **92**
Resource Clo. TS6 —3C **54**
Retford Clo. TS19 —1F **47**
Retford Gro. TS25 —1C **14**
Rettendon Clo. TS19 —5F **31**
Revesby Rd. TS3 —2A **76**
Reynoldston Av. TS19 —5E **31**
Rhodes Ct. TS17 —1E **87**
Rhondda Av. TS19 —1F **47**
Rhoosegate. TS17 —5F **71**
Rhyl Clo. TS19 —5F **31**

Ribble Clo. TS22 —4B 18
Ribble Ct. DL1 —5A 116
Ribble Dri. DL1 —5A 116
Ribbleton Clo. TS7 —3A 92
Ribchester Clo. TS19 —5E 31
Riccall Ct. TS10 —2C 42
 (off Hambleton Av.)
Riccarton Clo. TS19 —5D 31
Richard Ct. DL1 —4B 112
Richard Ct. TS26 —5E 7
Richard Hind Wlk. TS18 —3A 70
Richardson Av. DL14 —5B 102
Richardson Rd. TS17 —5C 70
Richardson Rd. TS18 —2A 70
Richardson St. TS26 —4E 7
Richardson Wlk. DL5 —4F 107
Richards St. TS12 —1F 81
Richard Ter. DL14 —5F 103
Richmond Av. DL14 —3B 102
Richmond Clo. DL3 —3C 110
Richmond Clo. DL17 —3A 101
Richmond Clo. TS6 —1E 77
Richmond Ct. TS6 —4F 55
Richmond Cres. TS23 —1F 33
Richmond Fields. DL16 —3E 99
Richmond Rd. TS10 —1F 43
Richmond Rd. TS18 —2F 69
Richmond St. TS2 —2F 51
Richmond St. TS18 —4C 48
Richmond St. TS25 —2F 11
Ricknall Av. DL5 —3F 109
Ricknall Clo. TS5 —2C 88
Ricknall La. DL5 —1F 109
Ridge, The. TS12 —3D 63
Ridgeway. DL3 —2A 112
Ridgeway. DL5 —2C 108
Ridley Av. TS5 —3D 73
Ridley Ct. TS20 —5B 32
Ridley Ct. TS26 —4E 7
Ridley Dri. TS20 —5A 32
Ridley St. TS10 —4D 29
Ridley's Yd. TS20 —5C 32
Ridley Ter. TS13 —1B 66
Ridley Ter. TS26 —4E 7
Ridlington Way. TS24 —4C 4
Ridsdale Av. TS19 —1E 47
Ridsdale St. DL1 —3C 116
Rievaulx Av. TS23 —5D 19
Rievaulx Clo. TS19 —5E 31
Rievaulx Ct. DL16 —1B 98
Rievaulx Dri. TS5 —4F 73
Rievaulx Rd. TS12 —1E 81
Rievaulx Wlk. TS6 —1E 77
Rievaulx Way. TS14 —3F 97
Rifts Av. TS12 —1C 62
Riftswood Dri. TS11 —5C 44
Rigden Ho. TS2 —2F 51
 (off Silver St.)
Riggston Pl. TS26 —3B 6
Rigg, The. TS15 —5D 95
Riley St. TS18 —1A 70
Rillington Clo. TS19 —5D 31
Rillston Clo. TS26 —4B 6
Rimdale Dri. TS19 —4B 46
Rimswell Pde. TS19 —4C 46
Rimswell Rd. TS19 —3B 46
Ring Rd., The. TS19 & TS20
 —3F 47
Ringway. TS17 —5F 71
Ringwood Cres. TS19 —1F 47
Ringwood Rd. TS3 —1B 76
Ripley St. TS3 —5B 54
Ripley Rd. TS20 —4A 32
Ripon Clo. TS19 —1E 47
Ripon Dri. DL1 —4C 116
Ripon Rd. TS7 —2C 92
Ripon Rd. TS10 —1A 44

Ripon Rd. TS12 —4D 65
Ripon Way. TS6 —5F 55
Rise, The. DL3 —3E 115
Rise, The. TS7 —3B 92
Rishton Clo. TS19 —1E 47
Rissington Wlk. TS17 —1F 87
Ritson Rd. DL5 —1D 109
Rium Ter. TS24 —4F 7
Riverbank Trading Est. DL1
 —5B 112
River Ct. TS2 —5D 35
Riverdale Ct. TS5 —2C 72
Rivergarth. DL1 —3F 113
Riverhead Av. TS19 —1E 47
Rivermead Av. DL1 —3F 113
Riversdene. TS9 —4D 119
Riverside. DL14 —4F 103
Riverside. TS18 —1C 70
Riverside Bus. Pk. TS2 —2D 51
Riverside Dri. DL1 —3F 113
Riverside M. TS15 —2C 94
Riverside Pk. Ind. Est. TS2
 —1E 51 & 2D 51
Riverside Pk. Rd. TS2 —2D 51
Riverside Rd. TS2 —3F 37
Riverside Way. DL1 —4D 113
Riverslea. TS9 —4D 119
Riverston Clo. TS26 —3A 6
Riversway. TS7 —2F 91
River View Ind. Est. DL1 —5C 112
Robert Av. TS6 —3E 55
Robert Huggins Ho. TS4 —1C 88
Roberts St. TS6 —3E 55
Robert St. DL16 —4B 98
Robert St. TS17 —2D 71
Roberts Wlk. DL1 —2C 116
Robin Clo. TS17 —4C 86
Robinson Ct. TS13 —4E 67
Robinson St. TS12 —5C 62
Robinson St. TS13 —5E 67
Robinson Ter. TS13 —4D 67
Robson Av. TS17 —4E 87
Robson Ct. TS24 —1E 7
Robson Dri. DL4 —2C 104
Robson St. TS23 —3E 35
Rochdale Av. TS19 —1F 47
Rochdale Clo. TS3 —2E 75
Rochester Clo. DL14 —3A 102
Rochester Clo. TS17 —1D 71
Rochester Dri. TS10 —2F 43
Rochester Rd. TS5 —2F 73
Rochester Rd. TS19 —5F 31
Rochester Rd. TS23 —5F 19
Rochester Way. DL1 —4F 113
Roche Wlk. DL3 —4A 110
Rockall Av. TS19 —5D 31
Rockcliffe Ct. TS13 —1E 67
Rockcliffe Ho. DL1 —4C 116
Rockcliffe Ter. TS13 —2A 66
Rockcliffe View. TS13 —2A 66
Rocket St. DL1 —2C 116
Rocket Ter. TS10 —4B 28
Rockferry Clo. TS19 —5D 31
Rockingham Dri. DL14 —3A 102
Rockingham St. DL1 —3A 116
Rockliffe Rd. TS5 —2D 73
Rockpool Clo. TS24 —1F 7
Rockport Ct. TS18 —4D 49
Rock Rd. DL16 —4B 98
Rockwell Av. DL1 —3E 113
Rockwood Clo. TS14 —4F 97
Rodmell Clo. TS3 —2B 76
Rodney Clo. TS23 —5E 33
Rodney St. TS26 —4E 7
Roebuck Clo. TS17 —4D 87
Roecliffe Gro. TS19 —5C 30
Roedean Dri. TS16 —5D 85

Rogeri Pl. TS24 —4D 5
Rokeby Av. TS4 —3B 74
Rokeby St. TS18 —2A 70
Rokeby St. TS24 —1A 8
Roker Clo. DL1 —5E 113
Roker St. TS24 —5F 7
Roker Ter. TS18 —2A 70
Rolleston Av. TS19 —5E 31
Romaine Pk. TS24 —1A 8
Romald Kirk Rd. TS2 —1D 51
Romaldkirk Wlk. DL1 —4D 117
Romanby Av. TS19 —1F 47
Romanby Clo. TS24 —1A 8
Romanby Gdns. TS5 —2F 89
Roman Rd. TS5 —1E 73
Romany Rd. TS9 —3B 120
Romford Rd. TS19 —5E 31
Romney Clo. TS10 —3F 43
Romney St. TS1 —4F 51
Romsey Rd. TS19 —1F 47
Ronaldshay Ter. TS11 —4E 45
Rookery Dale. TS12 —4C 80
Rookhope Gro. DL14 —4A 102
Rook La. TS20 —3C 32
Rookwood Hunt. DL5 —4A 106
Rookwood Rd. TS7 —3C 92
Ropery St. TS18 —5B 48
Ropner Av. TS18 —2F 69
Rosa St. DL16 —3B 98
Roscoe Rd. TS23 —5F 33
Roscoe St. TS1 —4B 52
Rose Av. TS11 —4B 44
Rosebank. TS26 —1D 11
Rosebay Ct. DL3 —1E 115
Rosebay St. TS14 —4B 96
Roseberry Av. TS9 —3C 120
 (Great Ayton)
Roseberry Av. TS9 —3F 119
 (Stokesley)
Roseberry Cres. TS6 —5B 56
Roseberry Cres. TS9
 —2B 120 to 3B 120
Roseberry Cres. TS26 —4C 32
Roseberry Dri. TS8 —5D 89
Roseberry Dri. TS9 —2B 120
Roseberry Flats. TS23 —1E 33
Roseberry M. TS26 —4D 7
Roseberry Rd. TS4 —5B 52
Roseberry Rd. TS9 —3B 120
Roseberry Rd. TS10 —2B 42
Roseberry Rd. TS20 —4C 32
Roseberry Rd. TS23 —1D 33
Roseberry Rd. TS26 —4D 7
Roseberry Sq. TS10 —2C 42
Roseberry Ter. DL4 —2D 105
Roseberry View. TS19 —3D 71
Rosebery St. DL3 —5F 111
Rose Cotts. DL4 —2C 104
Rosecroft Av. TS4 —2A 74
Rosecroft Av. TS13 —5C 66
Rosecroft La. TS13 —5C 66
Rosedale. DL16 —2B 98
Rosedale Av. TS4 —1A 74
Rosedale Av. TS26 —5D 7
Rosedale Clo. TS21 —3B 118
Rosedale Cres. DL3 —4B 110
Rosedale Cres. DL4 —3E 105
Rosedale Cres. TS13 —3C 66
Rosedale Cres. TS14 —4A 96
Rosedale Gdns. TS12 —5F 81
Rosedale Gdns. TS19 —5E 31
Rosedale Gdns. TS23 —4E 19
Rosedale Gro. TS10 —1A 42
Rosedale Rd. TS7 —3C 92
Rosehill. TS9 —4B 120
Rose Hill Dri. TS9 —4E 119
Rose Hill Way. TS9 —4E 119

St Andrew's Rd. TS11 —2A **60**
St Andrew's Rd. E. TS6 —3F **55**
St Andrew's Rd. W. TS6 —3F **55**
St Andrew's Rd. DL1 —4B **112**
St Andrew's Ter. DL14 —3D **103**
St Andrews Way. DL5 —5E **109**
St Anne's Rd. TS11 —2A **60**
St Ann's Ct. TS24 —5B **8**
St Ann's Ind. Est. TS18 —4D **49**
St Ann's Ter. TS18 —4D **49**
St Augustine's Way. DL3 —1A **116**
St Austell Clo. TS8 —4D **89**
St Barbara's Wlk. DL5 —4F **107**
St Barnabas Rd. TS5 —1E **73**
St Bees Wlk. TS24 —5A 8
(off Lamb St.)
St Bernard Rd. TS18 —1B **70**
St Catherines Ct. TS3 —1D **75**
St Catherine's Ct. TS24 —5A **8**
St Chad's Clo. DL14 —4E **103**
St Charles Rd. DL16 —1D **99**
St Columba's Av. TS22 —2D **33**
St Crispins Ct. TS19 —3A **48**
St Cuthbert St. TS17 —3D **71**
St Cuthbert's Av. TS23 —2D **33**
St Cuthbert's Pl. DL3 —2E **115**
St Cuthbert's Rd. TS18 —2B **70**
St Cuthbert's Ter. DL17 —2B **100**
St Cuthbert St. TS24 —1C **8**
St Cuthbert's Wlk. DL14 —4D **103**
St Cuthbert's Wlk. TS13 —5B **66**
St Cuthbert's Way. DL1 —2B **116**
St Cuthbert's Way. DL5 —2E **109**
St David's Clo. DL16 —1E **99**
(in two parts)
St David's Clo. TS23 —2D **33**
St David's Grn. DL1 —4F **113**
St David's Rd. TS6 —3F **55**
St David's Wlk. TS26 —3B **6**
St Edmund's Grn. TS21 —4C **118**
(in two parts)
St Edmund's Ter. TS21 —4C **118**
St Elizabeth's Clo. DL5 —2E **107**
St George's Bungalows. TS6
—3F **55**
St George's Cres. TS11 —2B **60**
St George's Rd. E. TS6 —3F **55**
St George's Rd. W. TS6 —3F **55**
St George's Ter. TS13 —5B 66
(off Liverton Ter.)
St Germain's Clo. TS11 —4D **45**
St Germain's La. TS11 —4E **45**
St Giles Clo. DL3 —2B **114**
St Godrics Rd. DL5 —1D **109**
St Helen's Clo. TS6 —1E **77**
St Helen's St. TS24 —1C **8**
St Helen's Wlk. TS13 —5B **66**
St Hilda's Chare. TS24 —3D **9**
St Hilda's Cres. TS24 —2D **9**
St Hildas Flats. DL1 —2B **116**
St Hilda's Pl. TS13 —4D **67**
St Hilda's Ter. TS13 —3B **66**
St Hilda St. TS24 —3E **9**
St Hild Clo. DL3 —2C **114**
St James Ct. TS6 —2E **55**
St James' Gdns. TS2 —2A **52**
St James Ho. TS18 —4D **49**
St James M. TS1 —5E **51**
St James' Pl. TS24 —5A **8**
St Joan's Gro. TS25 —3F **11**
St John's Clo. TS18 —4B **48**
St John's Cres. DL1 —2C **116**
St John's Gro. TS10 —5E **29**
St John's Pl. DL1 —2B **116**
St John's Rd. DL4 —4C **104**
St Joseph's Ct. TS26 —5E **7**
St Leonard's Clo. TS13 —5B **66**

St Leonard's Rd. TS14 —4B **96**
St Luke's Av. TS17 —3E **71**
St Luke's Cotts. TS4 —2C **74**
St Luke's Ct. TS26 —3D **7**
St Margaret's Gro. TS5 —3E **73**
St Margaret's Gro. TS6 —4C **54**
St Margaret's Gro. TS10 —1E **43**
St Margaret's Gro. TS17 —5E **71**
St Margaret's Gro. TS25 —3F **11**
St Margaret's Way. TS12 —4C **64**
St Mark's Clo. TS11 —4D **45**
St Mark's Clo. TS19 —4C **46**
St Martin's Clo. TS13 —5A **66**
St Marys Clo. DL14 —5C **102**
St Mary's Clo. TS18 —4C **48**
St Mary's Ct. TS6 —3F **55**
St Mary St. TS24 —2D **9**
St Mary's Wlk. TS5 —4E **73**
St Matthew's Ct. TS6 —2E **55**
St Mawes Clo. TS26 —3B **6**
St Michael's Clo. TS13 —5B **66**
St Michael's Ct. TS20 —2C **48**
St Michael's Gro. TS20 —2C **48**
St Nicholas Ct. TS6 —2E **55**
St Nicholas Gdns. TS15 —4F **95**
St Nicholas Ind. Est. DL1 —4C **112**
St Ninian's Clo. DL3 —2B **114**
St Oswald's Clo. DL14 —4E **103**
St Oswald's Ct. DL5 —4F **107**
St Oswald's Cres. TS23 —2D **33**
St Oswalds Ct. TS24 —3E **7**
St Oswald St. TS24 —2D **9**
St Oswald's Wlk. DL5 —4F **107**
St Patrick's Clo. TS6 —3F **55**
St Patrick's Rd. TS6 —3F **55**
St Paul's Clo. DL16 —3B **98**
St Paul's Ct. TS19 —4A **48**
St Paul's Gdns. DL16 —3B **98**
St Paul's Pl. DL1 —4B **112**
St Paul's Rd. TS1 —4E **51**
St Paul's Rd. TS17 —3D **71**
St Paul's Rd. TS19 —4A **48**
St Paul's Rd. TS26 —5E **7**
St Paul's St. DL16 —3B **98**
St Paul's St. TS19 —5A **48**
St Paul's Ter. DL1 —4B **112**
St Paul's Ter. DL4 —2D **105**
St Paul's Ter. TS19 —4A **48**
St Peter's Gro. TS10 —5E **29**
St Peter's Rd. TS18 —2A **70**
St Peter's Sq. TS17 —1E **87**
St Thomas Gro. TS10 —1E **43**
St Vincent Ter. TS10 —4C **28**
St Wilfrid's Wlk. DL14 —4F **103**
(in two parts)
Salcombe Clo. TS8 —1C **90**
Salcombe Dri. TS25 —1E **15**
Salcombe Way. TS10 —3F **43**
Salisbury Gro. TS10 —1A **44**
Salisbury Pl. DL14 —2E **103**
Salisbury Pl. TS26 —2C **6**
Salisbury St. TS17 —3E **71**
Salisbury Ter. DL3 —5F **111**
(in two parts)
Salisbury Ter. DL4 —3B **104**
Salisbury Ter. TS24 —2A **52**
Salisbury Ter. TS20 —2C **48**
Saltaire Ter. TS25 —5D **15**
Saltburn Bank. TS12 —1E **63**
Saltburn La. TS12
—5D **63** to 1E **63**
Saltburn Rd. TS12
—1E **63** to 4C **64**
Saltburn Rd. TS17 —4E **71**
Saltcote. TS7 —1F **91**
Salters Av. DL1 —4D **113**
Salters Clo. DL1 —3D **113**

Saltersgate Rd. DL1 —1C **112**
Saltersgill Av. TS4
—3A **74** to 1C **90**
Saltersgill Clo. TS4 —3A **74**
Salters La. DL1 —4F **117**
(Firth Moor)
Salter's La. DL1 —1C **112**
(Harrowgate Village)
Salter's La. TS21
—3B **118** to 1C **118**
Salter's La. N. DL1 —1B **112**
Salter's La. S. DL1 —3D **113**
Salter Wlk. TS24 —1C **8**
Saltholme Clo. TS2 —4F **35**
Saltney Rd. TS20 —1A **48**
Salton Clo. TS5 —2C **72**
Saltram Clo. TS17 —5C **86**
Saltram Gro. TS7 —1D **91**
Saltscar. TS10 —2F **43**
Saltview Ter. TS2 —5B **36**
Saltwells Cres. TS4 —5C **52**
Saltwells Ind. Est. TS4 —4B **52**
Saltwells Rd. TS4 —4B **52**
Salt Yd. DL3 —2A **116**
Salutation Rd. DL3
—3B **114** & 3C **114**
Salvin St. DL16 —2E **99**
Samaria Gdns. TS5 —2E **89**
Sambrook Gdns. TS5 —2E **89**
Samphire St. TS2 —5A **36**
Sampson Pl. DL5 —4D **107**
Samsung Av. TS22 —1B **18**
Samsung Ind. Pk. TS22 —1B **18**
Samsung Roundabout. TS22
—1B **18**
Samuelson Ho. TS3 —2E **75**
Samuel St. TS19 —4A **48**
Sandalwood Ct. TS5 —2F **89**
Sandbanks Dri. TS24 —4B **4**
Sanderson Clo. DL5 —4E **107**
Sanderson St. DL1 —2B **116**
Sand Flatts La. TS5 —2F **89**
Sandford Bus. Pk. TS6
—1C **54** & 2D **55**
Sandford Clo. TS4 —3B **74**
Sandgate Ind. Est. TS25 —2B **12**
Sandhall Clo. TS23 —2A **20**
Sandling Ct. TS7 —2F **91**
Sandmartin La. TS20 —3C **32**
Sandmoor Clo. TS6 —2F **77**
Sandmoor Rd. TS11 —2A **60**
Sandown Dri. DL5 —2E **107**
Sandown Pk. TS10 —2E **43**
Sandown Rd. TS23 —5E **19**
Sandown Way. TS17 —2A **72**
Sandpiper Clo. TS10 —3F **43**
Sandpiper Wlk. TS2 —4F **35**
Sandport Wlk. TS18 —4D 49
(off Alnport Rd.)
Sandriggs. DL3 —4C **110**
Sandringham Ho. TS3 —3E **75**
Sandringham Rd. TS3 —3E **75**
Sandringham Rd. TS6 —4F **55**
Sandringham Rd. TS10 —4D **29**
Sandringham Rd. TS17 —3E **71**
Sandringham Rd. TS18 —1A **70**
Sandringham Rd. TS26 —4E **7**
Sandsend Rd. TS6 —5A **56**
Sandsend Rd. TS10 —1B **42**
Sands Hall Roundabout. TS21
—5A **118**
Sandwell Av. TS3 —3A **76**
Sandwell Chare. TS24 —3D **9**
Sandwich Gro. TS27 —4B **4**
Sandwood Pk. TS14 —5A **96**
Sandy Flatts Ct. TS5 —2F **89**
Sandy Flatts La. TS5 —2F **89**

Sandy La. TS11 —5E **59** to 4A **60**
Sandy La. TS22 —1C **32** & 2D **33**
(in two parts)
Sandy La. W. TS24 —4A **18**
Sapley Clo. TS17 —2E **87**
Sarah St. TS25 —2A **12**
*Sark Wlk. TS14 —4A **96***
(off Hutton La.)
Satley Rd. TS23 —3A **20**
Saunton Av. TS10 —3F **43**
Saunton Rd. TS23 —1A **34**
Sawley Clo. DL3 —4A **110**
Sawley Gro. TS18 —2B **68**
Sawtry Rd. TS3 —2A **76**
Saxby Rd. TS20 —2C **48**
Saxon Ct. DL14 —2C **102**
Saxonfield. TS8 —3C **90**
Scalby Gro. TS10 —2F **43**
Scalby Gro. TS19 —5B **46**
Scalby Rd. TS3 —1C **74**
Scalby Sq. TS17 —4E **71**
Scaling Ct. TS14 —4D **97**
Scampton Clo. TS17 —2C **86**
Scanbeck Dri. TS11 —4E **45**
Scarborough St. TS6 —3B **54**
Scarborough St. TS13 —4B **66**
Scarborough St. TS17 —3D **71**
Scarborough St. TS24 —5A **8**
Scargill. DL1 —4C **116**
Scargill Ct. DL1 —4D **117**
Scargill Dri. DL16 —1C **98**
Scarteen Clo. TS14 —4D **97**
Scarth St. DL3 —2F **115**
Scarth Wlk. TS18 —5B **48**
Scarthwood Clo. TS17 —5D **87**
Scawfell Gro. TS25 —3F **11**
Scawton Ct. TS10 —2C **42**
Scholars Path. DL5 —5A **106**
School Av. TS5 —2C **72**
School Aycliffe La. DL5 —3A **108**
School Clo. TS11 —4E **45**
School Clo. TS18 —2B **70**
School Croft. TS1 —2A **52**
School La. TS13 —5B **66**
School St. DL3 —4C **110**
*School Wlk. TS18 —2B **70***
(off School Clo.)
Schooner Ct. TS24 —4B **8**
Scira Ct. DL1 —3C **112**
Scolars Ct. TS15 —2C **94**
Scotforth Clo. TS7 —3A **92**
Scotney Rd. TS23 —5E **19**
Scott Dri. TS20 —5A **32**
Scott Gro. TS25 —3B **10**
Scotton Clo. TS18 —3C **68**
Scotton Ct. TS3 —2B **76**
Scott Pl. DL5 —4C **106**
Scott Rd. DL14 —4C **102**
Scott Rd. TS6 —2C **76**
Scott's Rd. TS2 & TS3 —2B **52**
Scotts Ter. DL3 —2B **112**
Scott St. DL4 —4C **104**
Scott St. TS10 —4D **29**
Scrafton Pl. TS11 —5D **45**
Scruton Clo. TS18 —2C **68**
Scugdale Clo. TS15 —5C **94**
Scurfield Rd. TS19 —1B **46**
Seaford Clo. TS10 —3E **43**
Seaham Clo. TS20 —5F **31**
Seaham St. TS20 —4C **48**
Seaham View. TS20 —5F **31**
Sealand Clo. TS17 —3E **87**
Sealey St. TS1 —3B **52**
Seal Sands European Chemical Pk.
                    TS2 —5B **24**
Seal Sands Link Rd. TS23
               —2E **19** to 2B **36**

Seal Sands Rd. TS2
               —2C **36** to 4C **24**
Seamer Clo. TS5 —4F **73**
Seamer Gro. TS18 —2E **69**
Seamer Rd. TS8 —5C **88**
Seathwaite. TS5 —2C **88**
Seaton Carew Rd. TS2 & TS25
               —5B **36** to 3C **22**
Seaton Clo. TS10 —3A **44**
Seaton Clo. TS19 —5B **46**
Seaton La. TS25 —5F **11**
Seatonport Ct. TS18 —4D **49**
Seaton St. TS1 —4A **52**
Sea View Ter. TS6 —1E **55**
Sea View Ter. TS24 —1C **8**
Secker Pl. DL5 —5F **107**
Sedgebrook Gdns. TS3 —3B **76**
Sedgefield Ind. Est. TS21 —3C **118**
Sedgefield Rd. TS5 —2D **89**
Sedgemoor Rd. TS6 —3F **77**
Sedgemoor Way. TS23 —4B **20**
Sedgwick St. DL3 —5F **111**
Sefton Rd. TS3 —1B **76**
Sefton Way. TS15 —5B **94**
Selbourne St. TS1 —4E **51**
Selbourne Ter. DL3 —1F **115**
Selby Cres. DL3 —4B **110**
Selby Gro. TS25 —4E **11**
Selby Rd. TS7 —3C **92**
Selkirk Clo. TS4 —4A **74**
(in two parts)
Selset Av. TS3 —4F **75**
Selset Clo. DL1 —4D **117**
Selwood Clo. TS17 —2E **87**
Selworthy Grn. TS17 —5A **86**
Selwyn Dri. TS19 —2C **46**
Semmerwater Gro. TS10 —1D **43**
Serpentine Gdns. TS26 —4C **6**
Serpentine Rd. TS26 —4C **6**
Seton Wlk. DL5 —2F **109**
Severn Clo. TS14 —4C **96**
Severn Gro. TS12 —5D **63**
Severn Gro. TS22 —5B **18**
Severn Rd. TS10 —5B **28**
Severn Way. DL1 —5A **116**
Severn Way. TS10 —5B **28**
Severs Dri. TS8 —4D **89**
Severs St. TS6 —2A **54**
Seymour Av. TS16 —1C **94**
Seymour Clo. TS11 —5F **45**
Seymour Cres. TS16 —1B **94**
Seymour Dri. TS16 —1B **94**
Seymour Gro. TS16 —1B **94**
*Seymour Hill Ter. TS13 —4D **67***
(off North Rd.)
Seymour St. DL14 —4D **103**
Shackleton Clo. TS17 —1E **87**
Shadforth Dri. TS23 —3A **20**
Shadwell Clo. TS6 —4D **77**
Shaftesbury Rd. TS6 —5D **55**
Shaftesbury St. TS18 —1B **70**
Shafto St. DL16 —3B **98**
Shafto Way. DL5
               —5E **107** to 1E **109**
Shakespeare Av. TS6 —4A **56**
Shakespeare Av. TS25 —2E **11**
Shakespeare Rd. DL1 —4B **116**
Shaldon Clo. TS10 —3F **43**
Shannon Ct. TS25 —4C **14**
Shannon Cres. TS19 —4B **46**
Shannon Way. DL1 —5A **116**
Sharp Cres. TS24 —1E **7**
Sharp Rd. DL5 —1E **109**
Sharrock Clo. TS3 —4C **52**
Shawbrow View. DL3 —2A **114**
Shawbrow View. DL14 —5D **103**
Shaw Cres. TS6 —4F **55**

Shawcross Av. TS6 —3E **55**
Shaw Gro. TS25 —3B **10**
Shaw St. DL16 —3C **98**
Shearwater Av. DL1 —2E **117**
Shearwater La. TS20 —3B **32**
Sheepfoote Hill. TS15 —4C **94**
Sheerness Gro. TS24 —5A **8**
Sheerness Way. TS10 —3F **43**
Shelley Clo. TS23 —2E **19**
Shelley Cres. TS6 —5D **55**
Shelley Gro. TS25 —2D **11**
Shelley Rd. DL1 —1C **116**
Shelley Rd. TS4 —3A **74**
Shelton Ct. TS3 —2A **76**
Shepherd Clo. TS17 —5C **70**
Shepherd St. TS12 —4C **80**
Shepherdson Ct. TS6 —2B **54**
Sheppards Croft. DL5 —2A **108**
Shepton Clo. TS17 —5F **71**
Sheraton Clo. DL5 —1E **109**
Sheraton Pk. TS19 —2F **47**
Sheraton Rd. DL5 —1E **109**
Sheraton St. DL3 —4A **112**
Sheraton St. TS18 —1A **70**
Sherborne Clo. DL3 —4A **110**
Sherburn Av. TS23 —4F **19**
Sherburn Clo. TS5 —1D **89**
Sheridan Gro. TS25 —2D **11**
Sheriff St. TS26 —4E **7**
Sherwood Clo. TS7 —1C **92**
Sherwood Dri. TS11 —5C **44**
Sherwood Rd. TS17 —2D **87**
Shetland Clo. TS5 —3E **89**
Shetland Dri. DL1 —2E **113**
Shevington Gro. TS7 —3F **91**
Shibden Rd. TS3 —5D **53**
Shields Ter. TS24 —1A **8**
Shield Wlk. DL5 —5E **107**
Shildon By-Pass. DL4 —4A **104**
Shildon Clo. TS23 —4E **19**
Shildon Ct. DL4 —4C **104**
Shildon Ind. Est. DL4 —4D **105**
Shildon St. DL1 —4B **112**
Shincliffe Rd. TS23 —3A **20**
Shinwell Cres. TS6 —3B **54**
Ship Inn Yd. TS18 —1B **70**
Shipley Gro. DL14 —5A **102**
Shirley Av. TS5 —2C **72**
Shoreham Clo. TS10 —3F **43**
Shoreswood Wlk. TS5 —2E **89**
Short Clo. TS18 —4B **70**
Short St. DL14 —4C **102**
Short St. TS3 —3C **52**
Shotley Clo. TS23 —4E **19**
Shotton Ct. TS23 —5A **20**
Shrewsbury Rd. TS3 —1A **76**
Shrewsbury St. TS25 —2E **11**
Shropshire Wlk. TS25 —2F **11**
Shutts Ct. DL3 —2F **115**
Sid Chaplin Dri. DL5 —4C **106**
Sidcup Av. TS3 —4F **75**
Siddington Wlk. TS3
               —2E **75** & 1F **75**
Sideling Tails. TS15 —4D **95**
Sidlaw Av. TS12 —5D **63**
Sidlaw Rd. TS23 —5D **19**
Sidmouth Clo. TS8 —1C **90**
Sidney Ter. DL14 —1D **103**
Siemens St. DL17 —2B **100**
Sildale Clo. DL3 —4F **111**
Silkin Way. DL5 —5C **106**
Silton Gro. TS18 —2E **69**
Silver Chambers. TS18 —5C **48**
Silver Ct. TS18 —5C **48**
Silverdale. TS7 —3A **92**
Silverdale Pl. DL5 —5B **106**
Silver St. DL1 —2B **116**

Silver St. DL16 —3C **98**
Silver St. TS2 —2F **51**
Silver St. TS9 —4D **119**
Silver St. TS15 —2C **94**
Silver St. TS18 —5C **48**
Silver St. TS24 —5F **7**
Silverton Rd. TS14 —5E **97**
Silverwood Clo. TS27 —3A **4**
Silverwood Ct. TS17 —3D **71**
Simcox Ct. TS2 —2D **51**
Simonside Gro. TS17 —4A **86**
Simonside Wlk. TS7 —3B **76**
Simpasture Ct. DL5 —2D **109**
Simpasture Ga. DL5 —1D **109**
Simpson Clo. TS6 —3C **54**
Simpson Grn. TS6 —3B **54**
Simpson St. TS5 —1F **73**
Sinclair Rd. TS25 —4B **10**
Sinderby Clo. TS23 —4F **19**
Singapore Sq. TS16 —3B **84**
Sinnington Clo. TS14 —4E **97**
Sinnington Rd. TS17 —2D **87**
Sir E. D. Walker Homes. DL3
　　　　　　　—4D **115**
Sir Hugh Bell Ct. TS10 —4F **27**
Siskin Clo. TS20 —3B **32**
Sitwell Wlk. TS25 —3B **10**
Skeeby Clo. TS18 —2C **68**
Skeeby Rd. DL1 —4C **116**
Skeldale Gro. DL3 —4F **111**
Skelton Ct. TS14 —1E **97**
Skelton Dri. TS10 —1F **43**
Skelton Dri. TS11 —4F **45**
Skelton Ind. Est. TS12 —5F **63**
Skelton Rd. TS12 —1A **82**
Skelton Rd. TS17 —4E **71**
Skelton St. TS24 —5D **5**
Skelwith Rd. TS3 —2D **75**
Skerne Rd. DL5 —3E **109**
Skerne Rd. TS20 —1B **48**
Skerne Rd. TS24 —1E **7**
Skerries Cres. TS10 —4C **42**
Skerries Wlk. DL1 —2E **113**
Skiddaw Clo. TS16 —4C **84**
Skiddaw Ct. TS7 —3A **92**
Skinnergate. DL3 —2A **116**
Skinner St. TS18 —1B **70**
Skinningrove Bank Rd. TS13
　　　　　　　—1B **66**
Skinningrove Rd. TS13 —3A **66**
Skiplam Clo. TS8 —4D **89**
Skipper's La. TS6 —3A **54** to 2D **77**
Skipper's La. Ind. Est. TS6
　　(in three parts) —3A **54** & 4B **54**
Skipton Clo. DL5 —5C **106**
Skipton Clo. DL17 —3E **101**
Skipton Gro. DL14 —4C **102**
Skipton Moor Clo. DL1 —5D **117**
Skipton Rd. TS23 —5F **19**
Skirbeck Av. TS3 —2B **76**
Skirlaw Rd. DL5 —5E **107**
Skirlaw Rd. TS15 —4C **94**
Skottowe Cres. TS9 —3A **120**
Skottowe Dri. TS9 —3A **120**
Skripka Dri. TS22 —5B **18**
Skye Wlk. DL1 —2E **113**
Skye Wlk. TS14 —4C **96**
Slake Ter. TS24 —3B **8**
Slater Rd. TS6 —4A **56**
Slater St. TS26 —4E **7**
Slater Wlk. TS6 —4A **56**
Slayde The. TS15 —5D **95**
Sledmere Clo. TS23 —2A **20**
Sledmere Dri. TS5 —4F **73**
Sledwick Rd. TS23 —1A **34**
Sleights Ct. TS14 —2E **97**
Sleights Cres. TS6 —5A **56**

Slingsby Clo. TS5 —5F **73**
Slip Inn Bank. TS10 —1C **90**
Smeaton St. TS3 —4C **52**
Smirks Yd. TS20 —2C **32**
Smithfield Rd. DL1 —4B **116**
Smith's Dock Pk. Rd. TS6 —2D **77**
Smith's Dock Rd. TS6 —1B **54**
Smith St. TS18 —5B **48**
Smith Wlk. DL5 —5E **107**
Smyth Pl. TS24 —5E **5**
Smythsons Clo. DL5 —3A **108**
Snipe La. DL2 —5E **115** to 5C **116**
Snipe St. TS10 —4F **27**
Snowden St. TS6 —5E **55**
Snowdon Cres. TS10 —2C **42**
Snowdon Gro. TS24 —4B **4**
Snowdon Rd. TS2 —2F **51**
Sober Hall Av. TS17 —4A **86**
Soho Cotts. DL4 —4D **105**
Soho St. DL4 —4C **104**
Somerby Clo. TS24 —1A **8**
Somerby Ter. TS3 —1E **75**
Somersby Clo. TS24 —1A **8**
Somerset Cres. TS12 —1B **80**
Somerset Gro. DL1 —5C **112**
Somerset Rd. TS6 —4F **55**
Somerset Rd. TS14 —4D **97**
Somerset Rd. TS20 —1B **48**
Somerset St. TS1 —4B **52**
Somerset Ter. TS23 —2A **34**
Somerville Av. TS3 —3A **76**
Somerville Ct. DL1 —3B **112**
Somerville Ho. TS3 —4F 53
(off Purfleet Av.)
Soppett St. TS10 —4D **29**
Sorbonne Clo. TS17 —1C **70**
Sorrel Clo. TS19 —3C **46**
Sorrel Ct. TS7 —1D **91**
Sorrell Gro. TS14 —4B **96**
Sorrell Wynd. DL5 —2E **107**
Sotherby Rd. TS3 & TS6 —4E **53**
Southampton St. DL1 —5A **112**
Southampton St. TS10 —5E **29**
S. Arden St. DL1 —2A **116**
South Av. TS10 —2F **41**
South Av. TS23 —5E **33**
S. Bank By-Pass. TS3 & TS6
　　　　　　　—3E **53**
Southbank By-Pass. TS6 —2B **54**
S. Bank Rd. TS3 —3D **53**
Southbrooke Av. TS25 —3D **11**
Southburn Ter. TS25 —1F **11**
S. Church Enterprise Pk. DL14
　　　　　　　—5E **103**
S. Church Rd. DL14 —2D **103**
Southcliffe. DL14 —5F **103**
South Cotts. DL5 —3A **108**
South Ct. DL16 —5A **98**
South Ct. TS6 —3B **54**
South Cres. TS24 —3E **9**
Southdean Clo. TS8 —3F **89**
Southdean Dri. TS8 —3F **89**
South Dri. TS7 —1E **91**
　　(Marton)
South Dri. TS7 —4B **76**
　　(Ormesby)
South Dri. TS26 —4C **6**
Southend. TS4 —1B **74**
South End. TS25 —1C **16**
Southend Av. DL3 —3F **115**
Southend Pl. DL3 —3F **115**
Southfield Cres. TS20 —2D **49**
Southfield La. TS1 —4F **51** & 4A **52**
Southfield Rd. TS1
　　　　　　　—4F **51** to 4A **52**
Southfield Rd. TS11 —5E **45**
Southfield Rd. TS20 —2C **48**

Southfield Ter. TS9 —3B **120**
S. Gare Rd. TS10 —2C **26**
Southgate. TS6 —1B **78**
Southgate. TS24 —2C **8**
Southgate St. DL14 —2D **103**
South Grn. TS18 —2B **70**
South Gro. DL5 —5F **109**
S. Lackenby. TS6 —5B **56**
Southland Av. TS26 —1D **11**
Southland Gdns. DL4 —2B **104**
Southlands Dri. TS7 —1C **92**
Southmead Av. TS3 —4F **75**
S. Mt. Pleasant St. TS20 —2C **48**
South Pde. TS25 —1F **11**
South Pk. Av. TS6 —3E **77**
Southport Clo. TS18 —4E **49**
South Rd. TS20 —1C **48**
South Rd. TS26 —5E **7**
South Row. DL5 —5F **109**
South Row. DL14 —1D **105**
South Side. (Dean Rd.) DL17
　　　　　　　—3C **100**
S. Slip Rd. TS6 —3E **55**
South St. DL3 —4A **112**
South St. DL4 —4C **104**
South St. DL16 —3C **98**
South St. TS6 —2A **78**
South St. TS14 —3D **97**
South Ter. DL1 —3A **116**
South Ter. DL4 —5A **104**
South Ter. DL14 —2D **103**
South Ter. DL16 —2D **99**
South Ter. TS6 —3B **54**
South Ter. TS10 —4E **29**
South Ter. TS12 —1B **80**
　　(in two parts)
S. Town La. TS13 —5D **67**
South View. DL4 —2D **105**
South View. DL14 —2D **103**
South View. DL16 —5A **98**
South View. DL17 —2D **101**
South View. TS13 —4C **66**
South View. TS16 —1C **94**
South View. TS23 —4E **33**
S. View Ter. TS3 —4D **53**
Southwark Clo. TS6 —4D **77**
Southway. TS6 —2E **57**
South Way. TS20 —1D **49**
Southwell Grn. DL1 —4F **113**
Southwell Rd. TS5 —2A **74**
Southwell Sq. TS5 —2A **74**
Southwick Av. TS4 —1C **90**
Sowerby Cres. TS9 —3D **119**
Sowerby Way. TS16 —3C **84**
　　(in two parts)
Spain Hill. TS11 —4D **45**
Spalding Rd. TS25 —2B **14**
Spalding Wlk. TS20 —1D **49**
Spark Sq. TS19 —3E **47**
Sparrow Hall Dri. DL1 —2D **113**
Spaunton Clo. TS8 —4D **89**
Spearman Wlk. TS27 —4B **4**
Speeding Dri. TS24 —4B **4**
Speedwell Clo. DL1 —2C **116**
Speeton Av. TS5 —5F **73**
Speeton Clo. TS23 —2F **19**
Spenborough Rd. TS19 —3E **47**
Spencely St. DL4 —2C **104**
Spencerbeck Ho. TS7 —3C **76**
Spencer Clo. TS11 —4D **45**
Spencerfield Cres. TS3 —5B **54**
Spencer Gro. DL1 —4D **117**
Spencer Hall. TS18 —1C **70**
Spencer Rd. TS6 —5E **55**
Spennithorne Rd. TS18 —1F **69**
Spenser Gro. TS25 —2D **11**
Spilsby Clo. TS25 —2C **14**

Spinnaker Ho. TS24 —4B **8**
(off Warrior Quay)
Spinney, The. DL3 —5E **115**
Spinney, The. DL5 —2E **107**
Spinney, The. DL16 —2F **99**
Spinney, The. TS26 —1A **10**
Spitalfields. TS15 —4C **94** & 4D **95**
Spital Ga. TS15 —4D **95**
Spital, The. TS15 —4D **95**
Spitfire Clo. TS11 —4C **44**
Spout La. DL4 —4E **105**
Springbank Rd. TS7 —5C **76**
Spring Clo. TS17 —3D **71**
Spring Ct. DL3 —4D **111**
Springfield. TS9 —3E **119**
Springfield Av. TS12 —5B **64**
Springfield Av. TS18 —3F **69**
Springfield Clo. TS16 —5C **84**
Springfield Gdns. TS9 —3E **119**
Springfield Rd. DL1 —3C **112**
Springfield Rd. TS5 —1C **72**
Springfields. DL5 —3A **108**
Spring Garden Clo. TS7 —1C **92**
Spring Garden La. TS7 —1B **92**
Spring Garden Rd. TS25 —2F **11**
Spring Head Ter. TS13 —4D **67**
(in two parts)
Spring Hill. DL3 —3A **112**
Springhill. TS7 —4C **76**
Springhill Gro. TS17 —3B **86**
Springholme. TS7 —4C **76**
Springholme Yd. TS18 —2A **70**
Spring La. TS21 —5B **118**
Springlea. TS7 —4C **76**
Springmead. TS7 —4C **76**
Spring Rise. TS6 —4D **77**
Spring Rd. DL5 —5D **109**
Springston Rd. TS26 —3B **6**
Spring St. TS2 —2A **52**
Spring St. TS18 —2A **70**
Springvale Ter. TS5 —2C **72**
Springwalk. TS7 —4C **76**
Spring Way. TS18 —3F **69**
Springwell Clo. TS23 —2A **20**
Springwell Flatlets. TS26 —2C **6**
Springwell Ter. DL1 —4D **113**
Spruce Ct. DL4 —4D **105**
Spruce Gro. DL3 —2D **115**
Spruce Rd. TS19 —2F **47**
Spurn Wlk. TS24 —5A **8**
Spurrey Clo. TS17 —4C **86**
Square, The. TS6 —1A **78**
Square, The. TS13 —1B **66**
Square, The. TS18 —5C **48**
(in two parts)
Square, The. TS21 —4B **118**
Stable Ct. TS13 —4C **66**
Stadium Ct. TS6 —4B **54**
Stafford Clo. TS17 —3C **70**
Stafford Rd. TS6 —4F **55**
Stafford Rd. TS14 —4D **97**
Stafford St. TS18 —2B **70**
Stag La. DL5 —2E **107**
Staincliffe Rd. TS25 —4C **12**
Staindale. TS14 —4A **96**
Staindale Clo. TS15 —3F **95**
Staindale Gdns. TS19 —4F **47**
Staindale Pl. TS25 —3D **11**
Staindale Rd. TS17 —5E **71**
Staindrop Cres. DL3 —5C **110**
Staindrop Dri. TS5 —1D **89**
Staindrop Rd. DL3 —5A **110**
Staindrop St. TS24 —5A **8**
Stainforth Clo. DL5 —5C **106**
Stainforth Ct. TS3 —4E **75**
Stainforth Gdns. TS17 —5D **87**
Stainmore Clo. TS19 —5A **48**

Stainmore Cres. DL5 —4B **106**
Stainmore Wlk. DL5 —5B **106**
Stainsby Ga. TS17 —4A **72**
Stainsby Rd. TS5 —3B **72**
Stainsby St. TS17 —3D **71**
Staintondale. DL5 —4A **106**
Staintondale Av. TS10 —2A **42**
Stainton Gro. TS20 —2B **48**
Stainton Rd. TS22 —5C **18**
Stainton St. TS3 —5D **53**
Stainton Way. TS8 & TS7
—4D **89** to 3A **92**
Stainwood Ct. DL3 —5D **111**
Staithes Ct. TS25 —5B **8**
Staithes Rd. TS10 —1A **42**
Stakesby Clo. TS14 —1D **97**
Stamford Ct. TS23 —4A **20**
Stamford St. TS1 —4B **52**
Stamford Wlk. TS25 —1D **15**
Stamp St. TS18 —5B **48**
Stanfield Rd. DL5 —5F **107**
Stanford Clo. TS17 —1D **71**
Stanghow Rd. TS12
—1D **81** to 5F **81**
Stanhope Av. TS26 —5E **7**
Stanhope Clo. DL16 —1D **99**
Stanhope Clo. DL17 —3E **101**
Stanhope Gdns. TS4 —2C **74**
Stanhope Gro. TS5 —3E **73**
Stanhope Rd. TS18 —4F **47**
Stanhope Rd. TS23 —1A **34**
Stanhope Rd. N. DL3 —1F **115**
Stanhope Rd. S. DL3 —2F **115**
Stanhope St. TS12 —1D **63**
Stanley Clo. TS17 —3D **71**
Stanley Gro. TS10
—4E **29** & 5E **29**
Stanley Rd. TS25 —3F **11**
Stanley St. DL1 —2C **116**
Stanley St. TS20 —5B **32**
Stanley Wlk. TS18 —5B **48**
Stanmore Av. TS4 —4B **74**
Stanmore Gro. TS25 —5B **12**
Stannage Gro. TS17 —4D **71**
Stanstead Way. TS17 —1F **87**
Stapleford Rd. TS3 —3B **76**
Stapleton Bank. DL2 —5C **114**
Stapleton St. TS20 —4B **32**
Stapylton Ct. TS6 —2E **55**
Stapylton St. TS6 —2E **55**
Starbeck Clo. TS11 —2A **60**
Starbeck Wlk. TS17 —3F **87**
Starbeck Way. TS7 —3C **76**
Stargate Clo. DL5 —2E **107**
Starmer Cres. DL1 —4C **116**
Startforth Rd. TS2 —1D **51**
Statham Pl. DL3 —1A **112**
Station App. DL14 —2D **103**
Station App. TS24 —4A **8**
Station Av. TS25 —4C **14**
Station Clo. TS11 —5D **45**
Station Cres. TS23 —3E **33**
Station La. TS12 —5D **63**
Station La. TS25 —5B **12**
Station Pde. TS23 —2D **33**
Station Rd. DL3 —5A **112**
Station Rd. DL5 —5C **108**
Station Rd. TS6 —2F **77**
(Eston)
Station Rd. TS6 —5E **39**
(Grangetown)
Station Rd. TS9 —4C **120**
(Great Ayton)
Station Rd. TS9 —4F **119**
(Stokesley)
Station Rd. TS10 —3D **29**
Station Rd. TS13 —5C **66**

Station Rd. TS16 —3D **85**
Station Rd. TS20 —3B **32**
Station Rd. TS21 —5A **118**
Station Rd. TS23 —2D **33** to 4E **33**
Station Rd. TS25 —4C **14**
Station Sq. TS12 —1D **63**
Station Sq. Shopping Cen. TS12
—1D **63**
Station St. DL4 —4C **104**
Station St. TS1 —2F **51**
Station St. TS12 —1D **63**
Station St. TS17 —2D **71**
Station St. TS20 —4C **48**
Station Ter. DL5 —5F **109**
Station Vs. TS11 —5D **45**
Staveley Ct. TS3 —1D **75**
Staveley Gro. TS19 —2F **47**
Staveley Wlk. TS7 —4B **76**
Stavordale Rd. TS19 —4A **48**
Stead Clo. DL5 —5C **106**
Steele Cres. TS6 —2C **54**
Steeplejack Way. DL1 —2B **116**
Stephen Ct. DL1 —4B **112**
Stephenson Ct. TS6 —4B **54**
Stephenson Ind. Est. TS25
—4C **16**
Stephenson St. DL3 —5A **112**
Stephenson St. DL17 —3B **100**
Stephenson St. TS1 —4A **52**
Stephenson St. TS17 —2D **71**
Stephenson Way. DL5 —5C **106**
Stephenson Way. TS18 —1C **70**
Stephens Rd. TS6 —2C **54**
Stephen St. TS26 —4D **7**
Stevenage Clo. TS17 —4F **71**
Stevenson Clo. TS15 —3F **95**
Stewart Ct. TS20 —3C **48**
Stewart Rd. TS20 —3C **48**
Stewart St. DL3 —5F **111**
Stileston Clo. TS26 —3B **6**
Stirling Clo. DL14 —3A **102**
Stirling Gro. DL1 —2C **112**
Stirling Rd. TS10 —1F **43**
Stirling St. TS25 —2F **11**
Stirling Way. TS17 —2E **87**
Stirrup, The. DL5 —4A **106**
Stockdale Av. TS10 —1A **42**
Stockley Clo. DL3 —2A **112**
Stocks Grn. DL5 —5A **106**
Stocksmoor Clo. DL1 —4D **117**
Stockton Almshouses. TS18
—1B **70**
Stockton Rd. DL1
—4F **113** & 3F **113**
Stockton Rd. TS5 —1A **72**
Stockton Rd. TS21 —5C **118**
Stockton Rd. TS22 —2E **19**
Stockton Rd. TS25 & TS22
—1F **11** to 4A **14**
Stockton St. TS2 —2F **51**
Stockton St. TS23 —4E **33**
Stockton St. TS24 —5F **7**
Stockton-Thornaby By-Pass. TS21,
TS16, TS18, TS17 & TS5
—3B **68** to 2F **71**
Stockwell Av. TS17 —4E **87**
Stockwith Clo. TS3 —3B **76**
Stokesley By-Pass. TS9 —5D **119**
Stokesley Cres. TS23 —3E **33**
Stokesley Rd. TS7 —1D **91**
(Marton)
Stokesley Rd. TS7 —4C **92** to 5D **93**
(Nunthorpe)
Stokesley Rd. TS8 —4B **90**
Stokesley Rd. TS9 —4A **120**
Stokesley Rd. TS14 —3A **96**
Stokesley Rd. TS25 —5C **12**

Stoneacre Av. TS17 —5C **86**
Stonebridge. DL1 —2A **116**
Stonechat Clo. TS17 —5B **86**
Stonecliffe Dri. DL3 —3D **115**
Stonecrop Clo. TS18 —2E **69**
Stonedale Cres. DL3 —1E **115**
Stonedale Wlk. TS5 —2D **89**
Stonegate. TS6 —1A **78**
Stone Hall Clo. TS9 —3E **119**
Stonehaven Way. DL1 —2F **113**
Stonehouse Clo. TS15 —5F **95**
Stonehouse St. TS5 —1F **73**
Stonehurst Dri. DL3 —3D **115**
Stoneleigh Av. TS5 —4C **72**
Stoneleigh Ct. DL5 —3F **107**
Stone Row. TS13 —1B **66**
Stone St. TS4 —3B **52**
Stonethwaite Clo. TS24 —2F **7**
Stoneyhurst Av. TS5 —3B **72**
Stonor Wlk. TS3 —4F **75**
Stooperdale Av. DL3 —4C **110**
Stornoway Clo. TS19 —5B **46**
Stotfold St. TS26 —5E **7**
Stotfold Wlk. TS26 —3B **88**
Stoupe Gro. TS10 —2A **44**
Stourport Clo. TS18 —4D **49**
Stowe St. TS1 —4F **51**
Stowmarket Clo. TS25 —2D **15**
Strait La. TS8 —4C **88**
Straker St. TS26 —4E **7**
Strand St. DL4 —4C **104**
Strand, The. TS10 —2A **44**
Stranton. TS24 —1F **11**
Stranton Ho. TS24 —5F **7**
Stranton St. DL14 —1D **103**
Stranton St. TS17 —3D **71**
Stratford Cres. TS5 —1C **72**
Stratford Gdns. DL17 —2D **101**
Stratford Rd. TS25 —2E **11**
Strathaven Dri. TS16 —5D **85**
Stratton Ct. DL1 —3F **115**
Stratton St. DL16 —3C **98**
Strauss Rd. TS6 —2C **54**
Strawberry La. DL17 —1C **100**
Stray, The. DL1 —2D **117**
Stray, The. TS21 —5A **68**
Streatlam Rd. DL1 —4C **116**
Streatlam Rd. TS23 —5B **20**
Strensall Clo. TS11 —2B **60**
Strome Clo. TS17 —5D **87**
Strona Wlk. TS14 —4C **96**
Stuart St. TS24 —3F **7**
Studland Dri. TS24 —3B **4**
Studland Rd. TS10 —3A **44**
Studley Rd. TS5 —2D **73**
Studley Rd. TS17 —5E **71**
Studley Rd. TS19 —4A **48**
Studley Rd. TS25 —1F **11**
Stump Cross. TS14 —3D **97**
Sturt Dri. TS20 —5A **32**
Sudbury Rd. TS20 —5D **33**
Suffield St. TS2 —2F **51**
Suffolk Clo. TS12 —2B **80**
Suffolk Clo. TS25 —2F **11**
Suffolk Pl. DL14 —4D **103**
Suffolk Rd. TS5 —2A **74**
Suffolk St. TS18 —1A **70**
Suggitt St. TS26 —4D **7**
Sulby Av. TS3 —1E **75**
Summerhouse Gro. DL3 —2A **114**
Summerhouse Sq. TS20 —5C **32**
Sunbury. TS7 —4F **97**
Sundell Ct. TS18 —1A **70**
Sunderland Rd. TS22 —2D **19**
Sundial M. TS22 —3D **19**
Sunley Av. TS4 —2B **74**
Sunningdale. DL5 —2E **107**

Sunningdale Ct. TS6 —2F **77**
Sunningdale Dri. TS16 —5D **85**
Sunningdale Grn. DL1 —3E **113**
Sunningdale Gro. TS27 —4B **4**
Sunningdale Ho. TS6 —2F **77**
Sunningdale Rd. TS4 —4A **74**
Sunningdale Rd. TS11 —2B **60**
Sunningdale Wlk. TS16 —5D **85**
(in two parts)
Sunniside. TS24 —2D **9**
Sunnybank Rd. TS7 —5C **76**
Sunnybrow Av. TS23 —4E **33**
Sunnydale. DL4 —2D **105**
Sunnyfield. TS7 —4B **76**
Sunnyfield. TS9 —4A **120**
Sunnygate. TS6 —1B **78**
Sunnyside. TS8 —3A **90** & 3B **90**
Sunnyside Av. DL4 —3D **105**
Sunnyside Av. TS4 —3A **74**
Sunnyside Gro. TS18 —3D **69**
Sunstar Gro. TS7 —1D **91**
Sun St. DL3 —1A **116**
Sun St. DL14 —3D **103**
Sun St. TS17 —3C **70**
Sun St. TS18 —2A **70**
Surbiton Rd. TS19 & TS18
                              —5A **46**
Surgery La. TS24 —1E **7**
Surrey Pl. DL14 —5D **103**
Surrey Rd. TS20 —1D **49**
Surrey St. TS1 —5E **51**
Surrey Ter. TS23 —3F **33**
Surtees Av. DL4 —3C **104**
Surtees St. DL3 —5F **111**
Surtees St. DL14 —1C **102**
Surtees St. TS18 —1B **70**
Surtees St. TS24 —5A **8**
Surtees Ter. DL17 —5F **101**
Surtees Wlk. DL5 —1E **109**
Sussex St. TS2 —2F **51**
(in two parts)
Sussex St. TS25 —2F **11**
Sussex Wlk. TS20 —2D **49**
Sussex Way. DL1 —5D **113**
Sutcliffe Ct. DL3 —2A **112**
Sutherland Gro. TS20 —4B **32**
Sutton Clo. DL3 —2B **114**
Sutton Ct. TS10 —2C **42**
Sutton Pl. TS23 —5A **20**
Sutton Way. TS4 —3A **74**
Swainby Clo. TS5 —4F **73**
Swainby Rd. TS20 —3C **48**
Swainby Rd. TS25 —1C **16**
Swainson Pl. TS24 —5F **7**
Swainson St. TS24 —5F **7**
Swainston Clo. TS5 —1C **88**
Swale Av. TS17 —5E **71**
Swalebrooke Av. TS25 —3C **10**
Swale Clo. TS16 —1C **94**
Swaledale Av. DL3 —1C **114**
Swaledale Clo. TS17 —4B **86**
Swaledale Cres. TS23 —3E **33**
Swaledale Rd. TS4 —3A **74**
Swale Rd. TS20 —1B **48**
Swallow Clo. TS14 —3A **96**
Swallowfields. TS8 —5B **90**
Swallow La. TS20 —4B **32**
Swanage Clo. TS8 —2C **90**
Swanage Dri. TS10 —3A **44**
Swanage Gro. TS24 —4B **4**
Swan St. DL1 —2B **116**
Swan Wlk. DL5 —1F **109**
Swift Gro. TS25 —3C **10**
Swilly La. TS12 —1C **80**
Swinburne Ho. TS25 —3C **10**
Swinburne Rd. DL3 —2F **115**
Swinburne Rd. TS16 —3D **85**

Swinburne Rd. TS25 —3C **10**
Swinburn Rd. TS20 —3B **48**
Swinton Rd. TS18 —2C **68**
Swyfte Clo. TS21 —5C **118**
Sycamore Av. TS12 —2B **62**
Sycamore Av. TS17 —5D **71**
Sycamore Cres. TS6 —5D **55**
Sycamore Dri. TS12 —4B **64**
Sycamore Rd. TS5 —2F **73**
Sycamore Rd. TS7 —5C **76**
Sycamore Rd. TS10 —5F **29**
Sycamore Rd. TS16 —2E **85**
Sycamore Rd. TS19 —2F **47**
Sycamore Sq. DL4 —3D **105**
Sycamores, The. DL3 —1D **115**
Sycamores, The. TS25 —3D **11**
Sycamore Ter. TS2 —5F **35**
Sycamore Wlk. TS13 —4C **66**
Sydenham Rd. TS18 —2A **70**
Sydenham Rd. TS25
                        —2F **11** & 2A **12**
Sydney Clo. TS5 —2C **72**
Sydney Rd. TS7 —2E **91**
Sydney St. TS18 —5B **48**
Sylvan Gro. DL3 —3A **115**
Sylvan Wlk. TS3 —3F **75**
Symington Wlk. DL1 —2C **116**
Symons Clo. TS18 —1B **68**
Syon Gdns. TS20 —4F **31**

Tailrigg Clo. TS19 —4A **48**
Talbot Ho. TS24 —2D **9**
Talbot St. TS1 —4B **52**
Talbot St. TS20 —3C **48**
Talbot Yd. DL3 —2A **11**
(off Post Ho. Wynd)
Talgarth Rd. TS20 —4C **32**
Talland Clo. TS27 —4A **4**
Tamarisk Clo. TS17 —4C **86**
Tame Rd. TS3 —4D **53**
Tameside. TS9 —2E **119**
Tame St. TS23 —3E **35**
Tamworth Rd. TS23 —5F **19**
Tandridge Ct. DL3 —5D **111**
Tanfield Pl. DL5 —3D **107**
Tanfield Rd. TS25 —3E **11**
Tangmere. DL16 —1B **98**
Tanhill Wlk. TS3 —2E **75**
Tankersley Rd. TS11 —2A **60**
Tankerville St. TS26 —4E **7**
Tanner Clo. TS17 —4C **86**
Tannery Yd. DL1 —2B **116**
Tansley Av. TS3 —1F **75**
Tansley Gdns. DL1 —3E **117**
Tanton Gro. TS22 —5C **18**
Tanton Rd. TS9 —2E **119**
Tanwell Clo. TS19 —4C **46**
Tanya Gdns. TS5 —2F **89**
Tanya Gdns. TS19 —5D **47**
Taransay Wlk. DL1 —2E **113**
Tarnside Path. DL5 —5B **106**
Tarnston Rd. TS26 —3B **6**
Tarran St. TS5 —5D **51**
Tarring St. TS18 —1B **70**
Tarr Steps. TS17 —5A **86**
Task Ind. Est. TS18 —4D **49**
Task Rd. TS18 —4D **49**
Tasman Dri. TS18 —2C **68**
Tasmania Sq. TS7 —3F **91**
Tatham St. TS4 —4B **92**
Tattersall Clo. DL5 —2E **107**
Taunton Clo. TS8 —1C **90**
Taunton Gro. TS26 —3B **6**
Taunton Vale. TS14 —5E **97**
Tavistock Rd. TS5 —1E **73**
Tavistock St. TS5 —1E **73**

Tawney Clo. TS6 —4E **55**
Tawney Rd. TS6 —4E **55**
Taybrooke Av. TS25 —3D **11**
Taylor Rd. DL14 —4D **103**
Taylor Sq. DL14 —5B **102**
Taylor Wlk. DL5 —4E **107**
Tay Side. DL1 —2F **113**
Teak St. TS1 —4A **52**
Tealby Wlk. TS3 —2B **76**
Teal Rd. DL1 —2E **117**
Teare Clo. TS1 —4E **51**
Tebay Clo. TS7 —3B **76**
Tedder Av. TS17 —1E **87**
Ted Fletcher Ct. DL1 —4E **113**
Tedworth Clo. TS14 —5D **97**
Tees Bank Av. TS16 —3E **85**
Tees Barrage Way. TS17 —1F **71**
Tees Barrage Way. TS18 —5F **49**
Tees Bay Bus. Pk. TS25 —4B **16**
Tees Bay Retail Pk. TS25 —4A **54**
Tees Cres. DL16 —2C **98**
Teesdale Av. DL3 —3B **114**
Teesdale Av. TS23 —3E **33**
Teesdale Av. TS26 —5D **7**
Teesdale Boulevd. TS17 —5C **48**
Teesdale Pk. TS17 —1D **71**
Teesdale Ter. TS17 —3E **71**
Teesdale Wlk. DL4 —3E **105**
Teesdale Wlk. DL14 —5A **102**
(in two parts)
Tees Dock Rd. TS6
                      —2D **39** & 2F **55**
Tees Dri. DL1 —5A **116**
Teesgate. TS17 —4F **71**
Tees Grange Av. DL3 —2A **114**
Teeside Ho. TS1 —4A **52**
Teeside Ind. Est. TS17 —4F **87**
Tees (Newport) Bri. App. Rd. TS18
                      & TS23 —3B **50**
Tees Rd. TS10 —1C **42**
Tees Rd. TS14 —4C **96**
Tees Rd. TS25 —3C 22 to 5D **13**
Teesside Pk. Dri. TS17 —2A **72**
Teesside Pk. Interchange. TS17
                      —2A **72**
Teesside Retail Pk. TS17 —2A **72**
Tees St. TS6 —1B **54**
Tees St. TS13 —5E **67**
Tees St. TS23 —3E **35**
Tees St. TS24 —4F **7**
Tees St. Ind. Est. TS23 —3E **35**
Tees Viaduct. TS18 —3A **50**
Teesway. TS18 —3A **50**
Teignmouth Clo. TS27 —5A **4**
Telford Clo. TS24 —1A **8**
Telford Dri. DL1 —2C **116**
Telford Rd. TS3 —3F **53**
Temperance Av. 4 —2C **104**
Temperance Pl. DL3 —1A **116**
Temperance Ter. TS24 —1D **9**
Tempest Anderson Ho. DL3
                      —5D **111**
Tempest Ct. DL1 —2C **112**
Tempest Rd. TS24 —4C **4**
Templar St. TS18 —2A **70**
Temple Ct. TS20 —4C **48**
Tenby Clo. TS6 —5F **55**
Tenby Wlk. TS26 —2C **6**
Tenby Way. TS16 —1D **85**
Tennant St. TS18 —5B **48**
Tennyson Av. TS6 —3F **55**
Tennyson Av. TS25 —2D **11**
Tennyson Clo. TS6 —4F **55**
Tennyson Gdns. DL1 —5B **116**
Tennyson Rd. TS23 —2E **19**

Tennyson St. TS1 —5F **51**
Tenters St. DL14 —1D **103**
Ternbeck Way. TS17 —3F **87**
Tern Gro. TS10 —3F **43**
Terry Dicken Ind. Est. TS9
                      —5F **119**
Tetcott Clo. TS14 —5D **97**
Tewkesbury Av. TS7 —4F **91**
Thackeray Gro. TS5 —3F **73**
Thackeray Rd. TS25 —2B **10**
Thames Av. TS14 —4C **96**
Thames Av. TS17 —5E **71**
Thames Av. TS24 —1E **7**
Thames Cen. DL5 —5D **107**
Thames Rd. TS10 —1B **42**
Thames Rd. TS12 —5D **63**
Thames Rd. TS22 —4B **18**
Thames Way. DL1 —5A **116**
Thatch La. TS17 —4D **87**
Theakston Gro. TS18 —2B **68**
Therby Clo. DL3 —4F **111**
Thetford Av. TS3 —2A **76**
Thetford Rd. TS25 —2C **14**
Thickley Ter. DL4 —5D **105**
Thinford Gdns. TS5 —2E **89**
Thirlby Clo. TS3 —2D **75**
Thirlmere. DL16 —1B **98**
Thirlmere Av. TS5 —4D **73**
Thirlmere Ct. TS23 —5F **33**
Thirlmere Cres. TS6 —2E **77**
Thirlmere Dri. TS12 —1C **80**
Thirlmere Rd. DL1 —3C **116**
Thirlmere Rd. DL17 —3C **100**
Thirlmere Rd. TS10 —1C **42**
Thirlmere St. TS26 —1E **11**
Thirsk Gro. TS25 —4F **11**
Thirsk Rd. TS9 —5D **119**
Thirsk Rd. TS15 —4D **95**
Thistle Grn. TS18 —5C **48**
Thistle Rise. TS8 —3A **90**
Thistle Rd. TS19 —1F **47**
Thistle St. TS1 —4A **52**
Thomas Ct. DL1 —3C **116**
Thomas St. DL1 —3C **116**
Thomas St. DL4 —5D **105**
Thomas St. DL16 —3C **98**
Thomas St. TS3 —4D **53**
Thomas St. TS12 —1E **81**
Thomas St. TS18 —5C **48**
Thomlinson Rd. TS25 —2A **12**
Thompson Gro. TS24 —1E **7**
Thompson Rd. DL14 —3D **103**
Thompsons Clo. TS22 —3D **19**
Thompson's Rd. TS12 —2B **80**
Thompson St. DL16 —2C **98**
Thompson St. TS18 —4B **48**
Thompson St. TS24 —1F **11**
Thompson St. E. DL1 —2B **112**
Thompson St. W. DL3 —2A **112**
Thomson Av. TS5 —1C **72**
Thomson St. TS14 —3D **97**
Thorgill Clo. TS4 —3A **74**
Thorington Gdns. TS17 —5D **87**
Thornaby Pl. TS17 —2D **71**
Thornaby Rd. TS17
                      —2D **71** to 5E **87**
Thornberry Ct. TS5 —2D **73**
Thornbrough Clo. TS18 —3C **68**
Thornbury Rise. DL3 —1D **115**
Thorncliffe Gro. DL14 —4E **103**
Thorn Clo. DL16 —5A **98**
Thorn Clo. TS17 —4C **86**
Thorndike Rd. TS6 —5F **55**
Thorndyke Av. TS4 —3B **74**
Thornfield Clo. TS16 —4B **84**

Thornfield Gro. TS5 —3D **73**
Thornfield Rd. DL3 —1D **115**
Thornfield Rd. TS5 —2D **73**
Thornhill Gdns. DL4 —2B **104**
Thornhill Gdns. TS26 —3C **6**
Thornhill Pl. TS26 —3C **6**
Thornley Av. TS23 —3F **19**
Thorn Rd. TS19 —1F **47**
Thorn Side. TS17 —4C **86**
Thorn St. TS1 —3F **51**
Thornthwaite. TS5 —2C **88**
Thornton Clo. DL5 —4D **107**
Thornton Clo. TS8 —5C **88**
Thornton Cotts. TS8 —5C **88**
Thornton Cres. TS22 —1C **32**
Thornton Garth. TS15 —4D **95**
Thornton Gro. TS20 —2B **48**
Thornton Rd. TS8 —5C **88**
Thornton St. DL3 —1A **116**
Thornton St. TS3 —4D **53**
Thornton St. TS26 —5E **7**
Thornton Vale. TS8 —5C **88**
Thorntree Av. TS3
                      —4F **53** & 5F **53**
Thorntree Ct. TS17 —4E **71**
Thorntree Ho. TS3 —1A **76**
Thorn Tree La. TS25 —5D **15**
Thorntree Rd. TS17 —4D **71**
Thornville Rd. TS26 —4E **7**
Thornwood Av. TS17 —4C **86**
Thorpe St. TS24 —1B **8**
Thorphill Way. TS23 —4F **19**
Throckley Av. TS5 —1D **89**
Thropton Clo. TS23 —4E **19**
Throstlenest Av. DL1 —5D **113**
Throston Clo. TS26 —1D **7**
Throston Grange Ct. TS26 —2C **6**
Throston Grange La. TS26 —2B **6**
(in two parts)
Throston St. TS24 —2D **9**
Thrush Rd. TS10 —5D **29**
Thrushwood Cres. TS11 —5F **45**
Thruxton Way. TS20 —5A **32**
Thurlow Grange. TS21 —5C **118**
Thurlow Gro. DL5 —4D **107**
Thurlow Rd. TS21 —5C **118**
Thurlstone. TS7 —4F **97**
Thurnham Gro. TS7 —3F **91**
Thursby Clo. DL5 —2A **106**
Thursby Dri. TS7 —3B **76**
Thursby Gro. TS25 —2B **14**
Thurso Clo. TS19 —5A **46**
Thwaites La. TS10 —5E **29**
Thweng Way. TS14 —4B **96**
Tibbersley Av. TS23 —4F **33**
Tibthorpe. TS7 —3A **92**
Tidkin La. TS14 —4B **96**
Tilbury Rd. TS6 —2A **54**
Tilery Ct. TS20 —3D **49**
Tilery Way. TS20 —3C **48**
(in two parts)
Timberscombe Clo. TS17 —4A **86**
Timothy Ter. DL16 —4C **98**
Tindale. TS14 —4A **96**
Tindale Clo. TS15 —5C **94**
Tindale Grn. DL5 —5A **106**
Tindale Wlk. TS5 —2D **89**
Tintagel Clo. TS27 —5A **4**
Tintern Av. DL3 —4A **110**
Tintern Av. TS23 —1E **33**
Tintern Rd. TS12 —1E **81**
Tipton Clo. TS17 —5F **71**
Tiree Gdns. DL1 —2E **113**
Tirril Way. TS7 —4A **92**
Tithe Barn Rd. TS19 —1B **46**
Tiverton Gro. TS26 —2C **6**
Tivoli Pl. DL14 —3C **102**

Toddington Dri. TS20 —5F **31**
Todd St. DL16 —3B **98**
Tod Point Rd. TS10 —4E **27**
Tofts Clo. TS11 —4F **45**
Tofts Farm E. Ind. Est. TS25
—2B **16**
Tofts Farm W. Ind. Est. TS25
—3A **16**
Tofts Rd. E. TS25 —2B **16**
Tofts Rd. W. TS25 —3A **16**
Tollerton Clo. TS19 —4E **47**
Tollesby Bri. TS8 —2C **90**
Tollesby La. TS7 —1C **90** & 3D **91**
Tollesby Rd. TS5 —3F **73**
Tollgate Garth. DL1 —3F **113**
Tom Browns Wynd. TS15 —2C **94**
Tomlin St. DL4 —5C **104**
Tom Raine Ct. DL1 —2B **116**
Topcliffe Dri. TS5 —2D **89**
Topcliffe St. TS17 —1F **87**
Topcroft Clo. TS3 —4F **75**
Topham Grn. TS3 —1D **75**
Topping Clo. TS24 —1B **8**
Torbay Clo. TS8 —1C **90**
Torbay Gro. TS26 —2C **6**
Torbay Wlk. TS26 —2C **6**
Torcross Clo. TS27 —4A **4**
Toronto Cres. TS4 —1B **74**
Torquay Av. TS25 —1D **15**
Torrance Dri. DL1 —2F **113**
Torrington Ho. TS3 —4F 53
(off Purfleet Av.)
Torver Mt. TS7 —3A **92**
Torwell Dri. TS19 —4C **46**
Tothill Av. TS3 —2B **76**
Tovil Clo. TS19 —2B **46**
Tower Flats. TS24 —5A 8
(off Tower St.)
Tower Grn. TS2 —1A **52**
Tower Rd. DL3 —1E **115**
Tower St. TS18 —1C **70**
Tower St. TS24 —5A **8**
Town Farm Ct. TS21 —5B **118**
Town Hall Ct. TS15 —2C **94**
Town Sq. TS8 —4C **90**
Town Sq. TS23 —1E **33**
Town Wall. TS24 —2C **8**
Towthorpe. TS7 —3A **92**
Trafalgar Ct. TS6 —2B **54**
Trafalgar St. DL17 —4F **101**
Trafalgar Ter. DL3 —5F **111**
Trafalgar Ter. TS10 —4C **28**
Trafford Clo. DL1 —5F **113**
Tranmere Av. DL3 —1F **75**
Tranter Rd. TS4 —3A **74**
Travellers Ga. TS25 —4F **11**
Travellers Grn. DL5 —2F **109**
Tredegar Wlk. TS26 —2B **6**
Treelands. DL3 —2C **114**
Trefoil Clo. TS14 —4B **96**
Trefoil Wood. TS7 —1D **91**
Tregarth Clo. TS4 —3A **74**
Trenchard Av. TS17 —2E **87**
Trenholme Rd. TS4 —5C **52**
Trent Av. TS17 —5E **71**
Trentbrooke Av. TS25 —3D **11**
Trentham Av. TS3 —2A **76**
Trent Pl. DL1 —5A **116**
Trent Rd. TS10 —1B **42**
Trent St. TS20 —2C **48**
Tresco Wlk. TS14 —4C **96**
Trevino Ct. TS16 —4E **85**
Trevithick Clo. DL1 —2C **116**
Trevor Grn. N. DL5 —4F **107**
Trevor Wlk. DL5 —4F **107**
Trident Bus. Cen. TS2 —1E **51**

Trident Ct. TS24 —4B **8**
Trigo Clo. TS7 —2D **91**
Trimdon Av. TS5 —1C **88**
Trimmer Ho. TS2 —1F 51
(off West St.)
Trinity Ct. TS14 —2D **97**
Trinity Cres. TS3 —4C **52**
Trinity M. TS17 —1D **71**
Trinity Rd. DL3 —2E **115**
Trinity St. TS18 —1B **70**
Trinity St. TS24 —2D **9**
Tristram Av. TS25 —2D **11**
Tristram Clo. TS6 —2D **77**
Troon Av. DL1 —3E **113**
Troon Clo. TS4 —4A **74**
Troon Clo. TS22 —5B **18**
Troutbeck Clo. DL16 —1B **98**
Troutbeck Rd. TS10 —1C **42**
Trout Hall La. TS12 —2C **80**
Troutpool Clo. TS24 —1A **8**
Troutsdale Clo. TS15 —5C **94**
True Lovers' Wlk. TS15 —2C **94**
Trueman Gro. DL3 —1A **112**
Trunk Rd. TS6 & TS10
—4A **54** to 5B **28**
Truro Clo. DL1 —4F **113**
Truro Dri. TS25 —1D **15**
Tubwell Row. DL1 —2A **116**
Tudhoe Moor. DL16 —2F **99**
Tudhoe Pk. Ct. DL16 —1D **99**
Tudhoe Pk. Vs. DL16 —1D **99**
Tudor Ct. TS3 —1B **76**
Tunstall Av. TS23 —3F **19**
Tunstall Av. TS26 —4D **7**
Tunstall Ct. TS26 —4C **6**
Tunstall Gro. DL14 —5A **102**
Tunstall Gro. TS26 —4C **6**
Tunstall Hall La. TS26 —5B **6**
Tunstall Rd. DL5 —1C **108**
Tunstall Rd. TS18 —3C **68**
Tunstall St. TS3 —4D **53**
Tunstall Ter. DL1 —4C **116**
Turford Av. TS3 —5F **53**
Turnberry Av. TS16 —5D **85**
Turnberry Dri. TS11 —3A **60**
Turnberry Gro. TS27 —4A **4**
Turnberry Way. TS8 —5F **91**
Turnbull St. TS24 —3F **7**
Turner St. TS10 —3C **28**
Turner Ter. TS6 —4D **57**
Turner Wlk. TS25 —3B **10**
Turnpike Clo. DL1 —3F **113**
Turton Rd. TS15 —4C **94**
Tuson Wlk. TS24 —3F **7**
Tweed Av. TS17 —5E **71**
Tweed Ho. TS18 —4D 49
(off Tweedport Rd.)
Tweed Pl. DL1 —5B **116**
Tweedport Rd. TS18 —4D **49**
Tweed Rd. DL16 —1E **99**
Tweed Rd. TS10 —1B **42**
Tweed St. TS12 —1D **63**
Tweed St. TS13 —4E **67**
Tweed Wlk. TS24 —3E **7**
Twickenham Rise. DL1 —5F **113**
Twizzie Gill View. TS13 —2F **67**
Tynebrooke Av. TS25 —3D **11**
Tyne Ct. TS6 —4A **54**
Tyne Cres. DL1 —5A **116**
Tyne Cres. DL16 —2C **98**
Tynedale St. TS18 —1A **70**
Tynedale Wlk. DL4 —4E **105**
Tyneport Grn. TS18 —4D 49
(off Eastport Rd.)
Tyne Rd. TS10 —1B **42**
Tyne St. TS6 —2B **54**
Tyne St. TS13 —4E **67**

Tyrone Rd. TS19 —4B **46**

Udale Dri. TS16 —1D **95**
Ullapool Clo. TS19 —5B **46**
Ulla St. TS1 —5F **51** & 4F **51**
Ullswater Av. TS5 —4D **73**
Ullswater Clo. DL16 —2E **99**
Ullswater Clo. TS6 —4A **56**
Ullswater Dri. TS12 —5C **62**
Ullswater Gro. TS10 —5C **28**
Ullswater Rd. DL17 —3C **100**
Ullswater Rd. TS18 —5F **47**
Ullswater Rd. TS23 —5F **33**
Ullswater Rd. TS25 —2A **12**
Union Pl. DL1 —2B **116**
Union Rd. TS24 —1A **8**
Union Sq. TS18 —5B **48**
Union St. DL3 —1A **116**
Union St. DL14 —2D **103**
Union St. TS1 —4E **51**
Union St. TS14 —2E **97**
Union St. TS24 —2D **9**
Union St. E. TS18 —4D **49**
University Boulevd. TS17 —1D **71**
Uplands Rd. DL3 —2F **115**
Upleatham Gro. TS19 —1C **68**
Upleatham St. TS12 —1D **63**
Up. Archer St. DL3 —1A **116**
Up. Beveridge Way. DL5 —5E **107**
Up. Branch St. TS6 —2B **54**
(in two parts)
Up. Church St. DL16 —2E **99**
Up. Church St. TS24 —5F **7**
Up. Garth Gdns. TS14 —2D **97**
Up. Graham St. TS6 —2B **54**
(in two parts)
Up. Green La. TS17 —5D **71**
Up. Jackson St. TS6 —2B **54**
Up. Napier St. TS6 —2B **54**
Up. Norton St. TS18 —4C **48**
Up. Oxford St. TS6 —2B **54**
Up. Princess St. TS6 —2B **54**
Up. Russell St. DL1 —1B **116**
Up. Westbrook. DL3 —5A **112**
Uppingham St. TS25 —2E **11**
Upsall Dri. DL3 —4F **115**
Upsall Gro. TS19 —1C **68**
Upsall Pde. TS19 —5C **46**
Upsall Rd. TS3 —2E **75**
Upsall Rd. TS7 —2C **92**
Upton Ct. TS17 —5C **86**
Upton St. TS1 —4A **52**
Upton Wlk. TS25 —2C **14**
Urford Clo. TS19 —4F **95**
Urlay Gro. TS5 —1E **89**
Urlay Nook Rd. TS16
—4A **84** to 1C **94**
Urra Ct. TS10 —2C **42**
Usway Ct. TS17 —3A **86**
Usworth Rd. TS25 —4F **11**
Usworth Rd. Ind. Est. TS25
—4F **11**
Uvedale Rd. TS6 —3C **54**

Vale Dri. TS17 —4F **71**
Vale, The. TS4 —2A **74**
Vale, The. TS19 —3E **47**
Vale, The. TS26 —5B **6**
Valiant Way. TS17 —2D **87**
Valley Clo. TS11 —4D **45**
Valley Clo. TS15 —4E **95**
Valley Clo. TS26 —5A **6**
Valley Dri. TS15 —3E **95**
Valley Dri. TS26 —1A **10**
Valley Ecology Pk. TS23 —3D **33**

A-Z Middlesbrough 171

Valley Gdns. TS11 —3E **45**
Valley Gdns. TS16 —5B **84**
Valley Gdns. TS19 —3E **47**
Valley Rd. TS4 —2A **74**
Valley St. DL1 —1B **116**
Valley St. N. DL1 —1B **116**
Vancouver Gdns. TS4 —5B **52**
Vancouver Ho. TS1 —3A **52**
Vancouver St. DL3 —5F **111**
Vane Ct. TS21 —5A **68**
Vane Rd. DL5 —5F **107**
Vane St. TS18 —5B **48**
Vane St. TS24 —1C **8**
Vane Ter. DL3 —1F **115**
Van Mildert Rd. DL5 —1F **109**
Varo Ter. TS18 —1A **70**
Vart Rd. DL14 —5C **102**
Vasser Way. TS17 —1C **70**
Vaughan Ct. TS6 —2E **55**
Vaughan Shopping Cen. TS3
—2B **76**
Vaughan St. DL3 —2A **112**
Vaughan St. DL4 —3A **104**
Vaughan St. TS1 —3F **51**
Vaughan St. TS12 —1F **81**
Venables Rd. TS14 —2D **97**
Ventnor Av. TS25 —3E **11**
Ventnor Rd. TS5 —2E **73**
Verity Rise. DL3 —1A **112**
Verner Clo. TS24 —3A **4**
Verner Rd. TS24 —3A **4**
Vernon Ct. TS8 —5D **89**
(in two parts)
Vernon Gdns. DL1 —1B **112**
Vernons Gdns. DL1 —1B **112**
Veronica St. TS3 —4C **52**
Verwood Clo. TS19 —2B **46**
Veryan Rd. TS23 —1A **34**
Viaduct, The. TS17 —1F **71**
Vicarage Av. TS19 —5A **48**
Vicarage Ct. TS25 —1F **11**
Vicarage Dri. TS11 —4E **45**
Vicarage Gdns. TS25 —1F **11**
Vicarage Rd. DL1 —1C **116**
Vicarage Row. TS25 —4C **14**
Vicarage St. TS19 —4A **48**
Vickers Clo. TS11 —3B **44**
Vickers Clo. TS18 —4A **70**
Vickers Ct. DL5 —1F **109**
Vickers St. DL14 —2D **103**
Victoria Av. DL14 —1D **103**
Victoria Av. TS10 —1E **43**
Victoria Av. TS20 —2C **48**
Victoria Clo. TS11 —2B **60**
Victoria Ct. TS6 —3B **54**
Victoria Embkmt. DL1 —3A **116**
Victoria Gdns. DL16 —4B **98**
Victoria Gdns. TS3 —3A **76**
Victoria Gro. TS19 —4D **47**
Victoria Homes. TS25 —1E **11**
Victoria Ho. TS18 —5C **48**
Victoria Pl. TS24 —2D **9**
Victoria Rd. DL1 —3A **116**
(in two parts)
Victoria Rd. TS1 —4F **51**
Victoria Rd. TS6 —3E **55**
Victoria Rd. TS12 —3D **63**
Victoria Rd. TS16 —3D **85**
Victoria Rd. TS17 —3D **71**
Victoria Rd. TS19 —5D **47**
Victoria Rd. TS26 & TS24 —5E **7**
Victoria Sq. TS1 —3A **52**
(off Albert Rd.)
Victoria St. DL1 —3B **116**
Victoria St. DL4 —4D **105**
Victoria St. DL14 —1D **103**
Victoria St. DL16 —4B **98**

Victoria St. TS1 —4D **51**
Victoria St. TS6 —3B **54**
Victoria St. TS18 —5B **48**
Victoria St. TS23 —4D **35**
Victoria St. TS24 —2D **9**
Victoria St. TS25 —5C **12**
Victoria Ter. TS2 —5A **36**
Victoria Ter. TS12 —2D **63**
Victoria Ter. TS13 —4D **67**
Victoria Ter. TS24 —4A **8**
Victoria Ter. TS25 —5C **12**
Victor Way. TS17 —2E **87**
Victory Sq. TS24 —5F **7**
Victory Ter. TS10 —4C **28**
Viewley Cen. TS8 —4F **89**
Viewley Cen. Rd. TS8 —3F **89**
Viewley Hill Av. TS8 —3A **90**
Villa Av. TS3 —5A **54**
Village Clo. DL5 —3E **107**
Village Paddock. TS18 —3E **69**
Villas, The. DL17 —3B **100**
Villa St. DL16 —4B **98**
Villa Ter. TS18 —1B **70**
Villiers Clo. DL3 —1C **114**
Villiers Pl. DL5 —4E **107**
Villiers St. DL16 —2C **98**
Villiers St. TS24 —5F **7**
Vincent Rd. TS5 —1A **74**
Vincent Rd. TS23 —4E **19**
Vincent St. TS24 —1A **8**
Vine Clo. TS14 —4E **97**
Vine St. DL3 —5E **111**
Vine St. DL16 —2C **98**
Vine St. TS2 —2F **51**
Violet Gro. DL1 —2D **117**
Virginia Clo. TS19 —2E **47**
Virginia Gdns. TS5 —2E **89**
Vollum Rise. TS24 —2C **8**
Vulcan St. DL1 —5B **112**
Vulcan St. TS2 —1F **51**
Vulcan Way. TS17 —2E **87**
Vyners Clo. DL16 —5D **99**
Vyner St. DL16 —3B **98**

Waddington St. DL14 —3D **103**
Wade Av. TS18 —4C **48**
Wadham Gro. DL1 —3A **112**
Waine Cres. DL14 —4C **102**
Wainfleet Rd. TS25 —2B **14**
Wainstones Clo. TS9 —4A **120**
Wainstones Ct. TS9 —5F **119**
Wainstones Dri. TS9 —5A **120**
Wainwright Clo. TS25 —3C **12**
Wainwright Wlk. TS25 —4C **12**
Wakefield Rd. TS5 —1F **73**
Wake St. TS3 —4D **53**
Walcher Rd. DL5 —5D **107**
Waldon St. TS24 —1F **11**
Waldridge Gro. TS23 —3B **20**
Waldridge Rd. TS19 —1C **46**
Waldron St. DL14 —1C **102**
Wales St. DL3 —4A **112**
Walker Dri. DL14 —5B **102**
Walker La. DL5 —1D **109**
Walkers Row. TS14 —2E **97**
Walkers Ter. DL3 —2B **112**
Walker St. TS10 —4D **29**
Walker St. TS17 —3D **71**
Walker Ter. DL17 —4F **101**
Walkley Av. TS17 —4D **71**
Walkworth La. DL16 —1C **98**
Wallas Rd. DL5 —1D **109**
Wallington Ct. TS23 —3F **19**
Wallington Dri. TS21 —1B **118**
Wallington Rd. TS23 —3E **19**
Wallington Wlk. TS23 —3F **19**

Wallington Way. TS23 —3F **19**
Wallis Rd. TS6 —4A **54**
Walmer Av. DL14 —4C **102**
Walmer Cres. TS11 —2A **60**
Walnut Clo. TS17 —5D **71**
Walnut Gro. TS10 —1F **43**
Walpole Rd. TS25 —3C **10**
Walpole St. TS1 —4F **51**
Walsham Clo. TS19 —3D **47**
Walsingham Ct. TS23 —4F **33**
Walter St. DL4 —5D **105**
Walter St. TS18 —2A **70**
Waltham Av. TS18 —1D **69**
Waltham Clo. DL3 —4C **110**
Walton Av. TS5 —3E **73**
Walton Ct. TS18 —4E **49**
Walton Heath. DL1 —3E **113**
Walton Ho. TS2 —2F **51**
(off Stockton St.)
Waltons, The. TS9 —4C **120**
Walton St. DL1 —3B **116**
Walton St. TS18 —4E **49**
Walton Ter. TS14 —3E **97**
Walworth Clo. TS10 —2F **43**
Walworth Cres. DL3 —4C **110**
Walworth Gro. TS5 —5D **73**
Walworth Rd. DL5 —3E **109**
Walworth Rd. DL17 —2D **101**
Walworth Rd. TS19 —1D **47**
Wand Hill. TS12 —4D **81**
Wand Hill Gdns. TS12 —4D **81**
Wand Hills Av. TS12 —5F **63**
Wansbeck Clo. DL16 —1B **98**
Wansbeck Gdns. TS26 —1E **11**
Wansford St. TS23 —2A **20**
Wanstead Clo. TS11 —4D **45**
Warbler Clo. TS17 —4B **86**
Warburton Clo. DL5 —5F **107**
Warcop Clo. TS7 —4A **92**
Wardale Av. TS5 —2D **89**
Ward Clo. TS18 —1B **70**
Wardell Rd. TS15 —5E **95**
Warden Clo. TS19 —1D **47**
Wardley Clo. TS19 —1D **47**
Wardman Cres. TS10 —1F **43**
Warelands Way. TS4 —5C **52**
Ware St. TS20 —3C **48**
Warkworth Av. DL14 —4B **102**
Warkworth Dri. TS26 —4B **6**
Warkworth Rd. TS23 —5D **19**
Warkworth Way. DL1 —2D **113**
Warner Gro. DL3 —2A **112**
Warrenby Ct. TS10 —4F **27**
Warren Clo. TS24 —1E **7**
Warren Ct. TS24 —1E **7**
Warrenport Rd. TS18 —4E **49**
Warren Rd. DL5 —2D **109**
Warren St. TS24 —1D **7**
Warren St. DL3 —1F **115**
Warren St. TS1 —4E **51**
Warren St. TS25 —4B **12**
Warrior Dri. TS5 —4B **12**
Warrior Quay. TS24 —4B **8**
Warrior Ter. TS12 —1D **63**
(off Windsor Rd.)
Warsett Cres. TS12 —1F **81**
Warsett Rd. TS11 —4F **45**
Warton St. TS3 —4D **53**
Warwick Clo. DL16 —1D **99**
Warwick Clo. TS16 —1C **94**
Warwick Cres. TS23 —2A **34**
Warwick Gro. TS20 —2D **49**
Warwick Gro. TS26 —5D **7**
Warwick Pl. TS24 —5A **8**
Warwick Rd. DL14 —3B **102**
Warwick Rd. TS10 —1E **43**
Warwick Rd. TS14 —4D **97**

Warwick Sq. DL3 —3C **110**
(in two parts)
Warwick St. TS1 —5E **51**
Warwick St. TS6 —3B **54**
Wasdale Clo. TS24 —1F **7**
Wasdale Dri. TS16 —1D **95**
Wasdale Gro. TS19 —2F **47**
Washbrook Dri. DL3 —1A **112**
Washford Clo. TS17 —4A **86**
Washington Cres. DL5 —4F **107**
Washington Gro. TS20 —1A **48**
Washington St. TS2 —2F **51**
Waskerley Clo. TS19 —1D **47**
Waskerley Gro. DL14 —5A **102**
Waskerley Wlk. DL5 —5A **106**
Wass Way. TS16 —3C **84**
Watchgate. TS7 —3B **92**
Waterford Rd. TS20 —2B **48**
Waterford Ter. TS1 —5D **51**
Water La. TS13 —5D **67**
Waterloo Rd. TS1 —4F **51**
Waterloo Ter. DL4 —3B **104**
Waterside. DL3 —5D **111**
Watersmeet Clo. TS17 —5A **86**
Watling Clo. TS20 —5A **32**
Watling Rd. DL14 —5C **102**
Watness Av. TS12 —5E **63**
Watson Gro. TS17 —3C **70**
Watson Rd. DL5 —2C **108**
Watton Clo. TS25 —3C **14**
Watton Rd. TS17 —4A **72**
Watt St. DL17 —2B **100**
Waveney Gro. TS12 —5D **63**
Waveney Rd. TS10 —1B **42**
Waverley St. TS1 —4E **51**
Waverley St. TS18 —2A **70**
Waverley Ter. DL1 —3B **116**
Waverley Ter. DL4 —2D **105**
Waverley Ter. TS25 —3D **11**
Wayland Ter. DL3 —4E **111**
Waymar Clo. TS5 —2D **73**
Wayside Rd. DL1 —2B **112**
Wayside Rd. TS3 —5B **54**
Wear Chare. DL14 —1D **103**
Wear Ct. TS6 —4A **54**
Wear Cres. TS16 —1C **94**
Weardale. TS14 —5A **96**
Weardale Cres. TS23 —3E **33**
Weardale Dri. DL14 —5A **102**
Weardale Gro. TS5 —3F **73**
Weardale Pl. TS18 —4F **47**
Weardale St. DL16 —2E **99**
Weardale Wlk. DL4 —3E **105**
Wearport Grn. TS18 —4D 49
(off Eastport Rd.)
Wear St. DL16 —3C **98**
Wear St. TS6 —2B **54**
Wear Ter. DL14 —1D **103**
Weastell St. TS1 —1F **73**
Weatherhead Av. TS5 —2B **72**
Weaver Clo. TS17 —4D **87**
Weaverham Rd. TS20 —1A **48**
Weavers Ct. TS9 —3E **119**
Weavers Way. DL1 —1A **116**
Weaverthorpe. TS7 —3A **92**
Webb Clo. DL5 —5D **107**
Webb Rd. TS6 —3A **54**
Webster Av. TS5 —2A **74**
Webster Clo. TS18 —1B **70**
Webster Rd. TS6 —2F **77**
Webster Rd. TS22 —1D **33**
Webster St. TS18 —1B **70**
Wederly Clo. DL3 —4F **111**
Weir St. DL1 —1A **116**
Welbeck Av. DL1 —4E **113**
Welbeck Cotts. DL1 —4B 11
(off Welbeck St.)

Welbeck St. DL1 —4B **116**
Welburn Av. TS4 —2B **74**
Welburn Gro. TS7 —4B **76**
Welbury Clo. TS18 —2C **68**
Welbury Gro. DL5 —5F **107**
Welbury Way. DL5 —4E **109**
Welland Clo. TS5 —2D **89**
Welland Cres. TS19 —3C **46**
Welland Rd. TS10 —1B **42**
Welland Rd. TS25 —2C **14**
Well Bank. DL5 —5F **109**
Wellbeck St. TS12 —5E **63**
Wellbrook Clo. TS17 —3B **86**
Wellburn Ct. TS19 —5C **46**
Wellburn Rd. TS19 —5C **46**
Welldale Cres. TS19 —4C **46**
Welldeck Gdns. TS26 —4D **7**
Welldeck Rd. TS26 —4D **7**
Wellesley Rd. TS4 —4B **52**
Wellfield Grn. TS19 —1C **46**
Well Ho. Dri. DL5 —3D **107**
Well Ho. Ride. DL5 —3D **107**
Well Ho., The. TS11 —5D **61**
Wellington Clo. TS2 —2F **51**
Wellington Clo. TS11 —4C **44**
Wellington Clo. TS18 —5F **69**
Wellington Ct. M. DL1 —2A 11
(off Grange Rd.)
Wellington St. TS2 —2F **51**
Wellington St. TS18 —5B **48**
Wellmead Rd. TS3 —5A **54**
Wells Av. TS24 —1E **7**
Wells Clo. DL1 —4F **113**
Wells Clo. TS6 —1F **77**
Well's Cotts. TS16 —2D **95**
Wells Gro. TS10 —1A **44**
Wellspring Clo. TS5 —1C **88**
Wells St. TS24 —2D **9**
Welton Ho. TS3 —2B **76**
Wembley Ct. TS18 —1A **70**
Wembley St. TS1 —4D **51**
Wembley Way. TS6 —4D **77**
Wembley Way. TS18 —1A **70**
Wensleydale Rd. DL1 —3B **112**
Wensleydale Sq. DL14 —5A **102**
Wensleydale St. TS25 —2F **11**
Wensley Rd. TS18 —1E **69**
Wensley Ter. DL17 —5F **101**
Wentworth Ct. TS6 —2F **77**
Wentworth Cres. TS11 —2A **60**
Wentworth Gro. TS27 —4B **4**
Wentworth St. TS1 —4E **51**
Wentworth Way. DL3 —3B **110**
Wentworth Way. TS16 —5D **85**
Wesleyan Rd. DL16 —3C **98**
Wesley Ct. DL1 —2C **116**
Wesley Cres. DL4 —2C **104**
Wesley Gro. DL14 —2C **102**
Wesley Mall. TS1 —3F **51**
Wesley Pl. TS20 —2C **48**
Wesley Row. TS1 —4E **51**
Wesley St. DL1 —2C **116**
Wesley Ter. TS13 —2A **66**
W. Auckland Rd. DL2 & DL3
—1B **110** to 5D **111**
W. Auckland Rd. DL4 —3A **104**
West Av. TS12 —1C **62**
West Av. TS23 —5E **33**
Westbank Rd. TS7 —5C **76**
Westbeck Gdns. TS5 —3F **73**
W. Beck Dri. DL3 —1A **114**
W. Beck Way. TS8 —3C **90**
Westborough Gro. TS18 —2B **68**
Westbourne Gro. DL3 —2E **115**
(in two parts)
Westbourne Gro. TS3 —4C **52**
Westbourne Gro. TS6 —5C **54**

Westbourne Gro. TS10 —4D **29**
Westbourne Rd. TS5 —2C **72**
Westbourne Rd. TS25 —2E **11**
Westbourne St. TS18 —2B **70**
Westbrook. DL3 —5A **112**
Westbrooke Av. TS25 —3D **11**
Westbrooke Gro. TS25 —3E **11**
Westbrook Ter. DL1 —5A **112**
Westbury St. TS17 —2D **71**
Westcliffe Ct. DL3 —3F **115**
West Clo. DL4 —3A **104**
W. Coatham La. TS10 —1E **41**
Westcott Dri. DL14 —3F **103**
Westcott St. TS18 —1B **70**
Westcott Ter. DL17 —3B **100**
Westcott Wlk. DL5 —1E **109**
West Cres. DL3 —1F **115**
West Cres. TS5 —2C **72**
Westcroft. TS3 —1D **75**
Westcroft Rd. TS6 —2E **55**
Westdale Rd. TS17 —5E **71**
W. Dyke Rd. TS10
—4D **29** to 4B **42**
West End. TS9 —4D **119**
West End. TS14 —3C **96**
West End. TS21 —5B **118**
W. End Av. TS14 —3C **96**
W. End Gdns. TS15 —2C **94**
Westerby Rd. TS3 —4E **53**
Westerdale. DL16 —2B **98**
Westerdale Av. TS10 —1A **42**
Westerdale Av. TS19 —4F **47**
Westerdale Ct. DL3 —3C **110**
Westerdale Gdns. DL4 —3E **105**
Westerdale Rd. TS3 —1D **75**
Westerdale Rd. TS25 —1B **14**
Westerham Gro. TS4 —4B **74**
Westerhope Ct. DL3 —3D **111**
Westerleigh Av. TS19 —5C **46**
Westerton Grn. TS19 —2C **46**
Westerton Rd. TS23 —3F **19**
Westfield Av. TS10 —5D **29**
Westfield Clo. TS6 —2C **76**
Westfield Clo. TS10 —1F **41**
Westfield Ct. TS19 —3F **47**
Westfield Cres. TS19 —2F **47**
Westfield Dri. DL3 —1C **114**
Westfield Rd. DL14 —3C **102**
Westfield Rd. TS6 —2D **77**
Westfield Rd. TS9 —3D **119**
Westfield Rd. TS11 —4B **44**
Westfields. DL5 —3A **108**
Westfields. DL16 —2B **98**
Westfield Ter. TS13 —4C **66**
Westfield Wlk. TS13 —4C **66**
Westfield Way. TS10 —2F **41**
Westfield Way. TS13 —4C **66**
Westgarth Clo. TS11 —4C **44**
Westgarth Ter. DL1 —5C **112**
Westgate. TS14 —3D **97**
Westgate. TS15 —2C **94**
Westgate Cres. DL3 —3D **111**
Westgate M. TS14 —3E **97**
Westgate Rd. DL3 —3D **111**
Westgate Rd. DL14 —1D **103**
Westgate Rd. TS5 —3D **73**
Westgate Rd. TS14 —2E **97**
West Grn. TS9 —4D **119**
W. Hartlepool Rd. TS22 —2D **19**
Westholme St. TS23 —5A **20**
Westkirk Clo. DL3 —2C **110**
Westland Av. TS26 —1D **11**
Westlands. TS9 —4D **119**
Westlands Av. TS20 —2C **48**
Westlands Rd. DL3 —5D **111**
Westlands Rd. TS16 —1C **94**
Westland Way. TS18 —4A **70**

West La. DL14 —5B **102**
West La. TS5 —5C **50** & 1C **72**
West La. TS6 —2E **55**
(in two parts)
Westlea Av. DL14 —3D **103**
W. Mill Cotts. DL14 —1B **102**
West M. TS15 —2C **94**
Westminster Clo. TS6 —1F **77**
Westminster Rd. DL1 —4D **117**
Westminster Rd. TS5 —1F **73**
Westmoor Clo. DL16 —4A **98**
W. Moor Clo. TS15 —3F **95**
W. Moor Rd. DL1 —5D **117**
Westmoreland Gro. TS20 —4A **32**
Westmoreland St. DL3 —3A **102**
Westmoreland St. TS25 —1F **11**
Westmoreland Wlk. TS25 —2F **11**
Westmorland Clo. DL16 —1E **99**
Westmorland Rd. TS5 —1E **73**
Westmorland Rd. TS10 —1C **42**
Westmorland Way. DL5 —5D **107**
Weston Av. TS3 —4F **53**
Weston Cres. TS20 —2C **48**
Weston Way. TS19 —1D **47**
(off Ingleton Rd.)
West Pk. TS26 —5B **6**
West Pk. Av. TS13 —4B **66**
West Pk. La. TS4 —5B **118**
Westpoint Rd. TS17 —1C **70**
Westport Clo. TS18 —4E **49**
W. Powlett St. DL3 —2F **115**
W. Precinct. TS23 —1E **33**
Westray. TS8 —5F **91**
Westray St. TS13 —2A **66**
West Rd. DL4 —3A **104**
West Rd. DL14 —1C **102**
West Rd. TS13 —4B **66**
West Rd. TS23 —4E **33**
West Row. TS4 —2A **116**
West Row. TS5 —2C **72**
West Row. TS6 —1A **78**
West Row. TS18 —1B **70**
West Row. TS25 —4C **14**
West Scar. TS10 —2E **43**
West Side. TS7 —1D **91**
West St. DL3 —2F **115**
West St. DL17 —3C **100**
West St. TS2 —5A **36**
(High Clarence)
West St. TS2 —1F **51**
(Middlesbrough)
West St. TS6 —1A **78**
(Eston)
West St. TS6 —2E **77**
(Normanby)
West St. TS11 —3D **45**
West St. TS15 —2C **94**
West Ter. DL5 —5F **109**
West Ter. DL16 —4A **98**
West Ter. TS3 —4C **52**
West Ter. TS9 —4A **120**
West Ter. TS10 —3D **29**
West Ter. TS11 —2B **60**
West Ter. TS12 —1B **80**
West View. DL3 —2B **114**
West View. DL14 —5F **103**
West View. DL17 —3D **101**
West View. TS10 —5D **117**
W. View Clo. TS16 —5C **84**
W. View Rd. TS27 & TS24
—5A **4** to 1B **8**
W. View Ter. DL4 —2B **104**
W. View Ter. TS16 —5C **84**
W. View Ter. TS25 —5C **12**
Westward Clo. TS1 —3F **51**

Westwick Ter. TS4 —1C **90**
Westwood Av. TS5 —3F **73**
Westwood Av. TS7 —3C **92**
Westwood La. TS17 —5D **87**
Westwood Way. TS27 —4A **4**
Westworth Clo. TS15 —4F **95**
Wetherall Av. TS15 —5C **94**
Wetherby Grn. TS7 —3B **76**
Wetherell Clo. TS11 —5F **45**
Wetherfell Clo. TS17 —4A **86**
Weymouth Av. TS8 —1C **90**
Weymouth Dri. TS24 —4B **4**
Weymouth Rd. TS18 —1E **69**
Whaddon Chase. TS14 —4F **97**
Wharfdale Av. TS23 —3E **33**
Wharfedale Clo. TS17 —4A **86**
Wharfe Way. DL1 —5A **116**
Wharf St. TS18 —1C **70**
Wharton Clo. TS15 —4F **95**
Wharton Pl. TS12 —4C **80**
Wharton St. TS12 —2F **81**
Wharton St. TS24 —4F **7**
Wharton Ter. TS24 —3E **7** & 3F **7**
Wheatacre Clo. TS11 —5E **45**
Wheatear Dri. TS10 —3E **43**
Wheatear La. TS17 —4C **86**
Wheatfields Ho. TS6 —3F **77**
Wheatlands. TS9 —3B **120**
Wheatlands Clo. TS14 —4F **97**
Wheatlands Dri. TS11 —5C **44**
Wheatlands Dri. TS13 —2F **67**
Wheatlands Pk. TS10 —3E **43**
Wheatlands Ter. TS13 —4D **67**
(off Springfield Est.)
Wheatley Clo. TS5 —1E **89**
Wheatley Rd. TS19 —1C **46**
Wheatley Wlk. TS19 —1D **47**
Wheeldale Av. TS10 —1A **42**
Wheeldale Clo. DL1 —4D **113**
Wheeldale Cres. TS17 —5E **71**
Wheeler Grn. DL5 —4E **10**
(off Defoe Cres.)
Whernside. TS7 —3A **92**
Whernside Cres. TS17 —4A **86**
Whessoe Rd. DL3
—1F **111** to 4A **112**
Whessoe Rd. TS19 —1D **47**
Whessoe Wlk. TS19 —1D **47**
Whickam Clo. TS19 —1C **46**
Whickham Clo. TS3 —3C **52**
Whinbank Rd. DL5 —3D **109**
Whinbush Way. DL1 —2E **113**
Whinchat Clo. TS17 —5C **86**
Whinchat Tail. TS14 —3B **96**
Whinfell Av. TS16 —4C **84**
Whinfell Clo. TS7 —4A **92**
Whinfield Clo. TS19 —3B **46**
Whinfield Dri. DL5 —5D **109**
Whinfield Rd. DL1 —2D **113**
Whinflower Dri. TS20 —5A **32**
Whingroves. TS17 —4A **72**
Whinlatter Clo. TS19 —5A **48**
Whinlatter Pl. DL5 —1B **108**
Whinney Banks Rd. TS5 —2C **72**
Whinston Clo. TS26 —4A **4**
Whinstone Dri. TS8 —4D **89**
Whinstone View. TS9 —3B **120**
Whin St. TS1 —3F **51**
Whisperdale Ct. TS3 —1F **75**
Whitburn Rd. TS19 —1C **46**
Whitburn St. TS24 —1F **11**
Whitby Av. TS6 —5F **55**
Whitby Av. TS14 —3F **97**
Whitby Clo. DL14 —4A **102**
Whitby Clo. TS12 —1E **81**
Whitby Cres. TS10 —1A **44**
Whitby Gro. TS24 —5A **8**

Whitby Ho. TS2 —1F **51**
(off Stockton St.)
Whitby Rd. TS7 —2C **92**
Whitby Rd. TS13 —4E **67** & 1E **67**
Whitby Rd. TS14 —3F **97**
Whitby Rd. TS17 —4E **71**
Whitby St. TS24 —5A **8**
Whitby St. S. TS24 —1A **12**
Whitby Wlk. TS24 —5A **8**
Whitby Way. DL3 —4A **110**
Whitebeam Ct. TS4 —3A **74**
Whitebridge Dri. DL1 —2C **112**
Whitecliffe Ter. TS13 —4C **66**
Whitehall Rd. TS16 —3B **84**
White Hart Cres. DL1 —5F **113**
Whitehead Wlk. DL5 —4F **107**
White Ho. Croft. TS21 —5B **68**
White Ho. Dri. TS21 —5B **68**
White Ho. Rd. TS17 —1C **86**
Whitehouse Rd. TS22 —5B **18**
Whitehouse Shopping Cen. TS19
—4E **47**
Whitehouse St. TS5 —5D **51**
Whiteley Gro. DL5 —4D **107**
Whitemeadows. DL3 —2C **114**
White Stone Clo. TS16 —2F **43**
White St. TS3 —5D **53**
Whitfield Av. TS4 —5B **52**
(off Angle St.)
Whitfield Bldgs. TS4 —4B **52**
(off Angle St.)
Whitfield Clo. TS16 —4C **84**
Whitfield Dri. TS25 —3F **11**
Whitfield Rd. TS20 —4A **32**
Whithorn Gro. TS8 —3F **89**
Whitley Rd. TS17 —2E **87**
Whitrout Rd. TS24 —4C **4**
Whittle Ho. TS2 —1F **51**
(off West St.)
Whitton Clo. DL5 —3E **107**
Whitton Clo. TS5 —5C **72**
Whitton Rd. TS19 —4D **47**
Whitwell Clo. TS18 —2B **70**
Whitwell Rd. DL1 —3E **117**
Whitwell Ter. TS14 —2D **97**
Whitworth Av. DL5 —4D **109**
Whitworth Clo. DL16 —4A **98**
Whitworth Dri. DL5 —4D **109**
Whitworth Rd. DL16 —3A **98**
Whitworth Rd. TS6 —2E **55**
(in two parts)
Whitworth Ter. DL16 —4B **98**
Whorlton Clo. TS14 —5D **97**
Whorlton Ct. TS10 —2C **42**
Whorlton Moor Cres. DL1 —5E **117**
Whorlton Rd. TS2 —5E **35**
Whorlton Rd. TS19 —1C **46**
Whorlton Rd. TS22 —1C **32**
Wibsey Av. TS3 —4F **75**
Wickets, The. TS25 —1C **16**
Wicklow St. TS1 —5D **51**
Widdowfield St. DL3 —5F **111**
Widdrington Ct. TS19 —3B **46**
Widecombe Wlk. DL17 —3F **101**
Widgeon Rd. DL1 —2E **117**
Wigton Sands. TS5 —2C **88**
Wilbore Croft. DL5 —2A **106**
Wilder Gro. TS25 —3B **10**
Wilfred St. TS18 —1A **70**
Wilken Cres. TS14 —1E **97**
Wilkes St. DL3 —5A **112**
Wilkinson Rd. DL5 —1F **109**
Wilkinson St. TS12 —5E **81**
Wilkinson St. TS20 —3C **48**
Willerby Grn. TS5 —3D **73**

Willey Flatt La. TS15 —5C **94**
William Crosthwaite Av. TS17
—5E **87**
Williamfield Way. DL5 —1B **108**
William Kerr Cres., The. DL17
—3A **100**
Williams Av. TS5 —2C **72**
Williams St. TS12 —1F **81**
William St. DL3 —4A **112**
William St. DL17 —5F **101**
William St. TS2 —2F **51**
William St. TS6 —1A **78**
William St. TS10 —4E **29**
William St. TS12 —1E **81**
William St. TS18 —1B **70**
(in two parts)
William Ter. TS20 —2C **48**
Willington Rd. TS19 —1C **46**
Willow Bank. TS8 —5C **90**
Willow Chase, The. TS21 —5A **68**
Willow Clo. TS12 —2B **62**
Willow Clo. TS17 —5D **71**
Willowdene Av. TS14 —2F **69**
Willow Dri. TS6 —3D **77**
Willow Dri. TS12 —5B **64**
Willow Gro. TS24 —2E **7**
Willow Rd. DL3 —5D **111**
Willow Rd. DL16 —5A **98**
Willow Rd. DL17 —2D **101**
Willow Rd. TS14 —2D **97**
Willow Rd. TS19 —3A **48**
Willow Rd. E. DL3 —5F **111**
Willows Ct. TS17 —5F **87**
Willows Rd. TS5 —2F **73**
Willows, The. DL14 —1E **103**
Willows, The. TS7 —2F **91**
Willows, The. TS10 —5F **29**
Willows, The. TS19 —3E **47**
Willows, The. TS21 —5B **118**
Willow Ter. TS2 —4F **35**
Willow Wlk. DL4 —3E **105**
Willow Wlk. TS13 —4C **66**
Willow Wlk. TS24 —2E **7**
Wilmire Rd. TS22 —1D **33**
Wilson St. DL3 —5F **111**
Wilson St. TS1 —2F **51**
Wilson St. TS12 —4C **64**
(Brotton)
Wilson St. TS12 —5E **81**
(Lingdale)
Wilson St. TS14 —3D **97**
Wilson St. TS17 —2F **71**
Wilson St. TS26 —4D **7**
Wilson Ter. TS13 —1B **66**
Wilson Wlk. DL5 —2D **109**
Wilstrop Grn. TS3 —4E **75**
Wilton Av. TS10 —2E **41**
Wilton Av. TS26 —5D **7**
Wilton Bank. TS12 —2B **62**
Wilton Clo. DL3 —2C **114**
Wilton Ct. DL5 —5A **106**
Wilton Dri. DL3 —1C **114**
Wilton Grn. TS6 —4C **56**
Wilton La. TS10 & TS14 —3F **57**
Wilton La. TS10 —1D **97**
Wilton Rd. TS26 —5E **7**
Wilton St. TS1 —5F **51**
Wilton St. TS10 —4D **29**
(in two parts)
Wilton Way. TS16 —5A **56**
Wiltshire Rd. TS12 —1B **80**
Wiltshire Wlk. TS20 —2D **49**
Wiltshire Way. TS26 —3C **6**
Wimbledon Clo. DL1 —5F **113**
Wimbledon Ct. TS5 —3D **73**
Wimbledon Rd. TS5 —3D **73**
Wimborne Clo. DL3 —4B **110**

Wimpole Rd. TS19 —4B **46**
Wincanton Rd. TS10 —1E **43**
Winchester Ct. DL16 —1B **98**
Winchester Rd. TS5 —1A **74**
Winchester Rd. TS10 —1A **44**
Winchester Rd. TS12 —4D **65**
Winchester Wlk. TS26 —2C **6**
Winchester Way. DL1 —4F **113**
Windermere. DL16 —1B **98**
Windermere Av. TS10 —1C **42**
Windermere Av. TS23 —5F **33**
Windermere Ct. DL1 —4B **116**
Windermere Dri. TS12 —5C **62**
Windermere Rd. DL17 —3C **100**
Windermere Rd. TS5 —2E **73**
Windermere Rd. TS18 —5F **47**
Windermere Rd. TS25
—3F **11** & 3A **12**
Windleston Clo. TS19 —1C **46**
Windleston Dri. TS3 —4E **75**
Windlestone Rd. TS23 —5A **20**
Windleston Wlk. DL5 —4F **107**
Windmill Ter. TS20
—2C **48** & 3C **48**
Windrush Gro. DL1 —1C **112**
Windsor Av. DL16 —4B **98**
Windsor Av. DL17 —2D **101**
Windsor Ct. DL4 —4C **104**
Windsor Ct. DL14 —2C **102**
Windsor Ct. TS5 —2F **73**
Windsor Ct. TS6 —4F **55**
Windsor Ct. TS12 —1D **63**
Windsor Cres. TS7 —2B **92**
Windsor Gdns. DL4 —3D **105**
Windsor Gdns. TS2 —2A **52**
Windsor Ho. TS2 —2A 52
(off Gosford St.)
Windsor Oval. TS17 —5D **71**
Windsor Rd. TS5 —1E **73**
Windsor Rd. TS6 —2E **77**
Windsor Rd. TS10 —1E **43**
Windsor Rd. TS12 —1D **63**
Windsor Rd. TS17 —5D **71**
Windsor Rd. TS18 —2F **69**
Windsor St. DL1 —5A **112**
Windsor St. TS1 —4F **51**
Windsor St. TS23 —3E **35**
Windsor St. TS26 —5F **7**
Windsor Ter. DL4 —3C **104**
Windsor Ter. TS13 —4E 67
(off Whitby Rd.)
Windy Hill La. TS11 —4E **45**
Wingate Av. TS23 —3A **20**
Wingate Rd. TS19 —1D **47**
Wingate Wlk. TS3 —4E **75**
Winlaton Clo. TS19 —1C **46**
Winpenny Clo. TS15 —4F **95**
Winsford Ct. TS17 —4B **86**
Winslade Av. TS3 —4A **54**
Winston Av. TS23 —3F **19**
Winston Churchill Clo. TS17
—2E **87**
Winston Dri. TS6 —1F **77**
Winston St. DL3 —2F **115**
Winston St. TS18 —2A **70**
Winterbottom Av. TS24
—5E **5** & 1E **7**
Winterburn Pl. DL5 —4B **106**
Winter Clo. TS15 —5C **94**
Winter Clo. TS25 —3F **11**
Winterton Cotts. TS21 —2B **118**
Winthorpe Gro. TS25 —2B **14**
Wisbech Clo. TS25 —3B **14**
Wiseman Wlk. DL5 —4E **107**
Wiske Clo. TS19 —3C **46**
Witbank Rd. DL3 —1E **115**
Witham Av. TS16 —2D **85**

Witham Gro. TS25 —2C **14**
Witham Ho. TS16 —2E **85**
Witney Ct. DL3 —3E **115**
Witton Ct. TS23 —5A **20**
Witton Cres. DL3 —4B **110**
Witton Dri. DL16 —1D **99**
(in two parts)
Witton Rd. DL17 —1D **101**
Woburn Av. DL3 —4A **110**
Woburn Gro. TS3 —3A **76**
Woburn Gro. TS25 —1E **15**
Woking Clo. TS6 —4E **77**
Wolfe Rd. TS20 —2B **48**
Wollaton Rd. TS23 —5A **20**
Wolseley St. DL17 —4F **101**
Wolsey Clo. DL5 —4F **107**
Wolsey Dri. TS20 —4F **31**
Wolsey Ho. TS24 —2D **9**
Wolsey Rd. DL16 —1E **99**
Wolsingham Clo. TS19 —1D **47**
Wolsingham Dri. TS5 —1E **89**
Wolsingham Dri. TS17 —5F **71**
Wolsingham Ter. DL1 —5D **113**
Wolveston Clo. DL5 —4B **106**
Wolviston Bk. La. TS23
—3F **19** & 3B **20**
Wolviston Ct. TS22 —5C **18**
Wolviston Interchange. TS22
—2C **18**
Wolviston Mill La. TS22 —4B **18**
Wolviston Rd. TS23 & TS22
—3D **33** to 3D **19**
Wolviston Rd. TS25 —2E **11**
Wolviston Wlk. TS19 —1C **46**
Woodbank Rd. TS7 —5C **76**
Woodbine Ter. TS25 —4C **14**
Woodborough La. TS19 —3E **47**
Woodbrook Clo. TS11 —3A **60**
Woodburn Clo. TS8 —3F **89**
Woodburn Dri. DL3 —4D **115**
Woodcock Clo. TS6 —2F **77**
Woodcrest Rd. DL3 —4E **115**
Woodford Clo. TS11 —4C **44**
Woodford Grn. TS16 —5D **85**
Woodford Wlk. TS17 —3D **87**
Woodgate Clo. TS25 —3C **14**
Woodhall Gro. TS18 —3C **68**
Woodham Ga. DL5 —2D **107**
Woodham Grn. TS19 —1C **46**
Woodham La. DL5 —2D **107**
Woodham Rd. DL5 —3E **109**
Woodham Rd. TS23 —3F **19**
Woodham Village. DL5 —3E **107**
Woodham Way. DL5 —2C **107**
Woodhay Av. TS5 —3B **72**
Woodhouse La. DL14 —3A **102**
Woodhouse Rd. TS14 —2C **96**
Woodhouse Roundabout. TS14
—2B **96**
Woodland Rise. DL5 —4A **106**
Woodland Rd. DL3
—5D **111** to 1F **115**
Woodlands Dri. TS6 —3F **77**
Woodlands Dri. TS15 —4E **95**
Woodlands Gro. TS26 —4B **6**
Woodlands Hall. TS1 —4A **52**
Woodlands Rd. DL14 —2E **103**
Woodlands Rd. TS1 —5A **52**
Woodlands Rd. TS6 —4E **77**
Woodlands, The. DL3 —1E **115**
Woodlands, The. TS7 —4C **92**
Woodlands, The. TS17 —5D **71**
Woodland St. TS18 —2A **70**
Woodland Ter. DL3 —1D **115**
Woodland Way. TS21 —5A **68**
Wood La. DL17 —2D **101**
Woodlea. TS8 —5C **90**

Every possible care has been taken to ensure that the information given in this publication is accurate and whilst the publishers would be grateful to learn of any errors, they regret they cannot accept any responsibility for loss thereby caused.

The representation on the maps of a road, track or footpath is no evidence of the existence of a right of way.

Printed and bound in Great Britain
by Cox & Wyman Ltd, Reading, Berkshire